TRANSFORMATIONAL TRENDS IN
GOVERNANCE AND DEMOCRACY
**National Academy of Public Administration**
Terry F. Buss, Series Editor

*Modernizing Democracy:*
*Innovations in Citizen Participation*
Edited by Terry F. Buss, F. Stevens Redburn, and Kristina Guo

*Meeting the Challenge of 9/11:*
*Blueprints for More Effective Government*
Edited by Thomas H. Stanton

*Transforming Public Leadership for the 21st Century*
Edited by Ricardo S. Morse, Terry F. Buss, and C. Morgan Kinghorn

*Foreign Aid and Foreign Policy:*
*Lessons for the Next Half-Century*
Edited by Louis A. Picard, Robert Groelsema, and Terry F. Buss

*Performance Management and Budgeting:*
*How Governments Can Learn from Experience*
Edited by F. Stevens Redburn, Robert J. Shea, and Terry F. Buss

*Innovations in Public Leadership Development*
Edited by Ricardo S. Morse and Terry F. Buss

D1715842

# About the Academy

The National Academy of Public Administration, like the National Academy of Sciences, is an independent, nonprofit organization chartered by Congress to identify emerging issues of governance and to help federal, state, and local governments improve their performance. The Academy's mission is to provide "trusted advice"—advice that is objective, timely, and actionable—on all issues of public service and management. The unique source of the Academy's expertise is its membership, including more than 650 current and former Cabinet officers, members of Congress, governors, mayors, legislators, jurists, business executives, public managers, and scholars who are elected as Fellows because of their distinguished contribution to the field of public administration through scholarship, civic activism, or government service. Participation in the Academy's work is a requisite of membership, and the Fellows offer their experience and knowledge voluntarily.

The Academy is proud to join with M.E. Sharpe, Inc., to bring readers this and other volumes in a series of edited works addressing current major public management and public policy issues.

The opinions expressed in these writings are those of the authors and do not necessarily reflect the views of the Academy. To access Academy reports, please visit our website at www.napawash.org.

# Innovations in Public Leadership Development

Edited by Ricardo S. Morse
and Terry F. Buss

NATIONAL ACADEMY OF
PUBLIC ADMINISTRATION

TRANSFORMATIONAL TRENDS IN
GOVERNANCE AND DEMOCRACY

*M.E.Sharpe*
Armonk, New York
London, England

**Library of Congress Cataloging-in-Publication Data**

Innovations in public leadership development / edited by Ricardo S. Morse
and Terry F. Buss.
    p. cm. — (Transformational trends in governance & democracy)
  Includes bibliographical references and index.
  ISBN 978-0-7656-2069-9 (cloth : alk. paper)—ISBN 978-0-7656-2070-5 (pbk. : alk. paper)
  1. Public administration—United States. 2. Leadership—United States. 3. Organizational
change—United States. 4. Political leadership—United States. I. Morse, Ricardo S.,
1971– II. Buss, Terry F.

JK421.I56 2008

352.23'6—dc22

2007030821

Printed in the United States of America

| BM (c) | 10 | 9 | 8 | 7 | 6 | 5 | 4 | 3 | 2 | 1 |
| --- | --- | --- | --- | --- | --- | --- | --- | --- | --- | --- |
| BM (p) | 10 | 9 | 8 | 7 | 6 | 5 | 4 | 3 | 2 | 1 |

Rick and Terry dedicate this book to their children,
Logan, Eli, Olivia, and Talen,
and
Abigail and Nathaniel,
respectively.

# Contents

# Preface

It is a pleasure to introduce this book, *Innovations in Public Leadership Development,* the sixth in a series—*Transformational Trends in Governance and Democracy,* of the National Academy of Public Administration—intended to capture the latest thinking in public management. This work is intended to be a companion to another edited book in the series, *Transforming Public Leadership for the 21st Century. Innovations* presents ideas, frames, and models for how to develop public leaders who are ethical, effective, and committed, while *Transforming* offers insight into what public leadership is, is not, or ought to be. Both books are offered in the context of the rapidly evolving field of public management, and both convey in a variety of ways the enthusiasm, inspiration, and dedication, indeed the honor, of working in the public service.

This book is grounded in several premises widely shared by our contributors. *First,* leaders can, and indeed must, be developed if the public sector is to meet its obligations to citizens and its constituents. It is just not the case or our experience that leaders are born and in short supply. *Second,* although it has some common attributes, public leadership differs from leadership in other contexts, such as military, sports, or business. Military models of leadership, for example, remain focused on hierarchical structures of authority, whereas public leaders now find themselves leading much more in a collaborative environment. *Third,* the practice of public leadership is in crisis, or at least in turmoil, necessitating new ways of leading and alternative ways of developing leaders. Public confidence in government is low, traditional ways of doing business are becoming obsolete, scandal appears to be permeating government, management and administration are becoming increasingly political, and the quality of public services seems on the decline. New leaders are desperately needed. And *fourth,* a wide variety of training and development innovations are underway that can, and are producing public leaders who have been or will be effective in today's environment. These innovations, many presented here, are grounded in practice rather than theory, have been tested and evaluated for effectiveness, and are beginning to attract a large following in the field.

The contributors hope that their work conveys the exciting times in which we find ourselves in the field of public management and the unprecedented opportunities for advancing leadership development.

## Acknowledgments

We would like to thank Jenna Dorn, President of the Academy, for her support and encouragement; Scott Belcher, former Executive Vice President, for marshaling Academy resources in developing and executing this project; Morgan Kinghorn, past Academy President, for promoting the project widely across the institution; Bill Shields, Vice President, for facilitating the project; and of course, our leader, Bill Gadsby, Vice President of the Academy's studies program. Ednilson Quintanilla, at the Academy, did a fine job managing the preparation of the manuscript. The Academy would also like to thank M.E. Sharpe, especially Harry Briggs, Elizabeth Granda, and Ana Erlić, for their assistance in preparing the manuscript for publication.

Terry F. Buss
Miami, Florida

# Innovations in
# Public Leadership
# Development

# 1

# Introduction

Ricardo S. Morse and Terry F. Buss

> All who have studied and thought about leadership development recognize that we know too little to permit definitive treatment of the subject. The best we can hope is to offer provisional clarification on the way to something better.
>
> —*John Gardner* (1990, 157)

Leadership and leadership development constitute an enormous, burgeoning field of inquiry and practice. There are thousands of books on leadership, along with hundreds, if not thousands, of various types of leadership development programs throughout the United States. To give some sense of scope, a subject search for "leadership" in the books category of Amazon.com (on May 3, 2007) yielded no less than 27,099 results. On that given day, Lee Iacocca's *Where Have All the Leaders Gone?* (2007) was the bestseller in the group. Remarkably, only 148 of the 27,099 results (one-half of one percent) were in the "public affairs and administration" category. On the other hand, 14,757 were classified under the "business and investing" category.

This should not come as a surprise to anyone familiar with the field of public administration. Indeed, leadership and leadership development *in public administration* has long been a vastly understudied field. There are literally only a few books written that specifically discuss leadership in public service—that is, leadership exercised by "regular" public managers. While there are scores of books on political leadership and significant literature on military leadership,[1] it is difficult to find many discussions of leadership that are aimed squarely at management-level agency staff, city and county managers and department heads, and so on.

However, public managers at all levels of government have many training and continuing education opportunities in the area of leadership development. The Federal Executive Institute (www.leadership.opm.gov) and the Senior

Executive Institute (www.coopercenter.org/leadership/SEI) are two prominent examples of well-established leadership development programs (www.
GovLeaders.org). Many state and federal agencies also have well-established
leadership development programs. In addition, professional associations, such
as the International City/County Management Association (ICMA) University
(www.icma.org/icmau), provide leadership development opportunities. Several
universities also house leadership institutes and programs for the public sector,
and a good number of professional degree programs in public administration
and public affairs include courses on leadership; however, very few programs[2]
include leadership courses in the core curriculum.

All this is to say that formal leadership development efforts are found in
the public sector, along with a smattering of books and articles on the topic.
But when compared to the private sector, there really is no comparison. As
the Amazon.com search revealed, the public sector is dwarfed dramatically
by the private sector in literature and training for leadership.[3] With this
compilation, we aim to make a contribution to the thinking and practice of
leadership development *for the public sector.* Specifically, we offer insights to
practitioners and academics who are engaged in the development of current
and future public leaders. This includes (at least) the following groups that
are all concerned with developing public leadership:

- those involved in Master's of Public Administration (MPA) and other
  public affairs professional programs,
- officers and staff of public service professional associations,
- executive leaders and human resources personnel in public agencies,
- individual trainers and other consultants that work with public organizations, and
- program administrators and trainers at leadership institutes across the
  country.

The chapters included in this volume offer innovations in thinking and practice that we hope will help move forward efforts to improve the leadership
effectiveness of current public leaders as well as to grow future leaders.

## Leadership Development in the Public Sector

So what exactly does public leadership development mean? First, it is important to untangle the meaning of "leadership development." The Center for
Creative Leadership (CCL) defines *leader development* as the "expansion of a
person's capacity to be effective in leadership roles and processes" (Van Velsor
and McCauley 2004, p. 2). "Leadership roles and processes" means "those that

facilitate setting direction, creating alignment, and maintaining commitment in groups of people who share common work" (p. 2). Traditionally, leadership development and leader development, as defined, were synonymous. Leadership has long been viewed "as an individual-level skill" (Day 2000, p. 583); thus, leadership development has been about developing leaders.

However, many in the leadership development arena now distinguish *leadership* and *leader* development. Leader development corresponds with the CCL definition above, being at the individual level, and leadership development is an organizational-level phenomenon (Day 2000). Leadership development is thus defined as "the expansion of the organization's capacity to enact the basic leadership tasks needed for collective work: setting direction, creating alignment, and maintaining commitment" (Van Velsor and McCauley 2004, p. 18). Where leader development focuses on developing human capital, leadership development focuses on developing social capital (Day 2000). Developing individual leadership capacity is then seen as a subset of a broader set of activities called leadership development.

It is important to note, though, that the majority of "leadership development programs" are in fact *leader* development programs aimed at developing individuals. We see the distinction, however, as important and corresponding with major, transformational shifts in public, as well as private, organizations. Top-down, hierarchical models of management and leadership are giving way to models of collaboration and networks (Goldsmith and Eggers 2004). Van Velsor and McCauley (2004) observe that "it is getting harder and harder for formal leaders to enact leadership effectively on their own." Furthermore, "today's challenges are often too complex for individual leaders to fully understand alone . . . shared meaning must be created in the midst of seeming chaos and uncertainty. Individuals, groups, and organizations must work collaboratively to explore, set and reset direction, create alignment, and maintain commitment" (p. 18). Thus, leadership development goes beyond developing individual capacities to developing connections "between individuals, . . . collectives, . . . and between the organization and key constituents and stakeholders in its environment. . . . It also means developing the individual and collective capacities to create shared meaning, to effectively engage in interdependent work across boundaries, and to enact the task of leadership . . . in a way that is more inclusive" (p. 19).

In placing "public" in front of leadership development, we are narrowing the scope to public service organizations and leaders. By public service we specifically mean those working in public organizations, although we recognize that expanded notions of governance mean expanded notions of what constitutes public and who constitutes the public service. Thus, those who might see themselves working for the public good, as opposed to private interests, could well fall under this definition. Another consequence of—and complication added by—placing "public" in front of leadership development is that the focus can be broader than the organization. On one level, we might speak of developing the leadership capacity of a public organization as a collective entity. But on another level, we might think in terms of service or issue networks, or even communities of place.

Therefore, public leadership development, as used here, is a broad term that describes developing the capacity of public organizations, or networks of organizations that serve public purposes, to enact "leadership tasks needed for collective work" (Van Velsor and McCauley 2004, p. 18). Developing or growing public leaders is a key part of this overall effort and involves expanding individual leadership capacity for public purposes. Leadership for public purposes includes leading public organizations and leading in collaborative settings for the public or common good. For the most part, this book focuses on the leader development component of this broader notion of leadership development. However, many chapters speak to new ways of thinking about public leadership, and hence, the broad purview of public leadership development. In addition, discussions of developing public leaders fold in nicely with this more comprehensive view of public leadership development that is emerging.

### Different Types of Leader Development

It is important to understand that there are several different, yet complementary, types of leader development. The first, and perhaps most basic, is what Van Wart calls "self-study" (2005, p. 398). Here we are speaking primarily of "learning that occurs outside formal training and structured developmental experience provided by the organization" (p. 399). This includes the practice of creating "work-specific development plans based on [one's] self-observations about what knowledge and competencies they need to enhance" (p. 399). Van Wart also noted that self-study corresponds with the idea of personal leadership, the skill of continual learning, and several traits that engender self-improvement behaviors.

The self-study approach to leader development also corresponds with the idea of reflective practice or "praxis." Denhardt (2004) explained: "In praxis, we find once again the connection between personal learning and the relationships between theory and practice" (p. 195). Through "critical reflection on our own situation and that of our society . . . we are compelled to act to increase our sense of autonomy and responsibility, both for ourselves and for our society" (Denhardt 2004, pp. 24–25). Thus, in a praxis approach, the individual leader is constantly seeking development in its broadest sense.

A second type of leader development is what Blunt (2003) called "leaders growing leaders." Within organizations, seasoned leaders can develop or "grow" the next generation of leaders by

- being "examples of character and capability,"
- developing "deep and lasting relationships" with future leaders "acting as mentors," and
- "coaching" them as they learn from "challenging and varied job experiences" (ibid., p. 10).

By consciously serving as an example, and through mentoring and coaching, leaders develop a "leader-centered culture" that begets new leaders. This is how leaders can best "leave a legacy" (ibid., p. 12).

A third and related type of leader development is what Blunt (2003) called "organizations growing leaders." In addition to efforts of individual leaders developing leaders, there is much that can be done at the organizational level to develop leaders. High-performing organizations have strong leadership-oriented cultures. This includes real commitment by senior leaders to the "leaders developing leaders" approach, as well as to more formal development initiatives within the organization. Many organizations' human resources departments offer leadership development programs; however, some are much more extensive than others.

Another key factor in leader development is "challenging job experiences" (Blunt 2003, p. 72). Van Wart (2005) noted that when "structured experience" is challenging, yet realistic in terms of expectations, it enhances "the developmental opportunities embedded in experience" (p. 399). It is also beneficial to create a variety of experiences, including "cross-organizational assignments or networking" (Van Wart 2005, p. 399; Blunt 2003, p. 72). The Intergovernmental Personnel Act (IPA) Mobility Program[4] is an interesting mechanism that can be used to facilitate development. Managers seeking advancement in their home agency rotate assignments within an agency or across agencies to learn how others lead and manage. Finally, quality feedback and rigorous, ongoing evaluation are included as "best practices" for organizations that are developing leaders (Blunt 2003).

The fourth type of leader development is through "off-site" formal leadership training and education. Here we include leadership academies and institutes, as well as professional education programs that offer certificates and degrees. These are likely the first to come to mind when people hear the term "leadership development." Indeed, most of the authors in this volume approach leadership development with formal training programs for individual leaders in mind. Gardner (1990) noted that "most conventional programs are essentially advanced courses in management" (p. 175). However, many programs go much deeper than managerial skills. For example, the Federal Executive Institute offers a program on Leadership for a Democratic Society that includes themes of "personal leadership, organizational transformation, . . . and global perspective[s]" (Van Wart 2005, p. 401). The extent to which professional degree programs such as the MPA offer leadership development components varies (Denhardt and Campbell 2005). In any case, many practitioners seek MPA and similar degrees to help them advance to higher leadership positions. Therefore, these programs should all carefully consider what they are doing to develop leadership and leaders (Fairholm 2006).

## A Critical Time for Leadership Development in the Public Sector

Leadership development has always been important in the public sector, but its importance is growing for a variety of reasons. For one, there is an ever-increasing recognition that leadership is a key aspect of public management (Behn 1998; Fairholm 2004). In the past, leadership and management followed the venerable policy/administration dichotomy. Political principals lead, administrative agents manage. However, this view has changed dramatically. Behn (1998, p. 209), pointing out the various deficiencies of governance in the United States, argued that leadership by public managers can provide a corrective, helping improve in governance. The notion of public managers as "agential leaders" further underscores a critical, legitimate *leadership* role for public managers (Wamsley 1990). Indeed, it is safe to say that there is now some degree of consensus in the field of public administration that leadership is "an obligation" of public managers (Behn 1998, p. 209). Thus, developing leaders and not just managers is a primary concern. Two other reasons it is such a critical time for public leadership development are briefly discussed below.

### *A Leadership Crisis?*

For some time now, there has been widespread recognition of a "quiet crisis" in government. This term comes from the National Commission on the Public Service (also known as the Volcker Commission), which was formed in 1987 to prepare recommendations to counter what was then viewed as a gradual erosion of human capital in the public sector (the focus being on the federal government). The National Commission (1989) viewed recruitment and retention trends pointing toward "a government of the mediocre." (p. 4). In the intervening time, the crisis has now turned into a looming "catastrophe" (Millick and Smith 2002). A second National Commission on the Public Service (2003) painted an even darker picture of the future. The bipartisan study group concluded that "too many of our most competent career executives and judges are retiring or leaving early" and "too few of our most talented citizens are seeking careers in government" (p. iv).[5]

The crisis—or catastrophe—has many dimensions that go beyond the scope of this book.[6] However, a major component of primary interest here is what the crisis means for leadership in the public sector. An erosion of (career) leadership in government should be of great concern. There are several drivers for the leadership crisis, including lack of leader preparation, lack of public confidence in government, the "age bubble," and the ascendancy of political leadership over civil service.

Soni (2004) reports on a U.S. Office of Personnel Management (OPM) study that found that supervisors and senior leaders in the federal government by and large are selected for their technical expertise, and they lack preparation for leadership. The majority of agencies surveyed did not have any type of leadership development program. Furthermore, senior leaders generally were "lacking in skills and abilities needed for leading agencies in the twenty-first century such as collaborative leadership, managing across sectors and levels of government, leading by shared values, ability to frame issues in new ways, and ability to motivate others" (Soni 2004, p. 164). The second National Commission on the Public Service (2003) reported that "few organizations in our society have paid so little attention [as the federal government] to leadership succession and leadership quality" (p. 18).

Another major driver that was recognized two decades ago by the National Commission (1989) was the general low public confidence in government. This makes it much harder for public agencies to attract the "best and brightest." Years of "bureaucrat bashing" took its toll; fewer than half of senior executives in government would recommend the public service as a career to their children (p. 12). A specific goal of the Commission (1989) was to "rebuild the public trust" (p. 13).

Sadly, not much ground has been gained on this front. A recent survey by Harvard's Center for Public Leadership found 70 percent of respondents agreed that there is a "leadership crisis" in the United States today. Furthermore, all levels of government fell below the "moderate amount" level of confidence in a question on "overall level of confidence in leadership" by sector (Pittinsky et al. 2006). While much of this is likely due mostly to dissatisfaction with *political* leadership, the antigovernment climate noted two decades ago that creates such a negative environment for public servants does not seem to have improved much, if any. In fact, major failures such the war in Iraq and the response to Hurricane Katrina, and rampant political corruption in all quarters, have likely exacerbated the problem.

Another major factor that contributes to the crisis is the "age bubble" that was created in large part by the baby boom generation. OPM director Linda Springer, in discussing the problems presented by an aging government workforce, said "this is not a retirement boom, or a retirement wave, but a retirement tsunami." Springer explained at OPM's Federal Workforce Conference in 2006 that "sixty percent of the [federal] government's 1.6 million employees, *including 90 percent of its 6,000 senior executives,* will be eligible to retire in the next decade" (Ziegler 2006, italics added). This "age bubble" seems to be impacting the public sector hardest, due to the other factors mentioned: "declining appeal of public service" and inadequate leader preparation, in addition to employment regulations in the public sector that in some cases makes it less competitive (Young 2003).

The impact goes beyond just the federal government. A 2002 survey of the Council of State Governments found a similar problem for state governments (cited in Young 2003, p. 37). The ICMA recognizes similar trends in local government management and is responding with several initiatives, including an "emerging leaders" program and the "Next Generation Initiative" designed to help "the next generation of local government managers to train and develop themselves" (Bobkiewicz n.d.).

Finally, another contributor to our leadership crisis is that in recent years, political appointees have begun to dominate government, especially at the federal level (Ink 2007). They have maintained their role as policymakers but also have expanded their direct influence on day-to-day operations of agencies and programs. Career civil servants have been pushed aside or pushed down in appropriations.

It is important to note that this crisis is recognized not only by human resource experts but by the practitioners themselves. Government managers at both the federal and local level recognize the need to focus on leadership development in the coming years. A 2007 survey[7] of nearly 400 senior federal government executives asked: "In thinking about your organization's management needs over the next five years, how would you evaluate the importance of each of the following types of management knowledge and skills?" The respondents (N = 392) rated 15 areas from "not important at all" (1) to "extremely important" (5). The area with the most votes for "extremely important" was "leadership," with 80 percent. The next three highest-rated areas are also all leadership related: decision making/problem solving (79 percent), communication skills (74 percent), and teamwork (74 percent). More technical skills rated much lower.[8]

Results of a similar survey completed by 403 city and county managers in 2006 yielded similar results. Eighty-two percent of respondents rated decision making/problem solving as "extremely important" for their organization's management needs over the next five years, with communication skills second (77 percent), and leadership third (72 percent).[9] Clearly, public leaders understand the "quiet crisis" and would agree that developing future leaders must be a top priority at all levels of government.

## The Transformation of Public Leadership

The other reason leadership development in the public sector has never been more important has to do with the changing nature of public leadership itself. As we described in *Transforming Public Leadership for the Twenty-First Century* (Morse, Buss, and Kinghorn 2007), the way public leadership is understood and practiced is undergoing a dramatic, transformational change. The so-called new governance is shifting leadership away from traditional command-and-control conceptions toward partnerships and networks. Leading from positions of formal authority is giving way to leading "from the middle" (Luke 1998, p. 187). Rather than focusing on leading followers in an organizational context, today's public leaders are "boundary crossers" who work in collaboration with other public sector partners, as well as those from the private and nonprofit sectors (Peirce and Johnson 1997).

This transformation of public leadership requires many leaders. They must not only be effective organizational leaders in the traditional sense but also be effective collaborative, interorganizational leaders. In so doing, they must not only promote organizational cultures of excellence but now must develop cultures of boundary-crossing collaboration. The twenty-first-century public leader must continue to conserve institutional mission and values (Terry 2003) but must also be adept at transcending the organization to create public value (DeSeve 2007).

Thus, with all that is involved with leading within the context of the new governance, greater attention must be paid to developing leadership capacity in current and future leaders, as well as within and across organizations more generally. Being a public manager today involves much more than POSDCORB (Planning, Organizing, Staffing, Directing, Coordinating, Reporting, and Budgeting), and thus the training and preparation of public managers to be public *leaders* is essential.

## Overview of the Book

The collection of chapters that follow all speak in one way or another to this central theme of developing public leaders. We recognize that we still "know too little to permit definitive treatment of the subject," and that "the best we can hope is to offer provisional clarification on the way to something better" (Gardner 1990, p. 157). The "way to something better," in our view, is a greater emphasis on developing public leaders within the ranks of public administration. Moreover, this greater emphasis should be informed by the understanding of what public leadership means in the twenty-first century context of the "new governance" and by real experience in designing and delivering leader development programs. The authors here offer such wisdom and experience, and it is our hope that their contributions will help advance the practice of developing public leaders now and for the future.

Part I sets the stage, with four essays that discuss and unpack some of the changing conceptions of leadership facing the public sector. In Chapter 2, Marc Holzer takes issue with the simplistic, authoritarian image of leadership that pervades our culture and offers a more complex picture in the form of two cases of federal leaders—Nancy Hanks and Colin Powell. In so doing, Holzer illustrates a richer, more nuanced picture of public leadership. Holzer's piece illustrates how simple, short cases can be powerful teaching tools for leader development.

In Chapter 3, Stephanie Newbold, with the late Larry Terry, addresses the question of leadership as it relates to a transition in the field of public administration from the New Public Management (NPM) to what they call the New Democratic Governance (NDG). They offer a thoughtful critique of the NDG from the perspective of the "old institutionalism." The discussion underscores the critical importance of maintaining constitutional values within any discussion of public leadership and reminds us that, above all, public administrative leadership is about conserving the constitutional values that underpin the existence of any public agency. Newbold and Terry's chapter offers a word of caution to both NPM and NDG and, as such, suggests an important frame for the other discussions of leadership that follow.

Chapter 4 offers another framing piece for the rest of the book. James Colvard's chapter discusses management and leadership—an important, if contested, distinction in any discussion of leadership development. He also discusses, based on his many years as a public leader, the required understandings of managers and leaders and the different forms of power available to both. He traces the development stages of public leaders, from "individual performers" fresh out of school all the way through future-focused "leadership."

In Chapter 5, Brian Gittens looks to developing leaders in a rather unusual place—the offices of academic department chairs. Public institutions of higher education are very much part of the public service, but are rarely treated as such. As a result, discussions of public leadership rarely include colleges and academic departments. Gittens argues that a context of heightened public accountability for educational outcomes and financial resources begs for effective leadership by academic department chairs. He connects transformational leadership behaviors with constructive departmental cultures and views that model as a promising opportunity for the development of department chairs as leaders.

Part II offers three chapters that speak directly to leadership development for the "new governance." The new governance is characterized by interorganizational collaboration and networks. In Chapter 6, Rick Morse identifies some key competencies of collaborative leadership that go beyond those already identified for organizational leadership. Important competencies for collaboration include personal attributes of systems thinking and sense of mutuality, skills such as strategic thinking and group facilitation, and behaviors such as stakeholder identification and strategic issue framing. He argues that developing collaborative behavioral competencies requires an inside-out approach that goes beyond learning tools and addresses the fundamental personal attributes that facilitate collaborative action.

Chapters 7 and 8 discuss experiences in developing and delivering formal leadership training in the vein of the new governance. In Chapter 7, Carl Stenberg, Vaughn Upshaw, and Donna Warner of the University of North Carolina–Chapel Hill School of Government, share lessons learned in designing and delivering the Public Executive Leadership Academy, an intensive leader development program for local managers with an explicit focus on the public manager as a community change agent. Their chapter offers insight into what the content and pedagogy of such programs can look like, as well as many other important lessons for designing and delivering executive leader development programs.

In Chapter 8, Ruth Ann Bramson discusses leader development in the context of the MPA program at Suffolk University in Boston. Bramson and colleagues developed an innovative specialty—Community Leadership and Public Engagement—within the program. Emphasizing collaborative leadership and community problem solving, the Suffolk program translates the New Public Service (Denhardt and Denhardt 2003) into a curriculum that is explicitly focused on leader development for the new governance. Although it is still a work in progress, Bramson's efforts in Boston illustrate the potential of leader development within MPA programs, as well as the difference of a focus on collaboration and engagement versus top-down leadership conceptions.

A major aspect of the transformation of governance and leadership is globalization. The chapters in Part III discuss public leadership in the global context. In Chapter 9, Ruth Zaplin and Sydney Smith-Heimbrock draw attention to the fact that the United States sends thousands of officials abroad annually to work with foreign governments, international organizations, nongovernmental organizations, and universities—officially or unofficially. Unlike their Foreign Service counterparts who receive extensive training in language, culture, and diplomacy, these representatives often lack a sound grounding in how to work in a global context. Some do damage to the United States as a result, but more often they simply miss opportunities to reflect positively on their country and what it is trying to accomplish. Zaplin and Smith-Heimbrock look at the competencies they feel are necessary to work effectively as leaders in a global context.

In Chapters 10 and 11, respectively, Ambassador Thomas Pickering and Daniel Spikes, recently retired from the Foreign Service, offer their views on competencies necessary for working abroad. Ambassador Pickering, an experienced career Foreign Service officer and key decision maker in a private sector, multinational firm, Boeing, offers his views on what global leaders need to know and how they can be developed. Pickering pays special attention to the skills required for effective negotiations with foreign entities and career development issues. Spikes, in Chapter 11, lays out in detail the global leadership competencies that the State Department requires for advancement in the Foreign Service. From this overview, it is easy to see why the Foreign Service has become so effective.

Part IV looks to a particularly important subset of public leadership: political appointees. The second National Commission on the Public Service (2003) highlighted the political appointee problem in Washington, DC (the proliferation of appointee positions as well as the politicization of the process) as a serious impediment to effective government leadership. Effective leadership by political appointees is critical to the overall public leadership landscape. One of the clear lessons of the Katrina debacle was how ineffective leadership by appointees can have a devastating effect on an organization that very recently was lauding its deep pool of career talent.

In Chapter 12, Frank DiGiammarino lays out a model that informs newly appointed leaders about how they can successfully manage agencies and programs in the short time horizon that most have to achieve their goals before moving on. Typically, high-level leadership, especially at the federal level, has somewhat less than two years to make a difference. As such, they need to hit the ground running. DiGiammarino, in a series of twenty-five case studies of effective leaders, instructs leaders in how to be successful. In a different approach to the issue, Cindy Williams, Steve Redburn, and Terry Buss, in Chapter 13, offer their thoughts on the ten most important things that newly appointed senior officials should do in the early days of their tenure if they wish to be successful. The authors convened a focus group of highly effective leaders and asked them to discuss what they tried to do as they assumed responsibility for leading their agency. The chapter presents the collective results of this exercise.

Part V offers four chapters that speak directly to the design and delivery of leader development programs in the public sector. In Chapter 14, Jed Kee, Kathryn Newcomer, and Mike Davis present a follow-up to their "transformational stewardship" model of public leadership that is presented in Morse, Buss, and Kinghorn (2007). Here they apply the model of transformational stewardship to leader development, outlining the attributes and skills of transformational stewards, and thus the competencies that must form the core of development efforts. Furthermore, they discuss the types of development approaches that are most appropriate for developing different transformational steward capabilities. Their chapter offers concrete guidance for anyone involved in designing and delivering a public leader development program.

In Chapter 15, Rich Callahan shares wisdom gained from many years "in the trenches" delivering leader development programs at the University of Southern California. He offers advice in terms of content and delivery, with an emphasis on helping leaders initiate and sustain change in their organizations. He argues that programs should operate at five different levels of leadership (individual, group, organization, community, and institutional) and focus on outcomes.

Chapter 16 offers a substantial treatment of the action learning approach to leader development by Robert Kramer, which is based on his work at American University (Washington, DC). Kramer observes that most leadership development programs, especially those for mid-level managers, tend to be offered off-site, often in the evening or on weekends. Consequently, it is difficult for program participants to make the leap from training to the real world of leadership at their workplace, which is often turbulent, chaotic, and complex. Kramer rectifies this dilemma in leadership development programs focused on action learning—learning and building capacity to learn in real time, in the here-and-now, while continuing to act in the swirling midst of permanent "white water" that is the context for today's leaders.

Chapter 17 offers a unique pedagogical approach to leader development called social artistry. Lisa Nelson offers a framework in which leadership development builds creative capacities in a culture-specific context. In her words, "social artistry uses a society's or organization's own stories, music, and other arts in combination with a set of principles of human development to evoke awareness and access to the sensory, psychological, mythic, and integrative resources that are available to all humankind." Nelson offers a means for leaders to achieve much greater creativity in solving problems or taking advantage of opportunities.

By way of concluding our book, we report, in the Appendix, the results of a daylong session held with some of the nation's top leaders who were asked to think about what it would take for government to grow effective leaders. Unlike theories that claim leaders are born, not developed, this session lays out an agenda detailing what might be done.

## Next Steps

While the 16 chapters that follow cover a lot of ground, we acknowledge that in terms of *public* leadership development, we still have a long way to go in scholarship and practice. In terms of scholarship, there needs to be more systematic study of leadership competencies and behaviors to inform the curriculum of leader development programs. We need to better understand how leadership (as distinguished from leader) development in and across public organizations can best be accomplished. What approaches and techniques can best develop organizational capacity for collective work? We also need more systemic study of leader development programs to determine which approaches yield the best results in terms of actual leader behaviors and organizational outcomes.

In practice, we need simply to see more emphasis on leadership and leader development within public organizations. In the OPM study cited by Soni (2004, p. 163), it was reported that only four of twenty agencies surveyed actually had formal, internal leader development programs. We also need to see a greater emphasis on leader development in MPA and other professional degree programs (Fairholm 2006). Producing competent managers is not enough. Data from the 2006 and 2007 National Association of Schools of Public Affairs and Administration (NASPAA) surveys (cited in notes 7 and 9) make it very clear that practicing managers recognize leadership as a top priority for the future of their organizations. Public affairs programs must acknowledge this and reflect it in their curricula.

Finally, in a time when "network" is supplanting "hierarchy" as the dominant organizational form, we need to consider how leadership development can be accomplished *across* organizations. That is, as we consider how leaders and organizational cultures can be more collaborative, we must also consider how to develop capacity for joint work across organizations or within networks. In the future, public leadership development is likely to be thought of less in terms of the organization and more in terms of the network. How this will take shape and what types of approaches and techniques will be most appropriate for this work are questions that will need to be answered.

## Notes

1. For lists of what military leaders are reading, see www.ndu.edu/Library/reading-list/PMReadingList.html or visit www.ndu.edu (accessed May 12, 2007).

2. Of 142 National Association of Schools of Public Affairs and Administration (NASPAA)–accredited schools in 2004, 42 percent had a course on leadership listed in the curriculum. However, only 9 percent reported a leadership course in their core requirements (Denhardt and Campbell 2005, p. 170).

3. It should be noted that many leadership books and programs from the private sector (otherwise known generically as the field of "management") assume to speak to public sector leaders as well. The tacit assumption is that "leadership is leadership," whether that is at IBM or the U.S. Department of Transportation. Of course, there are many problems with this assumption (see Rainey 2003, ch. 3, for a very thoughtful discussion of the distinctive aspects of management and leadership in the public sector).

4. "The Intergovernmental Personnel Act Mobility Program provides for the temporary assignment of personnel between the Federal Government and state and local governments, colleges and universities, Indian tribal governments, federally funded research and development centers, and other eligible organizations" (www.opm.gov/programs/ipa/ (accessed May 10, 2007).

5. The Volcker Commission was housed in and supported by the National Academy of Public Administration until it disbanded in May 2007.

6. The question of developing human capital in the public sector is the subject of another book in this series, *Innovations in Human Capital Management* (Sistare, Shiplett, and Buss 2008).

7. Data available at www.naspaa.org/naspaa_surveys/FederalEmployerSurvey.pdf (accessed May 10, 2007).

8. For example, budgeting and financial management (44 percent), performance measurement (54 percent), information technology (32 percent), policy analysis (31 percent), and statistical analysis (21 percent).

9. Data available at http://www.naspaa.org/naspaa_surveys/CityManagerSurvey.pdf (accessed May 10, 2007).

## References

Behn, Robert D. 1998. "What Right Do Public Managers Have to Lead?" *Public Administration Review* 58(3): 209–224.

Blunt, Ray. 2003. *Growing Leaders for the Public Service.* Washington, DC: IBM Center for the Business of Government, Human Capital Management Series.

Bobkiewicz, Walter J. n.d. "Welcome to ICMA's Next Generation Website." Quoted material on http://icma.org/main/ns.asp?nsid=1600&hsid=9 (accessed November 20, 2007).

Day, David V. 2000. "Leadership Development: A Review in Context." *Leadership Quarterly* 11(4): 583–613.

Denhardt, Robert B. 2004. *Theories of Public Organization,* 4th ed. Belmont, CA: Thomson/Wadsworth.

Denhardt, Janet V., and Kelly B. Campbell. 2005. "Leadership Education in Public Administration: Finding the Fit Between Purpose and Approach." *Journal of Public Affairs Education* 11(3): 169–179.

Denhardt, Janet V., and Robert B. Denhardt. 2003. *The New Public Service.* Armonk, NY: M.E. Sharpe.

DeSeve, Edward. 2007. "Creating Public Value Using Managed Networks." In *Transforming Public Leadership for the 21st Century,* eds. Ricardo S. Morse, Terry F. Buss, and C. Morgan Kinghorn, 203–220. Armonk, NY: M.E. Sharpe.

Fairholm, Matthew R. 2004. "Different Perspectives on the Practice of Leadership." *Public Administration Review* 64(5): 577–590.

———. 2006. "Leadership Theory and Practice in the MPA Curriculum: Reasons and Methods." *Journal of Public Affairs Education* 12(3): 335–346.

Gardner, John W. 1990. *On Leadership.* New York: The Free Press.

Goldsmith, Stephen, and William D. Eggers. 2004. *Governing by Network: The New Shape of the Public Sector.* Washington, DC: Brookings.

Iacocca, Lee. 2007. *Where Have All the Leaders Gone?* New York: Scribner.
Ink, Dwight. 2007. "Twenty-first Century Career Leaders." In *Transforming Public Leadership for the 21st Century,* eds. Ricardo S. Morse, Terry F. Buss, and C. Morgan Kinghorn, 47–68. Armonk, NY: M.E. Sharpe.
Luke, Jeffrey S. 1998. *Catalytic Leadership: Strategies for an Interconnected World.* San Francisco: Jossey-Bass.
Millick, Sujata S., and Linda Wines Smith. 2002. "From Crisis to Catastrophe." *PA Times* 25(5): 3.
Morse, Ricardo S., Terry F. Buss, and C. Morgan Kinghorn, eds. 2007. *Transforming Public Leadership for the 21st Century.* Armonk, NY: M.E. Sharpe.
National Commission on the Public Service. 1989. *Leadership for America: Rebuilding the Public Sector.* Washington, DC: National Commission on the Public Service, Paul A. Volcker, Chairman.
———. 2003. *Urgent Business for America: Revitalizing the Federal Government for the 21st Century.* Washington, DC: National Commission on the Public Service, Paul A. Volcker, Chairman.
Peirce, Neal, and Curtis Johnson. 1997. *Boundary Crossers: Community Leadership for a Global Age.* College Park, MD: Academy of Leadership Press.
Pittinsky, Todd L., Seth A. Rosenthal, Laura M. Bacon, R. Matthew Montoya, and Wei-chun Zhu. 2006. *National Leadership Index 2006: A National Study of Confidence in Leadership.* Cambridge: Center for Public Leadership, John F. Kennedy School of Government, Harvard University.
Rainey, Hal G. 2003. *Understanding and Managing Public Organizations.* 3rd ed. San Francisco: Jossey-Bass.
Sistare, Hannah, Melissa Smith, Myra Shiplett, and Terry Buss. 2008. *Innovations in Human Capital Management.* Armonk, NY: M.E. Sharpe.
Soni, Vidu. 2004. "From Crisis to Opportunity: Human Resource Challenges for the Public Sector in the Twenty-First Century." *Review of Policy Research* 21(2): 157–178.
Terry, Larry D. 2003. *Leadership of Public Bureaucracies: The Administrator as Conservator,* 2nd ed. Armonk, NY: M.E. Sharpe.
Van Velsor, Ellen, and Cynthia D. McCauley. 2004. "Our View of Leadership Development." In *The Center for Creative Leadership Handbook of Leadership Development,* 2nd ed., eds. Cynthia D. McCauley and Ellen Van Velsor, 1–22. San Francisco: Jossey-Bass.
Van Wart, Montgomery. 2005. *Dynamics of Leadership in Public Service: Theory and Practice.* Armonk, NY: M.E. Sharpe.
Wamsley, Gary L. 1990. "The Agency Perspective: Public Administrators as Agential Leaders." In *Refounding Public Administration,* eds. Gary L. Wamsley, Robert N. Bacher, Charles T. Goodsell, Philip S. Kronenberg, John A. Rohr, Camilla M. Stivers, Orion F. White, and James F. Wolf, 114–162. Newbury Park, CA: Sage.
Young, Mary B. (Principal Research Consultant). 2003. *The Aging-and-Retiring Government Workforce: How Serious Is the Challenge? What Are Jurisdictions Doing About It?* Lexington, MA: The Center for Organizational Research, a division of Linkage, Inc. Sponsored by CPS Human Resource Services and available online at http://www. cps.ca.gov/AboutUs/agebubble.asp (accessed May 10, 2007).
Ziegler, Mollie. 2006. "OPM Chief Urges New Vision to Recruit Younger Feds: Calls Boomer Retirements a 'Tsunami.'" *Federal Times,* March 9. Available online at http:// www.federaltimes.com/index.php?S=1575070 (accessed May 10, 2007).

# Part I

# Changing Conceptions of Public Leadership

# 2

# Culture and Leadership

Marc Holzer

## Leadership for Policy Implementation

The implementation of public policy is one of the enduring frustrations of government. In a comprehensive overview of the subject in the *International Encyclopedia of Public Policy and Administration,* David J. Houston (1998) held that "implementation typically involves a wide range of actors with diverse interests and competing goals, including formal policymakers, bureaucratic officials from all levels of government . . . , private sector organizations, nonprofit organizations, clientele groups, and other interested citizen groups" (p. 1093). Although he does include "planning, communicating, negotiating" among the "activities" of implementation, nowhere in his comprehensive review of the subject does he mention leadership or partnership per se. Rather, he describes comprehensive theories of policy implementation that involve many factors. Our first premise is that leadership is an equally important activity, perhaps the most important part of the activity mix.

Our second premise is that simplistic models of leadership are at odds with the complexities and subtleties of public policy implementation. Traditional, simplistic models of leadership pervade our society and condition our public managers from a very early age. Those ingrained top-down models frustrate policy implementers—or public servants—by making the least, rather than the most, of our critical human resources.

Models of excellent leadership can be especially powerful in informing the study of public administration/implementation. They offer salient models that can gain and maintain the attention of busy policy implementers. If better leadership "prescriptions" are to be constructed, they will have to rely on lessons of successful leadership through new lenses, and the literature of leadership offers especially powerful lenses, often focusing on partnerships as a means to the stated goals of a particular public policy.

Our third premise is that programs in public administration and public affairs, as well as in business and management, are expending much effort in undoing the assumptions that students bring to the classroom; as a corollary, they are ignoring the problems and constraints of such deep-seated, albeit simplistic, views. Those simplistic assumptions essentially follow an authoritarian, or Theory X, model.

- Leaders must be strong and decisive; under continuous pressure, they must act on the spot, reaching decisions without taking much time to consider the subtleties and implications.
- Leaders are expected to act as authoritarian, lone decision makers; they may solicit advice, but their operative paradigm is "the buck stops here," the adage that the decision is on their desk, on their watch. They are expected to act, and they do so as much to serve their egos as to respond to the expectations of their colleagues, superiors, and board members that they present a strong and decisive persona.
- The "team" must back up the leader, right or wrong. Team members do not argue; soldiers carry out their orders, athletes execute their plays, and subordinates follow directions.
- Authority emanates from the top and is to be automatically accepted. Members of an organization, paid or volunteer, rarely talk back or challenge top-down directives. And they are just as often ignored in the formulation of decisions and strategies.
- Leaders know best and the workforce must therefore follow. Generals and Secretaries of Defense view wars as too complex for the average soldier or citizen to understand. Principals view education as too complex for students, parents, and even teachers to comprehend.

Thus, public management is driven by assumptions of leadership that are widely accorded legitimacy by the workforce exposed to Theory X-type role models from birth.

- Young children are socialized to follow the authoritative directions of their parents. This is a necessary pattern of survival and cultural transference that often continues throughout the life cycle of parents' relationships with their children.
- As they grow and gain independence, other authority-oriented role models insert themselves.

  - Students are expected to follow the lead of their teachers and, later, their professors, who are given immense authority to direct, judge, punish, and reward.

- Student-actors must follow the directions of the drama coach or director of the school play.
- Student-athletes are acculturated never to question the edicts from their coaches.

Those role models are reinforced throughout adulthood. The prevailing stereotype of the authoritative leader is reinforced and appears in multiple venues.

- On the silver screen—In *Patton,* George C. Scott portrays the revered general as a larger-than-life figure, intimidating his troops into courageous actions, accusing slackers of cowardice, and exposing himself to enemy fire as an exemplar to his troops. That image, as portrayed by other actors who represent real and fictional characters, is a thread through movies of wartime "action" and Cold War deception, of the Wild West, and of police and firefighting heroics.
- On television—Shows offer prime-time stereotypes of those in command almost hourly: authoritative police commanders on *Law and Order,* a decisive doctor on *House,* and a confident president on *West Wing.* Commercials on both TV and radio almost invariably present the boss as a figure to be feared and to be pleased. The executive's voice is loud and strong, his or her manner is forceful, and his or her subordinates are relegated to inferior positions.
- Popular fiction—The genre of Michael Crichton and colleagues—deals primarily in stereotypes of powerful figures (albeit sometimes bumbling as he/she ignores the advice of subordinates). Novels of politics or crime trade in images of strong Presidents, CIA directors, admirals and generals, commissioners and commanders. The language is idiomatic, and the characterizations are two-dimensional.
- Sports—The image of the lone, aggressive decision maker is reinforced daily, and especially on the weekends, through athletic contests that are televised or in person: the football or basketball coach pacing the sidelines who is playing the role of chess master, while the players are simply pieces on the game board; the baseball manager sitting at the end of the bench strategizing; the Olympic coach directing the preparation of the compliant skater or runner; the World Cup coach shouting at the soccer team.
- Comics—Although the boss is often portrayed as insensitive, the power relationship is that of superior to inferior. In *Dilbert,* the staff typically suffers from the wrong-headed behavior of management, but the incumbent, incompetent managers seem to survive. In *Blondie,* the boss is the productivity figure while Dagwood is the buffoon.

Although simplistic assumptions are widely discredited in the research-based literature, few people are exposed to it or are taught those research findings. In the United States, tens of millions of people staff public and quasi-public organizations (nonprofits, private sector contractors). Only a very small percentage (in the range of tens of thousands) are educated in public management at the graduate level (Master of Public Administration [MPA], Master of Public Policy, and similar degrees), and even many of those graduates have never been exposed to courses on leadership per se. Most people in positions of public sector leadership come from fields in which there is little but the stereotypes to inform their expectations: law, medicine, engineering, social work, education, and so on.

## Leadership as a Complex Construction

As alternatives to the simplistic assumptions that inundate our children and that are reinforced through adulthood by the media, analyses and case studies of leadership offer a set of creative recommendations for how our courses on leadership, motivation, and behavior might more effectively reverse the notions of authority that our society so pervasively communicates, suggesting alternative models that would make much better use of our human resources in the quest for more effective public organizations and programs. We cannot govern in the twenty-first century from first-century models such as the Caesars.

As examples of the efficiency and power of leadership cases, we cite the examples of two federal administrators: Nancy Hanks of the National Endowment for the Arts (NEA) and Colin Powell of the Department of Defense. Both are examples of how cases may help develop models for leadership, and both offer insights on building and maintaining sometimes fragile partnerships.

### *The Case of Nancy Hanks*

According to Margaret Jane Wyszomirski (1997), Nancy Hanks, as the second chairperson of the NEA (1969–1977), is generally acknowledged to have been an especially successful policy implementer who executed a strategy for advancing and adapting the agency to a changing policy environment. Hanks brought unusually deep and broad leadership skills to the NEA.

During Hanks's tenure, the agency budget increased twelvefold. Its staff increased six-fold. The number of applications for funding increased tenfold. The number of grant awards rose by a factor of seven. Overall, Hanks nurtured an arts boom throughout the country. Theater audiences more than tripled. Dance audiences increased by a factor of ten. Other measures of the arts showed similar growth. Just as important, artists and government officials came to feel they were full partners in a set of long-term endeavors.

Wyszomirski characterizes the ingredients of Hanks's leadership—the "recipe" for implementation—as four major elements: environmental context, bureaucratic resources, political tactics, and personal style.

In terms of the context, Hanks was relatively nonpartisan. Although a Republican, she was acceptable to President Nixon as "neither an artist nor a politician"(p. 125). As a "neutral" figure, she was able to build partnerships (i.e., political coalitions) by avoiding any political or artistic labels. Rather, according to Wyszomirski, she described herself modestly as a budgeting specialist, an arts administrator who could creatively put a program into a political context. She was adept at partnering: building networks, convening panels of experts, coordinating advisory committee decisions, integrating diverse viewpoints, and reformulating information and opinion into an acceptable, practical product. She also has been described as an individual with great attention to detail and a facility for meticulous preparation.

In addition to her personal characteristics, Hanks defined a long-term financial growth strategy for the agency. Wyszomirski (p. 129) describes her three goals as:

1. Cultural resources development, targeting nonprofit arts agencies for competitive grants;
2. Availability of artistic resources to a much wider audience; and
3. Advancement of our cultural legacy by funding new creative opportunities for artists and new artistic experiences for audiences.

Each of these three goals was the basis for a new coalition of partners: arts agencies, audiences, and artists.

To fund these initiatives, Hanks took advantage of the newly passed Budget and Impoundment Control Act of 1974 to secure more than $10 million in transitional funding. In addition, by developing "challenge grants" as a new category of funding, which required a three-to-one match of private-to-federal dollars, she effectively stretched NEA's budget. Both actions required substantial coalition building in the arts and political communities, as well as alliance building with other federal agencies such as the U.S. Information Agency and the General Services Administration. To staff NEA's initiatives, she built a capable, loyal staff, in large part by drawing on her wide networks. That staff underscored and reinforced her own capabilities and was very much a fourth partner in building momentum for the arts.

Finally, Hanks became known for results-oriented programs (p. 133). She often relied on ideas that had been successfully piloted elsewhere, often at the state level. By paying attention to such innovations, she was able to adapt workable ideas rather than risk implementing something entirely new.

Compared to her successors who were notably less successful, Hanks is viewed as a person with the right qualities and the necessary skills to take advantage of a policy environment that presented opportunities for implementation of public policy. She is known as a leader who worked effectively with a broad range of allies, including bureaucrats in her own agency and in other federal venues, and politicians in the White House and Congress.

Overall, then, we can extract the following guidelines from the Hanks case.

1.   Build networks resulting in partnerships.
2.   Bring technical expertise to the position.
3.   Increase resources and disburse them to partners.
4.   Integrate diverse viewpoints.
5.   Adapt proven ideas.
6.   Demonstrate results.
7.   Build a capable, loyal staff as internal partners.
8.   Take advantage of opportunities in the policy environment.

### The Case of Colin Powell

Nancy Hanks had a clear mission, one in which she ardently believed: growth of the arts. General Colin Powell's most public implementation task, however, was to implement an even clearer mission, but one that he may not have initially supported, the Persian Gulf War. However, by all accounts he did so in an effective manner.

According to Jon Meacham (1997), Powell reportedly had reservations about going to war against Iraq. As an alternative, he favored a strategy of containment. But Powell's responsibility as Chairman of the Joint Chief's of Staff was to implement the President's decision to go to war. By all accounts, Powell was adroit in his support of the President, partnering with different players to build a supportive constituency.

Meacham characterizes Powell's skills as more than technical. In the White House, he was considered surprisingly adept politically and was a major player who knew how to work the levers of power at the departmental and interagency levels. Among members of the press, he was viewed as especially cooperative in helping to develop stories, a clear indication of his subtle skillfulness in enlisting the press as a policy implementation partner.

Like Hanks, Powell's attributes included an efficient manner and an ability to get things done. He was firmly committed to the principles of merit, and he attributed his success to the Army's objectivity in assessing the skills and accomplishments of its members. Powell clearly felt that his success in the military was based solely on his performance. That statement alone underscored his awareness of the need to build and maintain support within the military bureaucracy over the long haul (i.e., the course of his career).

By reputation, Powell was characterized, in terms of policy implementation, as a conservative manager. He is described by Meacham and others as someone who knew how far he could take an argument, and he was understandably reluctant to antagonize other decision makers who did not share his understanding of facts, strategies, or tactics. But his persuasive abilities enabled him to fight for federal funds for defense and to prevail. He proved an effective negotiator. In 1990 he took the initiative, convincing President George H.W. Bush and Defense Secretary Dick Cheney to maintain a "base force" of 1.6 million troops, and overall defense spending of $290 billion (Meacham 1997, p. 164). In arguing for those numbers, he used his ties with the press to "float" his own position in advance of that of the White House. He was able to preserve Cold War levels of funding without a Cold War enemy. He did this in part by building a coalition of interests within the Department of Defense, a mutually advantageous strategy of multiple, overlapping forces, thus begging the questions of efficiency and redundancy and minimizing opportunities for drastic budget cuts.

During the Gulf War, Powell was as adept at being a politician as he was at being a military strategist. According to General Norman Schwarzkopf, he was never sure whether Powell was representing his own views or those of others.

Overall, Powell emerged from the Persian Gulf War as a hero—highly respected and positioned for future leadership. The military had accomplished its mission, and he was perceived both as an effective leader, by his troops and the public, and as an effective soldier, by his civilian superiors. He had successfully implemented national policy largely by recruiting organizational allies and maintaining coalitions, much as he had done in earlier budgetary and intradepartmental "wars."

We can also extract guidelines for successful policy implementation from the Powell case, according to Meacham.

1. Know how to "partner" in the process of implementing desired policy.
2. Become a reliable source for potential press partners.
3. Project an image of efficiency.
4. Advocate principles of merit, thereby building a positive image for the organization.

5. Build both internal and external coalitions.
6. Be able to represent the views of other partners.
7. Argue preemptively, thereby facilitating partnership opportunities.
8. Be willing to implement orders to be an "inside" partner.

## The Leadership Literature

What implementation insights can we extract from the leadership literature as a whole? Perspectives on leadership are often framed as guides, and a sampling of those distillations may help a policy-level official build a salient overall model of leadership for implementation. For example, in addition to the personal and political attributes emphasized above, John Baldoni (1998), a well-known writer on leadership, defined six key attributes of leadership messages.

1. *Character:* Effective leadership over the long run should be moral.
2. *Bearing:* Confidence should emerge from bearing, which is the public presentation of character.
3. *Attitude:* Optimism holds more potential than pessimism.
4. *Words:* The public face of the inner person.
5. *Deeds:* A leader is ultimately the sum of his or her accomplishments.
6. *Wisdom:* A willingness to look ahead as well as a willingness to be flexible in changing conditions.

Although a distinctly different perspective than each of the two cases above, Baldoni's list offers a complementary perspective on partnering. The attributes he describes not only serve the individual, but also serve to attract and hold the support of superiors, peers, and subordinates who find it attractive and advantageous to be associated with such a leader. If the sum of these six points may be labeled as "charisma," then such charisma may be viewed as a collective signal to potential allies, or partners. Charisma itself will not ensure implementation, but by helping to recruit and hold allies, that set of attributes will certainly make policy implementation more likely.

Addressing the military, Maureen Leboeuf (1999) defined an alternative philosophy of leadership. It certainly complements the more pragmatic view of General Powell. Leboeuf presents a complex view of leadership, one that is rooted in abstractions rather than skills or personal chemistry:

1. *Vision:* Idealistic and a vision of the future organization.
2. *Values:* Loyalty, duty, respect, selfless service, honor, integrity, and personal courage.

3. *Care for soldiers/employees:* Quality of life, proper training and equipment, safety, family support, and timely recognition for a job well done.
4. *Leader development:* Formal schooling, leader training within the organization, and empowerment.
5. *Managing change:* Recognize that change is inevitable and strive to master it; clearly articulate the reasons for change and how it ties into the organization's mission and purpose.
6. *Diversity:* Value and listen to every member of the organization.
7. *Sense of humor:* To help build rapport and cooperation (pp. 30–33).

Much of Leboeuf's list is advice on partnering, especially with the organization's all-important internal partners: soldiers/employees and future leaders. She is suggesting that both abstractions and tangible improvements in their quality of life will build support for a leader's agenda. Her advice on diversity (number 6) is merely that everyone may have something valuable to offer in terms of strengthening the implementation system, and sometimes in terms of avoiding disastrous mistakes. Even the advice as to sense of humor offers help in partnering in terms of personal rapport and spirit of cooperation.

**Conclusion**

Overall, innovative partnerships between the public and nonprofit and private sectors, and across agencies, departments, levels, and even branches of the government, serve as models for significantly higher levels of accomplishment after we begin to think outside the usual bureaucratic box. Federal, state, and local officials need to encourage and support effective partnerships that accomplish government's policy-related goals. When permitted to approach problem solving creatively, public servants can create partnerships toward more productive, more responsive government.

In particular, implementation requires public sector managers who are willing to rethink human resource management. In a society with higher, quality-oriented expectations, the simplistic bureaucratic, hierarchical management style that our culture communicates is insufficient. Yet, too many organizations, public and private, fail to intelligently utilize or maintain their expensive human capital. The reason for this is simple: it is difficult and it takes much time and effort. The more enduring but more difficult way to implement improved performance is to develop each worker's individual capacity and desire to function at the highest level possible. Employees at all levels are the partners on which the success of every public organization rests.

The enlightened leadership and management of human resources is particularly important in the public sector because government's most extensive and expensive investments are people; most public organizations devote 50–85 percent of their budgets to employee salaries and benefits. Because those "human resources" have complicated needs, responsive public organizations have adopted enlightened human resource practices, rejecting an authoritarian, bureaucratic style. Public organizations have often recognized that a productive organization is humane, structured around not only the task but also its members and their human needs. They understand that the art of leadership inheres in getting people to work well for the organization by grasping and responding to their needs.

But organizational leaders also understand that intended services are achieved not by isolated individuals working alone and competing with each other, but by teams working cooperatively and supporting their colleagues. Thus, effective leaders recognize that partners within the organization are teams as well as individuals.

It might be tempting to adopt either of the cases or lists above as a model. It might even be tempting to develop a "leadership schematic." But we must caution that this type of schematic cannot and should not be considered a formula for leadership toward implementation. No single model is sufficient or specific to any individual's particular problem-solving situation. Each individual has to form his or her own schematic or roadmap. Each implementation situation will differ in significant ways. Some will necessarily emphasize a certain subset of skills. It would be naïve and misleading to consider each element of equal weight and import. Yet, over the long run, each is potentially important. At the same time, we must acknowledge that this picture is incomplete. What is salient will depend on the individual, the situation, the group, the resources, and so on. To implement policy effectively, one must be willing to search for and to adapt insights on leadership; thus, this schematic should differ on an individual basis and should evolve over time.

Leadership, in its simplest formulation as outlined in the first part of this chapter, may be taken as the "born leader." But few if any leaders are born to the job. Even those with the most powerful personal attributes learned such behaviors from family, friends, teachers, and even television and other media. The most effective leaders go beyond the simple prescriptions and assumptions communicated by the culture, and continue to learn about leadership. This learning empowers their ability to implement policies and priorities. Even for very busy decision makers, who are so busy implementing public policy that they do not have time to read the heavier texts and journal articles, effective means to learning for leadership may include:

- *Books:* A search of the Web will yield hundreds of titles on leadership. Similarly, a visit to any good bookstore will yield dozens. For example, Montgomery Van Wart has recently written *Dynamics of Leadership in Public Service: Theory and Practice* (2005). Amazon.com lists some fifty books on leadership as bestsellers.
- *Articles:* Short discussions of leadership are widely available in the print and electronic media, particularly in magazines in both formats and in electronic blogs. Searches under the term "leadership" on various search engines produce links to thousands of articles.
- *Online resources:* Excellent, thoughtful examinations of leadership are available via cases on the Web, such as the Hartwick Classic Film Leadership Cases (www.hartwickinstitute.org) and the Electronic Hallway (www.hallway.org). Diverse cases are found on such sites as the Wildland Fire Leadership Development Program (www.fireleadership.gov), including its Leadership in Cinema program. GovLeaders.org links to a wide range of publications, games and simulations, degrees, and institutes specifically focused on public sector leaders.

Leadership resources, in print or video or online, may offer richer, deeper visions of effective leadership. For the most part, those visions run counter to the relatively simplistic, top-down model that so pervades our culture. But perhaps the more thoughtful analyses and reflections on leadership are insufficient guides by themselves to the extent that they are simply overwhelmed by the leadership messages inherent in popular culture and bestselling titles, messages that are built on the lessons of a Patton, an Attila the Hun, or a prominent coach.

The most effective approach to leadership development may be to deliver sophisticated lessons as part of structured leadership development experiences. For example, many MPA programs, and in particular Executive MPA programs, offer courses in leadership, as do other degree programs, continuing education courses, and public management conferences. Those more thoughtful and structured approaches to the study of leadership—approaches characterized by partnering and collaborative behaviors—may effectively help undo the assumptions or behaviors many managers have subconsciously absorbed but have never consciously questioned.

## References

Baldoni, John. 1998. "The Leadership Message." Available at: http://www.bus.ualberta.ca/rfield/Speeches/John%20Baldoni%201998–1.htm (accessed April 9, 2007).

Houston, David J. 1998. "Implementation." In *International Encyclopedia of Public Policy and Administration,* ed. Jay M. Shafritz, 1093–1097. Boulder, CO: Westview Press.

Leboeuf, Maureen K. 1999. "Developing a Leadership Philosophy." *Military Review* 79(3): 28–34.

Loverd, Richard A. 1997. *Leadership for the Public Service.* Upper Saddle River, NJ: Prentice Hall.

Meacham, Jon. 1997. "Colin Powell: How Colin Powell Plays the Game." In *Leadership for the Public Service,* ed. Richard A. Loverd, 159–170. Upper Saddle River, NJ: Prentice-Hall.

Van Wart, Montgomery. 2005. *Dynamics of Leadership in Public Service: Theory and Practice.* Armonk, NY: M.E. Sharpe.

Wyszomirski, Margaret Jane. 1997. "From Nancy Hanks to Jane Alexander: Generating Support for Art's Sake at the National Endowment for the Arts." In *Leadership for the Public Service,* ed. Richard A. Loverd, 121–149. Upper Saddle River, NJ: Prentice-Hall.

# 3

# From the New Public Management to the New Democratic Governance

## Leadership Opportunities and Challenges

Stephanie P. Newbold and Larry D. Terry

The concept of governance is critical to the study and practice of public administration and even more central to the specific opportunities and challenges that affect public sector leadership. Scholars have defined governance in a multitude of ways and in a plethora of different contexts. The public administration community relies on the term frequently, but a single, agreed-on definition does not exist. This, as a result, leads to a great deal of confusion when scholars and practitioners emphasize the term "governance" as a means of comparing or critiquing different theoretical approaches to public administration, such as those associated with New Public Management (NPM) or New Democratic Governance (NDG).

Donald Kettl (2002) defines governance as "the way government gets its job done" (p. xi). He argues that traditions stemming from the administrative and political philosophies of Alexander Hamilton, Thomas Jefferson, James Madison, and Woodrow Wilson transformed the nation's governance structure. Carolyn Heinrich and Laurence Lynn (2000) maintain that governance "generally refers to the means for achieving direction, control, and coordination of individuals or organizations . . . and may be defined as regimes of laws, administrative rules, judicial rulings, and practices that constrain, prescribe, and enable activity" (pp. 2–3). Jon Pierre (2000), in a similar line of argument, supports the position that governance has two distinct meanings. The first focuses on "empirical manifestations of state adaptation to its external environment and the second denotes a theoretical representation of social systems co-ordination and the role of the state in that process" (p. 3).

Gary Wamsley et al. (1990) make the compelling case that governance should permeate the theoretical and practical underpinnings of public administration. Their definition integrates old institutionalism with normative, constitutional theory. The foundations of Wamsley's model are present in Peter Bogason and Juliet Musso's (2006) assumption that governance "can be understood as encompassing both structure and process, both institutional and procedural dimensions" (p. 5). Jos Raadschelders (1999) moves in this direction as well, arguing: "The purpose of public administration is to govern, and thus government and governance are the core concepts that help us to organize the study of Public Administration" (p. 288). Eva Sorensen (2006), by contrasting government with governance, contends that the latter "denotes a complex governing process in which a multitude of public and private actors interact to govern society" (p. 99). Lester Salamon (2002a) finds merit in this approach, but his definition of governance "relies on a wide array of third parties in addition to government to address public problems and pursue public purposes" (p. 8). Salamon's perspective complements key elements associated with NDG.

This discussion highlights how a select group of highly regarded public administration scholars define governance and apply it to the roles and responsibilities traditionally associated with governing. We recognize that other definitions for governance exist and that each provides a distinct way of conceptualizing how this concept affects the administration of public agencies and elements of public sector leadership—theoretically and practically.

For the purposes of this chapter we define governance as the historical, political, institutional, legal, and constitutional foundations that enable government to exist and function within the boundaries established by the U.S. Constitution. This definition builds on Jan Grell and Gary Gappert's (1992) notion that governance is a broader concept than government because it holds the potential "to influence government as well as its traditional institutions and actors" (p. 68). An interesting way of deepening the field's collective understanding of this process is by thinking of public administration as being part of an "ever-democratizing constitutional republic."[1] The administrative state is not perfect—as the history of the nation certainly reflects—and it has not always lived up to the grand normative principles embedded within U.S. constitutional tradition. The administrative state, however, is constantly seeking new ways to preserve constitutional tradition, to enhance its institutional legitimacy, to provide essential public services, and to ensure that it does not function in a hollow environment (Terry 2006; Milward and Provan 2000; Milward, Provan, and Else 1993). In a word, "good governance is vital for the protection of the rights of citizens and the advancement of economic and social development" (Kim et al. 2005, p. 647).

The purpose of this chapter is to raise important leadership questions associated with public administration's transition from NPM to NDG. Analyzing this transition is essential for deepening the field's ongoing debate regarding how we think about and define governance. First, this chapter describes the key elements of NPM and analyzes its institutional effects on the administrative state. Although many public administration scholars have focused on the theoretical foundations of NPM, questioned whether it represents a separate and distinct field of public management inquiry, and pondered its credibility, the field has not scrutinized the strengths and weaknesses of NDG in the same manner. Therefore, our second objective is to describe and evaluate the core elements of NDG, including transparency, networks, and civil society/participation. Finally, this chapter outlines the central tenets of old institutionalism as a means of providing a distinctive way of scrutinizing the theoretical underpinnings of NDG. Old institutionalism, as understood through the lens of Philip Selznick (1957), provides public administration with the necessary insight to examine important institutional dynamics associated with NDG, particularly leadership in the public sector.

**New Public Management**

*Description*

Since the 1980s, scholars and practitioners have meticulously described the strengths and weaknesses of NPM. The principles of microeconomic theory largely influenced the development of this line of inquiry. Terry (1998) was one of the first scholars to outline the different theoretical approaches of NPM. Quantitative/analytic management, liberation management, and market-driven management (pp. 195–196), as well as public choice theory, transaction cost economics, and principal-agent theory, led to his argument that the incorporation of these theoretical perspectives into public administration led to a specific form of neo-managerialism. Former Vice President Albert Gore's *Report of National Performance Review* (1993) and David Osborne and Ted Gaebler's *Reinventing Government* (1992) laid the foundation for the application of these theories to public sector management. Public administration, as a result, has been grappling with the implications of this movement ever since.

James Thompson's (2006) position that "management and performance shortcomings of federal agencies are rooted in the political rather than the managerial system" (p. 496) highlights an important dynamic associated with NPM. Supporters of this line of inquiry argue that government should do more with fewer resources, treat citizens as customers, and compete with the private sector to determine which sector can perform public services more economically, effectively, and efficiently. These political preferences in administrations have extraordinarily affected how agencies provide public service delivery, implement a wide range of policies, and manage programs (Kettl 1993; Milward 1994; Prager and Desai 1996; Wallin 1997; Johnstone and Romzek 1999; Milward and Provan 2000; Savas 2000; Van Slyke 2003).

### Key Elements

Liberation management and market-driven management are the core elements associated with NPM. The former supports the notion that civil servants are not only competent, capable, knowledgeable, and highly skilled, but they also recognize the value of quality management to the organization in which they serve (Peter 1992; Light 1997). Proponents of this approach argue that managerial problems develop because of the "bureaucratic system with its burdensome rules, controls, and procedures" (Terry 2006, p. 114). Market-driven management, by contrast, emphasizes competition and gives preference to private sector values, especially economy, efficiency, and effectiveness, over values associated with public sector management, such as responsibility, responsiveness, and representativeness (Loffler 1997; Considine 2001). Advocates of this approach maintain that encouraging public managers to rely on market forces as civil servants motivates them to improve performance (Terry 2006, p. 114).

### Critique

Public administration scholars have examined and critiqued the key elements of NPM extensively (Box 1998, 1999; de Leon and Denhardt 2000; Denhardt and Denhardt 2003). The Constitutional School is particularly sensitive to the liberation and market-driven managerial approaches espoused by NPM supporters. The Constitutional School is a group joined in a loose confederation that is characterized by an interest in the principles embodied in the U.S. Constitution, which is the basis for their research and practice.[2] These scholars' public administration is broader and deeper in both scope and perspective than what the theoretical and practical underpinnings of NPM provide. To make this case, we need look no further than Alexander Hamilton's observation in *Federalist 27:* "It may be laid down as a general rule that [the people's] confidence in and obedience to a government will commonly be proportioned to the goodness or badness of its administration" (Cooke 1961, p. 172). One way to measure citizen confidence in government is certainly through economic performance indicators, but in a separation-of-powers system of government, leaders must also take into account other considerations, particularly in cases affecting the protection of individual rights.

Public servants must protect and defend not only individual rights but also constitutional integrity, transparency, and rule of law (Rosenbloom 2007) for the citizenry to maintain confidence in government. NPM does not take into account these normative factors for policymaking, management, analysis, and evaluation techniques of public agencies, especially in matters affecting democratic governance. Christensen and Laegreid (2002) argue "under NPM accountability is based on output, competition, transparency and contractual relations, and thus represents a departure from public administration of the old school, where various forms of accountability were based upon process and procedures, hierarchical control, trust, and cultural traditions" (p. 277).[3] Finally, Kirlin (1996) presents an important critique of NPM's reliance on micro-economic theory: "Economists sometimes adopt a view of the functions of government to fit their tools of analysis. In support of their chosen approach, they distort the history of government, making it subordinate to economics when it clearly is not" (p. 170). The omission of normative, democratic, and constitutional principles from NPM provides an opportunity for theories associated with NDG to challenge this school of thought.

## New Democratic Governance

### Description

In comparison with NPM, NDG is a relatively new line of inquiry, intending to shift public administration's dialogue and understanding about the normative dimensions associated with democratic governance. NDG draws our attention to important areas of concern omitted by NPM and its micro-economic orientation. According to Bevir (2006), "If markets and networks are replacing bureaucracies, perhaps we need new means for ensuring that the latter mechanisms remain appropriately democratic" (p. 426). Salamon (2002a) describes the new governance process, especially as it relates to the theoretical underpinnings and elements of NDG.

> It finds commonalities flowing from the tools of public action that they employ. It thus shifts the unit of analysis from the individual program or agency to the distinctive tools or technologies that programs embody. Underlying this approach is the notion that the multitude of different government programs really embody a more limited number of basic tools or instruments of action that share common features regardless of the field in which they are deployed (p. 10).

This way of thinking also supports one of the central themes from the Sixth Global Forum on Reinventing Government in 2005, which focused on the idea that "good governance is vital for the protection of the rights of citizens and the advancement of economic and social development" (Kim et al. 2005, p. 647).

A number of scholars have pointed out serious theoretical and practical concerns with NPM and support a new approach or line of inquiry for examining the relationship between the state and its citizenry (King and Stivers 1998; Box 1998, 1999; DeLeon and Denhardt 2000; Denhardt and Denhardt 2003; Boyte 2005). The key elements associated with NDG provide a thoughtful response and well-argued critique of NPM.

## *A Closer Look at Civil Society/Participation, Transparency, and Networks*

NDG pays particular attention to civil society/participation, transparency, and networks. It examines the need for greater citizen collaboration not only with government agencies but also with civil society initiatives and programs (Hirst 1994; Stivers 1994). Stoker (2006) outlines broader elements associated with NDG, including defining public intervention by the search for public value; affording greater legitimacy to a wider range of stakeholders; building and maintaining a strong commitment to a public service ethos; and requiring an adaptable, learning-based approach to the challenges of public service delivery.[4]

The key elements of NDG present a way for citizens to express any possible frustration when dealing with the undemocratic structure of Weberian democracy (Golembiewski and Vigoda 2000; Vigoda 2002; Thompson 1983). More specifically, civil society initiatives, according to Cooper and Musso (1999), provide a meaningful and productive way for citizens to articulate dissatisfaction with administrative agencies and public services at all levels of U.S. government. NDG's emphasis on collaboration, cooperation, and public-private partnerships provides a well-grounded response to NPM's microeconomic orientation that treats citizens as customers (Osborne 2000; Teisman and Klijn 2002; Salamon 2002a).

The modern-day third sector emerged to meet the growing needs of citizens in large part because government agencies could no longer provide the multitude of services needed and requested by the citizenry at large. Hansmann (1987) argued that government failure theory played a major role in this contemporary transformation. As Young (2001) pointed out:

> This body of [governmental failure] theory has been used to explain why private nonprofit organizations arise to provide public goods and services on a voluntary basis, even in the presence of governmental provision. . . . Moreover,

since government must provide its services universally to all its citizens, it is limited in its ability to experiment on a scale with new programs, which creates another niche for private nonprofit organizations (p. 190).

Salamon (2002b) provides complementary support for these arguments in his defense of why the nonprofit sector is a resilient aspect of American society. Salamon maintains that the third sector "embodies two seemingly contradictory impulses that form the heart of American character: a deep-seated commitment to freedom and individual initiative and an equally fundamental realization that people live in communities and consequently have responsibilities that extend beyond themselves" (p. 3). DeLeon (1997) argues that civic associations are linked to a specific type of political education. Building on the ideas of Alexis de Tocqueville, he recognized the considerable role that local governments and townships play with regard to encouraging active citizen participation in local, state, and national politics.

Civil society initiatives and programs are an important element of this conversation. Edwards (2004) outlines three distinct roles and responsibilities associated with civil society: (1) civil society emerged as an arena for collective action distinct from states and markets; (2) civil society is part of a normative tradition that emphasizes the importance of preserving values associated with trust, cooperation, tolerance, and nonviolence; and (3) civil society underscores noteworthy democratic values associated with public deliberation and active citizenship. Edwards and Foley (2001) argue that the most important role attributed to civil society is the notion that these types of organizations "play a major role, if not *the* major role, in building citizenship skills and attitudes crucial for motivating citizens to use these skills" (p. 5, emphasis in original). In addition, they illustrate a variety of public and quasi-public functions that civil society organizations provide, including, "healing the sick, counseling the afflicted, supporting the penniless, educating both young and old, fostering and disseminating culture, and generally providing many of the necessities and adornments of a modern society" (p. 5).

One dimension of the NDG philosophy is that strengthening communities helps facilitate a more open and active dialogue between citizens, public administrators, and government agencies. Citizens, as a result, are more likely to make a more active and meaningful contribution to the policy process. As Musso et al. (2006) note, "The building blocks of political activity— organizing, working with others, compromise—depend on high levels of trust and tolerance, norms of reciprocity, and commitments to community" (p. 81). Transparency is crucial to this conversation. Perry, Mesch, and Paarlberg (2006) astutely observe that one way civil servants contribute to increasing the public's knowledge of organizational performance is through "being more transparent; partnering with researchers to assess organizational intervention; and engaging in more experiments to determine what works" (p. 511).

Increased public support for the community as a whole establishes what Denhardt and Denhardt (2000) call "the creation of shared interests and shared responsibility" (p. 554), and if interests and responsibilities are shared, a more transparent, open administrative state will be more likely to emerge. Rosenbloom (2000) also underscores the significance of transparency in building a legislative-centered public administration. The Freedom of Information Act (1966), Privacy Act (1974), Government in the Sunshine Act (1976), Inspector General Act (1978), Paperwork Reduction Acts (1980, 1995), and Government Performance and Results Act (1993) represent legislation passed to create more transparency.

Like transparency, networks are important to NDG. Salamon (2002a) maintains that the defining characteristic of networks is their "establishment of interdependencies between public agencies and a host of third-party actors" (p. 11). Networks are effective tools for policy implementation that involve one or more public or nonprofit agency. O'Toole (1997) argues that public administration should take networks seriously because of their broad impact on administration and the increased importance of the third sector and its collaboration with government agencies, and because the policy process is becoming increasingly more complex.

### Critique

At first glance, it appears that the tenets of NDG are benign and representative of the values inherent to democratic governance and the Constitutional School, but this line of inquiry, like NPM, deserves scrutiny. Bevir's (2006) commentary on system governance, which he argues is "committed to the ideals of dialogue, participation, consensus, empowerment, and social inclusion" (p. 426), highlights an important concern associated with NDG and one that merits serious scholarly consideration. System governance represents a clear and direct shift from NPM to NDG because of its emphasis on new institutionalism and communitarianism. However,

> [System Governance] should not be treated as a viable substitute for representative democracy, as if a process of top-down consultation with organized interests were enough to offset the democratic deficits associated with multilevel networks. And it certainly should not be mistaken for a radical, participatory democracy that fosters pluralism and dialogue. System governance generally consists of attempts to improve the effectiveness of established institutions by means of officially sponsored and managed participation .... If it ever succeeded

in genuinely broadening participation, it would run up against the possibility that citizens and associations act as catalysts for change, overturning existing norms, practices, and institutions instead of enhancing their legitimacy and effectiveness (Bevir 2006, p. 434).

This perspective resonates with O'Toole and Meier's (2004) concern regarding the dark side of networks: political dynamics do not disappear when agencies operate in a network environment. Instead, they are more likely to increase. Raab and Milward (2003) draw attention to the problems of "dark networks."[5] They make the case that dark networks should be contained because of their reliance on secrecy, use of physical force, and information processing. Salamon (2002a) has contributed by addressing the organizational and institutional concerns that often arise when government agencies lose control and oversee their programs when they transition from a traditional hierarchical structure to a network model.

Vigoda (2002) raises a principal concern regarding civil society/participation initiatives. He maintains that this element of NDG more closely resembles NPM than its supporters are willing to acknowledge. In a blistering critique, he argues:

> The motivation to meet the demands raised by citizens is equivalent to satisfying the needs of a regular customer in a regular neighborhood supermarket. Responsiveness in the public arena closely complies with business-oriented statements such as "the customer is always right" and "never argue with the clients' needs" that every salesperson memorizes from the first day at work. (p. 529)

With regard to transparency, an important question that public administration needs to address is whether too much transparency hinders the ability of government to act in an efficient and effective manner. We have assumed that transparency is a concept that stands alone without meriting serious scrutiny or critique because of the normative values that it embodies as being representative of an open and responsive government. This, like any idea influencing the theoretical and practical dynamics of the field, should not be the case.

Scholars and practitioners should examine every theory and scrutinize its strengths and weaknesses in order to develop a more comprehensive understanding of its application to the administrative state and its governance structure. This critique, therefore, provides an opportunity to examine how the tenets of old institutionalism provide the scrutiny needed to examine how the key elements of NDG hold the potential to undermine the constitutional and institutional integrity of the U.S. administrative state.

## Old Institutionalism

### *Description*

Philip Selznick is regarded as the leader of the old or traditional institutional movement. In his seminal work, *Leadership in Administration* (1957), Selznick illustrates the importance of leadership and statesmanship to the study and practice of good administration. In the opening sentence of this work, Selznick maintains:

> The nature and quality of leadership, in the sense of statesmanship, is an elusive but persistent theme in the history of ideas. Most writers have centered their attention on *political* statesmen, leaders of whole communities who sit in the high places where great issues are joined and settled. In our time, there is no abatement of the need to continue the great discussion, to learn how to reconcile idealism with expediency, freedom with organization. (p. 1)

In connecting leadership to statesmanship, Selznick serves as the intellectual foundation for this chapter. For leaders of the public service, maintaining, conserving, and connecting leadership with statesmanship provides a critical way of thinking about the relationships between career civil servants and the state they serve, and building citizen confidence in the administration of U.S. government. This was one of Hamilton's objectives in *Federalist 27*.

Selznick's (1996) conceptualization of old institutionalism preserves thick institutions, whereas NPM and NDG practices have a tendency to advance a hollow state with thin institutions. According to Selznick (1957), organizations become institutions through a process in which they are infused with value beyond their technical specializations. Selznick (1996) vigorously defended this position thirty-nine years after he wrote *Leadership in Administration* when contrasting "old" and "new" institutionalism: "Values do have a central place in the theory of institutions. We need to know which values matter in the context at hand; how to build them into the organization's culture and social structure; and in what ways they are weakened and subverted" (p. 271). Institutional leadership, therefore, is an essential component of old institutionalism. Institutional leaders, according to Selznick, play an integral role in preserving *and* conserving institutional integrity. They are experts "in the promotion and protection of values," which work to protect an institution's distinctive competence, mission, and roles—an essential component of Selznickian thought. Selznick's argument is important to the idea that the key elements associated with NPM undermine the integrity of administrative institutions by creating a hollow state with thin institutions (Terry 2006).

Selznick's later work, *The Moral Commonwealth* (1992), lays the foundation from which to examine the key elements of NDG with greater scrutiny. For our purposes, one of the most important aspects of this work is Selznick's expanded understanding of institutional integrity as it relates to leadership:

> We cannot know what integrity requires unless we have *a theory of the institution*. What counts as integrity and what affects integrity will be different for a research university and a liberal arts college; for a constitutional court and a lower court; for a regulatory agency and a highway department. Each institution, or each type of institution, has special functions and values; each has a distinctive set of unifying principles. When an institution is charged with lack of integrity, the charge always contains an implicit conception of what the institution is or should be (1992, p. 324, emphasis in original).

The historical, political, institutional, legal, and constitutional foundation of U.S. governance determines the type of integrity essential to the maintenance and preservation of the state and its administrative agencies. As important as civil society programs and networks are to meeting the growing needs of citizens, the institutional values and norms essential to preserving the integrity of these organizations are different from the values of public sector agencies. Governmental organizations emphasize institutional integrity by preserving and conserving constitutional tradition, which is not only an essential element of U.S. governance but also, to borrow from Selznick, an important aspect of "political statesmanship" (1957, p. 1).

Civil servants safeguard the institutional integrity of their respective agencies in several important and distinctive ways. Rohr (1986) argues that the oath of office is critical for developing a constitutional theory of public administration. Once civil servants take their oath of office to defend the Constitution, they must use their discretionary powers wisely "in order to maintain the constitutional balance of powers in support of instilling individual rights" (Rohr 1986, p. 181). Rosenbloom, Carroll, and Carroll (2000) build upon Rohr's argument in their support of constitutional competence for public managers because, as they correctly point out, "whole areas of public management are permeated by constitutional law" (p. 1). Protecting the individual rights of citizens is one of the most important responsibilities of the career civil service. Leaders of civil society programs and nonprofit organizations are not bound by a constitutional oath of office or by the legal environment of public management, which requires a high level of competence in constitutional law in an effort to ensure that individual rights are protected as much as possible.

## How Old Institutionalism's Key Elements Provide a Needed Critique of NDG

Charles Perrow (1986) called attention to the most important and distinctive element of traditional institutional thought—its emphasis on the environment. The process of institutionalization, according to Perrow, "is the process of organic growth, wherein the organization adapts to the strivings of internal groups and the values of the external society" (p. 167). Institutional leadership, according to Selznick (1957), has important environmental functions, which is why he was interested in developing a political orientation as a means of underscoring the significance of institutional leadership to the institutional environment. Selznick (1957) argues, "The link between 'polity' and 'politics' must constantly be kept in mind. To be sure, the political process always involves an actual or potential contest of wills, but it also includes the continuous redefinition of public interest and the embodiment of those definitions in key institutions" (p. 61).

This argument is an intellectual parallel to Madison's observation in *Federalist 51,* where he reminds us that we can find ourselves only in something greater than ourselves: "The interest of the man must be connected to the constitutional rights of the place" (Cooke 1961, p. 349). When public servants no longer view themselves as a product of the Constitution and of the nation's democratic institutions, public virtue diminishes. When this occurs, according to Madison, ambition becomes an "auxiliary precaution." Ambition, therefore, works to safeguard the separation-of-powers system since it ensures that people's personal interests are connected directly to the government. In a word, the same government that controls the people will also control itself. Theories associated with NDG do not provide the type of institutional environment Publius created in 1787 as a corrective institutional tool for protecting and legitimating the government's administrative institutions vis-à-vis constitutional tradition.

Beyond the grand theoretical and constitutional foundation that Publius (Cooke 1961) established, contemporary scholars have also articulated concerns associated with contracting out traditional government or public services. Kirlin (1996) built on Selznick's argument regarding institutionalization. He maintained, "Government action creates value without which private creation of value would be rare and very difficult. By providing the frameworks and institutions within which individuals, businesses, and other nongovernmental social groupings can create value, governments create a broader and more pervasive value for society" (p. 163). Kirlin's point speaks directly to why our definition of governance is crucial to this conversation. If we interpret the concept of governance as meaning the historical, political, institutional, legal, and constitutional foundations that enable government to exist and function within the confines of the American state, then we can begin to grapple with the structural and institutional consequences NDG brings in its effort to critique the microeconomic orientation of NPM. What NPM omits in its efforts to make government resemble the private sector and what NDG overlooks in its attempt to emphasize civil society, participation, networks, and transparency is the connection and legitimacy of the state's governance heritage to its administrative institutions.

## Conclusion

The purpose of this chapter has been to scrutinize the key elements of NDG, particularly civil society/participation, transparency, and networks. A careful and thoughtful examination of NDG reveals that it is not as benign as it first appears. This analysis, however, does not weaken the importance of NDG's critique of NPM. What this argument does provide, is a cautionary framework in which to understand what the state has the potential to lose when government agencies are no longer the primary source for public service delivery. As Paul Appleby (1945) noted over six decades ago, the essential character of government is different from other sectors because of its size, political character, scope of responsibility, and measures of accountability. He went on to argue that leadership in government is also different from what the private sector demands of its executives or, as this research indicates, what advocates of NDG require of its organizational and network leaders.

Selznick's (1957) incorporation of statesmanship into his discussion about what leadership qualities are needed for good administration should not be lost on the field. Statesmanship is important to any serious intellectual exchange regarding democratic governance (Newbold 2005). Public service leaders safeguard the nation's constitutional tradition and protect the normative and constitutional values embedded in the state's governance structure. When we, as scholars and practitioners, preference the key elements of NPM or NDG at the expense of the state's institutional integrity, we are less able to protect the distinctive competence, mission, and roles that are uniquely characteristic to public administration.

## Notes

Larry and I outlined this chapter together and submitted a proposal to the 2007 American Society for Public Administration's Annual Conference in Washington, DC, in June 2006. Unfortunately, he passed away before we completed this work. On matters of leadership in the American administrative state, his voice is greatly missed.

1. Gary L. Wamsley, Virginia Tech, coined the term "ever-democratizing constitutional republic," many years ago and uses it frequently to discuss ideas relating to public administration theory.

2. This label was agreed on by Richard Green, Karen Hult, Doug Morgan, Stephanie Newbold, John Rohr, and David Rosenbloom at the 2007 Southern Political Science Conference, New Orleans, Louisiana.

3. The unit of analysis regarding how the authors apply the concept of transparency in this article is significant. Transparency, in this context, refers to an economic orientation whereas NDG scholars maintain that transparency is citizen and/or service oriented.

4. Boyte (2005) maintains that democratic governance is comprised of "(1) translation of methods of citizen organizing elsewhere by naming its practices and ideas as a politics that can be practiced generally; (2) the democratization of professional practices; and (3) a renewal of the concept of democracy as a society, centered on shared civic responsibility for the creation and sustenance of public goods" (p. 542).

5. Raab and Milward (2003) use three examples of dark networks: heroin trafficking, Al Qaeda, and arms and diamond smuggling.

## References

Appleby, Paul. 1945. *Big Democracy.* New York: Alfred A. Knopf.

Bevir, Mark. 2006. "Democratic Governance: Systems and Radical Perspectives." *Public Administration Review* 66(3): 426–436.

Bogason, Peter, and Juliet Musso. 2006. "The Democratic Prospects of Network Governance." *American Review of Public Administration* 36(1): 3–18.

Box, Richard. 1998. *Citizen Governance: Leading American Communities into the 21st Century.* Thousand Oaks, CA: Sage.

———. 1999. "Running Government Like a Business: Implications for Public Administration Theory and Practice." *American Review of Public Administration* 29(1): 19–43.

Boyte, Harry. 2005. "Reframing Democracy: Governance, Civic Agency, and Politics." *Public Administration Review* 65(5): 536–546.

Christensen, Tom, and Per Laegreid. 2002. "Symposium on Accountability, Publicity, and Transparency: New Public Management: Puzzles of Democracy and the Influence of Citizens." *Journal of Political Philosophy* 10(3): 267–295.

Considine, Mark. 2001. *Enterprising States: The Public Management of Welfare-to-Work.* Oakleigh, Victoria, Australia: Cambridge University Press.

Cooke, Jacob. 1961. *The Federalist.* Middletown, CT: Wesleyan University Press.

Cooper, Terry, and Juliet Musso. 1999. "The Potential for Neighborhood Council Involvement in American Metropolitan Governance." *International Journal of Organization Theory and Behavior* 2(1&2): 199–232.

deLeon, Linda, and Janet Denhardt. 2000. "The Political Theory of Reinvention." *Public Administration Review* 60(2): 89–97.

deLeon, Peter. 1997. *Democracy and the Policy Sciences.* Albany, NY: State University of New York Press.

Denhardt, Janet, and Robert Denhardt. 2000. "The New Public Service: Serving Rather Than Steering." *Public Administration Review* 60(6): 549–559.

———. 2003. *The New Public Service: Serving, Not Steering.* Armonk, NY: M.E. Sharpe.

Edwards, Bob, and Michael Foley. 2001. "Civil Society and Social Capital: A Primer." In *Beyond Tocqueville: Civil Society and the Social Capital Debate in Comparative Perspective,* ed. B. Edwards, M. W. Foley, and M. Diani, 1–16. Hanover, CT: University Press of New England.

Edwards, Michael. 2004. *Civil Society.* Cambridge, UK: Polity Press.

Freedom of Information Act, 5 U.S.C. § 552 (1966).

Golembiewski, Robert, and Eran Vigoda. 2000. "Organizational Innovation and the Science/Craft of Management." In *Current Topics in Management,* vol. 5, eds. M. A. Rahim, R. T. Golembiewski, and K. D. Mackenzie, 263–280. Greenwich, CT: JAI Press.

Gore, Albert. 1993. *From Red Tape to Results: Creating a Government that Works Better and Costs Less: The Report of the National Performance Review.* Washington, DC: Government Printing Office.

Government in the Sunshine Act, 5 U.S.C. § 552b (1976).

Government Performance and Results Act of 1993, Pub. L. No. 103-62, § 20, 107 Stat. 285 (1993).

Grell, Jan, and Gary Gappert. 1992. "The Future of Governance in the United States." *Annals of the American Academy of Political and Social Science* 522(1): 67–78.

Hansmann, Henry. 1987. "Economic Theories of Nonprofit Organization." In *The Nonprofit Sector: A Research Handbook,* ed. W. W. Powell, 27–42. New Haven, CT: Yale University Press.

Heinrich, Carolyn, and Laurence Lynn, eds. 2000. *Governance and Performance: New Perspectives.* Washington, DC: Georgetown University Press.

Hirst, Paul. 1994. *Associative Democracy: New Forms of Economic and Social Governance.* Amherst: University of Massachusetts Press.

Inspector General Act of 1978, Pub. L. 95-452, § 1 (1978).

Johnstone, Joycelyn, and Barbara Romzek. 1999. "Contracting and Accountability in State Medicaid Reform: Rhetoric, Theories, and Reality." *Public Administration Review* 59(5): 383–399.

Kettl, Donald. 1993. *Sharing Power: Public Governance and Private Markets.* Washington, DC: Brookings Institution.

———. 2002. *The Transformation of Governance: Public Administration for Twenty-First Century America.* Baltimore, MD: Johns Hopkins University Press.

Kim, Pan Suk, John Halligan, Choel H. Namshin, and Angela M. Eikenberry. 2005. "Toward Participatory and Transparent Governance: Report of the Sixth Global Forum on Reinventing Government." *Public Administration Review* 65(6): 646–654.

King, Cheryl, and Camilla Stivers. 1998. *Government Is Us: Public Administration in an Anti-Government Era.* Thousand Oaks, CA: Sage.

Kirlin, John. 1996. "What Government Must Do Well: Creating Value for Society." *Journal of Public Administration Research and Theory* 6(1): 161–185.

Light, Paul. 1997. *The Tides of Reform: Making Government Work, 1945–1995.* New Haven, CT: Yale University Press.

Loffler, Elke. 1997. *The Modernization of the Public Sector in an International Comparative Perspective: Implementation in Germany, Great Britain and the United States.* Speyer, Germany: Forshungsinstitut Fur Offentliche Verwaltung.

Milward, H. Brinton. 1994. "Implications of Contracting Out: New Roles for the Hollow State." In *New Paradigms for Government: Issues for the Changing Public Service,* eds. P. Ingraham and B. Romzek, 41–62. San Francisco: Jossey-Bass.

Milward, H. Brinton, and Keith Provan. 2000. "Governing the Hollow State." *Journal of Public Administration Research and Theory* 10(2): 359–379.

Milward, H. Brinton, Keith Provan, and Barbara Else. 1993. "What Does the Hollow State Look Like?" In *Public Management Theory: The State of the Art,* ed. Barry Bozeman, 310. San Francisco: Jossey-Bass.

Musso, Juliet, Christopher Weare, Nail Oztas, and William E. Loges. 2006. "Neighborhood Governance Reform and Networks of Community Power in Los Angeles." *American Review of Public Administration* 36(1): 79–97.

Newbold, Stephanie. 2005. "Statesmanship and Ethics: The Case of Thomas Jefferson's Dirty Hands." *Public Administration Review* 65(6): 669–677.

Osborne, David, and Ted Gaebler. 1992. *Reinventing Government.* Reading, MA: Addison-Wesley.

Osborne, Stephen, ed. 2000. *Public-Private Partnerships: Theory and Practice in International Perspective.* London: Routledge.

O'Toole, Laurence. 1997. "Treating Networks Seriously: Practical and Research-Based Agenda in Public Administration." *Public Administration Review* 57(1): 45–52.

O'Toole, Laurence, and Kenneth Meier. 2004. "Desperately Seeking Selznick: Cooptation and the Dark Side of Networks." *Public Administration Review* 64(6): 681–693.

Paperwork Reduction Act of 1980, 45 U.S.C. Ch. 35 (1980).

Paperwork Reduction Act of 1995, 45 U.S.C. Ch. 35 (1995).

Perrow, Charles. 1986. *Complex Organizations: A Critical Essay.* 3rd ed. New York: McGraw Hill.

Perry, James, Debra Mesch, and Laurie Paarlberg. 2006. "Motivating Employees in a New Governance Era: The Performance Paradigm Revisited." *Public Administration Review* 66(4): 505–514.

Peter, Thomas. 1992. *Liberation Management: Necessary Disorganization for the Nanosecond Nineties.* New York: Alfred A. Knopf.

Pierre, Jon, ed. 2000. "Introduction: Understanding Governance." In *Debating Governance,* ed. J. Pierre, 1–10. Oxford: Oxford University Press.

Prager, Jonas, and Swati Desai. 1996. "Privatizing Local Government Operations." *Public Productivity and Management Review* 20(2): 185–203.

Privacy Act of 1974, 5 U.S.C. § 552a (1974).

Raab, Jorg, and H. Brinton Milward. 2003. "Dark Networks as Problems." *Journal of Public Administration Research and Theory* 13(4): 413–440.

Raadschelders, Jos. 1999. "A Coherent Framework for the Study of Public Administration." *Journal of Public Administration Research and Theory* 9(2): 281–303.

Rohr, John A. 1986. *To Run a Constitution: The Legitimacy of the Administrative State.* Lawrence, KS: University Press of Kansas.

Rosenbloom, David. 2000. *Building a Legislative Centered Public Administration: Congress and the Administrative State, 1946–1999.* Tuscaloosa: University of Alabama Press.

———. 2007. "Reinventing Administrative Prescriptions: The Case for Democratic-Constitutional Impact Statements and Scorecards." *Public Administration Review* 67(1) 28–39.

Rosenbloom, David, James D. Carroll, and Jonathan D. Carroll. 2000. *Constitutional Competence for Public Managers.* Itasca, IL: Peacock.

Salamon, Lester, 2002a. "The New Governance and the Tools of Action: An Introduction." In *The Tools of Government: A Guide to the New Governance,* ed. Lester Salamon, 1–47. Oxford: Oxford University Press.

———. 2002b. "The Resilient Sector: The State of Nonprofit America." In *The State of Nonprofit America,* ed. Lester Salamon, 3–61. Washington, DC: Brookings Institution Press.

Savas, E. S. 2000. *Privatization and Public-Public Partnerships.* New York: Chatham House.

Selznick, Philip. 1957. *Leadership in Administration: A Sociological Interpretation.* Berkeley: University of California Press.

———. 1992. *The Moral Commonwealth: Social Theory and the Promise of Community.* Berkeley: University of California Press.

———. 1996. "Institutionalism 'Old' and 'New.'" *Administrative Science Quarterly* 41(2): 270–277.

Sorensen, Eva. 2006. "Metagovernance: The Changing Role of Politicians in Processes of Democratic Governance." *American Review of Public Administration* 36(1): 98–114.

Stivers, Camilla. 1994. "The Listening Bureaucrat: Responsiveness in Public Administration." *Public Administration Review* 54(4):364–369.
Stoker, Gerry. 2006. "Public Value Management: A New Narrative for Networked Governance?" *American Review of Public Administration* 36(1): 41–57.
Teisman, Geert, and Erik-Hans Klijn. 2002. "Partnership Arrangements: Governmental Rhetoric or Governance Scheme?" *Public Administration Review* 62(2): 197–205.
Terry, Larry. 1998. "Administrative Leadership, Neo-Managerialism, and the Public Management Movement." *Public Administration Review* 58(3): 194–200.
———. 2006. "The Thinning of Administrative Institutions." In *Revisiting Waldo's Administrative State,* eds. D. H. Rosenbloom and H. E. McCurdy, 109–128. Washington, DC: Georgetown University Press.
Thompson, Dennis. 1983. "Bureaucracy and Democracy." In *Democratic Theory and Practice,* ed. G. Duncan, 235–250. Cambridge: Cambridge University Press.
Thompson, James. 2006. "The Federal Civil Service: The Demise of an Institution." *Public Administration Review* 66(4): 496–503.
Van Slyke, David. 2003. "The Mythology of Privatization in Contracting for Social Services." *Public Administration Review* 63(3): 296–315.
Vigoda, Eran. 2002. "From Responsiveness to Collaboration: Governance, Citizens, and the Next Generation of Public Administration." *Public Administration Review* 62(5): 527–540.
Wallin, Bruce. 1997. "The Need for a Privatization Process: Lessons from Development and Implementation." *Public Administration Review* 57(1): 11–20.
Wamsley, Gary L., et al. 1990. *Refounding Public Administration.* Thousand Oaks, CA: Sage.
Young, Dennis R. 2001. "Government Failure Theory." In *The Nature of the Nonprofit Sector,* ed. J. S. Ott, 190–192. Boulder, CO: Westview.

# 4

## Developing Future Leaders

James E. Colvard

Leadership and leaders must be defined before they can be rationally discussed. A leader is someone you follow because you want to, not because you have to. Leadership is convincing someone to do what you want them to do and convincing someone not to do that which you do not want them to do. Leadership is an experientially acquired skill. It is not abstract, like science or mathematics, and thus cannot be taught in the classic manner. Much like the effect of oxygen on combustion, teaching in the classic manner of expounding abstraction can support and enhance the development process for leaders by furthering their understanding of experience.

Management is often viewed as the same as leadership. However, they are not the same. Management is historically dependent, is impacted by the state of technology, and can be taught. Leadership is historically independent, is not technology sensitive, and cannot be taught. Managers can be made; leaders are self-made. Management can be performed by machines: for example, a computer can manage a person's schedule. Leadership is personal; only the person can decide what to put on the calendar. The act of deciding is the heart of leadership; the execution of the decision is management. Most organizations train many managers but develop few leaders. Historically, leadership has been the premium capability that determines the difference between success in organizations and among nations. In a future fraught with uncertainty, leadership is essential.

### How Do We Develop Future Leaders?

It is said that generals always prepare to fight the last war, suggesting that military leaders have no vision. However, this statement means one only knows that which has previously occurred. Anticipating what will occur is problematic at best. Yogi Berra put it more simply when he said: "Prediction is very hard, especially when it's about the future." Thus, whether you are a military leader or any other kind of leader, there is uncertainty about how to best prepare your staff to be leaders in an unknowable future. The only thing that is certain to them is that it will be different from what they have experienced.

Many things will indeed change. Techniques, whether the tools of technology or the structures of organizations, will change. Simply listing the technology changes that have occurred during our professional lifetimes would be a simple but time-consuming exercise. Take the process of communicating between a manager and his or her staff. The manager used to dictate a memo to a secretary who prepared a memo that the manager reviewed, signed, and then distributed to the staff. Today, the manager sits down and types a message on a computer, and it is then transmitted instantly to each member of the staff. Think of the many different human actions and interactions that something as common as e-mail has changed in office routines—the impact of technology becomes obvious.

When voice mail is included, the historical roles of the secretary and the supervisor or boss have dramatically changed. Technology changed the roles of the actor and the speed at which events occur, but the important fundamentals of communicating thoughts to a staff have not changed.

This is also the case in developing future leaders. The technology of the future, the institutional structures, and the social environment will change, but the fundamentals will not. This discussion will focus on those fundamentals, which are the individuals and their relationships to others in an outcome-focused activity. Organizations exist to achieve intended outcomes through purposeful activity. Such outcomes can be defined as work. In the complex processes of organizations, outcomes are determined by coordinated activities, which requires management. Desired outcomes change over time and require changes in the activities intended to achieve them. Anticipating and adapting to those changes requires leadership.

## The Functions of Managers Versus Leaders

Recognizing the difference between management and leadership is critical to the development of leaders because the process is different in both. The following highlight their differences by describing the functions they perform.

- A manager takes care of where you are; a leader takes you to a new place.
- A manager deals in the present; a leader is concerned with the future.
- A manager deals with determinism; a leader deals with probability.
- A manager deals with short time frames; a leader deals with long time frames.

- A manager deals with complexity; a leader deals with uncertainty.
- A manager is concerned with the finding of facts; a leader makes decisions.
- A manager is concerned with doing things right; a leader is concerned with doing the right things.
- A manager's critical concern is efficiency; a leader's critical concern is effectiveness.
- A manager creates policies; a leader establishes principles.
- A manager sees and hears what is going on; a leader hears when there is no sound and sees when there is no light.
- A manager finds answers and solutions; a leader formulates the questions and identifies the problems.
- A manager looks for similarities between present and previous problems; a leader looks for differences.
- A manager thinks a successful solution to a management problem can be used again; a leader wonders if the problem, set in a new environment, may not require a different solution.

This is not meant to be an exhaustive list of things that define differences between management functions and leadership functions, but rather is sufficient to illustrate the point. If these differences in functions are accepted, people with different characteristics developed by different approaches will be required to effectively perform the roles. For example, good managers must pay great attention to detail, whereas good leaders must have exceptional conceptual skills and a propensity for the larger view. People who are restless and become bored with routines might better perform in a leadership role than a management role. Of course, they might be good at neither. It must be emphasized at this point that management roles include some leadership functions and that leadership roles include some management functions; the area between the two is a zone rather than a sharp line of demarcation.

**Required Understandings for Managers and Leaders**

What, then, should a person who is either going into a management position or will assume a leadership role learn? It can be argued that, among other things, he or she must learn how to:

- deal with the specific and the conceptual and how to separate the two;
- balance the experiential and the cognitive or abstract in their development process;
- deal with the objective and subjective and not confuse the two;

- deal with uncertainty and manage risk;
- use technology without becoming a machine;
- deal with the short term and long term and recognize the value of each;
- deal in a virtual world populated by "real" people; and
- understand the different forms of power and the strengths and weaknesses of each form.

It is useful to look at each of these in more detail. Professionals tend to advance in their careers by applying the specifics of their academic training. Effective engineers, for example, are relentlessly attentive to each detail in their work. This is critical for successful accomplishment of their assigned tasks, and it is essential at the individual product or project level because they often have trouble moving to the general or conceptual level. For example, they might be very effective at designing an automobile but cannot visualize other forms of transportation. The great railroad corporations in this country declined because they did not understand that their business was transportation and that railroads were only one of many ways to transport things.

Those who may become managers and leaders must first master the details of their profession in solving real problems. This allows them to fully understand their profession, develop a record of accomplishment, and, most importantly, develop the confidence to act when they advance to positions in which the individual details are not available to them but they must make decisions anyway. This mastery of detail and progression to the general and conceptual requires attention to employee development, which is the responsibility of those currently in positions of leadership because it is they who have the power to make it happen.

In the development process, a plan must be laid out that takes cognitive and abstract preparation, commonly called formal education, and adds to it the experiential dimension of applying knowledge. A new employee comes into an organization having been taught that all problems can be solved and that there are definitive answers to all questions. The employee needs to develop the understanding that abstraction simulates reality and that in the "experienced world" (compared with the "theoretical world") there are problems for which there are no obvious solutions and that answers do not exist for all questions. Telling a person about reality does not allow them to understand reality, they must experience it. Experience is the process that turns data into knowledge and knowledge into wisdom. A critical judgment that the existing leader must make is when an employee in a development stage should move on to the next stage.

In the early phases of development, future managers and leaders do specific things that have objective outcomes. An engineer may design a given device, or an accountant may have to balance the books. As their roles change and they move into management, their activities involve less objective outcomes. They will have to develop a vision and make a plan or a decision. These activities involve subjectivity and require that the manager or leader be comfortable with an outcome that has no objective manifestation. This is often hard for specialists who are used to being able to "prove" that they have solved the problem.

Uncertainty and risk are part of decision making, in which outcomes cannot be proven and the path not taken cannot be evaluated. Again, specialists have trouble with this—it is probably the greatest emotional barrier they have to cross to become a successful leader. The key is self-confidence that will allow the decision maker to deal with failure when a decision is later proven wrong.

Modern technology depersonalizes the management process to the point at which managers can become mechanistic. It is critical for managers to retain a personal touch and contact through such things as informal meetings with their employees and social activities that allow human-to-human contact. This becomes more difficult as organizations go international, since managers may never see the people who work for them. E-mail and video teleconferencing will not totally compensate for this depersonalization. Maintaining the personal touch in an impersonal world may become the management challenge of the current century.

As future managers progress from individual task execution to oversight functions, they must develop the ability to visualize the aggregation of short-term outcomes into a coordinated set that forms a desired long-term outcome. The attainment of coordinated, intended outcomes represents organizational work. The conceptualization of that composite is called vision.

With digitalization, our reality becomes more abstract or virtual, yet humans have not changed significantly and must accommodate to that virtual world. Managers and leaders will lag the technology consciousness of their younger employees and must recognize this in dealing with them.

The next section covers the forms of power and the strengths and weakness of each.

## Forms of Power Available to Managers and Leaders

In organizations, power comes in three primary forms: authority, competence, and value. Authority is based on force and is the basis for most of today's management structures. It is the gravitational model of power, where the higher you sit in the organization, the more force you have when you come down on a subordinate. Position in the organization is the manager's basis of power; the power belongs to the position, not the individual. Authority as the basis of power leads to pyramidal organizations. Authority-based organizations are very effective at executing tasks that are understood, because the process for their accomplishment is defined and the results of their accomplishment are observable.

Such organizations are based on command and control; only that which can be observed can be controlled. To be effective, authority-based organizations must have the means of imposing sanctions on those who do not perform or on those who defy the organization. The military, churches, manufacturing industries, and certain government agencies effectively utilize authority-based organizations. In the public service, authority is critical in that it is the legitimating power behind action. Authority-based organizations have severe limitations in dealing with a cognitive-based work world where ideation, discovery, and problem solving are dominant over observable task execution. It is not possible to observe what people are thinking; thus, it cannot be controlled.

Therefore, currently, even though hierarchic, authority-based organizations are necessary, another basis of power is needed—personal competence. Using this second form of power, competency-based organizations are becoming more common today. Such organizations tend to be flatter, with less weight given to where you sit and more emphasis placed on what you know. They tend to be more fluid and ad hoc in nature, with integrated teams that deal with problems as they emerge. Some of their limitations include ambiguity in the minds of employees who miss the certainty of a more structured organization. In addition, the use of expertise tends to depersonalize the individual and alienates him or her from the organization. Long-term development of individual expertise often falls through the cracks of the matrix organization.

Effective management and leadership in such organizations are critically dependent on the manager's or leader's ability to understand the level of competence of each individual, and thus to know where and how to effectively utilize them. The competence of an individual is a function of a very limited set of parameters and can be evaluated relatively easily. It begins with what a person is born with in terms of innate intelligence and energy. This innate capability is a given that people have nothing to do with; however, how well they use that innate capability can control  their attitude. The final parameter is the opportunity people have to develop their innate capability through the abstraction of formal education and the experiential dimension of practical experience. The manager or leader can quickly tell who in the organization has the smarts, energy, and attitude to succeed. As the holders of authority who legitimize development opportunities, managers and leaders have the responsibility to provide development opportunities for employees.

The final form of power that is often undervalued is value and belief, which is based on emotions. Collective values and beliefs are a culture, and each organization has its own culture. Culture provides the unstated reflexive response to routine situations that an organization encounters. It is what sustains an organization and creates timesaving routines, but it also inhibits change. Breaking the "way we do things in this organization" pattern is the greatest barrier to organizational change.

Individual values and beliefs define character. A leader's followers assess his or her character based on what he or she does—not what he or she says. If the values of the organization are consistent with the values of the individuals in the organization, they will be loyal to the organization. If the individual leader has positive values such as honesty, courage, and integrity, the followers will trust the leader. Trust in a leader magnifies their power of competence and authority. Authority allows a person to hold a position of leadership; the followers' trust makes it possible for the person to lead.

## Evolution of the Forms of Power

The previously discussed forms of power are based on an evolution of technology that progressed from physical to intellectual understanding. Civilizations began by understanding their physical world, how it was shaped, its size, and the nature of the physical elements that comprised it. It took a relatively long time for our understanding to evolve from thinking the Earth was flat to knowing it is spheroid. Grasping the nature of the elements that comprise the Earth took more time. During the physical era, humans mainly functioned as task executors. Functions that were performed could be observed. Organizations, if they existed, were small, collegial, and male-dominated. Leadership was exercised through fear of physical force of the leader.

Once humans understood the limits of their world and its composition, they began to explore ways to change it to meet their needs and desires. That change progressed through a set of technological eras of chemistry, physics, and biology. In the era of chemistry, humans learned how to combine natural elements to form synthetic or man-made elements. One of the critical discoveries of this era was how to extract nitrogen from the air to make synthetic fertilizers. This discovery freed humans from agricultural tasks that were required to feed themselves and allowed concentration on other forms of technology. The industrial revolution grew out of this era. The complexity of multiple coordinated tasks that were required for factories, compared with the individual labor of agriculture, gave rise to organizations and required management. The role of humans changed to add management to the function of task execution. The nature of work was still physical, had visible outcomes, and was understandable to the average person. Organizations of this era were large, hierarchy-based, and male-dominated. Power, in the chemistry era, still belonged to the leader.

The era of chemistry, which created synthetics at the macro level through the combination of natural elements, led to the era of physics, during which humans began to understand and alter the fundamental composition of natural elements. From this came the discovery of solid-state devices that created an explosive expansion in worldwide communication. Solid-state electronics gave way to massive computers and, as they became smaller and lighter, spawned satellites, cell phones, and international connectivity through the Internet. The era of physics shifted the role of humans from predominant task execution to problem solving and task execution. As a result, power became more intellectual and less physical and moved from the leader to the follower. The person in authority must solve the problem, but the person who knows how to solve the problem has the power. As power diffused, management approaches had to change. It was no longer possible to manage through command and control. It is not possible to control that which you cannot see. Thus, organizations became flatter, and management became more participative. Gender roles became more neutral as brainpower replaced muscle power, but cultural lag still gave a slight dominance to males.

The current era of technology is focused on biology. The major technical debates today are over gene altering, human cloning, and stem cell research. The questions today are not about the possibility of technology but rather about the moral and ethical questions surrounding the use of technology. Because this involves decision making (the essence of leadership) rather than task execution (the heart of management), it suggests that the future demands leadership.

## Development Stages for Managers and Leaders

Given that the future will demand leaders, what is the best way to develop them? One way to look at the development process is to break it into stages or phases and make some judgments about when the employee should move from one stage or phase to the next.

Phase one is the entry or individual performer phase when a person transitions from the formal or academic education world into the reality of everyday work. This is the most critical and formative stage of professional development. It is when individuals develop the self-confidence they will need for later stages in their career. This is the only phase in which there is a direct and clear association with the individual's effort and outcomes, and thus is a true measure of the person's professional competence.

It is critical in this phase that employees be given an assignment that challenges them sufficiently that they feel they have accomplished something worthwhile when they complete it. This is essential for developing a sense of self-confidence. It is also important that they not be given tasks beyond their capability, causing them to fail and forever have doubts about their abilities. This phase should encompass the first five to seven years of a professional career. People need enough time to accomplish something for which they can be held accountable, but not to stay so long that they are repeating the same experience. In this phase, the individual is doing work for others. In the next phase, he or she will begin to do work with others.

This second phase transitions the person from being an individual performer to being part of a team. This can occur as either a supervisor with responsibilities for the outcomes of other efforts or as a member of a team in which the individual's input is part of a collective effort and becomes homogenized into the team product. In either case, the individual becomes dependent on others for the ultimate execution of assigned tasks and cannot achieve them alone. This is an intermediate stage and should span no more than three years. It is in this stage that the person's focus begins to transition from the objective to the subjective. At this point in a career the individual should be well aware that other people do not like to be treated as objects. Therefore, the individual must make a decision whether to stay in the professional discipline, such as engineering or accounting, or move into management. If this person moves onto the next phase, it is difficult to return to the technical function. There is a balance in this phase between task execution and coordination. Transition to the next phase shifts that balance decidedly toward planning, coordinating, and overseeing, and away from task execution.

The third phase is management, in which the person becomes responsible for things in which they do not have sufficient expertise to effectively perform the individual tasks alone. Managers clearly must depend on others to achieve the organization's objectives. The previous stage should have prepared them for this. At this point, their role is clearly changing. They have moved to the general and must know the relationships among the specific, but are now responsible for making the whole work as opposed to working on each of the pieces. The challenge is to acquire resources, assign tasks, motivate people to perform them, and evaluate outcomes. It is here that the objective and subjective become clearly differentiated. Subjects are much more difficult to "control" than objects, and a manager quickly learns that controlling strategies will only work for things that can be seen and understood. The manager cannot see the cognitive processes of the staff, but he or she can react to the manner in which the staff is treated. An object, such as a computer, may fail to perform, but the staff does not get angry or upset by how the manager treats this situation. This transition to dealing with the subjective rather than the objective is often difficult, particularly for those who are very expert in their technical fields. This is why the best technical experts often do not make the best managers. It is not axiomatic that good technical people cannot become good managers, but it is more difficult because their prowess in the details makes them less tolerant of the limitations of the workers in that field, and they may tend to micro-manage.

Development as a manager is an experiential process because it requires interacting with humans, who cannot be abstracted. *The world of things may be made virtual, but humans cannot.* Therefore, to generalize management skills, the individual must manage in more than one situation involving different groups of people. Since management, unlike science, is inductive, this is axiomatic. If the individual decides to move to the next phase, which is leadership, he or she should have spent from five to seven years in more than one assignment involving management.

The final phase in career development, before accepting the irresponsibility of retirement, is the executive, or leadership, phase. It is in this phase that the individual perfects the ability to lead by returning to the role of working for others. While the leader may be the executive in charge of the organization, that leader's actions must be focused on serving and supporting the organization— hence, working for the organization that works for him or her. The leader's role in this stage focuses on the future, and thus, the timeframe shifts from the short to the long. Managers below the leader are responsible for achieving the short-term objectives of the organization, while the leader is responsible for seeing that those objectives are met, the greater responsibility now becoming that of preparing the organization for the future.

The critical aspect of preparing the organization for the future is the development of future leaders. The current leader now has the power of authority to legitimatize the activities of others, the most critical of which is their development. The leader establishes the principles of the organization, which the managers then translate into executable policy directives. Thus, the leader creates the values of the organization.

## Summary

The foregoing discussion focuses on the difference between management and leadership, the forms of power that undergird both, the evolution of technology that informs that power, and a logical set of stages of development that can be useful in preparing individuals to become managers and leaders.

Management and leadership are inductive, not deductive; they are experiential and not abstract. Thus, managers and leaders must be developed through a combination of abstract education, which prepares them to learn, and a variety of experience assignments, from which they actually learn and generalize that learning.

Critical to this discussion are the evolution of technology and the implications of that evolution on management. Those implications include the following:

- The complex demands of technology led to organizations, which evolved from vertical to horizontal organizations to distributed organizations.
- Power went from being physically based to being intellectually based and shifted from the leader to the followers.
- The role of humans evolved from doing to deciding.
- Human interactions became more depersonalized and abstract.
- Management by command-and-control no longer worked, and leadership became required.

# 5

## Transformational Leadership Behavior

## An Opportunity for Academic Department Chairs

Brian Gittens

Transformational leadership exhibited by academic department chairs has the potential to substantively and positively impact academic departments by positioning them to face challenges and be more adaptive to environmental changes. Positioning academic departments refers to shaping the departmental culture so that it is reflective of what Cooke and Lafferty (1983) termed "constructive organizational cultural norms." Constructive cultural norms are characterized by organizational learning that is facilitated by open communication and striking a balance between organizational goals and members' needs. This chapter explores the leadership context of higher education, including the challenge for academic department chairs. Finally, this chapter identifies opportunities for academic department chairs to increase their leadership capacity.

### Leadership Context of Public Higher Education

Public higher education faces challenges that need to be addressed at every level of leadership, including academic department chairs. Higher education is being required to provide improved evidence of its effectiveness (Hincker 2005; Miller and Malandra 2006). In an environment of scarce resources, all constituencies—concerned citizens and public officials—are demanding justification for the higher costs of education and questioning the qualifications of current college graduates (Miller and Malandra 2006). Constituencies are calling for systems of accountability for the use of public funds to meet societal needs and for assessing student learning outcomes from academic departments (Gmelch and Miskin 2004; Guskin and Marcy, 2002; Hecht et al. 1999; Miller and Malandra 2006; Newman, Couturier, and Scurry 2004; Rodd 2001; U.S. Department of Education 2006). "Higher education in this new century faces the paradox of being more critical than ever to society's future while at the same time being under great pressure to prove its worth in educating students and justifying its use of financial resources" (Guskin and Marcy 2002, p. 4).

Department chairs, because of their role in fiscal operations and their responsibility for the integrity of the discipline and related student learning outcomes, are directly affected by the increased call for accountability. To better understand the issues affecting higher education and ultimately academic department chairs, it is helpful to examine the impact of increased accountability for financial resources and assessing learning outcomes as they present challenges for them.

### Accountability for Financial Resources

A salient challenge facing higher education is the need for developing accountability systems that address the use of financial resources. Declining state subsidies and rising operating costs have prompted a call for increased fiscal accountability in higher education. States play a critical role in funding higher education, but most face long-term budget shortfalls. As a result, higher education is receiving a diminishing proportion of appropriations (Miller and Oldham 2006). While most state budgets showed improvement in 2006, analysis conducted by the National Center for Higher Education Management Systems (NCHEMS) concluded they all face potential deficits that will limit the funding of higher education (Jones 2006).

The NCHEMS study also found that in forty-six states, the growth in demand for other public services (K–12 education, social services, corrections, and Medicaid) will outpace the demand for higher education (Jones 2006). Support for these other services will result in lower levels of support for higher education (Guskin and Marcy 2002; Jones 2006; Leaming 1998; Newman et al. 2004). As state financial support for higher education continues to decline, expenses for operating institutions continue to rise because of the increased competition for students (Wellman 2006). "Higher education institutions operate under what economist Howard Bowen coined the revenue theory of cost—which is that institutions raise all the money they can, and spend all the money they have" (Wellman 2006, p. 8). There is an assumption that resource availability is equated with quality and prestige, which is reinforced by common ranking measures that use measures of funds as key metrics (Wellman 2006).

The system of financing higher education is in a dysfunctional state since subsidies are declining, cost per student is increasing, and public concerns about rising costs are eroding the credibility of higher education (U.S. Department of Education 2006). In an environment of decreased funding and increased competition for existing financial resources, department chairs, as leaders in higher education, need to address the call for fiscal accountability that preserves academic quality and credibility (Dickeson 2006; Miller and Oldham 2006; Wellman 2006).

## Accountability for Assessing Student Learning Outcomes

The preservation of academic quality and credibility means that higher education institutions must also develop accountability systems for assessing student-learning outcomes. Poor academic preparation of recent graduates and the need for an educated workforce necessitate a system of accountability for assessing student-learning outcomes (Miller and Malandra 2006). The performance of recent college graduates is cause for concern. In the most recent (2003) National Assessment of Adult Literacy survey,[1] less than a third of recent college graduates could demonstrate an ability to read complex texts and make inferences (Miller and Malandra 2006). In the same survey, only 25 percent of college graduates scored high enough to be considered proficient from a literacy standpoint (Miller and Malandra 2006). In the 2006 National Survey of America's College Students (NSACS), the American Institutes for Research found that 20 percent of four-year-degree holders have only basic quantitative literacy skills, and 50 percent did not score at the proficient level of literacy, meaning that they lack basic skills such as summarizing arguments in a newspaper editorial (Miller and Malandra 2006).

These statistics that belie the lack of academic preparedness of recent college graduates lend support to employers' assertions that students are not being prepared for the workplace and that they lack the skill necessary for successful employment. Economic demand for a better-prepared workforce is critical for the competitive global environment (U.S. Department of Education 2006; Miller and Malandra 2006; Newman et al. 2004). The new skill sets that employers need include problem solving, critical thinking, and written communication skills (Miller and Malandra 2006). Currently, there are no agreed-on tests or assessments of student learning outcomes, but without sound data and an improved, objective accountability system that addresses the learning outcomes for student learning, policy and subsequent change are uninformed (Miller and Malandra 2006). Because of their leadership, knowledge of the academic discipline, and a relationship with faculty, department chairs are in a unique position to shape departmental culture toward greater accountability of program quality and student learning (Gmelch and Miskin 2004).

*Summary*

According to the U.S. Department of Education (2006), improved systems of accountability for financial resources and assessing student-learning outcomes serve as the bases for reform in the U.S. higher education system. Improved accountability systems would result in institutions that are more nimble, more efficient, and more effective. For individuals, this means access to educational opportunities that allow them to be more productive workers and engaged citizens.

**Leadership Challenge for Academic Department Chairs**

The leadership challenge for chairs is that despite the increased importance of their role, there is limited focus on developing a leadership paradigm that helps them shape an adaptive departmental culture. Adaptive departmental cultures refer to organizations that are flexible and responsive to external challenges (Denison 1990; Kotter and Heskett 1992). Such organizations are positioned to effectively address the call for increased accountability for financial resources and student-learning outcomes (U.S. Department of Education 2006).

Greater accountability for financial resources and assessing student-learning outcomes has direct implications for academic department chairs (Gmelch and Miskin 2004; Hecht et al. 1999; Lucas 2000; Wergin 2004). Chairs are responsible for making decisions about allocating limited resources while sustaining academic quality in the department (Hecht et al. 1999; Rodd 2001; Wergin 2003, 2004). The remainder of this chapter discusses the importance of the department chairs' role and their responsibility for developing systems of accountability, and outlines departmental culture and the need for department chair transformational leadership behaviors. Finally, the association between department chair transformational leadership behaviors and departmental culture is discussed.

*The Importance of the Role of the Department Chair*

The importance of chairing a department involves three interrelated factors: operational oversight, decision making, and curriculum responsibility (Hecht et al. 1999; Murray 2000; Seagren, Creswell, and Wheeler 1993; Wergin 2004). First, the chairs' daily contact with students, administrators, and faculty makes them an integral part of the operational oversight of the department (Weinberg 1984). Seagren et al. (1993) refer to chairs as the mechanism through which the intentions of top management flow down and information flows up. This role places the chair in the position of negotiator between departmental goals and individual goals (Hecht et al. 1999; Seagren et al. 1993; Murray 2000). Second, chairs are important decision makers. The decisions that chairs make have implications for financial resources, curriculum, and faculty development (Bennett 1983; Carroll 1990; Rodd 2001). Finally, the chair is responsible for the curriculum, ensuring that the individual faculty members' talents are aligned with instructional needs, encouraging continued personal and professional growth, and attesting to the adequacy of instruction and research (Bennett and Figuli 1990; Hecht et al. 1999; Murray 2000; Wergin 2003, 2004). The chair is the official on campus who provides important operational oversight and makes key decisions that affect the academic curriculum.

## *Department Chairs and Accountability*

Because chairs provide significant operational oversight and are responsible for the curriculum, they are positioned to play an important role in the development of systems of accountability for financial resources and assessing learning outcomes (Hecht et al. 1999; Jones 2006; Murray 2000; Rodd 2001). Mandates that monitor the cost-effectiveness and quality of higher education have increased the importance of the chair's role (Hecht et al. 1999) and expectations for their leadership in the change process within higher education institutions (Gmelch and Miskin 2004; Hecht et al. 1999; Lucas 1994; Murray 2000; Rodd 2001; Seagren et al. 1993). This section discusses how chair leadership can shape accountability systems for financial resources as well as assessing student learning outcomes.

The development of accountability systems for financial resources requires the leadership of department chairs. Chairs are responsible for allocation and accountability of financial resources within the department and determining priorities in an environment of diminishing resources (Gmelch and Miskin 2004; Hecht et al. 1999; Lucas 2000). Chairs can shape and determine priorities by allocating resources to reward and recruit new faculty, in alignment with departmental goals. The allocation of resources sends a clear message about who and what is important in an academic department since financial resources are aligned with departmental and institutional priorities, thus creating a system of accountability that links funds to results (Gmelch and Miskin 2004). Chairs, because of their role in managing the operational budget of their departments, are best positioned to develop accountability systems for the use of financial resources (Gmelch and Miskin 2004; Lucas 1994).

The development of accountability systems for assessing student-learning outcomes also requires the leadership of department chairs. The leadership of department chairs is important in developing accountability systems for assessing student learning outcomes, since chairs are responsible for the quality of the academic program, including its courses, curriculum, teaching, and research (Diamond 1998; Gmelch and Miskin 2004; Hecht et al. 1999; Lucas 1994; Murray 2000; Wergin 2003, 2004). Department chairs are best positioned to assess the quality of a particular discipline and areas of need since they are the only administrators with the requisite discipline knowledge and vantage point (Hecht et al. 1999). Furthermore, the daily contact with faculty and students provides opportunities for chairs to receive informal feedback about learner outcomes or convene more formal forums to assess program quality (Hecht et al. 1999; Wergin 2003). The department chairs' responsibility for the curriculum and for preparing students creates an imperative for leadership that is focused on creating a system of accountability for assessing learner outcomes (Brown and Moshavi 2002; Hecht et al. 1999; Wergin 2003).

Overall, the department chair plays a significant role in addressing the call for increased accountability in higher education. The chair is the representative of the administration and acts as the change agent, entrepreneur, mediator, strategic planner, and consensus builder within the department (Diamond 1998). "Faculty may be viewed as the heart and soul of the institution, but the department chair is the glue, serving as the link between faculty and administration, between the discipline and the institution, and occasionally between parents and faculty" (p. ix). Chairs are also in a position to articulate the needs of upper-level administrators in a manner that motivates faculty and causes them to act (Birnbaum 1988; Rodd 2001; Gmelch and Miskin 2004; Wergin 2004). These multifaceted roles make chairs important leaders in addressing the call for increased accountability.

**Departmental Culture**

Before department chairs can address specific challenges of developing accountability systems for financial resources and assessing learner outcomes, they must understand and effectively negotiate factors that shape departmental culture. Academic departmental culture is characterized as individualistic, disjointed, and thereby difficult to manage or change (Brown and Moshavi 2002; Lucas 2000; Wergin 2003). Because of these characteristics, there is a strong resistance to leadership found in traditional hierarchical organizations, and in most institutions, it may be more appropriate to think of faculty as constituents rather than as followers (Birnbaum 1988; Hecht et al. 1999; Murray 2000; Rodd 2001; Wergin 2004). Cultural norms in higher education interact to dictate expectations of behavior and modes of influence. This section outlines how dualism of control, lack of mission clarity, sources of power and control, and higher education as an open organizational system affect departmental culture.

First, dualism of control has a profound effect on departmental culture. Dualism of control refers to the organizational structure of colleges and universities in which the conventional administrative hierarchy and the structure through which faculty make professional decisions exist in parallel (Corson 1960). The two structures are based on different systems of authority (Etzioni 1964). In conventional organizations, those who are higher in rank rely on administrative authority to make decisions and to direct the activities of others. In addition to this conventional administrative hierarchy, higher education has experts (faculty) who are not involved in coordinating business goals but rather have professional authority to provide specialized knowledge and judgments (Birnbaum 1988, pp. 9–15). Dualism of control sets the expectation that faculty are an integral part of decision making, thus a cultural norm of shared governance is established.

Second, the lack of mission clarity shapes departmental culture. Clarity of mission enables organizations to create systems of accountability and to establish performance standards. In a business setting, this often involves measuring earnings or profits. In higher education, however, there is no metric that is comparable to profits or money (Birnbaum 1988, pp. 9–15). A comparable metric does not exist "because of a disagreement on goals and in part because neither goal achievement nor the activities related to their performance can be satisfactorily quantified into an educational balance sheet" (Birnbaum 1988, p. 11). Lack of mission clarity contributes to a departmental culture in which ambiguity is the norm and the measurement of outputs is not emphasized.

Third, the various forms of power exercised in higher education affect departmental culture. French and Raven (1959) have identified five types of power that influence social groups: coercive power, reward power, legitimate power, referent power, and expert power. Coercive power refers to the ability to punish to gain compliance. Reward power is the ability to offer rewards or to decrease negative influences to gain compliance. Legitimate power refers to a common code or standard that grants authority and obliges another party to comply. Referent power results from the willingness to be influenced because of one's identification with another. Expert power stems from the acceptance of influence from another because of the belief that the other has some special knowledge or competence. Overall, faculty are likely to be influenced more by internalized principles of academic freedom and ethical behavior and communications from colleagues who are seen as sharing their values than by other forms of power or influence (Birnbaum 1988; Gmelch and Miskin 2004; Lucas et al. 2000). The various sources of power help shape expectations and behaviors within departments by dictating reward systems and sources of influence, and thus directly impacting its culture.

Finally, departmental culture is influenced by higher education's open organizational system. Organizations are considered open systems to the extent that external factors are allowed to enter the system and alter its elements (Birnbaum 1988, pp. 31–40). Closed systems have rigid boundaries that limit environmental interaction. Inputs into closed systems are defined and controlled, do not change the elements of the system, and thus cause and effect can be predicted with great accuracy. In contrast, open systems, such as colleges and universities, have boundaries that are more permeable and that allow various interactions between the external environment and elements of the system (Birnbaum 1988). The open system of colleges and universities creates a complex web of constituents that contributes to dualism of control and lack of mission clarity, and defines sources of power that affect departmental culture (Birnbaum 1988).

Dualism of control involves the constant negotiation of administrative and professional subsystems, each beholden to external constituents. For faculty, these include their professional networks of colleagues and funding sources, while administrators must be sensitive to the needs of the president, trustees, and lawmakers (Birnbaum 1988). Similarly, the lack of mission clarity is facilitated as different elements of the institution attempt to attend to the needs of the community through service and outreach, to students through teaching, and to funding agencies through research. All the major missions of the university may overlap, are interrelated, and shape one another without clear focus on any. Lastly, the sources of power and control are shaped by an open system because faculty view themselves as part of a system that extends beyond the formal boundaries of the university (Birnbaum 1988). Faculty form national and international networks based on their research interests and, as mentioned before, are influenced more by this expert or referent power (Birnbaum 1988). Administrative authority influences them to the extent that the authority aligns with and serves to support their professional activity (Birnbaum 1988; Gmelch and Miskin 2004). Understanding departmental culture is critical to ensuring alignment with institutional needs and the professional activities of faculty (Gmelch and Miskin 2004; Lucas 2000).

The nature of departmental culture forces chairs to rethink how traditional concepts of leadership should be applied (Leaming 1998). Hallmarks of departmental culture include academic autonomy, complex professional networks, and shared governance (Birnbaum 1988). Therefore, traditional hierarchical approaches to leadership do not fit in higher education settings, and their applicability may likely cause resistance and dissonance and thus be ineffective (Birnbaum 1988). The recognition of the cultural context of academic departments and its attendant nuances, however, can assist department chairs in recognizing the limitations of and opportunities for effective influence on faculty.

## Opportunities for Department Chairs

Transformational leadership provides a leadership paradigm that enables chairs to influence faculty within the cultural context of academic departments. The new higher education landscape demands leadership that fosters innovation and flexibility from the institutions that serve the nation's learners (U.S. Department of Education 2006). Transformational leadership has been empirically shown to facilitate a leader's ability to develop a shared vision, foster innovation, and empower others to achieve higher levels of performance (Bass 1985; Burns 1978; Brown and Moshavi 2002; Erdman 2002; Eppard 2004). This section discusses the opportunities for transformational leadership behaviors of department chairs and its impact on influencing faculty.

Private sector experience suggests that the human resource practices that promote success in an environment of rapid change, complexity, and unpredictability support at least three values: flexibility, access to information at all levels, and risk taking (Gilliland 1997, p. 32). Transformational leadership has been empirically proven to promote flexibility and access to information by inspiring creativity through intellectual stimulation (Bass 1985) and the influence orientation theme (Roueche, Baker, and Rose 1989). Transformational leadership also has been empirically linked to facilitating flexibility through creative problem solving (Woods 2004). Unfortunately, higher education in the United States has become increasingly risk adverse and at times self-satisfied (U.S. Department of Education 2006). Transformational leadership is characterized by leaders who assume risk as the status quo is challenged and the way of operating is redefined (Kouzes and Posner 1995). If universities are to prosper and change, then risk taking must be a controlling factor in university management (Leaming 1998).

Because of its emphasis on referent and expert power, transformational leadership can assist chairs in influencing faculty. Faculty, like others in professional organizations, are influenced by referent and expert power (Birnbaum 1988). Transformational leadership allows department chairs to exert referent and expert power through the tenets of idealized influence (Bass 1985) and the values orientation theme (Roueche et al. 1989). Idealized influence has been empirically found to be positively associated with perceptions of organizational effectiveness and satisfaction of faculty (Brown and Moshavi 2002). Idealized influence refers to leaders behaving in ways that result in their being role models for their team members. The leaders are admired, respected, and trusted. Team members identify with their leaders and want to emulate them because the leaders are perceived as having extraordinary capabilities, persistence, and determination (Bass 1985).

Development of the values orientation theme (Roueche et al. 1989)—defined by exemplifying the moral fiber of the leader to include commitment, quality, integrity, trust, and respect through modeling—represents another opportunity for department chairs to exercise referent power. Brown and Moshavi (2002) found empirical evidence that supports that the extent to which department chairs can model desired behavior and build trust determines their effectiveness in influencing faculty (Bass 1985; Birnbaum 1988).

## Department Chairs' Transformational Leadership Behaviors and Departmental Culture

Most importantly, the transformational leadership behaviors of academic chairs can develop departmental cultures that position departments to address increased mandates for accountability by creating a shared vision and by fostering learning that leads to creativity and adaptability. Transformational leadership behaviors as described by Roueche et al. (1989) have as central components the development of a shared vision through open communication and through demonstrating enthusiasm for goal achievement. This shared vision and the attendant motivation, support, and development of subordinates may contribute to establishing a constructive organizational culture—characterized by open communication and adaptability (Cooke and Lafferty 1983; Eppard 2004). This section briefly describes how department chairs' employment of the transformational leadership tenets of creating a shared vision and fostering learning may contribute to the adaptability of academic departments.

The context of higher education demands that chairs have the ability to create a shared vision and to create a culture that brings people together to work effectively (Rodd 2001; Wergin 2004). When departmental leadership is strong and adopts a transformational style, it is assumed that the climate exudes excitement and enthusiasm about the department's work (Lucas 1994). The department chair, functioning as a team leader, can create a climate in which members can be supportive of each other as they develop and implement a shared vision. There is empirical evidence that suggests that campuses with transformative leaders will flourish because they will create an environment or culture in which issues are openly debated and all constituents' interests are considered (Balthazard and Cooke 2004; Rodd 2001; Wergin 2004).

Roueche et al. (1989) developed a model of transformational leadership that was found to be effective in higher education through five themes summarized in Table 5.1. These themes, based on Burns's (1978) conception of transformational leadership, describe behaviors that have been found to be effective in higher education settings.

Fostering learning in the department empowers faculty to engage in addressing challenges that face the department through creative problem solving.

Table 5.1

**Attributes of Transformational Leaders**

| Theme | Attributes |
| --- | --- |
| Vision | Possesses a future orientation<br>Demonstrates a positive orientation toward change<br>Takes appropriate risks to bring about change<br>Demonstrates commitment to making appropriate changes<br>Is mission-oriented<br>Develops a shared vision |
| Influence Orientation | Places responsibility with authority<br>Is action-oriented<br>Causes team members to feel powerful<br>Employs appropriate decisional style<br>Demonstrates willingness to be influenced by the team<br>Builds a collaborative environment<br>Encourages open communication<br>Is in touch with team members<br>Demonstrates high energy |
| People Orientation | Understands the organizational ethos<br>Rewards appropriately<br>Demonstrates respect toward others<br>Considers individual needs<br>Is student-centered<br>Values others |
| Motivational Orientation | Is flexible in dealing with issues and people<br>Encourages creativity<br>Assists in the development of others<br>Helps clarify expectations<br>Attempts to inspire others |
| Values Orientation | Demonstrates commitment to learning<br>Advocates quality education<br>Demonstrates high standards<br>Demonstrates sound judgment<br>Demonstrates openness and trust<br>Demonstrates sense of humor<br>Leads by example |

*Source:* Drawn from Rouche et al. 1989.

Lucas (1994) asserts that a chair empowers others by creating a learning organization characterized by individuals who strive for personal mastery and team learning and a chair who is committed to self-discovery and self-growth. Chairs can accomplish this change by demonstrating behaviors consistent with transformational leadership themes (Brown and Moshavi 2002). Personal and professional learning is intentional and goes beyond the discipline for which the department is educated (Lucas 1994). This learning has been empirically shown to facilitate creative problem solving that engages organizational members and creates an organizational culture better positioned to address external challenges in organizations in general (Eppard 2004; Kotter and Heskett 1992; Schein 2004) and asserted as important for academic departments (Rodd 2001; Wergin 2003, 2004). Optimally, transformational leadership behaviors can shape what Cooke and Lafferty (1983) termed constructive organizational cultures. Constructive cultures in which members are encouraged to interact with others and to approach tasks in ways that will help them meet their higher-order satisfaction needs are characterized by achievement, self-actualizing, humanistic encouraging, and affiliative norms. The four norms associated with constructive cultures have been empirically shown to facilitate knowledge management and organizational performance through participatory decision making (Balthazard and Cooke 2004). The norms are characterized as follows.

1. A humanistic-encouraging culture characterizes organizations that are managed in a participative and person-centered way. Members are expected to be supportive, constructive, and open to influence in their dealings with one another.
2. An achievement culture characterizes organizations that do things well and that value members who set and accomplish their own goals. Members of these organizations set challenging but realistic goals, establish plans to reach these goals, and pursue them with enthusiasm.
3. A self-actualization culture characterizes organizations that value creativity, quality over quantity, and task accomplishment and individual growth. Members of these organizations are encouraged to gain enjoyment from their work, develop themselves, and take on new and interesting activities.
4. An affiliative culture characterizes organizations that place a high priority on constructive interpersonal relationships. Members are expected to be friendly, open, and sensitive to the satisfaction of their work group.

Transformational leadership behavior has been empirically linked to constructive organizational cultures (Eppard 2004; Woods 2004) but there has been little research focusing on department chairs. Given the evolving landscape of higher education, the need to develop chairs as transformational leaders that shape departmental culture toward greater accountability is critical.

**Conclusion**

The development of accountability systems for financial resources and assessing student learning outcomes requires significant change that can be enabled by department chair transformational leadership (Altbach, Berdahl, and Gumport 1999; Gmelch and Miskin 2004; Guskin and Marcy 2002; Hecht et al. 1999; Newman et al. 2004; Rodd 2001; Wergin 2004). Guskin and Marcy (2002) warn that "ignoring the future fiscal realties and the need to focus on student learning can, and probably will have a devastating impact on colleges and universities" (p. 7). They add that "maintaining the present structures will eventually undermine the two things on which higher education has found its past success and must base its future: the quality of faculty work life and student learning" (p. 7).

Today's educational climate requires transformational leaders who are capable of serving as agents of change (U.S. Department of Education 2006). Complexity and the need for change require academic department chairs who are capable of creating a vision; communicating that vision to others; stimulating people to think in different ways; formulating problems in a sophisticated, knowledgeable fashion that inspires creative solutions; and providing an organizational culture in which people achieve and feel appreciated (Lucas 1994). Department chairs should be transformational leaders. That is precisely the type of leader who can perform these essential tasks: revitalizing faculty and improving their professional development, using the untapped talents of the faculty, helping faculty formulate departmental goals and identifying new directions, creating a quality curriculum responsive to major changes in the discipline, and leading the development of departmental culture (Lucas 1994). Such skills do not come naturally for most department chairs; hence, the critical need to explicitly consider the development of this group of public leaders.

**Note**

1. See http://nces.ed.gov/naal/ (accessed November 26, 2007).

# References

Altbach, Philip G., Robert Berdahl, and Patricia Gumport, eds. 1999. *American Higher Education in the Twenty-first Century: Social, Political, and Economic Challenges.* Baltimore: Johns Hopkins Press.

Balthazard, Pierre A., and Robert Cooke. 2004. "Organizational Culture and Knowledge Management Success: Assessing the Behavior–Performance Continuum." In *Proceedings of the 37th Hawaii International Conference of System Sciences*, Island of Hawaii, January 5–8, 2004, by the University of Hawaii at Manoa College of Business. Available at http://doi.ieeecomputersociety.org/10.1109/HICSS.2004.1265577 (accessed November 26, 2007).

Bass, Bernard M. 1985. *Leadership and Performance Beyond Expectations.* New York: Free Press.

Bennett, John B. 1983. *Managing the Academic Department.* New York: ACE/Macmillan.

Bennett, John B., and David J. Figuli, eds. 1990. *Enhancing Departmental Leadership: The Roles of the Chairperson.* New York: ACE/Macmillan.

Birnbaum, Robert. 1988. *How Colleges Work: The Cybernetics of Academic Organization and Leadership.* San Francisco: Jossey-Bass.

Brown, F. William, and Dan Moshavi. 2002. "Herding Academic Cats: Faculty Reactions Transformational and Contingent Reward Leadership by Department Chairs." *Journal of Leadership Studies* 8(3): 79–92.

Burns, James MacGregor. 1978. *Leadership.* New York: Harper & Row.

Carroll, James. 1990. "Career Paths of Department Chairs: A National Perspective." *Research in Higher Education* 32(6): 669–688.

Cooke, Robert, and J. Clayton Lafferty. 1983. *Level V: Organizational Cultural Inventory— Form I.* Plymouth, MI: Human Synergistics.

Corson, John. 1960. *Governance of Colleges and Universities.* New York: McGraw-Hill.

Denison, Daniel R. 1990. *Corporate Culture and Organizational Effectiveness.* New York: John Wiley & Sons.

Diamond, Robert M. 1998. *Academic Leadership: A Practical Guide to Chairing the Department* (Foreword). Bolton, MA: Anker.

Dickeson, Robert C. 2006. "Frequently Asked Questions About College Costs." *The Secretary of Education's Commission on the Future of Higher Education.* Available at: http://www.ed.gov/about/bdscomm/list/hiedfuture/reports/dickeson2.pdf (accessed August 18, 2006).

Eppard, Randy. 2004. *To What Extent Does Transactional and Transformational Leadership Predict Constructive and Defensive Cultures.* PhD dissertation, Virginia Tech.

Erdman, Howard. 2002. *Transformational Leadership Congruence: A Comparison Between University and Community College Presidential Leadership.* PhD dissertation, Texas A&M University.

Etzioni, Amitai. 1964. *Modern Organizations.* Englewood Cliffs, NJ: Prentice-Hall.

French, John, and Bertram Raven. 1959. "The Bases of Social Power." In *Studies in Social Power,* ed. D. Cartwright. Ann Arbor, MI: Institute for Social Research, University of Michigan.

Gilliland, Martha. 1997. "Organizational Change and Tenure." *Change* 29(3): 30–33.

Gmelch, Walter, and Val Miskin. 2004. *Chairing an Academic Department.* Madison, WI: Atwood.

Guskin, Alan, and Mary Marcy. 2002. "Pressures for Fundamental Reform: Creating a Viable Academic Future." In *Field Guide to Academic Leadership,* ed. R. Diamond. San Francisco: John Wiley and Sons.

Hecht, Irene D., Mary Lou Higgerson, Walter Gmelch, and Alan Tucker. 1999. "Roles and Responsibilities of Department Chairs." In *The Department Chair as Academic Leader,* chapter 2. Phoenix, AZ: ACE Oryx Press.

Hincker, Larry. 2005. "The Restructured Higher Education Financial and Administrative Operations Act Update." *Virginia Tech News.* Available at: http://www.vtnews.vt.edu/story.php?relyear=2005&itemno=531 (accessed November 13, 2006).

Jones, Dennis. 2006. "State Shortfalls Projected to Continue Despite Economic Gains: Long-Term Prospects for Higher Education No Brighter." *The Secretary of Education's Commission on the Future of Higher Education.* Available at: http://www.ed.gov/about/bdscomm/list/hiedfuture/reports/jones.pdf (accessed August 20, 2007).

Kotter, John P., and James L. Heskett. 1992. *Corporate Culture and Performance.* New York: Free Press.

Kouzes, James, and Barry Posner. 1995. *The Leadership Challenge: How to Get Extraordinary Things Done in Organizations.* San Francisco: Jossey-Bass.

Leaming, Deryl. 1998. *Academic Leadership: A Practical Guide to Chairing the Department.* Bolton, MA: Anker.

Lucas, Ann. 1994. *Strengthening Departmental Leadership: A Team-Building Guide for Chairs in Colleges and Universities.* San Francisco: Jossey-Bass.

Lucas, Ann F. 2000. *Leading Academic Change: Essential Roles for Department Chairs.* San Francisco: Jossey-Bass.

Miller, Charles, and Geri Malandra. 2006. "Accountability/Context." *The Secretary of Education's Commission on the Future of Higher Education.* Available at: http://www.ed.gov/about/bdscomm/list/hiedfuture/reports/miller-malandra.pdf (accessed August 23, 2006).

Miller, Charles, and Cheryl Oldham. 2006. "Setting the Context." *The Secretary of Education's Commission on the Future of Higher Education.* Available at: http://www.ed.gov/about/bdscomm/list/hiedfuture/reports/miller-oldham.pdf (accessed August 19, 2007).

Murray, Douglas J. 2000. "Leading University-wide Change: Defining New Roles for the Department Chair." *The Department Chair* (Summer). Bolton, MA: Anker. Available at: http://www.acenet.edu/resources/chairs/docs/murray.pdf (accessed August 27, 2006).

Newman, Frank, Lara Couturier, and Jamie Scurry. 2004. *The Future of Higher Education: Rhetoric, Reality, and the Risks of the Market.* San Francisco: John Wiley and Sons.

Rodd, Laurel R. 2001. "The Art of Chairing: What Deming Taught the Japanese and the Japanese Taught Me." *Association of Departments of Foreign Languages Bulletin* 32(3). Available at: www.mla.org/adfl/bulletin/V32N3/323005.htm (accessed August 29, 2007).

Roueche, John E., George A. Baker, and Robert Rose. 1989. *Shared Vision: Transformational Leadership in American Community Colleges.* Washington, DC: Community College Press.

Schein, Edgar H. 2004. *Organizational Culture and Leadership,* 3rd ed. San Francisco: Jossey-Bass.

Seagren, Alan T., John W. Creswell, and Daniel W. Wheeler. 1993. *The Department Chair: New Roles, Responsibilities and Challenges.* ASHE-ERIC Higher Education Report No. 1. Washington, DC: George Washington University, School of Education and Human Development.

U.S. Department of Education. 2006. *A Test of Leadership: Charting the Future of US Higher Education.* Washington, DC: U.S. Department of Education.

Weinberg, Scott S. 1984. "The Perceived Responsibilities of the Departmental Chairperson: A Note of a Preliminary Study." *Higher Education* 13(3): 301–303.

Wellman, Jane V. 2006. "Costs, Prices and Affordability: A Background Paper for the Secretary's Commission on the Future of Higher Education." *The Secretary of Education's*

*Commission on the Future of Higher Education.* Available at: http://www.ed.gov/about/
bdscomm/list/hiedfuture/reports/wellman.pdf (accessed August 29, 2006).

Wergin, Jon L. 2003. *Departments that Work: Building and Sustaining Cultures of Excellence in Academic Programs.* Bolton, MA: Anker.

———. 2004. "Leadership in Place." *The Department Chair* 14(4):1–3.

Woods, Regina. 2004. *The Effects of Transformational Leadership, Trust, and Tolerance of Ambiguity on Organizational Culture in Higher Education.* PhD dissertation, Regent University.

# Part II

## Public Leadership and Collaboration

# 6

# Developing Public Leaders in an Age of Collaborative Governance

Ricardo S. Morse

"Collaboration," "collaborative governance," and "collaborative public management" have become central to the language of public administration. A casual review of recent public administration literature in journals such as *Public Administration Review* and *Journal of Public Administration Research and Theory* finds dozens of articles on collaboration and network management. The theme of the 2007 conference of the American Society of Public Administration was "Monumental Possibilities: Capitalizing on Collaboration." Indeed, a paradigm shift is taking place in public administration. The image of public administration as Weberian hierarchy is giving way to an image of the interorganizational network; an emphasis on command-and-control is being eclipsed by collaborate-and-connect. This, of course, is not unique to public administration, but rather is part of larger global trends that transcend sector and place (Friedman 2005).

So what does all this mean for public leadership? What does public leadership[1]—as practiced by public managers—mean in this age of collaborative governance? And more to the point of this volume, what competencies should be at the forefront of efforts to develop collaborative public leaders? Does a collaborative context require additional or enhanced competencies, or are standard organizational leadership competencies sufficient?

Historically, the field of public administration has paid too little attention to the topic of leadership (Terry 2003; Fairholm 2004; Morse, Buss, and Kinghorn 2007). This is particularly true for interorganizational leadership in the public sector. Most contemporary treatments of public leadership—research and professional development—emphasize *intra*-organizational leadership (e.g., Behn 1998; Terry 2003; Van Wart 2005). In other words, the focus of leadership development in public administration is on *leading organizations*. However, today's public managers "often must operate across organizations as well as within hierarchies" (Agranoff and McGuire 2003, p. 1), meaning organizational leadership, while necessary, is not sufficient. We must now consider how to develop collaborative or *inter*organizational public leaders.

In this chapter, I highlight contributions from research on collaborative leadership—mostly from civic and private sectors—and collaborative public management, to consider what personal attributes, skills, and behavioral competencies are needed for public leadership in a collaborative context, for leadership across boundaries. I begin with a brief discussion of the concept of collaborative governance, follow with the research on collaborative management and leadership, and then highlight competencies that seem to stand out as different from those identified for organizational leadership.

## Collaborative Management and Governance

The December 2006 special issue of *Public Administration Review* on "Collaborative Public Management" highlights a somewhat dramatic shift in emphasis away from the management and leadership *of* public organizations to management and leadership *across* organizations. A focus on hierarchy is giving way to a focus on networks and other forms of interorganizational partnerships. O'Leary, Gerard, and Bingham (2006) define collaborative public management as:

> a concept that describes the process of facilitating and operating in multiorganizational arrangements to solve problems that cannot be solved or easily solved by single organizations. Collaborative means to *co-labor*, to cooperate to achieve common goals, working across boundaries in multisector relationships. Cooperation is based on the value of reciprocity. (p. 7)

This understanding of collaborative public management grows out of a larger stream of scholarship on an expanding, if still muddled, notion of governance.

The term governance has come to be understood by many as the subject of public administration. Generally speaking, it is a term to describe how the public's business is accomplished. The so-called steering of society is viewed as a collective accomplishment of many actors—public and private—as opposed to a traditional view that equates governance with government. Frederickson and Smith (2003) explain that governance "refers to the lateral and interinstitutional relations in administration in the context of the decline of sovereignty, the decreasing importance of jurisdictional borders, and a general institutional fragmentation" (p. 222). Agranoff and McGuire (2003) explain "governance as involving multiple organizations and connections that are necessary to carry out public purposes" (p. 21).

Growing out of this broad understanding of governance is a call for collaborative governance, or rather a recognition that effective governance is the product of collaboration. Collaboration includes the variety of ways public organizations work across boundaries. Crossing organizational, jurisdictional, and sectoral boundaries has always been part of public management and governance, but the recent emphasis on collaborative governance and collaborative public management recognizes that the frequency of such interorganizational efforts has dramatically increased and is likely to continue to increase. Furthermore, there is a growing normative preference for collaborative efforts that transcends philosophic orientations. Indeed, collaboration is at the center of New Public Management (Kettl 2005) as well as the alternative, critical perspective that has been named New Public Service (Denhardt and Denhardt 2003). While the former may emphasize market values and the latter community values, in practice, both correspond with an increased focus on networks, partnerships, and collaboration.

All this is not to say that hierarchy and intra-organizational leadership are no longer important. On the contrary, it is likely that working effectively in an interorganizational environment requires even more intra-organizational management and leadership. At the very least, research on networks finds that public managers still spend most of their time "working within the hierarchy" (Agranoff 2006, p. 57). Agranoff's (2006) study of public managers across fourteen "public management networks" revealed, "there is a premium on the ability to understand and function across boundaries, but this skill has not necessarily replaced the need for internal skills" (p. 57).

But the context of public management is clearly changing. Boundaries are more permeable, and "network" seems to better describe the operational environment of today's public manager than does "hierarchy." We live in an age of collaborative governance, in which the so-called steering of society is now, more than ever, a process that includes the public, private, and civil sectors together, and not simply a monolithic public sector.

## Collaborative Leadership

The research on collaboration, particularly collaboration for public purposes, is consistent in recognizing the significant role of leadership in the success or failure of collaborative endeavors. Linden's (2002) study of collaboration in government and nonprofit agencies concluded that "leadership makes a huge difference" (p. 146). Similarly, Luke (1998), following the work of Crosby and Bryson (2005), found that in today's interconnected world, public leadership (which he distinguishes from organizational and public sector leadership) is essential. Public leadership "is a type of leadership that evokes collaboration and concerted action among diverse and often competing groups toward a shared outcome" (Luke 1998, p. 33).

Leadership for collaboration is different from traditional notions of leadership that are organizational (hierarchical) and ultimately about authority and motivating "followers." Collaborative leadership is about partnership and mutual learning. It emphasizes shared power or "power-with" rather than "power-over" (Follett 1924). It is leadership from the middle as opposed to the top. Thus, the argument here is that yes, there are additional competencies required for effective leadership across organizations.

Several scholars have articulated models of collaborative—sometimes called "facilitative"—leadership directly applicable to public managers. Chrislip and Larson (1994), Chrislip (2002), Luke (1998), Linden (2002) and Crosby and Bryson (2005) all discuss leadership from a collaborative governance perspective. The focus is on leadership as a process of pulling stakeholders together to solve public problems, and thus none of them are explicitly public sector. Put another way, rather than thinking of leadership in terms of accomplishing organizational objectives, these authors focus on solving public problems. Thus, "collaborative" leadership is exercised across all sector, and "public" leadership, in this respect, is not confined to government organizations.

The task here is to distill out specific leadership competencies that apply to the collaborative context. Numerous attributes, skills, and behaviors—collectively referred to as competencies—have been identified for public organizational leadership. Van Wart's excellent *Dynamics of Leadership in Public Service* (2005), for example, describes in some detail ten traits, six "meta-skills," and twenty-one behaviors, to total thirty-seven competencies for developing organizational leadership in the public sector (see Table 6.1). Most or all are generic competencies that cut cross all sectors; however, Van Wart is deliberate in tailoring his message to a public administration audience.

Van Wart's "Leadership Action Cycle" and competencies included therein (summarized in Table 6.1) constitute the baseline for thinking about what competencies are required for collaborative leadership. Clearly, many of the traits, skills, and behaviors are as applicable to leading in an interorganizational setting as they are within organizations. The task is to determine what additional competencies are required for the collaborative context. To do this, we turn to the literature on collaboration and collaborative leadership, as well as literature within public administration coming to be known as "collaborative public management."

There are many recently published works that discuss the process of

Table 6.1

**Public Organizational Leadership Competencies**

| Traits | Skills | Behaviors |
|---|---|---|
| Self-confidence | Communication | Task-oriented |
| Decisiveness | Social skills | Monitoring and assessing work |
| Resilience | Influence skills | Operations planning |
| Energy | Analytic skills | Clarifying roles |
| Need for achievement | Technical skills | Informing |
| Willingness to assume | Continual learning | Delegating |
| responsibility | | Problem solving |
| Flexibility | | Managing innovation and creativity |
| Service mentality | | People-oriented |
| Personal integrity | | Consulting |
| Emotional maturity | | Planning and organizing personnel |
| | | Developing staff |
| | | Motivating |
| | | Building and managing teams |
| | | Managing personnel conflict |
| | | Managing personnel change |
| | | Organization-oriented |
| | | Scanning the environment |
| | | Strategic planning |
| | | Articulating the mission and vision |
| | | Networking and partnering |
| | | Performing general management |
| | | functions |
| | | Decision making |
| | | Managing organizational change |

*Source:* Drawn from Van Wart (2005).

collaboration for public purposes[2] and, to varying degrees, requirements of leadership for collaboration. Table 6.2 summarizes and synthesizes several different models of collaboration into a generic overview of the collaborative process. This overview implies some of the competencies that fall outside the standard competencies for organizational leadership. The key element to consider is that in a collaborative process, no one is really "in charge," and power and authority are shared. Thus, a "leader" in a collaborative process does not have the positional authority and built-in "followers" that the same individual would have in his or her organization.

The process sketched in Table 6.2 illustrates a remarkable amount of consistency across different treatments of collaborative processes. Most scholars identify specific prerequisites that need to be in place before the process can begin. One of the most important prerequisites is the presence of a champion, a catalyst or sparkplug, or rather a leader. The next phases of the process,

Table 6.2

**The Process of Collaboration**

1. **Prerequisites**
   Boundary-crossing problem or opportunity
   Complex problem that requires "adaptive work"
   Shared-power environment
   At least some willingness to work together
   A "sparkplug" or "catalyst" to initiate process
2. **Convening**
   Identifying stakeholders
   Issue framing
   Getting stakeholders "to the table"
3. **Exploring and Deciding**
   Choosing an appropriate process and facilitator
   Reframing the problem (or opportunity) as a group
   Identifying shared interests and desired outcomes
   Exploring and identifying strategies
   Identifying and gathering additional information necessary for decision making
   Forging agreements
4. **Doing and Sustaining**
   Building support outside the group
   Appropriate institutionalization
   Monitoring outcomes
   Network facilitation to maintain and strengthen commitment

*Sources:* Drawn from Gray (1989); Heifetz (1994); Luke (1998); Chrislip (2002); Linden (2002); and Crosby and Bryson (2005).

from convening through determining the appropriate institutional mechanism and maintenance of the partnership, can all be viewed as tasks of collaborative leadership. These tasks are specific leader behaviors supported by certain attributes and skills.

Several works specifically discuss competencies for collaborative leadership, both within and without the field of public administration. I include in this the path-breaking work of Agranoff and McGuire (2001, 2003) who use the broader term of management—as in network management. While the differences and relationship between management and leadership (see Chapter 4) are subject to debate, it is apparent that many features of collaborative "management" are actually leadership behaviors. Management behaviors can be thought of as operational, concerned with the "three E's" and so on. Leadership is about adaptation and change. Certainly, leaders must manage, and managers must lead. Here we focus on the leading aspect.

As mentioned, many competencies span organizational and interorganizational leadership. For example, the service mentality discussed by Van Wart (2005) is consistently mentioned as a trait of collaborative leaders. Certainly,

Table 6.3

**Collaborative Leadership Competencies**

| Attributes | Skills | Behaviors |
|---|---|---|
| • Collaborative mindset<br>• Passion toward outcomes<br>• Systems thinking<br>• Openness and risk taking<br>• Sense of mutuality and connectedness<br>• Humility | • Self-management<br>• Strategic thinking<br>• Facilitation skills | • Stakeholder identification<br>• Stakeholder assessment<br>• Strategic issue framing<br>• Convening working groups<br>• Facilitating mutual learning processes<br>• Inducing commitment<br>• Facilitating trusting relationships among partners |

the six meta-skills are all applicable to leading across boundaries. But there are some competencies that are either unique to the collaborative environment or at least expand significantly on the organizational competencies identified in Table 6.1. These competencies, summarized in Table 6.3, represent a starting point for thinking about what additional elements of leadership development are needed for collaborative governance.

Following Van Wart (2005), I organize the competencies in terms of attributes (Van Wart uses the term "traits"), skills, and behaviors. A simple content analysis of related literature[3] identified dozens of competencies. Those already included in Van Wart's summary of public organizational leadership competencies (either exact wording or different wording but same meanings) were taken out.[4] The remaining competencies, summarized in Table 6.3, represent a starting point for articulating the enhanced or additional attributes, skills, and behaviors needed for collaborative leadership in the public sector. What follows is a brief discussion of these competencies.

*Personal Attributes*

In this section, I discuss several personal attributes that have been identified in the research as contributing to effective collaborative leadership. I use the term attribute rather than the more commonly used term trait because trait connotes a fixed characteristic; something that is inborn and not subject to change (think genetic traits). To speak of leadership traits implies that "leaders are born, not made." Speaking of a personal attribute seems to be less restrictive. A personal attribute is a characteristic quality, but not necessarily one that is hardwired or fixed.

The way attribute is used here, however, is interchangeable with the way

Van Wart (2005) described traits. According to Van Wart, traits (or here, attributes) "are all relatively stable dispositions by adulthood." Yet, "they are all amenable to significant improvement, and a few, to substantial improvement by training and education in specific situational environments" (p. 93).

In scanning the literature on collaborative leadership, several specific personal attributes are identified that clearly stand out from the list discussed in Van Wart (2005) for organizational leaders. One of the most commonly cited attributes is what Linden (2002) refers to as "*a collaborative mindset*" (p. 152, emphasis added). Collaborative leaders "see across boundaries" (Rosabeth Moss Kanter, quoted in Linden 2002, p. 161). They have "a vision of what collaboration can accomplish" (Gray 1989, p. 279). Luke (1998) explains this mindset as "understand[ing] the need to be inclusive and interactive, working across systems and agencies, connecting with other efforts, and involving key networks, partners, and stakeholders to pursue outcomes" (p. 226).

The collaborative mindset means seeing "*connections and possibilities* where others might see barriers or limitations" (Linden 2002, p. 161, emphasis in original). This collaborative mindset is one that understands, values, and seeks out what Covey (1989) describes as the principle of synergy: "You begin with the belief that parties involved will gain more insight, and that the excitement of that mutual learning and insight will create momentum toward more and more insights, learnings, and growth" (p. 264).

Another critical attribute identified across the collaboration literature is what Luke (1998) describes as a "*passion toward outcomes*" (p. 223, emphasis added). This clearly overlaps with the trait Van Wart (2005) labeled "need for achievement" (pp. 103–105). However, there are some important distinctions. As described in Van Wart, need for achievement is based primarily on self-interested motivations of personal advancement or winning. It is a "drive for excellence" that propels organizational leaders toward success (p. 103). Collaborative leaders have a different focus. Their passion or personal desire is "to bring about change and to make a difference" (Luke 1998, p. 223). For them, "the desired result or outcome for the public good becomes the passionate focus and spark that energizes and mobilizes" (Ibid.). Thus, more than having a need for personal and organizational achievement, the collaborative leader is passionate about the common good, about creating public value. That passion is "an emotional spark that mobilizes and sustains energy . . . build[ing] support and trust in an interdependent web of diverse stakeholders" (p. 224). Passion for results becomes a strong motivator for collaborative leaders, giving them "energy and sense of focus" that make them "clearly driven people" (Linden 2002, pp. 152–153).

Collaborative leaders also "see the big picture" and "take the long view." In other words, they are systems thinkers. *Systems thinking* is both an attribute and a skill. Senge (1990) explains system thinking as "a discipline for seeing wholes" as well as "a specific set of tools and techniques" (p. 68). Therefore, it is a habit of thinking (or attribute) as well as a set of skills that can be learned. Luke (1998) explains that this habit of thinking involves "thinking about impacts on future generations"; "thinking about . . . ripple effects and consequences beyond the immediate concern"; and "thinking in terms of issues and strategies that cross functions, specialties, and professional disciplines" (p. 222). Jurisdictionally and/or organizationally bound public leaders have many incentives to think short-term and stay internally focused. Being a systems thinker and considering the "forest *and* the trees" (Senge 1990, p. 127, emphasis in original) requires mental discipline and moral courage.

Collaborative leaders are often described as entrepreneurs, and are noted for their *openness and risk taking* (Morse and Dudley 2002; Henton, Melville, and Walesh 2004). Willingness to experiment and take risks is a critical attribute identified by many observers of collaborative leadership (Luke 1998; Sullivan and Skelcher 2002; Henton, Melville, and Walesh 2004). "They are risk takers. They are not afraid of failure" (Henton, Melville, and Walesh 2004, p. 209). Risk taking involves being comfortable with uncertainty, being able to make trade-offs, and "accommodating the unexpected" (Sullivan and Skelcher 2002, p. 101). Luke (1998) describes this attribute as a "committed openness . . . to identifying and testing new and diverse ways to achieve" the desired outcomes that drive them (p. 225). They are willing to be wrong, to revise their thinking, and to "understand that no project, program, or policy should be seen as final or definitive" (pp. 224–225).

A strong undercurrent in most treatments of collaborative leadership that receives very little explicit attention has to do with the leaders' psychological connection with others. I label this a *sense of mutuality and connectedness* with others. This attribute is expressed in its ideal form in Buber's *I and Thou* (1958). Essentially, it is a sense of being in relation to others, of being part of a whole; being a part of, rather than apart from, others. In its deepest sense, this attribute is a worldview reflected in the philosophical pragmatism of George Herbert Mead, William James, and John Dewey, as well as modern-day communitarianism (Etzioni 1996). The work of Mary Follett also speaks to this attribute in a compelling way for a public administration audience (Morse 2006). However, one need not delve deeply into philosophy or social psychology to understand this attribute. The interpersonal quality of mutuality and connectedness can be thought of in terms of perspective taking ("putting oneself in another's place") and concern for others (Luke 1998, p. 227). Ability to "understand others' concerns and perspectives" and ultimately having an "underlying concern for others" is a foundation for the application of collaborative skills and ultimately successful collaborative action (Luke 1998, pp. 226–228).

Trust[5] is a widely recognized factor in successful collaboration. Williams (2002) finds a "consensus that trust must underpin effective relationships at both an individual and organizational level" (p. 116). Clearly, the attribute of personal integrity, identified in Van Wart (2005) and most other compilations of leadership traits, is a component of this trust. But the genuine recognition and understanding of the other that stems from the attribute of mutuality and connectedness also connects in important ways with trust and trustworthiness (Covey 1989).

The "sense of relatedness" and genuine concern for the "larger public good" that runs through all the preceding attributes, "cannot occur without first shifting one's attention away from a preoccupation with oneself and toward looking outward to relationships and interpersonal networks" (Luke 1998, pp. 226–228). Collaborative leaders have a good degree of *humility,* an attribute Linden (2002) describes as a "strong but measured ego" (p. 154). They "don't have to grab the headlines for every success. Quite the opposite, they seem to take great satisfaction when they can share credit for accomplishments with many others. Their ambitions are directed more toward organizational success than personal glory" (Linden 2002, p. 154). Collaborative leaders are entrepreneurs, they are ambitious and driven. Yet, at the same time they are humble. Luke (1998) connects this to what psychologists call "ego-strength." Persons with ego-strength "don't have the internal motivation to be in charge of everything . . . [there is a] willingness to share credit, which is crucial in forging agreements and sustaining action" (pp. 230–231).

These six attributes appear to be fundamental to effective leadership in collaborative settings. They work in concert with other fundamental attributes that are associated with organizational leadership (see Table 6.1), although in some instances there may be tension between what makes for good organizational leadership and what makes for good collaborative leadership. For example, decisiveness, an attribute prized in organizational settings, might contradict the openness and humility needed for successful collaboration. The need for achievement in personal and organizational terms might be a source of tension with the passion for outcomes for the common good that transcend organizational boundaries. In practice, the public leader is constantly balancing competing personal and organizational commitments.

### Skills

We now turn to skills, or "broadly applied learned characteristics," that appear essential in the practice of collaborative leadership (Van Wart 2005, p. 92). Van Wart's six "skills" (Table 6.1) are broad categories for a much larger set of skills. For example, "communication skills" include oral, written, and nonverbal communications, as well as active listening skills—all certainly required in interorganizational settings as much as or even more than within organizations. In like fashion, there are three broad categories or skill sets specifically discussed in the collaborative leadership literature that seem to be *in addition to* the six skill sets noted in Table 6.1. These are labeled here as self-management, strategic thinking, and facilitation (or process) skills.

*Self-management* refers to the ability to prioritize and manage time effectively (Sullivan and Skelcher 2002, p. 102). A very large "self-help" literature is available that places self-management at the center of not only personal effectiveness but leader effectiveness (Covey 1989). In fact, some might consider self-management so basic to management skills in general that it is already included in Van Wart's (2005) "technical" skill set that includes "basic management knowledge/skills" (pp. 145–147). But this is a stretch. Self-management seems to be a fundamental skill set that stands apart from the others, and while relevant for leading organizations, is particularly relevant when working across boundaries. The personal habits of being proactive, beginning with the end in mind, and putting first things first (Covey 1989) are at the very foundation of what it takes to be a collaborative leader.

*Strategic thinking* covers a wide range of skills that are only partially covered in the "analytic skills" cluster identified by Van Wart (2005) and other lists of leadership skills. Luke (1998, pp. 151–184) offers an excellent discussion of the various components of strategic thinking for collaborative work. He argues that four sets of analytic skills are involved:

- "Framing and reframing issues and their strategic responses." This means defining problems "in ways that focus attention, stimulate an urgency for action, and provide a framework for the debates on action strategies."
- "Identifying and defining end-outcomes or desired results." Multiparty problem-solving efforts are enhanced by focusing on desired outcomes rather than detailing deficiencies. Effective leaders help groups identify outcomes and keep them separate from problems and inputs. They also clarify and "separate end-outcomes from intermediate outcomes."
- "Assessing stakeholder interest to discover common and complementary interests." Identifying stakeholders and determining their "goals, concerns, or stakes" is also a key component of the collaborative process.
- "Systematic thinking to reveal interconnections and strategic leverage points." This refers to the tools and techniques aspect of systems thinking mentioned earlier in this chapter. There are many "visual tools for communicating about and seeing multiple connections and interrelationships." These include various conceptual "mapping" exercises that can vary greatly in degree of complexity.

Senge's (1990) discussion of systems thinking includes additional insights and tools. Furthermore, Crosby and Bryson's *Leadership for the Common Good* (2005) offers much in the way of skills development in this area, including several exercises and models for stakeholder assessment.

Collaborative leaders also have "knowledge of the process tools" needed "for designing effective collaborations" (Gray 1989, p. 279). Again, Luke (1998, pp. 185–217) offers an excellent discussion of the *facilitation skills* needed to lead "from the middle" and help a diverse group work together effectively. The four primary skills involve:

- Helping the group generate "fresh ideas and new insights." This includes helping a group separate idea generation from evaluation and asking open-ended questions that "inquire and reveal."
- "Coping with conflict." This is a broad skill set within a skill set that is often included in discussion of leadership skills. The skills of principled negotiation articulated in Fisher, Ury, and Patton's *Getting to Yes* (1991) are essential here.
- "Getting a group unstuck and moving the debate forward." More often than not, collaborative groups can run out of steam or otherwise get in a rut. The skilled use of specific interventions can help a group get "unstuck." It is also important to know when it is time to call on an external facilitator.
- "Forging multiple agreements." Luke explains that "public leaders assist in forging agreement in three specific ways: they work to develop a nonconfrontational agreement-building process for selecting multiple strategies; they build larger agreements from smaller ones; and they seek high levels of consensus among diverse stakeholders."

Again, there are many great resources for developing facilitative leadership skills. Schwarz's *The Skilled Facilitator* (2002) is an excellent starting point.

Space does not allow full discussion of these three skill sets. The reader is referred to other works mentioned above that give in-depth coverage of these topics (especially Luke 1998; Covey 1989; Crosby and Bryson 2005; Schwarz 2002). The point to underscore here is that these broad skill sets are for the most part not found in those identified with organizational leadership (see Van Wart 2005). While these three skill sets can clearly contribute to better organizational leadership, they are especially important for interorganizational, or collaborative leadership and, along with the attributes discussed in the previous section, should form the core of leadership development for interorganizational collaboration.

## *Behaviors*

It is important to note that attributes and skills of leaders are relevant inasmuch as they contribute to effective leadership behaviors. Thus, competencies go beyond who you are (attributes) and what you can do (skills)—they also must include what you actually do. In fact, most of the research on collaborative leadership focuses on behavioral competencies, those behaviors or actions actually displayed by leaders in practice. The organizational leadership literature groups leader behaviors into task-oriented behaviors, people-oriented behaviors, and organization-oriented behaviors (Van Wart 2005, p. 157). Descriptions of collaborative leadership behaviors tend to cut across all three meta-categories. These behaviors naturally mirror the general process of collaboration (see Table 6.3).

Table 6.4 summarizes the leader behaviors identified from three different treatments of collaborative leadership. Chrislip and Larson (1994) and Luke (1998) are both broad treatments of collaborative leadership that are cross-sectoral, although each of them specifically addresses public sector practitioners as among their intended audiences. Agranoff and McGuire's research (2001; McGuire 2006), on the other hand, is specifically focused on public managers. The behaviors they identify are in terms of "collaborative public management." They don't distinguish leadership from management, although most of the behaviors they identify fall under what others label leadership.

While many leadership behaviors identified by Van Wart (2005, Table 6.1) overlap with the behaviors associated with collaborative leadership (e.g., team building, environmental scanning, networking, and strategic planning), there are many behaviors that are more specific to the collaborative context. These behaviors include stakeholder identification and assessment, strategic issue framing, relationship development with diverse stakeholders, convening working groups, facilitating mutual learning processes, inducing commitment, and facilitating trusting relationships among partners. It is likely that a more detailed analysis would yield a much longer list of behaviors that stand apart from those associated with organizational leadership (Table 6.1). Therefore, the list discussed here should be considered a starting point only and not a complete account of all the behavioral competencies for collaborative leadership.

*Stakeholder identification and stakeholder assessment* are two behaviors that work in tandem during the initial phases of a collaborative process. Identifying a broad array of stakeholders is "the first step in creating a constituency for change" and precedes efforts to get people involved (Chrislip and Larson 1994, p. 65). However, simply identifying stakeholders is not enough.

Table 6.4

**Collaborative Leadership Behaviors**

| Chrislip & Larson | Luke | Agranoff & McGuire |
|---|---|---|
| *Inspiring Commitment to Action*<br>• Convincing people that something can and should be done<br>• Convening stakeholders<br><br>*Leading as Peer Problem Solver*<br>• Helping groups create visions and solve problems<br>• Building relationships<br><br>*Building Broad-Based Involvement*<br><br>*Sustaining Hope and Participation*<br>• Promoting and protecting process | *Raising Awareness (Issue Framing)*<br>• Stimulate awareness and emotional concern that problem or opportunity exists<br>• Elevate issue to priority status by creating sense of urgency and "do-ability"<br>• Use "attentional triggers" to expand number of people concerned about the issue<br><br>*Forming Working Groups*<br>• Identify full spectrum of stakeholders<br>• Enlist core working group members and design multiple levels of participation<br>• Convene first meetings<br><br>*Creating Strategies*<br>• Build and nurture effective working group<br>• Facilitate mutual learning process<br>• Promote and facilitate strategy development<br><br>*Sustaining Action*<br>• Build commitment and political support<br>• Institutionalize cooperative behavior<br>• Network facilitation | *Activation*<br>• Identifying participants and stakeholders<br>• Tapping resources of those persons<br>• Recruiting potential members<br><br>*Framing*<br>• Facilitating agreement on leadership and administrative roles<br>• Helping establish identity and culture for the network<br>• Helping develop working structure for network, including strategic planning<br><br>*Mobilizing*<br>• Inducing commitment to the joint effort and building support from key players<br><br>*Synthesizing*<br>• Engendering productive and purposeful interaction among all actors<br>• Facilitating relationships to build trust and promote information exchange |

*Source:* Chrislip & Larson (1994, pp. 138–141); Luke (1998); Agranoff and McGuire (2001, pp. 289–301); and McGuire (2006, p. 37).

Stakeholders must be assessed in terms of what they might contribute to a collaborative effort, what interests they have in the issue, how they might define the problem (or opportunity), and so on. Effective leadership entails finding the right mix of stakeholders to involve and ways to involve them. There are several helpful frameworks and tools available to help leaders identify and assess stakeholders. The first place to start is Crosby and Bryson's *Leadership for the Common Good* (2005).

*Strategic issue framing* is another key behavior of collaborative leaders. Luke (1998) argues that "effective public leaders do not necessarily promote solutions; they promote problems." They become "advocates for issue emergence," creating a sense of urgency around a particular problem or opportunity (Luke 1998, p. 41). Strategic issue framing involves transforming a condition (a latent problem or opportunity) into a high-priority issue for the public—particularly those individuals and organizations seen as potential partners. Collaborative leaders use a variety of strategies for framing issues, such as leveraging dramatic (or "focusing") events and utilizing the media. They understand that how an issue is framed determines how fast it gets to the policy agenda, who gets involved, and what solutions are identified (Luke 1998, pp. 41–65). Linden (2002, p. 107) refers to this kind of issue framing as "creating high stakes."

Collaborative leaders also engage, on an ongoing basis, in *relationship development with diverse stakeholders*. Linden (2002) calls relationships "the glue to most collaborative efforts" (p. 92). An illustrative example involves the efforts of a U.S. Forest Service administrative officer, Rod Collins, and his "Friday chowders" with colleagues from the Bureau of Land Management (BLM). Seeing that formal, infrequent meetings between the two agency offices were not productive, he invited his BLM counterparts to meet his team for lunch at a local restaurant. This evolved into a monthly routine for over four years that produced relationships and tangible results (Linden 2002, pp. 101–102). Having chowder together seems almost trivial, but the research is very consistent in identifying these kinds of informal relationship-building efforts as essential and producing powerful outcomes. Indeed, Williams's (2002) study of "the competent boundary spanner" states plainly that "a necessary part of interorganizational working involves building and sustaining effective personal relationships" (p. 115).

*Convening working groups* is another clearly identified collaborative leadership behavior. Interorganizational groups simply do not come into being by happenstance. Bringing the right stakeholders together "to the table" is a critical act of leadership (Luke 1998, p. 67). Although there is no "one best way" to convene a working group of diverse stakeholders, Luke (1998) finds that successful beginnings usually involve a "safe or neutral space for meetings" and a process perceived as being legitimate or transparent, not "driven by hidden agendas." Collaborative leaders "pay close attention to first meetings and invest considerable time and energy in the initial process of convening" (p. 81).

After a working group has been convened, a key task of leadership becomes *facilitating mutual learning processes*. This involves "providing leadership to the *process* . . . setting the tone for the interactions, one that [is] respectful and hopeful" (Wondolleck and Ryan 1999, p. 122, emphasis in original). While the collaborative leader need not (ultimately) be the formal group facilitator, they do play a key role "establish[ing] high standards of communication, deliberation, open-mindedness, commitment, and hard work" for the group (Wondolleck and Ryan 1999, p. 122). The focus for the leader is in ensuring that the group "develop and nurture a deliberative process of mutual learning" (Luke 1998, p. 95). Leaders accomplish this by effectively "establishing and influencing the operating rules . . . [and] prevailing values and norms" of the working group (Agranoff and McGuire 2001, p. 299).

Throughout the process, collaborative leaders can be found *inducing commitment* both within and outside the working group. Leaders must induce commitment of participants early on during the convening stage and continue to induce commitment throughout the process, especially when the commitment level needs to go beyond talk (Agranoff and McGuire 2001, pp. 299–300; Linden 2002, pp. 173–174). Also, in order to sustain action during the implementation phase, commitment must be garnered from key decision makers. Effective commitment building at this stage involves identifying other "champions," including advocacy coalitions and other power holders who can help in the political process of allocating resources (Luke 1998, pp. 128–131).

Another ongoing collaborative leadership behavior is *facilitating trusting relationships among partners*. This is different than building relationships with partners, although it may involve similar strategies. As working groups come together, differences will naturally surface, and many relationship-based obstacles to collaboration will manifest themselves. Thus, in addition to having good relations with each of the partners individually, the collaborative leader makes efforts to build good relationships among the different actors in the group. Agranoff and McGuire (2001) explained that the leader "seeks to achieve cooperation between actors while preventing, minimizing, or removing blockages to cooperation" (p. 300). Luke (1998) described this as network facilitation. A network facilitator is a "multilateral broker" (Mandell 1984, 1988) that builds a "supportive relationship and strong bonds of trust among partners in the network" (Luke 1998, pp. 143–144).

Of course, much more could be said about each of these behaviors. The reader may turn to the resources cited in this chapter for more in-depth discussions of each of them. And again, there are likely many other discrete behaviors that could be added to the list here. This list is offered only as a starting point for thinking about the leader behaviors in a collaborative context that is distinct from those identified for organizational leadership.

### Leadership Styles

This discussion of competencies would not be complete without a word on leadership styles. In addition to attributes, skills, and behaviors, the study of leadership includes examining various overall "styles" of leadership. Van Wart (2005) reviews the various leadership styles identified in the literature. His "leadership action cycle" model views leader behaviors as being influenced by one's leadership style combined with specific competencies and the operational environment. Identified leadership styles include "laissez-faire," "directive," "supportive," and "participative" (Van Wart 2005).

The styles literature is very much from the organizational leadership point-of-view, with each implicitly assuming a leader–follower relationship. In other words, one's "style" refers to general patterns of leader behavior in relation to subordinates, tasks, goals, and so on. While the participative style seems consistent with the "inclusive" style of collaborative leadership discussed in Linden (2002), it may be that leadership for collaboration requires a different style altogether. Bardach's (1998) study of interagency collaboration identifies "facilitative" and "advocacy" styles that seem to best characterize effective collaborative leaders and also seem to be different from those identified in the organizational leadership literature.

Bardach (1998) notes that the facilitative style is a "kinder, gentler sort, sometimes called *servant* . . . leadership." He continues, "[A] good facilitative leader is someone with appropriate self-awareness about the nature of the role and a natural gift for diplomacy. It is often someone with a broad-gauge, general background or cross-disciplinary training and experience" (p. 226, emphasis in original). Those with a facilitative style often have "a relatively positive personal disposition . . . perceived as neutral, someone with 'no ax to grind.'" It is a "consensus-building style" (pp. 226–227).

In contrast, an advocacy style "approaches consensus building in a rallying spirit and carries it as far as it can reasonably do so" (p. 228). The essential difference between a facilitative and an advocacy style is that advocacy leaders have a vision and work with others who support it, while the facilitative leader essentially subordinates to the group (p. 228). In either case, the style of leadership is very different from the normal "top-down" ones that dominate discussions of organizational leadership. The collaborative leader's style stems from the attributes discussed above, attributes that engender joint-work and power-sharing.

More research could and should be done to explore the styles of collaborative leaders when they are working in an interorganizational setting versus when they are working within their "home" organizations. Is there a consistent organizational leadership style across collaborative leaders? Is it possible to be a directive leader within one's organization but a facilitative leader on the outside? These are just a few of the many interesting research questions for studying collaborative leadership as exercised by public managers.

**Developing Public Leadership for Collaborative Governance**

In reviewing the collaborative leadership literature for this chapter, it became apparent that the focus tends to be on tasks or behaviors. In other words, we know a lot about what collaborative leaders do. There is much less written about who collaborative leaders are, what makes them tick, and what attributes form the core of their character.

In considering what the competencies discussed in this chapter mean for public leadership development, two important observations should be made. First, if the aim is to develop public leaders who are better equipped to lead in a shared-power world, in an age of collaborative governance, then we need to start from the inside out. As Marc Holzer discusses in Chapter 2 of this volume, our culture seems to promote an image of leadership antithetical to what I have described as collaborative, or facilitative, leadership. If current or future public leaders are to work across boundaries effectively—creating public value in collaboration with actors across different jurisdictions and even sectors—then they have to have the mindset, the will, or habits of the heart to do so. The leader whose very character is rooted in command-and-control, top-down models of leadership may very well be able to learn the skills of collaboration, but it is unlikely those will be translated into behaviors.

Covey's (1989, 1990) simple, yet profound, approach to leadership development is called "inside-out." What he means by that is "to start first with self—to start with the most *inside* part of self—with your paradigms, your character, and your motives" (1990, p. 63, emphasis in original). In other words, if you want to be effective at leading change in an interorganizational setting, that is, a collaborative setting, then you have to *be* a collaborative person. Linden's (2002) "questions on your collaborative leadership" (p. 165) provide a nice starting point for self-reflection:

- Do you come across as someone who prefers to be the source of all new ideas?

Figure 6.1 **Four Levels of Public Leadership**

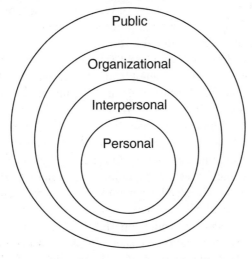

- Do others see you as someone who typically wants to find the answers to problems and challenges on your own?
- How do you react when others' perspective on an issue is very different from yours? Is that an irritation to be avoided? An inconvenience to be overcome? An asset to be used?
- When you are working on an issue with others, how likely are you to ask if there is anyone else with a stake in the issue?
- When you are trying to influence others, how much do you tend to push your own ideas, and to what extent do you use pull to invite others into the discussion?

In an age of collaborative governance, where shared problems and shared power is the norm, the public leader must truly *become* the type of person whom others can trust and respect. A focus on skills or tools will be useless if the personal attributes are not in alignment. The attributes must come first.

Public leaders operate on many different levels. Figure 6.1 is a simple illustration of this concept. Public leadership begins with personal leadership, the realm of what Covey (1989) calls "private victories." This is the realm of personal attributes and how they interface with one's world. The next level is that of interpersonal leadership or how one interacts with others. Leadership enacted at that level influences one's leadership at the organizational level. In other words, effective leadership of organizations is built on many interpersonal interactions. Organizational culture, for example, is developed through the sum product of countless interpersonal interactions. And organizations that work well "across boundaries" have cultures amenable to joint-work. Thus, effectiveness at the "public" (interorganizational) level is contingent on leadership at the organizational level, and so on.

Ultimately, leadership development for collaboration—the outer ring or "public" level in Figure 6.1—cannot be divorced from organizational, interpersonal, or personal leadership. They are all connected and begin with the self—the personal attributes one develops. This is the second observation regarding how the competencies discussed in this chapter fit into the broader discussion of public leadership development. That is, the inside-out approach can also be a way of thinking of leadership at all four levels. Whether a formal training program, mentoring, or self-reflection, the individual working to become a better collaborative leader can think about the competencies and what they mean at each level of leadership. What does being a collaborative leader mean for my own personal leadership? For my leadership in interpersonal situations? For my organizational leadership? And for my leadership across boundaries "for the common good" (Crosby and Bryson 2005)?

Development of leaders that can successfully lead change and create public value through partnerships and collaboration is of concern for the field of public administration today. This chapter offers a starting point for thinking about some of the specific competencies of public leadership for collaborative governance. Beyond the suggestions above regarding an inside-out approach to leadership development, I leave to others[6] more specific discussions of *how* to develop these leadership competencies in others. Several chapters in this book discuss specific models and experiences regarding the *how* of leadership development. The purpose of this chapter has been to stimulate more thought and discussion regarding the *what*.

## Notes

1. References to public leadership in this chapter will relate to leadership within the context of public administration. While the term can be and is used more broadly to encompass political leadership and even civic leadership, the effort here zeroes in on leadership as exercised by those in the public service.

2. There are many more treatments of interorganizational collaboration in the private sector that are likewise useful—especially the work of Huxham and Vangen (2005)—but not as directly as those that specifically focus on collaboration "for the common good." The primary difference has to do with interests. In private settings the profit motive and organizational interest are paramount; actors engage in collaboration to further their own interest. In the public sphere, self-interest certainly can be a factor, but the primary force bringing actors together is a shared interest in solving a public problem and/or in creating public value.

3. Although many relevant sources were consulted for this study, the primary sources used here that speak directly to the question of leadership competencies are Bardach

(1998), Luke (1998), Linden (2002), Chrislip and Larson (1994), Sullivan and Skelcher (2002), Straus (2002), Williams (2002), and McGuire (2006). This pool of literature is admittedly not complete; there are hundreds of sources that in one way or another are relevant to collaborative leadership in the public sector. However, these sources seemed relevant, and all, to one degree or another, identify leadership competencies in terms of behaviors and/or attributes and skills.

4. Many competencies identified as key to collaborative leadership are already part of the organizational leadership rubric. Personal integrity, for example, is as important to working within an organization as it is for working outside the organization. Energy and resilience are certainly required for successful collaboration as well. To keep this chapter reasonably short, a discussion of the items of overlap is not undertaken. Rather, the focus is on competencies identified that seem to fall outside the standard ones for organizational leadership.

5. Trustworthiness may also be viewed as a separate attribute. Luke (1998, pp. 233–236) included an excellent discussion of trust and personal integrity. It is not included as a separate attribute here, however, because it seems more of an outgrowth or product of integrity and the sense of mutuality that leads to authentic relationships rather than something that exists independently. In other words, one must have integrity and authentic relationships to build genuine interpersonal trust.

6. The following two chapters are especially good examples of efforts to develop leaders for collaborative governance.

## References

Agranoff, Robert. 2006. "Inside Collaborative Networks: Ten Lessons for Public Managers." *Public Administration Review* 66 (supplement): 56–65.

Agranoff, Robert, and Michael McGuire. 2001. "Big Questions in Public Network Management Research." *Journal of Public Administration Research and Theory* 11(3): 295–326.

———. 2003. *Collaborative Public Management: New Strategies for Local Governments.* Washington, DC: Georgetown University Press.

Bardach, Eugene. 1998. *Getting Agencies to Work Together: The Practice and Theory of Managerial Craftsmanship.* Washington, DC: Brookings Institution.

Behn, Robert D. 1998. "What Right Do Public Managers Have to Lead?" *Public Administration Review* 58(3): 209–224.

Buber, Martin. 1958. *I and Thou.* 2nd ed., trans. Ronald Gregor Smith. New York: Scribner.

Chrislip, David D. 2002. *The Collaborative Leadership Fieldbook: A Guide for Citizens and Civic Leaders.* San Francisco: Jossey-Bass.

Chrislip, David D., and Carl E. Larson. 1994. *Collaborative Leadership: How Citizens and Civic Leaders Can Make a Difference.* San Francisco: Jossey-Bass.

Covey, Stephen R. 1989. *The Seven Habits of Highly Effective People.* New York: The Free Press.

———. 1990. *Principle-Centered Leadership.* New York: The Free Press.

Crosby, Barbara C., and John M. Bryson. 2005. *Leadership for the Common Good: Tackling Public Problems in a Shared-Power World.* 2nd ed. San Francisco: Jossey-Bass.

Denhardt, Janet V., and Robert B. Denhardt. 2003. *The New Public Service: Serving, Not Steering.* Armonk, NY: M. E. Sharpe.

Etzioni, Amitai. 1996. *The New Golden Rule: Community and Morality in a Democratic Society.* New York: Basic Books.

Fairholm, Matthew R. 2004. "Different Perspectives on the Practice of Leadership." *Public Administration Review* 64(5): 577–590.

Fisher, Roger, William Ury, and Bruce Patton. 1991. *Getting to Yes: Negotiating Agreement Without Giving In.* 2nd ed. New York: Penguin Books.
Follett, Mary P. 1924. *Creative Experience.* New York: Longmans, Green.
Frederickson, H. George, and Kevin B. Smith. 2003. *The Public Administration Theory Primer.* Boulder, CO: Westview Press.
Friedman, Thomas L. 2005. *The World Is Flat: A Brief History of the Twenty-First Century.* New York: Farrar, Straus, and Giroux.
Gray, Barbara. 1989. *Collaborating: Finding Common Ground for Multiparty Problems.* San Francisco: Jossey-Bass.
Heifetz, Ronald A. 1994. *Leadership Without Easy Answers.* Cambridge, MA: Belknap Press of Harvard University Press.
Henton, Douglas, John Melville, and Kim Walesh. 2004. *Civic Revolutionaries: Igniting the Passion for Change in America's Communities.* San Francisco: Jossey-Bass.
Huxham, Chris, and Siv Vangen. 2005. *Managing to Collaborate: The Theory and Practice of Collaborative Advantage.* New York: Routledge.
Kettl, Donald F. 2005. *Global Public Management Revolution.* 2nd ed. Washington, DC: Brookings.
Linden, Russell M. 2002. *Working Across Boundaries: Making Collaboration Work in Government and Nonprofit Organizations.* San Francisco: Jossey-Bass.
Luke, Jeffrey S. 1998. *Catalytic Leadership: Strategies for an Interconnected World.* San Francisco: Jossey-Bass.
Mandell, Myrna P. 1984. "Application of Network Analysis to the Implementation of a Complex Project." *Human Relations* 37(6): 659-79.
_____. 1988. "Intergovernmental Management in Interorganizational Networks: A Revised Perspective." *International Journal of Public Administration* 11(4): 393-416.
McGuire, Michael. 2006. "Collaborative Public Management: Assessing What We Know and How We Know It." *Public Administration Review* 66 (supplement): 33–43.
Morse, Ricardo S. 2006. "Prophet of Participation: Mary Parker Follett and Public Participation in Public Administration." *Administrative Theory and Praxis* 28(1): 1–32.
Morse, Ricardo S., Terry F. Buss, and C. Morgan Kinghorn. 2007. *Transforming Public Leadership for the 21st Century.* Armonk, NY: M.E. Sharpe.
Morse, Rick, and Larkin Dudley. 2002. "Civic Entrepreneurs and Collaborative Leadership." *PA Times* 25 (August): 3.
O'Leary, Rosemary, Catherine Gerard, and Lisa Blomgren Bingham. 2006. "Introduction to the Symposium on Collaborative Public Management." *Public Administration Review* 66 (supplement): 6–9.
Schwarz, Roger. 2002. *The Skilled Facilitator.* Revised. San Francisco: Jossey-Bass.
Senge, Peter M. 1990. *The Fifth Discipline: The Art and Practice of the Learning Organization.* New York: Doubleday.
Straus, David. 2002. *How to Make Collaboration Work: Powerful Ways to Build Consensus, Solve Problems, and Make Decisions.* San Francisco: Berrett-Koehler.
Sullivan, Helen, and Chris Skelcher. 2002. *Working Across Boundaries: Collaboration in Public Services.* London: Palgrave.
Terry, Larry D. 2003. *Leadership of Public Bureaucracies: The Administrator as Conservator.* 2nd ed. Armonk, NY: M.E. Sharpe.
Van Wart, Montgomery. 2005. *Dynamics of Leadership in Public Service: Theory and Practice.* Armonk, NY: M.E. Sharpe.
Williams, Paul. 2002. "The Competent Boundary Spanner." *Public Administration* 80(1): 103–124.
Wondolleck, Julia M., and Clare M. Ryan. 1999. "What Hat Do I Wear Now? An Examination of Agency Roles in Collaborative Processes." *Negotiation Journal* (April): 117–133.

# 7

# From Local Managers to Community Change Agents

## Lessons from an Executive Leadership Program Experience

Carl W. Stenberg, Vaughn M. Upshaw, and Donna Warner

Since fall 2003, the Public Leadership faculty of the University of North Carolina at Chapel Hill (UNC) School of Government (SOG) has worked on the design and delivery of the Public Executive Leadership Academy (PELA), an advanced leadership program for local managers. PELA serves a diverse audience of twenty-five municipal and county managers, assistant managers, and department heads who aspire to leadership careers in local government and need to hone or develop their communication and collaboration skills. The program's curriculum is unique in its focus on the manager's role as community leader and change agent, and its emphasis on leading and managing in an intergovernmental and intersector context. Participants apply information and insights from class sessions to their "real world" change opportunity back home. To our knowledge, no other university-based public executive leadership program in the United States has this emphasis.

As we reflect on the past two years of experience, we have learned a great deal. The purpose of this chapter is to share these lessons with those interested in developing similar leadership programs. Our focus is on: (1) partnership management, (2) collaboration, (3) curriculum design, (4) team-building techniques, and (5) program evaluation.

### Partnership Management

The School of Government's Public Leadership faculty helps public officials lead and govern their communities and strengthen local governmental management. We work closely with the professional associations in the state to ensure that our research, consulting, and educational programs meet the needs of our clients. This approach served us well in the design and delivery of PELA. We believe the time devoted to managing partnerships paid significant dividends.

PELA was developed in partnership with the North Carolina City and County Management Association (NCCCMA) and the International City/County Management Association (ICMA). For several years, NCCCMA wanted the School of Government to launch an advanced professional development program for managers along the lines of the Senior Executive Institute (SEI) offered by the University of Virginia. ICMA was supportive of this initiative, and encouraged faculty to design a program that complemented rather than duplicated SEI, especially since nearly more than fifty managers from North Carolina were SEI alumni.

NCCCMA assisted us in conducting a needs assessment, creating an advisory committee to help design the program's structure, identifying major curricular components, and providing seed money and scholarships. We were able to call on the association for suggestions for managers who could serve as teaching faculty and give us feedback to ensure that what was developed was relevant to the "real world." The association also provided $10,000 each year toward program support and $7,500 for scholarships, to make PELA affordable and accessible to managers across North Carolina.

ICMA contributed the services of its Executive Director, Robert O'Neill, as a member of the PELA faculty and advice from other senior staff members, and it agreed to count PELA for 40 credit hours as part of its Voluntary Credentialing Program. For those seeking academic credit, the University of North Carolina–Chapel Hill agreed to offer six hours of graduate Continuing Education Units for completion of PELA at a modest additional tuition payment.

The partnerships with NCCCMA, ICMA, and the university were instrumental in building a program that is relevant and responsive. They also have been critical to containing PELA's costs. For the first two years of the program, tuition was set at $3,000. This amount covered all instructional costs and several meal functions. Travel and accommodations were paid by the participants. NCCCMA's financial support enabled us to discount tuition by $400 for its members and award scholarships for half of the remainder to managers in smaller and rural communities. Another important factor was that the School of Government contributed faculty and staff without charge. While there was a daily program charge for each participant to help pay for administrative services and parking, the budget did not need to cover salaries and benefits. Similarly, ICMA's staff services were reimbursed for only travel-related expenses.

In addition to collaborating closely with our partners on the program design, several individual managers also were engaged as advisors. Their input gave us confidence that PELA's program design and curriculum would meet the managers' interests and constraints. Our needs assessment and recruitment strategy exemplify some important lessons we learned about collaboration strategies.

### Needs Assessment

Regional meetings were held the winter of 2005 with municipal and county managers and assistant managers in eight locations across North Carolina. The primary purpose of the meetings was to hear from professional managers about: (1) major challenges and issues (personal and professional), (2) what was needed to manage these issues, (3) priorities for education and training programs, and (4) design and delivery preferences.

A wide range of challenges and issues were identified, and a number of common topics and themes emerged from the discussions, including manager–governing board relations, economic development, citizen engagement, intergovernmental relations, and change management. To address these challenges, the participants were interested in gaining skills in the following areas: communications, negotiations and conflict resolution, facilitation, collaborative decision making and consensus building, and interpersonal relations. There also was general interest in knowing more about "best management and leadership practices" and the emerging issues impacting North Carolina state and local government.

Participants also shared their views on scheduling sites, technology utilization, and tuition costs. A summary of these meetings was sent to the NCCCMA Executive Committee and to all participants and the PELA advisory committee.

A consistent message heard was the growing complexity of government and the need for managers to work with a wide range of stakeholders within their community and outside their jurisdiction. Public problems such as water and transportation no longer stop at county or municipal boundary lines, and managers find themselves working with other governments, nonprofit organizations, and businesses to craft a vision and plans for the future. This dimension of the manager's role is not new; in fact, during the 1960s an ICMA Future Horizons Committee "concluded that the manager was a community leader who deals with an array of conflicting community values, including issues of representation and equity, and who works in a facilitative style" (Nalbandian and Portillo 2006).

As we assessed this feedback, our challenge was to take an extensive "wish list" and design a curriculum with components that connected and built on each other within a reasonable instructional period. To help do so, we were advised to distinguish ourselves from SEI and other leadership development programs. We used the model of manager as a community leader and change agent as a guide and designed PELA to emphasize the significant *external* dimensions of the manager's job. The target audience was senior managers and those designated for leadership positions within their local government. We assumed managers would come to PELA with a basic understanding of their personal leadership style as well as significant experience managing an organization.

### Recruitment and Selection

We received thirty applications for twenty-five slots in the first year. The same number of applications was received for the 2006 session. Table 7.1 provides a breakdown of participants in 2005 and 2006. We anticipated a larger pool of applicants for the program based on the feedback on pent-up demand for leadership training we received during the needs assessment phase. North Carolina's public managers had expressed a strong interest in having a local government leadership program, but when the program was launched, only a fraction of those eligible actually applied. This was especially troublesome given the relatively sizable pool of managers in the state: 99 of the 100 counties have a county manager, and 206 of the 541 municipalities have a city or town manager.

After reviewing our approach to recruit, we wondered why senior managers —our target audience—were less inclined to apply than junior managers, assistant managers, and department heads. We are developing strategies for gaining feedback from this segment. One consequence of the light response from this audience has been the need to build more personal leadership and organizational leadership content into the program, which is important for participants to master before embarking on community leadership.

Another lesson we learned was that it takes time to get the message out—even when you think you have done a good job of communicating! Despite announcing the PELA rollout at multiple statewide meetings and in professional publications, the marketing materials were disseminated after the Thanksgiving holiday with a deadline for applications set for mid-January. We learned the importance of timing in disseminating promotional materials. Marketing materials mailed during the winter holiday season tended to be lost or overlooked, and with vacation schedules, many people had insufficient time to complete the application and get letters of recommendation (required for assistant managers and department heads).

We also learned the difference between advertising and recruitment. It is one thing to spread the word and quite another to generate participants. We

Table 7.1

**Demographics of PELA Participants in 2005 and 2006**

| Demographics | 2005 | 2006 |
|---|---|---|
| Number of Participants | 25 | 25 |
| Males | 20 | 19 |
| Females | 5 | 6 |
| African American | 3 | 5 |
| Caucasian | 22 | 20 |
| Managers | 13 | 11 |
| Assistant Managers | 6 | 10 |
| Department Heads | 6 | 4 |
| City | 18 | 18 |
| County | 7 | 7 |
| East | 4 | 6 |
| Central | 18 | 16 |
| West | 3 | 2 |
| Other | | 1* |

*One out-of-state participant from South Carolina

have come to better appreciate the importance of manager-to-manager marketing—at Association events and one-on-one communications between the faculty program director and managers—and plan to more fully utilize this strategy in promoting future programs.

The value of a "champion" in the manager community and among graduates cannot be overrstated. Having the program supported and encouraged by other managers and the Association's leadership is the best way we know to bolster participation. It is their endorsement and what they see as their results that encourage others to attend.

A recruitment strategy is also needed to ensure diversity. Diversity is an important factor in our selection process, and we were generally pleased with the class members' profiles (see Table 7.1). We sought to have a rich mix in terms of race, gender, municipal and county management, position (managers, assistant managers, and department heads), and representation from the various parts of the state (eastern coast, central piedmont, western mountain, urban, and rural). We learned the importance of using our networks of alumni and association members to help us gain representation from these sectors.

We understand that the face of our state will change dramatically in the next ten to fifteen years as the population grows and current managers retire. We want PELA to be a training ground and a resource for these new managers. Recruiting women and people of color was a particular challenge. Female participants in years one and two of PELA expressed feelings of being disconnected from their male counterparts, stating what they see as challenges of balancing their work and home given the stresses of a career in local government. An informal discussion and support group of female managers was formed in the second year. We hoped participation in PELA would be a first step to providing female managers and people of color with a cohort to help them to break into what some described as the "old boy" network of managers.

## Collaboration Considerations

During the pilot year, PELA was designed in collaboration with a wide range of people. Faculty and senior staff members from the School of Government's Public Leadership and Master of Public Administration (MPA) programs worked jointly to craft the curriculum. The 2005 planning committee also included faculty from the UNC Department of Women's Studies, a retired Raleigh assistant city manager who had assisted with the needs assessment, and the director of training from the North Carolina Administrative Office of the Courts. The committee structure changed in the second year because of the groundwork laid in year one. Collaboration was a central theme underlying PELA and as a faculty we committed to "walk the talk." In so doing, we learned that collaboration can be difficult and time-consuming.

One of the chief lessons we learned is the substantial time commitment it takes from faculty to both plan and deliver the program. The inaugural program included thirteen days of content over five sessions, and the second year involved fifteen days. The core faculty participated in planning the entire program. This model was a departure from the School of Government's traditional approach in which a single faculty director takes responsibility for a program's design, establishes learning objectives and outcomes, and invites faculty to teach specific topics.

The PELA faculty worked collaboratively to establish agendas, design each session, and decide how the program components should build on each other. Core faculty participated in all the PELA sessions too, even when they did not have teaching roles. The benefits realized from this participation were that the core faculty had intimate knowledge of the program, and were thus able to help tie elements together during the leadership dialogues, and in their teaching in subsequent segments of the program. As a result of the extensive groundwork, faculty were seen by participants as accessible and engaged in the total learning experience. The downside of this collaboration was that faculty had to balance their PELA commitment against their other responsibilities such as research, publishing, advising, and other course development and teaching for other clients.

In addition to the faculty time commitment, the collaborative approach required time to sort out roles and responsibilities and to determine how decisions were going to be made. As a result, creation of the design was slowed because many views had to be considered and schedules accommodated to ensure the segments of the curriculum built on each other and had a common thread to tie the pieces together. At times during the first year, it seemed like we were doing "just in time" content development.

In hindsight, we believe the program benefited from the richness of the knowledge and experience brought to the table, and the time commitment was worthwhile. It was especially important to have a representative from the NCCCMA and other non-SOG faculty to bring the "voice of reality" to the design meetings and to be sure the tie between theory and practice was strong.

A core value adopted by the group was that PELA's content and experience be fresh and focused on real world issues and problems and best practices from across the country. To achieve this objective, public administration leaders at the national and local levels have substantial teaching roles during the program. Participants also value the opportunity to listen and learn from others and to discover that others face similar challenges. Nationally recognized professionals enable participants to see examples of how leaders tackled problems similar to those they face, while academicians offer new tools and techniques to enhance their day-to-day practices.

Developing a new leadership program from the groundup allowed the faculty to experiment with a variety of different approaches to learning. We found adult learning techniques—including respect for participants' experiences, linking content to relevant work issues, and creating case-based experiential learning—were most effective with this audience. Participants were encouraged from the beginning to use their time in the program to take risks, explore, and experience new approaches and share the wealth of their knowledge and experience with their classmates and the instructors.

### Participants' Time Commitment

Like the program faculty, time was a key factor for PELA participants. An expectation of the program was that participants would attend every session. In addition to having classes during the day, two of each three-day block included evening sessions. Even though marketing materials listed two evening events on the schedule, some participants did not understand that the evening sessions were mandatory and felt the time demands were excessive.

When the participants were in class, the faculty and participants jointly established ground rules to help create a safe haven for learning. Among the agreements we made with each other were to turn off cell phones and leave behind Blackberries and other office distractions such as e-mail. Faculty understood that managers could not easily escape from the demands of the office, so thirty-minute breaks were scheduled in the mornings and afternoons to allow people to check in with the office, if necessary. However, a number of managers still left class sessions to take cell phone calls.

An important lesson during the first two years of PELA was finding out that we needed to give people more "down time." Participants felt they had little time to "hang out" with their fellow managers, build their networks, or talk about challenges facing them at home. Others said that they wanted more time to explore the Chapel Hill campus and surrounding area, but that this was impossible with such a tight and demanding program schedule.

## Curriculum Design

As noted earlier, the purpose of PELA is to help managers become change agents in their communities. The initial outline for the learning outcomes and curriculum evolved from the faculty and their understanding of leadership and community change as well as information gained from senior public managers in North Carolina and our organizational partners. We use the model shown in Figure 7.1 to guide our design.

The outcomes for the program are as follows:

- Understand participants' strengths and weaknesses as leaders and develop specific skills for personal learning and change.
- Diagnose problems and analyze situations within their organizations and communities.
- Engage elected officials and other leaders to develop a vision for their community.
- Encourage teamwork, community building, partnerships, and collaborative problem solving across jurisdictions and sectors.
- Develop and hone listening and communications skills in working with governing boards and professional staff.
- Assess risks and develop strategies to minimize negative consequences.
- Facilitate change to improve the quality of life in their community.
- Advocate the dignity and worth of public service.[1]

In the beginning, much time and attention was spent in determining the outcomes. We continue to refer to them as we design sessions and evaluate results. The time is well spent in being certain about what we want to deliver

Figure 7.1  **Community Leadership Model**

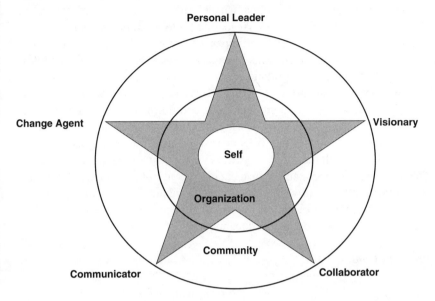

to our audience. We used the core learning outcomes to determine the specific topics covered in the program. The curriculum planning committee worked to ensure that each of these key outcomes was addressed in one or more sessions during the program. The outcomes also serve as the framework for the evaluation process.

We invested time not only in determining what the program should look like but also in how the program was to be delivered. For the planning committee, incorporating adult learning principles and practices into the PELA experience is a high priority. To address this goal, speakers are encouraged to include case studies or practical exercises in their presentations and to engage the participants by drawing out their personal experiences and leadership lessons. A significant amount of time was spent with each speaker sharing the outcomes of the program and the participant profile. We wanted customized programs that met the learning objectives. We worked with speakers to help them understand how their particular segment integrated with those before it or set the stage for subsequent sessions. As a result, the program sessions are highly interactive, giving participants an opportunity to apply theories to real-world situations and encouraging lively give-and-take among participants and instructors.

One of the initial goals expressed by senior managers was that PELA help build information technology skills among the participants. To address this interest, the pilot program was designed to include online learning tools. The University of North Carolina–Chapel Hill uses a password protected, electronic platform (Blackboard Academic Suite™) to deliver, support, and enhance course materials. All participants were given a password enabling them to access course documents (agendas, speaker biographies, schedules, reading materials, and presentations).

The experiment did not work well and was not carried forward to the next year. We learned there is a significant time commitment to be made in teaching participants and faculty how to efficiently use the technology. Some local governments did not have the software that would allow them to use it. Some faculty worked with their learning teams via the software and others did not. The information generated by the technology was not used in the classroom, so there was little incentive by students to participate. Participants asked us to go back to sending information via e-mail attachments and to use their time together in the classroom to build teams.

### Program Content

The 2005 and 2006 programs were designed as four three-day sessions, beginning on Tuesday and ending on Thursday. Based on our experience as a faculty and feedback from participants, a new residential program format was introduced in 2007. Table 7.2 shows the core components of the PELA curriculum in years one, two, and three.

Virtually all leadership programs face a common constraint—there is too much content to cover in too little time. In this, PELA was no exception. The program faculty used data from the needs assessment to craft a curriculum; but in addition, faculty had their own ideas about what was important to include in a leadership program. As a result, the curricula in the first two years were packed with good material but overly ambitious. Changes were made in years two and three to respond to both the faculty and the participants' suggestions for improvement and to give participants more "breathing room" and time to talk about and integrate the lessons learned from the previous program sessions. Our challenge remains how to maximize the time with participants and not exhaust them. The first year featured day and night programs, which exhausted some participants and presented logistical challenges to commuters. We reduced the number of evening programs to one per session in year two due to feedback.

The manager as community leader encompasses a myriad of skills and talents. Due to the strong response from mid-career and new managers, assistant managers, and department heads (as opposed to senior managers), the program was designed to work on multiple levels—helping managers understand their

Table 7.2

**Curricula for Years 1, 2, and 3 of PELA**

| Year 1 | Year 2 | Year 3 |
|---|---|---|
| **Session 1. Leadership Challenges and Styles** | **Session 1. Setting the Stage** | **Session 1. The Dynamics of Change and Implications for Leadership** |
| *Day 1*<br>Orientation to PELA<br>Leading in the Contemporary Governance Environment | *Day 1*<br>Orientation to PELA<br>21st-Century Manager<br>*World Café* | *Day 1*<br>21st-Century Manager<br>The Many Faces of Government<br>Economic and Demographic Forces at Work in the Region<br>Thinking Strategically and Systemically About Your Community<br>Exploring the Connections and Relationships |
| *Day 2*<br>Leadership Style and Behaviors<br>Dealing with Different Styles and Behaviors<br>Thinking Outside the Box | *Day 2*<br>The Many Faces of Government<br>*The Economic and Demographic Forces at Work in NC*<br>*Leadership Styles and Behaviors* | *Day 2*<br>Examining My Leadership Preferences and Styles<br>Leadership in the 21st Century<br>Stakeholder Analysis |
| *Day 3*<br>Systems Thinking<br>Social Systems and Trends<br>Stakeholder and Systems Analysis | *Day 3*<br>*Tragedy of the Commons Exercise*<br>Systems Thinking | *Day 3*<br>High-Performance Government: Governing Body and Staff Partnership<br>Manager's Competencies and Staff–Board Expectations<br>Strategies for Dealing with a Multigenerational Governing Body and Community |
| **Session 2. Building Relationships** | *Day 4*<br>Thinking Outside the Box<br>Introduction to Community Projects | |
| *Day 1*<br>Uses and Abuses of Power and Ethics<br>Communication and Persuasion Skills<br>Motivation and Team Building in Diverse Organizations<br>Managing Across Four Generations | **Session 2. Engaging Others in Change**<br><br>*Day 1*<br>*How Am I Doing? Importance of Feedback*<br>Stakeholders and Mapping | |

*(continued)*

Table 7.2 (continued)

| Year 1 | Year 2 | Year 3 |
|---|---|---|
| *Day 2* <br> Relationships between Managers and Elected Officials <br> Orienting and Coaching the Board <br> Strategic Thinking, Planning, and Implementation <br> Visioning and Long-Term Perspectives | *How Am I Doing? How to Get Feedback* <br> Risk Taking <br> Uses and Abuses of Power | *Day 4* <br> Leadership Styles and Trade-offs <br> Critical Competencies for Local Government Professionals <br> Consensus Building and Conflict Management Strategies <br> Cooking School |
| *Day 3* <br> Experiences in Citizen Participation <br> Diagnosing Power, Coalitions, and Relationship Structures <br> Communicating and Listening in the Community | *Day 2* <br> Managing and Motivating in Diverse Organizations <br> Cooking School | *Day 5* <br> Difficult Conversations: Building Trust with Your Board <br> Thinking Outside the Box <br> Taking Risks |
| **Session 3. Working with the Media** | *Day 3* <br> Leading and Managing Change <br> Project Groups: Mapping Change Exercise | **Session 2. Sustaining Your Leadership Through Collaboration** |
| *Day 1* <br> Framing and Communicating Your Message <br> Media Communication | **Session 3. Collaborating with Your Governing Board** | *Day 1* <br> Framing and Communicating Your Message <br> Media Communication |
| **Session 4. Leading Amidst Contradictions** | *Day 1* <br> Feedback from Your Board, Staff, and Community <br> Learning Team Meetings <br> Project Team Meetings | *Day 2* <br> Engaging and Empowering Citizens and Community Groups <br> *Local Management and Social Equity* <br> World Café |
| *Day 1* <br> Policy Negotiation and Dispute Resolution Techniques <br> Consensus Building | *Day 2* <br> Building a High-Performing Governing Body <br> Building a Sense of Community | |
| | *Day 3* <br> Developing Common Goals and Strategies | |

Developing Sustainable Decisions
Community Advocacy and Empowerment

*Day 2*
Organizational Systems
Balancing Policy and Administration
Facilitating and Formulating Policy
Cooking School

*Day 3*
Building Coalitions for Organizational Change
Taking Risks
Making Unpopular Decisions

**Session 5. Leading and Managing Change Inside and Out**

*Day 1*
Organized Living in a Disorganized World

Stress Management
Fitness and Nutrition

*Day 2*
Finding Time for Adaptive Leadership
Leading from the Heart: Living in Balance
Skits and Dinner

*Day 3*
Next Steps: Where Do We Go from Here?
Building a PELA Alumni Network
Graduation

**Session 4. Sustaining Leadership into the Future**

*Day 1*
Building a Community and Regional Vision
Engaging and Empowering Citizens
Manager's Role in Regional Visioning
Understanding Multiple Media Outlets

*Day 2*
Developing and Delivering Your Message
Project Time

*Day 3*
Conflict Management Strategies
Negotiation and Consensus Building
Project Time

**Session 5. Heart and Soul**

*Day 1*
Finding Time for Facilitative Leadership
Life, Work, and the Pursuit of Balance
Fitness and Nutrition

*Day 2*
Time Management and Organization
Skits and Dinner

*Day 3*
Leadership Dialogue
Graduation Lunch

*Day 3*
Strategies for Successful Collaborative Decision Making
Putting Collaborative Strategies into Action and Keeping Them Going

*Day 4*
Wellness for Life
Life, Work, and the Pursuit of Balance
Skits and Dinner

*Day 5*
Learning Teams: Leadership Project Debriefings
Graduation

*Note:* Items shown in *italics* reflect content changes from the previous year.

personal leadership, how they manage within their organization and work with their governing boards, and especially how to build relationships and communicate with external partners in their community and region. There was a constant tension in the program to ensure we were giving each dimension the attention and level of skill needed.

On a related note, we learned there is a continuing challenge to "meet people where they are." PELA's emphasis on facilitative leadership, adaptive change, and working as a community leader was difficult for participants—especially department heads and newer managers and assistants—who were concerned about internal organizational or personal management challenges such as time and stress management, delegation skills, and effective work team development. The first two PELA classes included a mixture of managers with a range of skill levels, years of experience, and educational and professional training, and the design was intended to encourage participants to learn from one another. For example, veteran managers shared insights about governing board relationships while younger managers talked about managing different generations in the workplace. The faculty had to remain flexible session-to-session to ensure we were adjusting the curriculum to meet the participants' needs.

In 2005, we used two leadership assessment tools to help connect individual behaviors with relevant course content. The Fundamental Interpersonal Relations Orientation-Behavior (FIRO-B; Consulting Psychologists Press 1996) was used as a way to help participants learn how they interact with others, and this provided a runway for talking about how to work more effectively with senior staff members and governing boards. The Thomas Kilmann Instrument (Consulting Psychologists Press 2001) was used to help people look at their behaviors when faced with a conflict situation. It served as a springboard to talking about how managers engage or avoid conflict in their communities. Participants valued having the opportunity to get feedback on their behavioral styles, but often wanted more time to explore how their behaviors helped or hindered their ability to lead in their organizations and communities. We also learned that, while informative, FIRO-B was not the best instrument for helping managers understand how they relate to change in their communities.

Based on faculty observations and participant feedback, we elected to use the Change Style Indicator (CSI) in PELA 2006 (Musslewhite and Ingram 2000). The CSI better reflected the content of the program and gave participants insights into their own preferences in making change and helped them recognize the value of alternate approaches. We kept the CSI for year three.

Another content change from 2005 to 2006 was the addition of an activity focused on identifying critical competencies for community leadership. Using behavioral competencies from the Career Architect Tool (Lombardo and

Eichinger 2003) and the ICMA's "Practices for Effective Local Government Management" (www.icma.org), participants ranked individually, in small groups and as a large group, the knowledge, skills, and abilities they thought were critical for effective community leadership. This exercise enabled the participants to compare their own perspectives on effective community leadership with those of their teams and with the class.[2] Further developing and refining competencies for effective community leadership is included in year three.

We begin the program by providing participants with information about the demographic, social, and economic changes occurring in our region as a way to provide context to think about changes affecting their communities and their role as a leader in the twenty-first century. As stated earlier, managers are living and managing in a time of significant change. It is helpful for them to have a sense of the various forces affecting their communities.

The content designed to help participants establish productive relationships for leading their local government organizations, governing boards, and communities has remained constant. These sessions look at the manager's relationship to his or her staff by exploring uses and abuses of power, building team leadership, and changing organizational culture to overcome obstacles to change. Professor John Nalbandian from the University of Kansas has led day-long sessions on building stronger board–manager relationships, and helping participants understand and learn how to address the growing knowledge gaps between public managers and local elected officials. We have retained and strengthened the presentations and exercises focused on helping managers build stronger relationships in their communities, conduct effective public meetings and community forums, work with the media, and engage citizens through community advocacy and empowerment activities.

Although the sequence of content differed in years one and two, by the fourth session, the goal was to begin integrating tools and strategies for working internally (with organizations and boards) and externally (with community partners and citizens) to effect community change. A second conceptual model (Figure 7.2) was developed that visually conveys the interdependence of these various components in community leadership as well as the concepts covered in the PELA curriculum supporting these dimensions. The model was designed to help participants better understand the relationships between their community context, their own leadership knowledge, skills and abilities, their organizations and governing boards, and their communities

In each of the first two years, the final PELA session emphasized, "Heart & Soul," drawing on the core text, Heifetz and Linsky's *Leadership on the Line* (2002). Because local government leaders often work long hours in full view of the public's eye, many managers indicated they neglected to take

Figure 7.2   **Community Context Model**

care of their personal needs. To address this problem, the conclusion of the PELA experience emphasized personal management skills, such as time and stress management as well as techniques for improving nutrition and exercise and work life balance. In addition, the final session provided participants feedback on their individual projects and time to reflect on their experience in the PELA program.

Participants evaluated the 2005 and 2006 programs at the end of each day as well as several weeks after graduation. The next sections describe the processes that were used and the feedback received. More lessons from participants about projects and case study assignments appear in the evaluation discussion below.

**Team-Building Approaches**

All the PELA sessions included team-building opportunities (including nonclass leadership experiences, the use of learning teams, and faculty as coaches). Evening sessions were an important component of the PELA learning experience and served to both accomplish and reinforce the PELA learning objectives to encourage teamwork, community building, partnerships, and collaborative problem solving across jurisdictions and sectors. Faculty designed the programs with the goal of providing a fun and creative way to integrate, enhance, and supplement concepts introduced in classroom-based sessions. A second goal was to provide participants with a customized learning experience, which demonstrated particular attention to their unique needs.

Given the stress of public service, the program aimed to create environments and events that built trust among participants and establish a network, which in turn enhanced sharing and learning in the classroom environment and acknowledged and reinforced their commitment to serving others. The evening programs were among the most highly rated by participants for the balance of learning and networking opportunities.

A sample of the activities from the first two iterations of PELA included:

1. A welcome dinner and reception on the evening before the program began provided participants and faculty with an informal chance to get to know each other and establish the network and learning environment that would prove crucial over the course of PELA.

2. A discussion of Machiavelli's *The Prince* using the Socratic method challenged many participants to reflect and think about power in ways that they never had before, leading to insights on how they use power to exert control on their boards and staffs.

3. The public nature of managers' work is like "life in the fishbowl." The program devoted an evening in a relaxed environment, giving participants a safe forum to discuss the fact they have little or no private space. Session evaluations revealed that participants greatly valued the chance to talk about the challenges they and their families face living in the public eye.

4. An evening session was held at a cooking school to provide a tangible illustration and application of how they work in a team, make decisions, delegate, and collaborate (or not). Insightful observations included "I undertook activities I never had before," "I realized how many hidden talents people have if you give them the chance to lead," and "I realized I did not want to share and I tried to hoard resources—well, at least the mushrooms—and I see that I may also do that with my staff."

5. PELA ended with an exercise incorporating risk taking, trust, reflection, and creativity. Teams were provided a box full of costumes and instructed to prepare a five-minute skit on what they learned from PELA. This chance to reflect in a lighthearted way provided a chance for participants to share important messages, learning, and laughter. This final session demonstrated the strength of the trust in the network they had created.

6. "Leadership Dialogues" that were conducted each morning provided a helpful technique to begin each session and to discuss and integrate the evening events. During these "dialogues," participants debriefed the previous night's experiences, asked questions, shared their "ah-has," and connected with or challenged the concepts introduced the day before.

7. In 2006, we held a half-day alumni reunion during the final session. The program featured John Nalbandian and Bob O'Neill speaking on the topic of "Professionalism in Local Government Management." While the program was well received, participants did not want to share class time with graduates, so future reunions will be free-standing events at the summer conference of the managers association.

### *Learning Teams and Faculty Coaches*

An essential part of the PELA learning experience was participating in learning teams. All of the PELA participants were assigned to learning teams of five members as a way to help foster networks across the group. Each team had a mix of gender, municipal, and county officials, and geographic base. One of the first assignments was for each team to name itself. These five-member learning teams served as a mechanism for networking, building trust, providing each other feedback, and offering advice and support for individual and community leadership challenges. In 2005, each learning team had a faculty advisor, someone who worked with the group consistently over the course of the program and who was a coach or resource, as needed. In 2006, faculty played a supportive role, encouraging more student leadership initiative within the learning teams. On reflection, the 2005 model provided more substantive focus and facilitated interaction, and we decided to return to using faculty advisors in 2007.

### Program Evaluation

The evaluation design for PELA's first two years was created to provide feedback on both formative and process measures. We plan to follow PELA participants over time to gain more information about the outcomes of their participation on their work as local government managers and the impact of their leadership in their communities. The evaluation design for the first and second years included the following components:

- pre- and a retrospective post-evaluation on PELA learning objectives;
- standard evaluation instruments distributed at the end of each day to

Table 7.3

**Pre-evaluation Data from PELA 2005 and PELA 2006**

| | Rate Your Knowledge, Skill, and Abilities Level | |
| --- | --- | --- |
| | At Start of PELA 2005 | At Start of PELA 2006 |
| PELA Learning Objectives | (n = 25) | (n = 25) |
| 1.  I know myself as a leader | 5.4 | 4.7 |
| 2.  I take a broad, systemic view of issues affecting my community | 5.4 | 5.4 |
| 3.  I engage key stakeholders in creating a vision for my community. | 4.6 | 4.7 |
| 4.  I encourage teamwork, community building, partnerships, and collaborative problem solving across jurisdictions and sectors | 5.8 | 5.2 |
| 5.  I develop and hone listening and communications skills in working with governing boards and professional staff | 5.1 | 4.8 |
| 6.  I assess risks and develop strategies to minimize negative consequences | 5.4 | 5.0 |
| 7.  I facilitate change to improve the quality of life in their community | 5.3 | 5.0 |
| 8.  I celebrate the dignity and worth of public service | 5.6 | 5.2 |

Rating for each item was on a Likert Scale from 1 (low) to 7 (high).

capture key learnings and identify the content most applicable to participants' practice and areas for improvement;
- specific evaluation questions for each program topic asking participants to rate how well the presenter addressed stated objectives for the topic and to rate the quality of the instruction;
- focus groups with participants in the final session (year one only); and
- follow-up, individual interviews with PELA participants.

*Pre-Evaluation and Retrospective Post-Evaluation*

At the first PELA session, all participants were asked to rate their knowledge, skill, and ability for each of the major program objectives. Table 7.3 summarizes pre-evaluation data from the first two years of PELA. Participants in the first cohort (PELA 2005) rated their knowledge, skills, and abilities at the start of the program higher than participants in the 2006 cohort on all but one item—engaging key stakeholders in creating a vision for the community.

After the program, participants rated themselves on these same measures and reflected back on their knowledge skill and abilities at the outset of the program using a retrospective post-evaluation or a "post-then-pre-evaluation" design. Asking participants to retrospectively rate their knowledge, skills, and abilities provides a better yardstick for interpreting the differences between perceived skills before and after the program because it minimizes the "response-shift bias" typically associated with self-reported pre–post test designs (Rockwell and Kohn 1989). The results of the retrospective post-evaluation appear in Table 7.4. At the end of the program, 2005 and 2006 PELA participants rated their initial knowledge, skills, and abilities lower than they had at the outset of the program. Similarly, 2005 and 2006 PELA participants reported that they had increased their knowledge, skills, and abilities on every measure. The differences between their perceived knowledge, skills, and abilities at the beginning and at the end of the program were statistically significant at the $p > .001$ level or higher. These results illustrate that participants thought they knew a lot about themselves and how to be strategic community leaders prior to attending the program. After attending the program, these participants realized they did not know as much coming in as they thought they did, and improved their community leadership as a result of participating in PELA.

## *Daily Evaluations*

Daily evaluation results were used by the program faculty to debrief each day's program and to identify areas to be addressed in the following day or session. Summaries of the feedback on specific presentations were provided to the individual faculty members following their participation. We found this rapid feedback particularly helpful in guiding adjustments making just-in-time changes to the program. For example, daily feedback let us know if there were particular concerns within the group or points needing additional clarification, or if things were going especially well. We also used their feedback to talk with presenters after the program, letting the presenters know what they did well and what needed improvement. Those who did not meet our learning objectives, or missed the mark with the participants, learned of this and in some cases were not invited back the following year.

## *Focus Groups*

External evaluators were engaged to assist with focus groups the first year and call participants after the program for in-depth follow-up interviews in both the first and second years. The focus groups were integrated into the final session of PELA in year one to ensure that all participants had a chance to provide feedback on their experience. Since marketing for the 2006 program

Table 7.4

**Comparison of PELA 2005 and PELA 2006 Retrospective Post-evaluation**

| | Rate Your Knowledge, Skill, and Ability Level[a] | | | | | |
| | 2005 PELA[b] | | | 2006 PELA[c] | | |
| PELA Learning Objectives: | Retrospective to Start of PELA 2005 (n = 15) | At the End of PELA 2005 (n = 15) | Difference | Retrospective to Start of PELA 2006 (n = 15) | At the End of PELA 2006 (n = 15) | Difference |
|---|---|---|---|---|---|---|
| 1. I know myself as a leader | 4.53 | 6.13 | 1.60* | 4.33 | 5.67 | 1.34* |
| 2. I take a broad, systemic view of issues affecting my community | 4.53 | 5.93 | 1.40* | 4.73 | 5.80 | 1.07* |
| 3. I engage key stakeholders in creating a vision for my community. | 4.33 | 5.93 | 1.60* | 4.40 | 5.53 | 1.13* |
| 4. I encourage teamwork, community-building, partnerships, and collaborative problem-solving across jurisdictions and sectors | 5.07 | 6.33 | 1.26* | 4.60 | 5.80 | 1.20* |
| 5. I develop and hone listening and communications skills in working with governing boards and professional staff | 4.33 | 5.93 | 1.60* | 4.53 | 5.93 | 1.40* |
| 6. I assess risks and develop strategies to minimize negative consequences | 4.93 | 6.00 | 1.07* | 4.87 | 5.73 | 0.86* |
| 7. I facilitate change to improve the quality of life in the community | 4.60 | 6.00 | 1.40* | 4.73 | 5.87 | 1.14* |
| 8. I celebrate the dignity and worth of public service | 4.93 | 6.60 | 1.67* | 4.93 | 5.87 | 0.94* |

*Significant at the .001 level or higher using a t-test paired for two sample means.

[a]Rating for each item was on a Likert Scale from 1 (low) to 7 (high).

[b]2005 PELA participants completed the retrospective post-evaluation on the last day of the program.

[c]2006 PELA participants completed the retrospective post-evaluation six months after the program.

was scheduled to commence two months following the end of year one, the planning committee wanted timely feedback and information from first-year participants to incorporate into the following year's program marketing, design, and schedule.

Focus group questions also invited feedback on the program structure. Generally, participants were happy with the schedule and Institute of Government location, and did not support moving to a week-long or two-week–long schedule. Participants said they liked the Tuesday to Thursday format and appreciated being able to return to work in their home offices on Mondays and Fridays.

Focus groups were also asked about the quality of administrative and faculty support during the program. Without exception, participants reacted positively to the level and quality of administrative and faculty support. They also said the opportunity to network with other managers was a significant benefit of participating in PELA.

In general, participants felt the value of PELA came in two distinct areas. One was in personal development, which they considered to be a part of leadership training. Several participants gave examples of how they used concrete skills learned in PELA in their day-to-day work. Being separated from their work environment made PELA a "safe" place for managers to consider their life-work-leadership issues. Second, participants enjoyed the opportunity to meet with peers and develop personal and work networks. Coming away from the program, most hoped they would be able to continue their relationships in some way in the future, and recommended annual get-togethers as a part of a PELA alumni program.

We also wanted participants' input on logistical issues such as the application process, meeting space, overnight accommodations, food, and transportation issues. Overall, the participants were comfortable with the application process, although many wanted more detail on the content and structure of the program. They liked having a variety of foods, both familiar and new, and enjoyed the hotel and meeting facilities at the School of Government on the UNC campus. The only drawback to the meeting location was that there was not enough free time to enjoy being in Chapel Hill or on campus. Our location is a wonderful asset, but the program did not take full advantage of it due to the demanding instructional schedule.

### Follow-Up Interviews

In the months following the final sessions, year one and two of PELA, an external evaluator conducted follow-up telephone interviews. Participants were specifically asked what they found most useful as a result of attending PELA, how their participation in PELA influenced their leadership practices, and how PELA affected their ability to bring about change in their own communities.

When participants in the first and second years were asked, "What did you gain from your PELA experience or find most useful?" the most common response was they benefited from the networking with other senior public managers and the faculty. In addition, they said being able to hear from opinion leaders in the profession helped them gain perspective on how to work differently with their communities, governing boards, and other organizations. First-year participants spoke about the benefit of learning to "step back and look at the big picture," while second-year participants commented on the value of taking "cultural differences into consideration."

Participants were asked what they wanted more of or less of in the program. Responses from both the first and second year reflected a desire for more "real world applications" and more opportunities to hear from "outside speakers" and "experts." The things people wanted "less of" included mandatory evening sessions, formal lectures, and theoretical sessions.

One of the unique aspects of the PELA curriculum is the inclusion of sessions to help people access their creativity. Several participants in the first and second years wanted more time to explore this topic and said it should definitely remain a part of the PELA program, while others reported the creativity sessions were too "touchy-feely" and poorly integrated into the rest of the program. A session focused on systems thinking also yielded mixed reactions with participants from both years, reporting that the sessions were either too complex or too simplistic and they would have liked to have spent less time on this topic.

Participants from years one and two were asked: "Has your leadership changed as a result of PELA, and if so, how?" The overwhelming majority of participants reported that their leadership had changed. In terms of *how* PELA had changed their leadership experience, participants most often indicated they were:

- more reflective on their own personal strengths and weaknesses as a leader;
- better able to understand others (employees, board, citizens, community partners); and
- better able to step back and take a broader perspective on issues facing their organizations and communities.

Following PELA, first- and second-year participants were asked: "How has PELA affected your daily work, your interactions with your board, your staff and your ability to bring about change in your community?" Participants said that following PELA they were more likely to:

- Communicate with staff more effectively;
- Engage staff more often in decision making;
- Better understand board members' expectations and perspectives;
- Be more confident working with members of the board;
- Build consensus with key stakeholders about community issues;
- Use media and communication tools with the public more effectively;
- Be able to see the big picture; and
- Take a more collaborative approach to complex issues.

Participants in the first year were equivocal about the benefits of the PELA community-application project, with many stating they got less out of the experience than they hoped. Some suggested the following improvements be made: making sure the project is completed during the course of the program, issuing clearer project guidelines in advance, and providing more faculty involvement in project selection. Because the project was focused on community, rather than organizational change, some participants felt that pursuing their project would put their personal or professional reputations at risk and that such projects were more appropriate as a learning exercise for PELA than as something to be implemented in the real world.

Based on feedback from the first year, the second-year participants were not required to do a community-application project. Instead, second-year participants were asked to write a series of reflective case studies on how the concepts and strategies that were taught in PELA applied to their work. In response to questions about the value of the case studies, half of second-year participants reported they benefited from applying PELA principles to their real work and reflecting on how they might use the concepts in their actual work. The other half suggested the case studies be (1) reduced in number or dropped altogether, (2) standardized so everyone uses the same situation rather than their own experiences, or (3) better integrated into the class and small group discussions. As a result of these reactions, a modified community-application project was reintroduced in the 2007 program.

Because the focus groups were dropped in the second year due to scheduling pressure, a few questions about reading assignments were added to the post-program interviews. Overall, the second-year participants agreed there was "too much reading" but thought the readings were relevant. Some participants suggested making some readings "mandatory" and others were "recommended" to help people better focus their attention on critical information. Eighteen of twenty second-year participants agreed that the primary text,

*Leadership on the Line* (Heifetz and Linsky 2002), should remain a part of the core curriculum because it was helpful and relevant to their work as public managers.

At the close of the interviews, the external evaluator asked if participants had other comments for the PELA faculty. Most often, first- and second-year respondents indicated that the program and the faculty were "great" or "wonderful." Some of the feedback from first-year participants focused on technical aspects of the program, such as start times and availability of program materials. But the predominant theme emerging from the first year's group was that the PELA experience was worthwhile and would pay dividends for many years, and they wanted to be involved with the program in the future. They suggested holding a half-day annual reunion, with a substantive program and speaker, as the preferred way to reinforce their network. They did not favor a newsletter or list-serve.

Similarly, second-year participants enjoyed having a chance to network with managers from a variety of jurisdictions and thought the informal activities, such as the cooking school, dinner events, and open dialogue sessions, contributed to improved interactions during the class itself. Both first- and second-year cohorts complimented the commitment and energy of the staff and faculty involved with the program. A number of people said the program faculty were "enthusiastic," "personable," and "invested in the students."

**Year Three: A New Format**

For the 2007 program, we will continue to integrate the sessions and give participants time to absorb and reflect on the content. We plan to strengthen the leadership-style-assessment components of PELA, using a variety of leadership-assessment instruments. We will deepen the focus on the manager as community change agent by expanding on the skills required to create a community vision and models and lessons learned from those in the field who are working across jurisdictions and collaborating on regional projects. We have added a session on social equity to raise awareness of the manager's role in ensuring fairness in service delivery and program responsiveness.

We have substituted Jeffrey Luke's book *Catalytic Leadership* (1998) as the core reading to help operationalize the three-part community context framework in the PELA curriculum—building leadership skills, fostering strong organizations and boards, and creating positive community relations (see Figure 7.2). *Leadership on the Line* will also continue to be used, and selected chapters from it are included among the readings.

Sustainability is a key issue facing leadership development programs. At the outset, ICMA staff and other advisors cautioned that single state-based programs usually exhaust their market within a few years. In the second year, we accepted an application from a manager outside of North Carolina as a way to "test the water." The ICMA staff also encouraged us to maintain our emphasis on managers, assistants, and key department heads, and not to open the program to middle managers to fill the available seats. In 2007, information about PELA and application materials were sent to the presidents of managers associations in the southeastern region as well as to selected SEI graduates. For 2008, a national recruiting strategy will be developed, including sponsoring a booth at the ICMA annual meeting.

The 2007 program was designed as a residential experience with two one-week sessions in August, and a two-week break in between. The curriculum was not significantly altered, but it was planned for delivery in a more condensed and integrated manner. This new format was adopted for the following reasons. First, one of the problems with spreading the program over seven months was the need for faculty and participants to devote time to reconnecting with material covered in previous sessions, which made threading and integration of content challenging. Second, with a program spread over seven months, the bonding and networking that are important benefits of leadership experiences were slow to develop. Third, the participants were often distracted by cell phone and Blackberry messages from the office, especially during the first two of the 2005 and 2006 sessions held in March and April, which competed with budget season in terms of a participant's time and priorities. We hope moving the program to the summer, when the pace of office business is relatively slower, will likely increase attention span and reduce distractions. Fourth, housing the program and the participants in the UNC School of Business's executive education facility will promote the retreat atmosphere critical for reflective practitioners' learning and will provide an environment more conducive to leaving the office behind. Fifth, a condensed format allows for more efficient use of faculty time. PELA faculty have several other responsibilities, including teaching in the MPA program and leadership training for elected officials and local government managers. Finally, a compressed summer format should make the program more appealing to out-of-state managers, who will be needed to sustain PELA.

The new format required raising the tuition to $4,000, which includes all instructional, housing, and meal costs. However, a financial analysis by PELA faculty revealed this amount to be comparable with total participant expenses for each of the two previous years, since participants paid separately for accommodations and several meals. The North Carolina City and County Management Association continued its financial support for the program, enabling us to discount the tuition by $500 for members and to offer scholarships. It will be interesting to gauge the response since some of the steps to sustain the program conflict with feedback we received during the needs-assessment phase.

In conclusion, the first two years of PELA offered a rich variety of learning opportunities for the program faculty and course development team. These ranged from the simplistic "No more hummus for breaks!" to the complexities of integrating and threading session content and working together as a team. We gained a deep appreciation for the sacrifice and commitment the local government managers make on the behalf of the citizens of our state.

There are two significant general lessons from the early PELA experience. The first lesson has to do with realizing the benefits of using a distinctive conceptual model to anchor and guide how the curriculum relates the complex community leadership roles with their managers personal and organizational leadership styles and strategies. This effort was also important in distinguishing PELA from other public leadership programs. The other lesson is the need to keep the program fresh and relevant by remaining in close contact with partners in the field, getting regular feedback from participants and graduates, and experimenting with new substantive topics and formats. With its unique approach to community leadership, PELA promises to be an essential component of the continuing education series for public managers in North Carolina and other states for years to come.

## Notes

1. Recent research has demonstrated the organizational value added of an enhanced level of public service motivation (Moynihan and Pandey 2005). The program overall helped reinforce the value of public service and develop commitment.

2. In 2006, PELA participants received a descriptive list of seventy-nine behavioral competencies. Each participant was asked to rate each competency as "high," "medium," or "low" for community leadership. Individuals then worked with their learning teams to reach a group consensus on critical competencies for community leadership. For the whole group, the competencies with the highest rankings in 2006 were dealing with ambiguity, approachability, political savvy, command skills, priority setting, composure, conflict management, decision quality, delegation, building effective teams, ethics and values, understanding others, hiring and staffing, managing vision and purpose, governance and political leadership, integrity and trust, citizen participation, facilitative leadership, listening, engaging people [creating public forums and arenas], building commitment and political support, and negotiating.

## References

Consulting Psychologists Press. 1996. *FIRO-B*. Palo Alto, CA: Author.
————. 2001. *Thomas-Kilmann Conflict Mode Instrument*. Palo Alto, CA: Author.
Heifetz, Ronald A., and Marty Linsky. 2002. *Leadership on the Line: Staying Alive Through the Dangers of Leading*. Boston: Harvard Business School Press.

Lombardo, Michael M., and Robert W. Eichinger. 2003. *The Career Architect.* Lominger Limited. Available at: www.lominger.com (accessed May 10, 2007).

Luke, Jeffrey S. 1998. *Catalytic Leadership: Strategies for an Interconnected World.* San Francisco: Jossey-Bass.

Moynihan, Daniel P., and Sanjay K. Pandey. 2005. "The Role of Organizations in Fostering Public Service Motivation." *Public Administration Review* 67(1): 40–53.

Musslewhite, W. Christopher, and Robyn P. Ingram. 2000. *Change Style Indicator.* Greensboro, NC: Discovery Learning.

Nalbandian, John, and Shannon Portillo. 2006. "Council-Manager Relations through the Years." *Public Management,* (July): p. 6.

Rockwell, S. Kay, and Harriet Kohn. 2007. "Post-Then-Pre Evaluation." *Journal of Extension,* 27(2). Available at: http://www.joe.org/joe/1989summer/a5.html (accessed April 30, 2007).

# 8

## Preparing MPA Graduates to Serve as Intermediaries in Community Building and Public Engagement

Ruth Ann Bramson

In 2004, the faculty of the public management department at Suffolk University in Boston made several curricular changes in the Master's in Public Administration (MPA) program to assist our graduates in grappling with a confluence of trends that impact community problem solving—governmental downsizing and decentralization, demands for greater stakeholder participation in decision making, increasing reliance on partnerships to address public problems, and, at the same time, a decline in many traditional forms of civic engagement. The department added a new course in collaborative leadership to the required core curriculum for all students receiving the MPA degree, we increased our course offerings in civic engagement, and we introduced an MPA specialization in Community Leadership and Public Engagement.[1] This chapter has three primary aims. The first is to present the rationale behind the curricular changes in the Suffolk MPA program. Second, the chapter describes the approach that the Suffolk University public management department is currently taking to prepare graduates in community leadership and public engagement. Third, the chapter discusses some of the questions, opportunities, and challenges our department has encountered in the process of making these program changes.

There is a young but crucial movement within public administration to reexamine the role of the public and public managers in policy making and implementation by looking at legitimate ways of engaging citizens more actively in deliberating about and solving community problems (Reich 1988; Thomas 1995; Behn 1998; Frederickson and Chandler 1984; Cooper 1991; Fox and Miller 1995; Wamsley and Wolf 1996; Nalbandian 1999; King and Stivers 1998; Denhardt and Denhardt 2003; Box 1998). This seems to be happening for a number of reasons. First, many scholars, officials, and thoughtful citizens have expressed concern about the health of American democracy and civic life (Buss and Redburn 2006; Barber 1984, 1998; Mansbridge 1990; Pateman 1970; Sandel 1996; O'Connell 1999; Mathews 1994; McSwite 1997). The need to strengthen community has become a persistent theme, with commentators from various disciplines and political perspectives focusing on different aspects of community in America (Bellah et al. 1985, 1991; Etzioni 1988, 1995; Wolfe 1989; Putnam 2000; Buss and Redburn 2006).

Second, there is increasing recognition that traditional hierarchical and bureaucratic approaches to public problem solving are no longer working. Today's public leaders are learning they must reach beyond their organizational boundaries and engage a much broader group of stakeholders to create sustainable strategies to address complex interconnected problems (Stone 1989; Frederickson and Smith 2003; Luke 1998; Linden 2002; Bryson 1992; Denhardt and Denhardt 2003).

And third, discourse theorists have sought to reconceptualize public administration through changes in how people talk and relate to one another in the policy-making process. This has bolstered interest in the underutilized approach to policy making known as public deliberation (Farmer 1995; Fox and Miller 1995; Reich 1988; McSwite 1997; Yankelovich 1999; Mathews 1994; Forester 1999).

## Civic Engagement Needed

Many social observers have expressed alarm as fewer Americans vote, participate in civic life, or involve themselves in voluntary organizations that meet regularly. Voting rates have dropped about 25 percent since the 1960s, and the proportion of people who tell pollsters that they "trust the federal government to do what is right" has fallen from three-quarters in the early 1960s to less than a third at the turn of the twenty-first century (Skocpol and Fiorina 1999). In *Bowling Alone*, Robert Putnam (2000) points to a decline in institutions such as clubs, professional groups, and other forms of communal and associational life. Recently, there have been numerous calls for reinvigorating the role of citizens in governance and in community problem solving, including from those within the profession of public administration (Frederickson and Chandler 1984; King and Stivers 1998; Box 1998; Buss and Redburn 2006). King and Stivers (1998) assert that public administrators should use their discretionary authority to foster collaborative work with citizens in deliberating, making decisions, and implementing public policy. Some even argue that the key role for public administrators today is to build community and encourage citizen involvement in public decision making (Nalbandian 1999).

## Public Managers are Key to Community Leadership and Public Engagement

If citizens are to be engaged in tackling public problems, public managers must help to make it so. By virtue of their positions, public managers have significant resources for playing an intermediary role in community problem solving.[2] Intermediaries may assume roles as facilitators, mediators, public process designers, organizers, coalition builders, capacity builders, public educators, as well as others, especially at the local community level.

Whether community involvement is procedurally required or generative, it is typically public managers who do the work of designing and implementing public involvement processes. Elected public officials, as well as other community leaders, have a crucial role as advocates for community engagement. Elected officials may request that a process be initiated, but it is generally public managers who make it happen. They can either use their authority to limit the role of the public to appearances in pro forma public meetings, which happens far too often, or they can design and implement processes crossing organizational and sector boundaries and engage diverse community members in the hard, noisy, and messy work of collective problem solving. Public managers also have staying power. Unlike elected officials who come and go with the election cycle, public managers typically stay in their positions for many years. Many public managers also share a common knowledge base and expertise gained in public administration programs and have opportunities for ongoing professional training to keep their skills current (Frederickson 1997a).

Christopher Gates (1996) of the National Civic League observed that, "the local city official or manager of the future is increasingly seen as a catalyst and facilitator of broad efforts by many different groups or individuals not as a stand alone problem solver" (p. 4).[3] William Ruckelshaus described this catalytic approach well in his 1996 Webb Lecture at the National Academy of Public Administration when he presented four or five instances in which public administrators stepped back from their accustomed roles and served as facilitators and supports, while citizens directly affected by a complex environmental problem hammered out solutions, that all, or most, could accept. He then went on to observe: "Historically, public administration has prided itself on its ability to apply the tools of rationality to complex problems. . . . I think that in the future many decisions will, rather, emerge from the sort of group processes I have been talking about. . . . The role of the public administrator will be largely to foster the process and make sure that it has technical support" (Ruckelshaus 1996, p. x).

## The Will/Skill Dilemma

To engage the public in community problem solving, public managers must believe it is important to do so and have the knowledge and skills to become effective intermediaries. The failure of public managers to engage community members in deliberation regarding public problems falls into the category of intractable problems that Daniel Yankelovich (1999) has called "will/skill dilemmas." Yankelovich writes, "Some problems resist solution because the will to solve them is lacking. Others resist solution because the knowledge to solve them is lacking. The worse kinds of problems are those cursed with a lack of will and a lack of skill, creating a vicious cycle. The skills remain undeveloped because of low motivation and motivation doesn't kick in because of lack of skills" (1999, p. 158).

Public managers face a will/skill dilemma in regard to public engagement. Many public managers are skeptical about whether the public has the knowledge, interest, and civic commitment to contribute anything of value to the public problem-solving process. From the apolitical rationalist point of view, the public's inferior level of information, relative to that of experts and professionals and the public's tendency to judge issues based on moral values, introduces random levels of subjectivity and misinformation into what they believe should be an objective and fact-based process. Engaging community members in public problem solving also requires knowledge and skills that have not traditionally been part of the preparation for careers in public administration, such as change management, systems thinking, community organizing, group process and facilitation, leadership, conflict resolution, and interpersonal skills (Luke 1998; Bryson 1992; Mathews 1994; Frederickson 1997b). This double bind leads to inaction and blocks the effort to engage community stakeholders in public problem solving.

This will/skill dilemma presents big challenges for public administration as it is currently constituted. Despite the need for public administrators to be more than technical experts, the curricula of many graduate programs in public administration, including Suffolk University, have centered on technical preparation in such areas as personnel management, administrative law, finance, budgeting, and program evaluation. These knowledge and skill areas are necessary but not sufficient for today's public managers.

## Early in the Learning Process

Unfortunately, while many academics and other opinion leaders have made a compelling case for civic engagement and for public managers as key agents in community problem solving, the effort to develop, document, and test new structures, processes, and norms is still in its infancy. We are at a very early stage of our process of learning what it means to prepare public managers for an intermediary role. We do not even have consistent language yet for this new way of doing business. Research on the goals, structure, and outcomes of collaborative public problem solving is limited, but we do have stories.

There are hundreds of case studies from communities all across the country, as well as internationally, where public professionals, primarily at the local level, are providing stakeholders with the opportunity to learn about the technical and political facets of policy options and creating opportunities for them to discuss and evaluate these options and their likely consequences, according to their own values and preferences. Through communal deliberation, decision making, and action, they are working with community members to address crime problems, school problems, environmental problems, and problems of ethnic and racial conflict, as well as many others. Can we share these case studies and engage our students in learning from them? Can we create learning experiences for our students that will help them to build both the will and skill to be intermediaries, facilitators, and community capacity builders? Can we develop an educational framing to assist public managers in thinking about when and how to involve community members in public deliberation and multistakeholder decision making? Can we help our graduates negotiate the complexities of community partnerships and alliances? Can we accelerate the emergence of this new model of public administrator?

These are some of the questions that faculty members in the public management department at Suffolk University asked themselves while conducting a yearlong curriculum review in 2002–2003. That discussion, along with a literature review, interviews with scholars and practitioners, a study of other MPA programs and a review of syllabi from other institutions, focus groups with current and former students, and a dialogue with colleagues in other departments of the university, led us to the decision to add a required course in collaborative leadership to our core curriculum for all MPA and Master of Health Administration (MHA) students, to increase our course offerings in community engagement, and to pilot a specialization in community leadership and public engagement for MPA students interested in providing guidance and technical assistance to public and nonprofit organizations on multistakeholder problem solving.

## Recent Suffolk Curriculum Changes

Suffolk University is an urban university located at the top of Beacon Hill in Boston, between the Massachusetts State House and Boston City Hall. The public administration department is housed in the School of Management along with undergraduate and graduate business programs. The Suffolk MPA program enrolls approximately 200 students, the majority of whom are part-time graduate students working in local, state, and federal government and nonprofit organizations, especially health care. Most classes are offered in the evenings and on Saturdays. Students who graduate with a straight MPA degree take fifteen three-credit courses; those who choose to graduate with a specialized MPA degree take an additional two courses for a total of seventeen three-credit courses. Currently, we offer four specialized degrees: state and local government, health care administration, nonprofit management, and, most recently, community leadership and public engagement.

In the process of deciding to introduce a new specialized MPA degree in Community Leadership and Public Engagement, our faculty had extensive conversations about our program, its identity, and its future. We had lively discussions about our individual philosophies regarding public administration and about personal and professional values and goals. Some colleagues questioned whether taking leadership by being a convener and facilitator in the policy-making process is a constitutionally proper role for a professional administrator. Public managers *must* lead, countered other department members (reflecting Robert Behn and others), because our current policy making process is broken and they are in a position to make it more democratic, at least potentially. Others argued, following Cooper (1991) and Frederickson (1997a), that public administrators are, properly, representative citizens who are employed by their fellow citizens to do the work of citizenship on their behalf, by reinforcing communal values and democratic processes. Several colleagues saw public deliberation and community problem solving as unrealistic and too removed from the machinations of the political process, especially in a part of the country dominated by strong mayor governments.

Faculty members questioned whether there was a market for a specialized MPA degree, which, unlike our other specialized MPA degrees, was not focused on a sector such as state and local government, health-care management, or nonprofit management, but rather on a body of process-oriented knowledge and skills that cuts across all sectors. Our focus groups with alumni and government, health care and nonprofit executives led us to believe that question could be answered affirmatively.

Underlying our differing views and priorities, we found a shared concern on the part of our faculty, that in order to address the complex interrelated problems facing organizations and communities, all of our graduates need leadership competencies for working collaboratively with multiple stakeholders. The best public managers have probably always operated this way: our students need to learn from the "best processes" that they have employed. We also need to bring together what has been learned in other fields, such as organizational development, systems thinking, and conflict resolution, about participative decision making in order to make policy making more democratic and more effective. We decided we want our program to provide graduates with a theoretical framework and practical skills for designing and implementing deliberative democratic processes and collaborative problem solving. We have taken the steps below to implement that decision.

## New Core Course on Leadership Strategies for an Interconnected World

We agree with Robert Behn (1998) and others who argue that public managers are obligated to lead because the U.S. system of governance is facing basic failures that public managers can help to correct (Denhardt and Denhardt 2003; Frederickson 1997a). Beginning in spring 2004, Suffolk University began requiring that all MPA students take a course that presents a collaborative leadership model, called Leadership Strategies for an Interconnected World. The decision to add this new course to our required core reflects recognition that public policy is increasingly being made through the interaction of many different interest groups and organizations with overlapping and often competing goals (Denhardt and Denhardt 2003; Luke 1998; Bryson 1992). Getting things done requires leadership to bring together diverse individuals and groups from multiple institutions, sectors, and jurisdictions in a collaborative manner. We decided all of our students, regardless of whether they worked in government, nonprofit organizations, or health care, needed to build knowledge and skills in collaborative leadership; therefore, we made this a required course in both MPA and MHA programs.

The course introduces a facilitative or collaborative model of leadership and applies it to the handling of societal problems in a system of distributed governance that requires partnerships among government agencies, nonprofit service providers, businesses, neighborhood groups, and educational institutions. Students are introduced to what Jeffrey Luke (1998) calls the tasks of catalytic leadership. Through readings, written and video case studies, experiential exercises, group work, and reflective writing, students are provided with opportunities to build knowledge and skills related to these leadership tasks.

Engaging the public in the collaborative process can be a risky and time-consuming activity. There is no guarantee it will succeed. People need commitment and drive to step out into the unknown. Having a sense of purpose helps public managers take unavoidable setbacks and failures in stride. In our new student orientation, held each September, we engage students in an appreciative inquiry process designed to help them identify personal and professional aspirations and goals. This new leadership course builds on the work done in the orientation by challenging students to do some hard thinking about their own values and priorities and how they define their purpose as public service professionals.

Much of the course is devoted to the dynamics of partnerships and alliances through the analysis of case studies and reflection on what it means to play a go-between role in public problem solving. By requiring that all MPA students take a course in collaborative leadership as part of the core curriculum, the precedent is set that all of our students need to understand this new way of doing business, can reflect on what it means in their own professional environment, and have an opportunity to develop and practice collaborative leadership skills.

## MPA Specialization in Community Leadership and Public Engagement

In spring 2004, Suffolk University began offering students seeking the MPA an option to pursue a specialized degree in Community Leadership and Public Engagement. Our goal in creating this degree is to provide a course of study that will prepare public service professionals with the specialized knowledge and skills to design, facilitate, and evaluate participative public processes and multistakeholder decision making. Students who choose the Community Leadership and Public Engagement specialized degree are those who wish to build a particular set of competencies that they can bring to careers in local, state, or federal government; international development; nonprofit organizations; or consulting.

If we want to engage the public more effectively in community problem solving, our public and nonprofit organizations are going to need people with the knowledge and skills to design, implement, and evaluate these processes. In 1999 and 2000, forty-two in-depth interviews were conducted with public managers, including many city managers, who are utilizing deliberative public processes in their communities. Almost without exception, the study participants said they had relied on a methodology developed elsewhere, such as Study Circles, or had worked closely with an outside consultant over an extended period. The overwhelming majority of the interviewees said they had no one on their staffs with knowledge of models for participative public decision making nor did they have the ability to design and guide the organization in implementing and evaluating such a process (Bramson 2000). This specialized MPA degree seeks to address this deficit by preparing a cadre of public service professionals with the advanced knowledge and skills to serve as coaches, consultants, and resources on democratic public processes for their organizations and communities.

In developing this new degree, the public management department went through a process of identifying what we believed to be the key content and skill areas needed for expertise in community leadership and public engagement. We found that many of our colleagues had academic and professional experience and interests, of which we were not fully aware, that would support this new specialization. We also reviewed our current course offerings to determine how they might support the new program. For example, if public managers are to function as catalysts and community capacity builders, they need a firm grounding in theories of democratic citizenship and in the history and political context of public administration. This is covered in Foundations of Public Organizational Administration, an entry-level required course for all MPA students. Community facilitators also need to understand the theories and practices of organizational development and change management. Organizational change management is the major focus of another required core course, Organizational Effectiveness in Government. Issue analysis, the analysis and communication of data, performance measurement, program design and evaluation, and strategic planning are other knowledge areas that are important for community problem solving and are taught elsewhere in our core curriculum.

The curriculum for the Community Leadership and Public Engagement specialized MPA degree takes a multidisciplinary approach. For example, from political science, we look at the role of citizen as it was conceived by the Founding Fathers and as it is being practiced today. From sociology, anthropology, and psychology, we draw concepts regarding community building, community organizing, and community problem solving. From organizational development, we draw practices and principles for implementing change and for involving whole systems in participatory processes. We agreed that students who specialize in community leadership and public engagement should be able to demonstrate:

- a theoretical understanding of leadership models, community organizing, issues of democracy versus bureaucracy, change management, conflict resolution, public communication, strategic planning, group process, and systems thinking, as they apply to bringing together diverse parties in communities to forge new solutions;
- the ability to work with a group to analyze a community issue and to design a process for engaging multiple stakeholders, resolving disputes, implementing changes, and evaluating results;
- the ability to analyze a participatory governance process in terms of its ability to advance democratic values such as equity, accountability, transparency, effectiveness, and representation;

- an advanced level knowledge of models and methods for large and small group democratic processes; and
- concern for democratic values and their role in enacting those values.

## Two New Courses Support Specialized Degree

Two new courses—Civic Innovation and Community Governance and Group Theory and Facilitation Practice—have been added to the curriculum to support this new specialized degree.

### *Civic Innovation and Community Governance*

Across a wide range of policy arenas, proponents of community engagement are developing innovative programs that apply deliberative democratic practices to public problem solving (Sirianni and Friedland 2001; Fung and Wright 2003). In this course, students examine cases that are drawn from areas as diverse as policing, restorative justice, public education, urban governance, youth development, civic journalism, environmental regulation, health care, community visioning, and international development. In each case, practitioners have developed institutional arrangements that engage the participation of ordinary citizens, empower groups made up of citizens and public servants, and hold these groups responsible for producing and measuring outcomes. Students analyze these programs, in detail, focusing on their goals and outcomes in terms of advancing the values of participation, fairness, deliberation, accountability, and effective governance (Fung and Wright 2003).

### *Group Theory and Facilitation Practice*

To effectively engage stakeholders in public problem solving, public managers need the ability to design and manage participative processes that assist community members in building a shared notion of the public interest. This new course is designed to integrate the theory and practice of group facilitation, with a particular focus on public participation. Students have "hands-on" opportunities to develop and demonstrate the competencies that are necessary to create arenas and to facilitate processes in which stakeholders can engage with one another in addressing public concerns. Coursework provides an overview as well as specific practice in participative process design, techniques, and tools for involving various stakeholders in defining problems, formulating policies or plans, making decisions, and implementing them. The course does not set forth a comprehensive theory of group facilitation. Instead, it describes a set of core values and congruent principles—elements of a theory—and shows how to use various methods to apply the principles in practice with both small and large groups. The course is taught by two instructors who provide students with extensive coaching. Specific methods covered include Institute of Cultural Affairs group facilitation methods, future search, open space technology, and appreciative inquiry, as well as others.

## Other Components of the Specialized MPA Degree

In creating this new specialized degree, we have brought together several courses that have been offered in the public administration department and in other departments of the university for many years. Community and Citizen Empowerment and Alternative Dispute Resolution are public management courses that have each had consistently high enrollments.

### *Community and Citizen Empowerment*

This course explores the major approaches currently being used in community-building efforts to strengthen community capacity. The course explores strategies intended to build a community's social capital and ways in which community organizing strengthens broader community-building efforts. Students are introduced to asset-based community building and contrast it with problem-oriented approaches. Recognizing that community change begins with changing the way people think and talk about issues, this course introduces students to theories and models for civic dialogue and public deliberation. Students examine such models as National Issues Forums, Study Circles, AmericaSpeaks, deliberative polling, citizens jury, citizen panels, and others. In the course, students develop a framework for public managers who are designing a public participation process and considering how much influence to share with the public, who to involve from the public, and how to choose among specific forms of public involvement.

A key component of the course involves students in leading an organizing project in connection with various institutions involved in community capacity building in the greater Boston area or on campus. The organizing projects involve students organizing other people to join them in achieving a clear outcome by the end of the semester.

### *Alternative Dispute Resolution or Conflict and Negotiation*

Engaging citizens in community problem solving requires public managers to have knowledge and skills in negotiation and conflict resolution. Coursework in alternative dispute resolution or negotiation is required of all students in this specialized degree. In the Public Management Alternative Dispute Resolution course, students learn guidelines for designing a dispute resolution system that will help handle conflicts effectively on an ongoing basis and avoid the damaging costs of attorney's fees, lost productivity, and emotional injury. Students examine key questions to be answered when analyzing a dispute and principles of dispute system design, such as designing procedures that encourage disputants to return to negotiation. Distinctions are made among negotiation, mediation, and arbitration, and each is explored extensively. Dispute resolution is discussed in settings that involve labor–management disputes, environmental issues, community disputes, construction claims, and business disputes. Special attention is paid to multistakeholder negotiations and public disputes.

Students also have the option of substituting a Master of Business Administration or MBA course in the theory and practice of negotiation for alternative dispute resolution. This course emphasizes that effective negotiation involves a combination of analytical and interpersonal skills. Analysis is important because negotiators cannot develop sound strategies without an understanding of the context of the situation, the interests of all parties, and the range of possible options. Interpersonal skills are important since negotiation is fundamentally a process of communicating, building trust (or not), and mutual persuasion.

**Multidisciplinary Electives and Practice-Oriented Capstone**

To examine the issue of public engagement in community problem solving through the eyes of scholars in various disciplines and fields of study and to gain knowledge and skills not included in the public administration curriculum, students in this specialized degree are encouraged to take selected electives in other departments of the university. For students in this program, the capstone course, which is required of all MPA graduates, takes the form of either an internship (for pre-professional students) or a practicum seminar (for in-service students) and is designed to provide opportunities for mentoring, experiential learning, working on real community problems, and reflection-in-action (Schon 1983).

**Unique Approach or Repackaging?**

The content of the courses in this specialization is not unique to the Suffolk program. Other MPA programs offer courses in conflict resolution, community organizing, collaborative leadership, and public participation methods.

In bringing these content areas together in this specialized degree, we are arguing that the public arena needs people with expertise that incorporates and builds on processes from organizational development, conflict resolution, community organizing, and group process and systems thinking, who can serve as intermediaries, facilitators, and change agents in public problem solving. To overcome the will/skill dilemma, public organizations need individuals whom they can turn to for assistance and who are grounded in democratic theory with knowledge and experience regarding the "who," "when," and "how" of civic engagement. To do this important work, we think people need an integrated course of study, not just scattered electives to develop the level of knowledge and skill and the confidence needed. They also need a chance to practice what they learn both in the classroom and in the community.

Developing a curriculum that prepares public management students to function as skilled intermediaries and facilitators in collaborative community problem solving takes our department to new and challenging territory. Our goal is to develop an educational framing for some practical guidance for public managers in thinking about when and how to involve citizens in public deliberation and multistakeholder decision making—a framework for practice. But skilled practice involves artistry as well as a theoretical framework. Can the interpersonal and communication skills necessary to be an effective community facilitator be taught? Will we need to develop teaching methods different from those usually found in graduate education to help community facilitators develop artistry through reflection-in-action? As we seek to teach our students to be reflective practitioners as community facilitators, how can we be more reflective practitioners in our own teaching?

Although this specialized degree program is less than one year old, members of the public management department faculty say that our focus on developing community change agents is having the effect of changing us. Our curriculum discussions provided us with a setting for dialogue about the core questions of public administration: Who are we? What is our core purpose? What is most meaningful and important about what we do? As we shared our basic assumptions and weighed options together, trust levels rose. We are a public management program that is housed within a school of business. This new specialized MPA degree, and the process we went through to develop it, has helped our department to clarify its purpose and role within the university. We are working more effectively across our own boundaries, collaborating with colleagues from other departments in the university to transcend turf issues and to create a multidisciplinary program. We have also strengthened long-time community partnerships and built new ones as we seek opportunities to give students hands-on experiences linked to class work. In some interesting ways, our internal process seems to be paralleling what we are seeking to create in the community at large.

This new specialized degree is influencing the way in which some of our courses are taught. For example, our budgeting course now includes cases involving participative budgeting; in the statistics course we decided we needed to send students into the community to conduct a program evaluation. It is also impacting hiring decisions; we expect to be adding new faculty to buttress our resources in organizational and community development in the near future.

The further we go in developing this new specialized degree program, the more conscious we are of how much more needs to be done. Public service educators who are committed to accelerating the emergence of a new brand of facilitative catalytic public managers need to be brought together to learn from one another and to promote the design, development, assessment, and dissemination of innovative learning methodologies and approaches. We need resource banks for sharing syllabi, readings, case studies, films, websites, and simulations, and developing and supporting research agendas.[4]

Public professionals have always been involved in the process of making public policy. But if policy making is to be made more democratic, public managers must overcome the will/skill dilemma that currently blocks them from providing leadership as community conveners, facilitators, and intermediaries. To mobilize the will to engage key stakeholders and the general public, the public manager must begin with himself or herself, with his or her own commitment to democratic values, and with a sense of personal purpose. Addressing the skill problem involves providing public managers with models, processes, theoretical frameworks, and practical experience for engaging the public in collaborative problem solving. Can we overcome these obstacles to democratic public problem solving? Can public administration rise to the challenge? We certainly hope so. Our democracy's future might depend on it.

## Notes

I want to acknowledge the support and assistance of my colleagues in the Public Management Department at Suffolk University in describing and reflecting on our process in developing this program. Earlier drafts of this chapter were presented at the international conference on "The Deliberative Position in Public Debate" in Tours, France, May 2003 and at the annual conference of the National Association of Schools of Public Administration and Affairs, October 2003 in Pittsburgh, PA.

## Appendix 8.1. Courses for a Specialization in Community Leadership and Public Engagement

*Civic Innovation and Community Governance*

In this course, students examine a variety of civic innovations that apply deliberative democratic practices to public problem solving by bringing together diverse parties across a variety of policy areas to forge new solutions.

*Community and Citizen Empowerment*

This course focuses on the theory and methods for community organizing, community development, and community learning, and explores ways that empowered citizens can bring about social and economic change.

*Group Theory and Facilitation Practice*

This course is for those who wish to increase their knowledge of group theory and build skills for designing processes to facilitate complex situations involving community. The course provides opportunities for practice and feedback and for reflection that integrates knowledge and application.

*Alternative Dispute Resolution*

This course reviews all areas of alternative dispute resolution: mediation, arbitration, negotiation, and conciliation, with an emphasis on resolving public disputes.

*Conflict and Negotiation*

This course emphasizes the theory and skills of win-win negotiation.

Four community leadership and public engagement elective courses selected from the following:

Public Liaison Strategies
Administrative Strategies of
   Local Government
Ethics and Management
Client and Community Relations
Leadership and Decision Making
Governmental Decision Making
Urban Politics and Government
Community Advocacy
Politics and the Media
Topics in Democracy
The Internet and Politics
Consultation

Systems Thinking
Communicating for Results
Organizational Development
Reflection and Dialogue
Interpersonal and Intercultural
   Communication
E-Community and the
   Digital Divide
Political Communication
Crisis Management
Managing Diversity
Restorative Justice

1. "Engagement" means that the people who are involved in a problem have a responsibility to work with others of differing views to try to devise a solution that will work and that will be accepted by most of those affected (See for example Widner University's approach to civil engagement in the Philadelphia metro region, www/wodemer/edi/Widener).

2. Intermediaries, as used here, refer to people and institutions who connect, support, and assist others in becoming more effective.

3. The term "catalyst" literally means an agent that initiates or speeds up a chemical reaction without itself being used up in the process (Webster's New World Dictionary).

4. There are a few noteworthy resources online: The Collaborative Democracy Network, www.csus.edu/ccp/cdn/, collects relevant syllabi; the new E-PARC website (Program on the Analysis and Resolution of Conflicts, The Maxwell School at Syracuse University), www.maxwell.syr.edu/parc/eparc/, includes syllabi, case studies, and simulations; and the National Coalition for Dialogue and Deliberation site indexes numerous resources that are useful for classroom use www.thataway.org

## References

Barber, Benjamin. 1984. *Strong Democracy: Participatory Politics for a New Age*. Berkeley, CA: University of California Press.

———. 1998. *A Place for Us*. New York: Hill and Wang.

Behn, Robert T. 1998. "What Right Do Public Managers Have to Lead?" *Public Administration Review,* 58(3): 209–221.

Bellah, Robert, Richard Madsen, William Sullivan, Ann Swidler, and Steve Tipton. 1985. *Habits of the Heart*. Berkeley, CA: University of California Press.

———. 1991. *The Good Society*. New York: Knopf.

Box, Richard C. 1998. *Citizen Governance: Leading American Communities into the 21st Century*. Thousand Oaks, CA: Sage.

Bramson, Ruth Ann. 2000. "The Deliberative Public Manager: Engaging Citizens in Productive Public Conversations." PhD diss., Union Institute.

Bryson, John. 1992. *Leadership for the Common Good*. San Francisco: Jossey-Bass.

Buss, Terry F., and F. Stevens Redburn, eds. 2006. *Modernizing Democracy*. New York: M.E. Sharpe.

Cooper, Terry L. 1991. *An Ethic of Citizenship for Public Administration*. Englewood Cliffs, NJ: Prentice Hall.

Denhardt, Janet V., and Robert B. Denhardt. 2003. *The New Public Service*. Armonk, NY: M.E. Sharpe.

Etzioni, Amitai. 1988. *The Moral Dilemma*. New York: Free Press.

———. 1995. *The New Communitarian Thinking*. Charlottesville, VA: University of Virginia Press.

Farmer, David John. 1995. *The Language of Public Administration: Bureaucracy, Modernity, and Postmodernity*. Tuscaloosa: University of Alabama Press.

Forester, John. 1999. *The Deliberative Practitioner*. Cambridge, MA: MIT Press.

Fox, Charles, and Hugh Miller. 1995. *Postmodern Public Administration*. Thousand Oaks, CA: Sage.

Frederickson, H. George. 1997a. *The Spirit of Public Administration*. San Francisco: Jossey-Bass.

———. 1997b. "Facing the Community." *Kettering Review* (December): 28–37.

Frederickson, H. George, and Ralph Clark Chandler, eds. 1984. "A Symposium on Citizenship and Public Administration." *Public Administration Review* 44 (Special Issue): 97–209.

Frederickson, H. George, and Kevin B. Smith. 2003. *The Public Administration Primer.* Boulder, CO: Westview Press.

Fung, Archon, and Erik Olin Wright. 2003. *Deepening Democracy: Institutional Innovation in Empowered Participatory Governance.* London: Verso.

Gates, Christopher. 1996. "Introduction to Citizens and Local Government: New Roles and Responsibilities." *National Civic Review* 85(3): 1–4.

King, Cheryl Simrell, and Camilla Stivers. 1998. *Government Is Us.* Thousand Oaks, CA: Sage.

Linden, Russell. 2002. *Working Across Boundaries.* San Francisco: Jossey-Bass.

Luke, Jeffrey. 1998. *Catalytic Leadership: Strategies for an Interconnected World.* San Francisco: Jossey-Bass.

Mansbridge, Jane, ed. 1990. *Beyond Self-Interest.* Chicago: University of Chicago Press.

Mathews, David. 1994. *Politics for People: Finding a Responsible Public Voice.* Urbana: University of Illinois Press.

McSwite, O.C. 1997. *Legitimacy in Administration.* Thousand Oaks, CA: Sage.

Nalbandian, John.1999. "Facilitating Community, Enabling Democracy: New Roles for Local Government Managers." *Public Administration Review* 59: 187–197.

O'Connell, Brian. 1999. *Civil Society: The Underpinnings of American Democracy.* Hanover, NH: University Press of New England.

Pateman, Carole. 1970. *Participation and Democratic Theory.* Cambridge: Cambridge University Press.

Putnam, Robert. 2000. *Bowling Alone.* New York: Simon and Schuster.

Reich, Robert, ed. 1988. *The Power of Public Ideas.* Cambridge, MA: Ballinger.

Ruckelshaus, William. 1996. "Restoring Public Trust in Government: A Prescription Restoration." *The Webb Lecture*, November 15. Washington, DC: National Academy of Public Administration.

Sandel, Michael. 1996, *Democracy's Discontent.* Cambridge: Belknap Press of Harvard University Press.

Schon, Donald. 1983. *The Reflective Practitioner.* New York: Basic Books.

Sirianni, Carmen, and Lewis Friedland. 2001. *Civic Innovation in America.* Berkeley: University of California Press

Skocpol, Theda, and Morris Fiorina. 1999. *Civic Engagement in American Democracy.* Washington, DC: Brookings Institution Press.

Stone, Clarence. 1989. *Regime Politics: Governing Atlanta 1946–1988.* Lawrence: University Press of Kansas.

Thomas, John Clayton. 1995. *Public Participation in Public Decisions: New Skills and Strategies for Public Managers.* San Francisco: Jossey-Bass.

Wamsley, Gary L., and James F. Wolf, eds. 1996. *Refounding Democratic Public Administration: Modern Paradoxes, Postmodern Challenges.* Thousand Oaks, CA: Sage.

Wolfe, Alan. 1989. *Whose Keeper.* Berkeley: University of California Press.

Yankelovich, Daniel. 1999. *The Magic of Dialogue.* New York: Simon & Schuster.

# Part III

## Global Public Leadership

# 9

# Developing Leaders in the New Age of Government

Ruth T. Zaplin and Sydney Smith-Heimbrock

There are increasing numbers of federal agencies finding the need for an overseas presence or that are experiencing global dimensions to their work. For example, Health and Human Services, whose Centers for Disease Control (CDC) and Prevention, the Food and Drug Administration, and the National Institutes of Health track and respond to health and medical developments worldwide; the Education Department's American Overseas Research Center promotes global exchange of ideas and innovations through American-funded academic research overseas; the Department of the Interior's U.S. Geological Survey must track global developments such as climate change and catastrophic events for their impact on American life; the Department of Transportation's Maritime Administration monitors shipping activities in an increasingly integrated global economy; and the Federal Aviation Administration assesses and monitors flight safety in airports and airspace covering the globe. Furthermore, many regulatory agencies have decision-making responsibilities that affect other nations and their nationals. In short, given the many bilateral and multilateral exchange agreements with other countries to which the United States is a party, there is almost no policy arena that does not require public administrators to engage with international counterparts and to monitor global trends and events. More and more, successful mission accomplishment for agencies requires the ability to influence events and ideas across national and cultural boundaries—in essence, to exercise effective global leadership (Dorfman 2003). This chapter addresses these three important questions:

- What is global leadership?
- What are the public dimensions of global leadership?
- How should government develop globally competent leaders?

**What Is Global Leadership?**

If leadership involves "people whose job or role it is to influence the thoughts and actions of others to achieve some finite set of . . . goals" (Gessner and Arnold 1999, in Hollenbeck 2001), then *global* leadership is exerting this role on a global scale. Global leadership is about having global influence and about asking the question, "How can I impact the world?" not "How do I impact my own organization?"

A global leader must have a global vision, looking well beyond traditional jurisdictions or identities. She must be able to communicate that vision across a diverse mix of peoples and interests and be heard (Hesselbein 2006). A global leader must also understand that in the twenty-first century traditional jurisdictions and identities are deeply interconnected with jurisdictions and identities around the globe. According to Bellamy (2006), Program Manager for Leadership and Knowledge Management of the U.S. Office of Personnel Management, "You can't break up a globe." The globe is one unit. Global leaders recognize that they and those whom they serve are part of that one, global unit. Speaking at the fiftieth anniversary of Japan's entry into the post–World War II "Bretton Woods" monetary accords, World Bank Vice President for South East Asia Mieko Nishimizu (as cited in Senge 2006, p. 21) stated:

> The future appears alien to us. It differs from the past most notably in that the Earth itself is the relevant unit with which to frame and measure that future. Discriminating issues that shape the future are all fundamentally global. We belong to one inescapable network of mutuality: mutuality of ecosystems; mutuality of freer movement of information, ideas, people, capital, goods and services; and mutuality of peace and security. We are tied, indeed, in a single fabric of destiny on Planet Earth. Policies and actions that attempt to tear a nation from this cloth will inevitably fail.

Effective leadership demands competencies specific to the global context. According to Senge (2006), two systems-thinking skills are vital: seeing patterns of interdependency and seeing into the future. It is one thing to say we are interdependent and another to understand what this means specifically, especially for problems created by the present systems that no one knows how to solve. In the public sector, global public leaders must be skilled in operating across national boundaries and drawing diverse national interests into a common global vision. Global public leaders must understand the forces of globalization itself to harness the power of deeply integrated economic, political, and social systems and dynamics to achieve public value.

They must redefine their "home" constituencies as fundamentally global in nature—connected through personal links and access to information with individuals, groups, and nations across the world. To effectively serve the public, leaders must address the ways in which the public is connected with others across the globe.

## What Are the Public Dimensions of Global Leadership?

Effective global leadership is urgent for the field of public administration in which the drive to provide needed policies and services intersects with the legitimate—and democratically legitimating—demand for public accountability (United Nations 2003). Specifically, the information revolution has converged with the steady integration of social, economic, and political structures and processes across nations to make public leaders accountable across the globe for their decisions and their actions. Indeed, the ability to hold leaders publicly accountable—a relatively new idea for some societies—is critical for democratic governance across the globe (Steinhardt 2006).

Effective public leadership thus requires a high level of competence in anticipating the service and accountability needs of an increasingly diverse constituency and integrating systems and operations across national boundaries to meet these needs. The latter responsibility—increasingly common for public administrators at all levels of American governance—requires attention to the concerns of "partner" agencies overseas and their constituents. The ability to anticipate and meet these concerns requires recognition and appreciation of the deep cultural and political differences that continue to characterize diverse populations across the globe. It is the validation of these differences and the ability to build on them to produce transparent and effective government services that mark the globally competent public leader.

The events of September 11, 2001, brought to every American's living room the immediate recognition that our own security and development depend to a great degree on the stability and development of other countries. Not just leadership, but specifically global leadership, has emerged from these events as a primary demand of the public. The public now understands, through satellite television networks as well as the Internet, that the government's everyday decisions, strategies, and operations are closely watched by nations, societies, and groups across the globe. The degree to which public administrators are able to incorporate a global perspective into their decision making and operations is now a significant part of how the public assesses the effectiveness of government services. But, despite the major shifts in demand for leadership that globalization and global movements have produced, the federal government still lags behind the private and nonprofit sectors in developing global leaders, perhaps with the exception of the Foreign Service. According to a 2003 RAND report, for example, the nation is producing too few future leaders who combine substantive depth with international experience and outlook (Bikson and Treverton 2003).

For public leaders, "going global" means holding oneself accountable for public outcomes on a global scale. Global leaders running domestic government agencies recognize that their policies impact other nations and peoples. They also recognize that their traditional constituencies are now interconnected with constituencies overseas. Global leaders running international government programs are held accountable to constituencies at home and abroad. The decision-making process of global leaders who run traditionally domestic government agencies and those who run international government programs must therefore take into account the increasingly global characteristics of domestic problems and constituencies, and the need to influence governments and groups overseas in order to achieve the public outcome sought. Global leadership therefore marks a fundamental shift in the relationship between U.S. public leaders and the rest of the world. In adapting the servant-leader model to public service and global leadership, U.S. leaders serve the world (Bellamy 2006). Complex policy problems facing the United States—such as global warming and international economic migration—demand this global service and leadership approach.

## How Should Government Develop Globally Competent Leaders?

Leading a public organization in this century requires some new principles and practices. At the same time, there remain three simple yet profound truths or laws about leadership that have not changed (Shrader 2006):

- Leadership is a matter of how to be, not how to do.
- Leaders succeed through the efforts of their people.
- Leaders build bridges.

In addition to these truths, there are basic leadership development principles and practices that are consistent with the traditional leadership development literature and are relevant and necessary for creating and maintaining a high-performance organizational culture in which talented people are motivated to reach their full potential to become global leaders. We discuss these basic leadership development principles and practices below—with illustrations from both the public and private sectors—from a global leadership development perspective.

## Start with Workforce Analysis

Leading organizations perform periodic, comprehensive, and detailed workforce analyses to determine their global leadership development needs. The workforce analysis includes continuous reexamination of the current leadership cadre's demographics; determining global leadership competencies needed in the short, mid, and long term; and identifying mission areas in which needed leadership capabilities should continue as they are or where an infusion may be needed to correct a surplus, shortage, or imbalance. Workforce analysis should include looking globally to identify current and projected shortages and excesses of leadership positions by level (supervisor, manager, and executive), organizational location, and mission area, including technical and managerial competencies. And it should also include ongoing analyses of external global challenges, emerging business opportunities/strategies, and benchmarks of leading global organizations' exemplary practices.

> To gather external perspectives, Shell joined the Global Research Consortium, a group of transnational companies that sponsor research on leadership and learning. The consortium gives its members the opportunity to hear and discuss the latest exemplary practices and lessons learned. Like other leading companies, Shell also works with consultants and professors to stay abreast of the latest leadership research. (Fulmer, Gibbs, and Goldsmith 2000).

## Create a Fair and Nurturing Work Environment for a Globally Diverse Workforce

We are all familiar with traditional organizations in which leadership is often viewed as residing within a small group of people at the top of the organization. In traditional (hierarchical) organizations, leadership development programs and resources are aimed at this elite group. Especially in today's global environment, where leadership responsibilities are dispersed geographically and organizationally, this view is no longer appropriate (Crabtree 2001). Effective leaders must create a context in which employees at all levels can achieve their full potential. This begins by ensuring a fair and nurturing work environment, in which all employees understand what they are trying to do and how they fit in, relevant parties move in roughly the same direction, and employees "live" the personal and organizational values by developing their own and others' skills necessary to get the work done (Hollenbeck and McCall 2001).

Creating a fair and nurturing work environment for a globally diverse workforce requires high levels of trust, competence, strong communities of practice, free flow of communication, and alignment of employee performance with the organization's global vision. In short, the leader who truly respects his or her employees and peers as human beings has a far greater chance of achieving organizational goals (Green et al. 2003). The type of respect that builds employee morale does not come from deference to power or from the expectation of reward, but from a sense of the intrinsic worth of human beings—all human beings. *Respect is the treatment of each person as unique and important* (Sirota, Mischkind, and Meltzer 2005). Fairness in the working environment has to do with equity. *Equity is the desire to be treated justly in relation to the basic conditions of employment* (Sirota et al. 2005). Employees expect these conditions in the employment relationship simply by virtue of being employed.

Thus, creating a fair and nurturing work environment is a necessary and practical step for meeting the universal human need for inclusion and respect. It also impacts an organization's ability to:

- attract the best global talent;
- become or remain an employer of choice;
- reduce voluntary turnover; and
- foster the growth of informal networks critical to effective work accomplishment, especially by knowledge workers.

A global environment characterized by dispersed leadership underscores the importance of a participatory approach. Additionally, in knowledge work, teams, not individuals, are the fundamental organizational unit. Skills that help people harmonize and remain satisfied within their teams will become increasingly valued as a workplace asset (Goleman 2005). In a fair and nurturing work environment, strong, cohesive teams—both ad hoc and standing—deliver work products that are critical to an organization in achieving its mission. Increasingly, strong, cohesive teams find their strength in loose networks of colleagues; different tasks can mean calling on different members of the network—often geographically dispersed—at different times. The extent to which workers feel included and respected is correlated with their willingness to call on different members of the network and to forgo engaging in a team when their specific skill set is not needed. This flexibility in specific work assignments—born of the confidence instilled by a culture of inclusion and respect—creates the chance for productive ad hoc groups, each with a membership tailored to offer an optimal array of talents, expertise, and placement. Just how well people can "work" a network—in effect, make it into a temporary, ad hoc team—is a crucial factor in on-the-job success (Goleman 2005).

The Centers for Disease Control uses a comprehensive internal review process to design global leadership development approaches that will support its new "net-centric" organizational structure. Based on lessons learned from the SARS outbreak, the CDC's Director, Dr. Julie Gerberding, determined that traditional hierarchies are no longer effective for responding to global health crises. Gerberding determined that she had to find new ways of bringing important knowledge, often held widely in organizations spanning the globe and falling well outside CDC lines of authority, to bear on problems threatening American public health. In response, the CDC restructured into a network that relies on leadership across the workforce and among partner organizations to activate the connections between concentrated centers of expertise and the front lines of operations. (Kettl 2005)

This phenomenon was demonstrated when the stars were studied in one division at Bell Labs, a unit that creates and designs the electronic switches that control telephone systems—a highly sophisticated and demanding piece of electronic engineering. Because the work is beyond the capacity of any one person to tackle, it is done in teams that can range from just 5 engineers to as many as 150. No single engineer knows enough to do the job alone and getting things done demands tapping into other people's expertise. To find out what made the difference between those who were highly productive and those who were only average, productivity researchers Robert Kelley and Janet Caplan had managers and peers nominate the 10–15 percent of engineers who stood out as stars. When they compared the exemplary contributors with everyone else, the most dramatic finding initially was the paucity of differences between the two groups. But after detailed interviews, the critical differences emerged in the internal and interpersonal strategies that the exemplary contributors used to get their work done. One of the most important differences turned out to be the stars' rapport with a network of key people (Goleman 2005). Such a skill is essential in effective teamwork.

Global leaders who create an inclusive work environment also create added value for organizational performance (Goleman 2005). Staff members who feel valued are encouraged in their pursuit of innovation, and hence do their best. If the organizational culture makes employees feel valued and the precondition of a fair and equitable work environment is met, employees will usually take the initiative to apply their skills and experiences in new ways to enhance their job performance (Thomas and Ely 2001). Since a globally integrated economy means that career decisions are no longer based on nationalism, as the labor pool shrinks in the years to come, being able to provide a work environment in which all kinds of employees can thrive—regardless of age, gender, discipline, social class, or geographic origin—will be a competitive edge for organizations.

In summary, the traditional managerial model of telling people what to do and how to do it is not effective for the global workplace. Today's global leaders instead must foster the growth of informal networks and be a partner to employees—guiding them, asking for their input, and sharing information. As the command-and-control model of power loses the respect and loyalty of the younger workforce, the need for globally competent, charismatic leaders is increasing (Greenberg-Walt and Robertson 2001). Finally, while the old functional model is obsolete, it has become increasingly clear that in terms of global leadership development, merely adding a few new interpersonal or charismatic competencies will not "fix" the old models. Nor can competency models, taken alone, ever explain the particular mix of competencies and personality traits that global leaders need to obtain outstanding results (Hollenbeck and McCall 2001).

### Demonstrate Support and Commitment of Top Leadership

Identifying and developing people with the needed competencies—specific to the global context in which an organization operates—must have the support and commitment of an organization's top leadership to succeed. Many top leaders understand the critical role their direct involvement plays and view their central task as developing other leaders, no matter how large the organization, and actively helping followers reach their own leadership potential.

> With 340,000 employees worldwide, GE [General Electric] could easily be an impersonal, difficult-to-navigate global company. With a highly competitive culture, it could be a place where ideas are hoarded and clever politicians squash good business people. With businesses ranging from medical equipment manufacturing to freight-car leasing, employees could be expected to have few skills and know few people outside their specialties. But GE has identified leadership as its core competence. Leadership development is understood as the company's most important business process. GE administrators report spending between one quarter and one half of their time on leadership issues. Largely because communities of practice permeate the organization, GE is remarkably informal and so successful at creating topflight administrators that it consistently produces more than it needs and exports its "trade surplus" in talent to companies around the world. With its networks, it seems that employees know people in every other GE business everywhere. (Stewart 2001)

Each year, Ontario's Secretary of the Cabinet—Ontario Public Service's top civil servant—convenes and actively participates in a two-day succession planning and management retreat with the heads of every government ministry. Agencies with international and domestic policy mandates discuss anticipated leadership needs across the government, as well as the individual status of about 200 high-potential administrators who may be able to meet those needs over the next year or two (U.S. Government Accountability Office [GAO] 2003).

Top global leaders also demonstrate support for leadership development when they regularly use these programs to develop, place, and promote individuals.

The Royal Canadian Mounted Police's (RCMP) senior administrator committee regularly uses leadership development programs when making decisions to develop, place and promote its top 500–600 officer and civilian employees. The RCMP's administrator committee, consisting of the agency's chief administrator, chief human capital officer and six other officials, meets quarterly to discuss the organization's succession needs and to make the specific decisions concerning individual staff necessary to address those needs. Since the Canadian government follows a multicultural model of governance, the degree to which staff represent their clients and their environment is a key factor in staffing decisions (GAO 2003).

Top global leaders demonstrate support for leadership development by ensuring that their organization's leadership development initiatives receive sufficient funding and staff resources. Such commitment is critical since leadership development initiatives can be expensive because of the emphasis placed on participant development. But in an increasingly competitive global environment, organizations have found this investment critical for their success.

GE and Shell International bring high-potential individuals into their training organizations on two-year rotational assignments to oversee leadership development. Hewlett Packard (HP) recruits key people from line positions for the same purpose. Taking "time out" from their operational duties to focus on leadership issues helps these individuals value and practice leadership skills for organizational effectiveness.

When James Wolfensohn joined the World Bank as president in 1995, he created a mission statement that affirmed the bank's longstanding commitment to dispersing knowledge and financial resources, but placed a stronger emphasis on the goal of reducing poverty worldwide. The new focus required significant change in institutional culture—change that had to be generated and sustained by leaders at all levels of the organization. Recognition of that need led to the Executive Development Program for managers, a unique collaboration among the Harvard Business School, the Kennedy School of Government, Stanford University, and IESE (the graduate business school of the University of Navarra, Spain). The program offers five weeks of classroom training and a leadership project that must help the Bank become more of a world leader (Fulmer et al. 2000).

> In addition to developing leaders from within their own organizational units, leading organizations reach out to access the experience of individuals in corporate education, human resources, and academia. For example, the Director of GE's Crotonville Center (Ossining, New York) came from a university setting. The head of the World Bank's Executive Development Program has a background in corporate education (GAO 2003). These two cases illustrate what some experts call the number-one leadership truth for effective global organizations—it is imperative that chief administrators not only support their organization's global leadership development efforts, but actively participate in them; communicate frequently about them; and provide the inspiration, passion, and necessary resources for their success. (Gandossy and Efrron 2004)

### Link Global Leadership Development to Strategic Planning

In too many organizations, administrator hiring decisions continue to be short-term and expedient, dominated by today's needs for operating the business and rarely including a developmental component for the future (Hollenbeck and McCall 2003). In contrast, leading global organizations use leadership development as a strategic planning tool to focus on current and future needs and to develop pools of high-potential staff to meet long-term goals. In these leading organizations, leadership development functions generally are geared toward specific strategic and global issues; more tactical management skills and business-specific challenges usually are left to business units that are better equipped to handle their own management skill training (GAO 2003).

> Every five years, the National Institutes of Health's National Human Genome Research Institute (NHGRI) draws on global expertise to develop new strategic goals and identifies the scientific and research capability needed to achieve them. National and international human genome experts discuss such topics as how skills critical to achieving previous goals may change during the coming years; how NHGRI should acquire, develop and shape these skills within universities and research programs; and whether it will need additional managers with similar scientific and medical skills to

oversee research activities. As one example, NHGRI's April 2003 strategic plan called for it to increase the number of scientists and managers with computer and clinical medical skills during the next five years. (Collins et al. 2003)

## Link Global Leadership Development to Succession Planning

Traditional approaches to succession planning attempt to fit the most highly qualified candidate with the job on the assumption that the candidate will carry out the responsibilities of the job efficiently and effectively. A drawback is that many succession planning functions focus on identifying and assessing talent and ignore development. What results is a list of candidates who might fill vacant positions rather than an understanding of the experiences candidates may need to be prepared for the job or how the job itself might fit the individual's development needs (Ohlott 2004).

Leading global organizations are aware that it is important to incorporate developmental considerations into job placement decisions. For this reason, they recognize the importance of aligning leadership development with other organizational functions and tying developmental efforts to formal succession planning. These organizations *marry succession planning and leadership development into one function and engage in broad, integrated succession planning and leadership development because these functions have the same fundamental goal: getting the right skills, in the right place, at the right time* (Fulmer et al. 2000).

GE openly ties leadership development to succession planning. All employees are rated in a nine-block system for the annual review, which includes discussion about individuals' performance and their adherence to GE's value statement. The system, which resembles a typical competency model, was created by former CEO Jack Welch and elaboration by his human resources team. It features a chart on which an employee's bottom-line performance is rated on one axis, and his or her adherence to GE values on the other. Those who do not make their performance numbers but do adhere to GE values are given a chance to improve and receive a higher rating. Those who make their numbers but do not demonstrate the GE values are rated low in the four-level model, which gauges promotion suitability. Those who do neither are rated lowest. (Fulmer et al. 2000)

Extending definitions and scope of succession planning and leadership development activities is becoming more important as global organizations take active steps to build high-performance, high-involvement work environments in which decision making is decentralized and leadership is diffused throughout the empowered global workforce. By collapsing the two functions into a single system, succession planning and leadership development can help an organization create new dimensions of performance rather than simply recreate the existing structure.

Aligning succession planning and leadership development with each other and with other corporate functions is particularly difficult for global organizations with multiple locations dispersed across geographic boundaries. Alignment can be strengthened by:

- Clearly identifying and establishing accountability for the roles and responsibilities of managers and administrators in succession planning, including the global leadership development component.
- Conducting periodic, comprehensive, and detailed workforce planning and analysis for global leadership positions that identify the current and projected leadership pool and pipeline.
- Strongly linking leadership development to the performance appraisal and promotion processes to help ensure they support the identification, assessment, and selection of leaders.
- Supporting and encouraging individual leadership development plans for participants and candidates in the global leadership pools.

Several critical steps must be taken to ensure that succession planning and global leadership development functions are aligned with organizational strategy. First, it is important to find out how the global leadership development functions will get the chief administrator and his or her team to where they want to be. Second, division heads across functions need to be consulted for input to learn what components are working, what components are not working, and what development needs are missing. Third, when top leadership articulates the focus and metrics of these functions, division directors can set the leadership development program priorities. This, in turn, should guide the focus and content of course development work.

One telling test of an aligned succession planning and global leadership development system is the extent to which an organization can fill important positions with internal candidates (GAO 2003).

> At Dow, an internal hire rate of 75 to 80 percent is considered a sign of success (the assumption is that the global company needs some external hires to maintain a fresh perspective and fill unanticipated roles). An outside hire for a critical role at the functional or corporate level is considered a failure in the internal development process. Dow also measures the attrition rate of its "future

leaders"—employees who are "precocious" in their development, perform at a competency level well above that of their colleagues and are believed to have the potential to fill jobs at much higher levels—against the attrition rate of its global employee population. In 2000, the future leaders' rate of attrition was 1.5 percent, compared with 5 percent globally, a signal to Dow's management that the company's future leaders are getting the developmental opportunities they want and need. It is worth noting that Dow's top 14 administrators all have had cross-functional developmental opportunities that prepared them for the demands of top management. (Conger and Fulmer 2003)

## Link Global Leadership to Individual and Organizational Performance

Performance appraisal systems in leading organizations should specifically hold managers and supervisors accountable for global leadership development and maintaining a global leadership culture in which all employees can develop to their full potential. This responsibility includes selecting participants for global leadership development programs, assessing global leadership potential and performance, holding subordinates accountable for global leadership development of their employees, assessing global leadership competency for selections and promotions, and supporting and contributing to diversity goals to create the synergy of a diverse workforce.

### Link to Individual Performance

For any global leadership development approach to be taken seriously, organizations must regularly assess managers' performance against rigorous global leadership, behavioral, and performance criteria. In leading organizations, Individual Development Plans (IDPs) are required for all employees. They include a focus on developing leadership competencies for team and organizational capabilities. On an aggregated basis, IDPs can help plan for global leadership development. They also can provide a baseline for assessing the extent to which employees meet identified developmental needs. In short, an agency-wide strategy for global leadership development can benefit from using IDPs to achieve more consistent and integrated leadership development experiences. According to Fred Hassan, chairman and CEO, Schering-Plough, "At Pharmacia and Upjohn . . . [w]e established new performance expectations that measured how well our employees demonstrated open-minded behaviors, including shared accountability, transparency, and collaboration across geographies. We called this behavior-based management and made it central to performance evaluation" (Green et al. 2003 p. 41).

"Developing people" is now part of the job description at Dell. Senior managers are measured and compensated on this objective. According to Dell CEO Kevin Rollins, "If we'd put in place a program without metrics, no one would have taken it seriously." (Stewart and O'Brien 2005 p. 110)

The current move to behavior-based management and performance-based pay systems that emphasize individual achievement and productivity does not preclude the use of performance awards to encourage the network-based global leadership competencies that are needed. But to achieve this balance, performance measurement systems—for programs as well as people—need to be carefully crafted to avoid the common pitfall of "inappropriately constraining the autonomy of lower level managers" (Stewart and O'Brien 2005). One approach is to make globally oriented outcomes part of performance standards at all levels of the organization, and to set performance expectations that measure how well employees "demonstrate open-minded behaviors, including shared accountability, transparency, and collaboration across geographies" (Green et al. 2003 p. 41). Other global leadership competencies that can be measured through performance appraisal systems include leading teams, creating and communicating a vision that speaks to global concerns, and fostering collaborative networks.

*Link to Organizational Performance*

Global leadership development strategies are moving away from individual learning and toward agency-wide performance, from exclusively building individual capabilities to developing team and organizational capabilities. Training and implementation support are tailored to specific programs or initiatives, often combining cognitive learning with the application of management and leadership competencies for specific issues. This broader scope emphasizes organizational performance, namely results and accountability, in which activities and outcomes are evaluated to determine the difference they make.

- In the Department of the Interior's Senior Executive Service (SES) performance management system, rating officials, Performance Review Board members, senior officials, and Executive Review Board members consider the results of the organizational assessment in determining summary performance rating and performance-based pay adjustments and awards. Disparities between individual and organizational performance results must be explained in the performance appraisal.

- The Department of the Treasury's SES pay for performance system emphasizes the identification of potential inconsistencies between organizational accomplishments (that others use to judge the department's performance) and recommended ratings, pay, and bonuses.

When linked to a strategic plan, individual and organizational performance creates a focus on management and global organizational challenges.

## Use the Hiring Process to Determine Global Leadership Potential

Leading global organizations that proactively manage their supply of leadership talent use the hiring process to determine potential. Recruiting is a prime task, not for the traditional human resources department but for operating managers at all levels, including the chief administrator. These organizations make a conscious effort to define selection criteria and global leadership competencies for new recruits when selecting new supervisors, managers, and administrators. Stephen Green, CEO, HSBC Group, stated:

> Our recruitment process is sophisticated, involving a complex process of tests, interviews, and exercises. We don't look so much at what or where people have studied but rather at their drive, initiative, cultural sensitivity, and readiness to see the world as their oyster. Whether they've studied classics, economics, history, or languages is irrelevant. What matter are the skills and qualities necessary to be good, well-rounded administrators in a highly international institution operating in a diverse set of communities. (Green et al. 2003, p. 40)

The selection criteria are also closely related to overall strategic plans and organizational performance needs. Some leading global organizations, such as sports teams, even recruit "the best talent available regardless of position," not to fill specific niches. Moreover, they consciously include leadership criteria in their recruitment profiles; they look for people interested in developing subordinates and view leaders as teachers rather than bosses (Kesner et al. 2003).

Once an employee is hired, leading global organizations lose no time in beginning the leadership development process wherever that employee may be. For example, Dell Computer provides its new managers with several types of training experiences at the point of initial hire, as well as at thirty, sixty, and ninety days following their hire. The training includes classroom learning and meetings with senior administrators to talk about managerial behaviors and how Dell operates as an organization. The training especially emphasizes

Dell's culture—how it is developed and sustained through its brand of effective management (O'Toole 2001).

Through the hiring process, leading global organizations maintain a database of knowledge workers they might want to employ at some time. Cisco Systems, the fast-growing maker of Internet equipment, already has such a database—containing sixty-five thousand potential employees worldwide. When someone applies for a job and there is no current opening, Cisco managers keep track of the applicant's skills and backgrounds for potential future use (O'Toole 2001).

There is no magic test to prove how effective someone will be as a global leader, but there are ways to get a good reading on potential. One way is to look at people's behavioral history and to assess whether they have already demonstrated effective global leadership in their academic career or previous work. Another way is to put people into realistic job previews or simulations that allow them to be observed interacting with others, tackling problems in teams, and behaving in situations that require management and global leadership skills.

Finally, leading global organizations have a good inventory of their human capital. In essence, they need to have individual profiles of their employees' skills, knowledge, and experience. In addition, they know how well individuals fit the "person" descriptions created to replace the job descriptions of the past. Evolving information technology allows priorities to be stored so that individuals at every level of the global organization can find what talents currently exist and decide who might be the best individuals to do particular types of work—wherever it may be (Lawler 2001).

### *Identify Talent Early from Multiple Organizational Levels*

When combined into a single system, effective succession planning and leadership development initiatives systematically identify high-performing employees from multiple levels throughout the organization early in their careers and track their upward mobility.

> According to Fred Hassan, Chairman and CEO, Schering-Plough, "The CEO has to see himself as the chief developer of talent, no matter how large the company. In 2000, we merged Pharmacia & UpJohn with Monsanto to create Pharmacia Corporation, a company with about 43,000 employees worldwide. I made it my business to know that large organization's top 200 managers personally—I don't mean the top 200 according to hierarchy, but according to their potential and the degree to which they contributed to the company's goals. Some of these people were quite junior, but I tried

to know who they were, what their strengths and weaknesses were, and I looked at their performance evaluations. In my last six months there, I had one-on-one meetings with approximately half of these people." . . . (Green et al. 2003, p. 41)

Avon's Andrea Jung takes the same kind of personal approach to identifying and nurturing global talent. She keeps a close eye on high-potential managers, even though they may be two or three or four levels below her. She also goes over the list at a private dinner held annually with the board. Her management team is graded not only on how it selects new managers but also on what it does to develop them as contributors to the global community (Green et al. 2003, p. 42)

Leading global organizations use the goals of their succession planning and leadership development programs as guides to putting the right people in the right programs.

At Sonoco Products, one of the world's largest manufacturers of packaging products, the leadership development process begins with lower-level employees perceived as having the potential to move up in the organization. The company considers the plant manager role to be a linchpin position because it is the first opportunity for managers to be responsible for multiple functions, as well as labor and community relations. Division vice presidents and their functional-area managers meet off-site for a full day with the division's human resources head to assess plant managers' performance and potential for promotion . . . The purpose is to . . . identify experience or performance issues that could affect a manager's promotion. The result is a pool of potential successors rather than a few leading contenders. (Conger and Fulmer 2003, p. 79)

### Emphasize Developmental Assignments and Relationships

Since the knowledge and breadth of skills needed by employees is growing and changing rapidly, global organizations must transform their training programs into an ongoing process of re-skilling and re-tooling. Continuous development is needed to keep up with changes in mission, technology, and work content. Continuous development will also help attract and retain younger people for whom self-development is a top priority. Developing global leaders is a process, not a competency taught solely in the classroom. It is best developed through experience and observation (Greenberg-Walt and Robertson 2001).

Research at the Center for Creative Leadership showed that participants often return to the office from training events energized and enthusiastic, only to be stifled by the reality of the workplace. Overall, the best leadership development efforts are those that combine classroom education, coaching, and strategically timed and designed job changes (McCauley and Douglas 2004). More and more, effective global leadership development and succession planning initiatives emphasize developmental or "stretch" assignments for high-potential employees in addition to more formal training components.

*Developmental Assignments*

In traditional, hierarchical organizations, rising leaders never had a reason to venture outside their silos. Now they do because silos become problematic when they deprive customers of better products and services. To build global leaders, global organizations must take people outside their comfort zones and offer them challenging assignments in different roles (Ready 2004). For global leadership development, these assignments should to the extent possible expose leaders to the broad geographic and substantive range of organizational operations and issues. Of particular importance will be exposing leaders to the conflicts that can arise in working with and in other cultures, and giving them an opportunity to practice conflict management competencies appropriate for the global environment.

Developmental job assignments place staff in new roles or unfamiliar job environments to strengthen skills and competencies and to broaden their experience. Challenge is the key element in a developmental job assignment. By tackling unfamiliar tasks and seeing the consequences of their actions, people learn from the challenges presented in their assignments. This learning may produce changes in how global leaders make decisions, take actions, handle risks, manage relationships, and approach problems.

> In Canada's Accelerated Executive Development Program, developmental assignments form the cornerstone of efforts to prepare senior administrators for top leadership roles in the public service. These assignments help enhance administrator competencies by having participants perform work in areas that are unfamiliar or challenging to them throughout the Canadian Public Service. For example, someone with a policy background could develop his or her managerial competencies through an assignment to manage a direct service delivery program in a different agency (GAO 2003).

Key to developmental assignments is the 80–20 development rule: Eighty percent of an employee's development should be attributed to on-the-job and life experiences; formal training should affect only 20 percent. Eighty percent of formal development occurs in the organizational units and only 20 percent occurs at the highest administrator level. It is imperative to identify the distinct stages in the careers of global administrators, development challenges at each stage, and levers the global organization can use, such as assignments and postings, to influence administrators' experiences (Kesner et al. 2003).

One challenge is that administrators and managers resist letting their high-potential staff leave their current positions to move to another organization as part of developmental assignments. Agencies in other countries have developed "portfolio" human capital approaches to respond to this challenge.

> Once individuals are accepted into Canada's Accelerated Executive Development Program, they are employees of the Public Service Commission, a central agency, and paid by it. Officials affiliated with the program said not having to pay participants' salaries makes administrators more willing to allow talented staff to leave for developmental assignments and fosters a government-wide, rather than agency-specific, culture among the program participants. (Kesner et al. 2003)

Governments would do well to follow Canada's lead and develop such a shared sense of responsibility among their agencies for leadership development. When government agencies view themselves as competing with each other for top talent, chances are slim that one agency would be willing to devote resources toward the development of promising individuals who might be expected to jump to another agency. On the other hand, if a government lessens the demand on agencies' internal resources where leadership development is concerned, the likelihood is far greater that an agency will be willing to cultivate promising individuals who may be expected to move to another agency. Moreover, agencies will enhance their sense that they are part of a greater and shared mission as opposed to operating disparately. Under such a system, agencies can expect to develop talented individuals with the abilities to lead effectively in a global working environment.

Similar opportunities for increasing the experiential depth of talented individuals are detail assignments and temporary promotions. These tools provide developmental opportunities for employees and an effective means of gapping positions between employees. Details may be internal to the bureau, department, or other federal agencies.

Intergovernmental Personnel Act (IPA) assignments authorize the temporary placement of employees between federal agencies and state, local and Indian tribal governments, institutions of higher education, and other eligible organizations. The purpose is for the sharing of information and skills in projects or programs of mutual interest or benefit to the two organizations involved.

*Developmental Relationships*

There is a growing understanding that individuals cannot rely solely on a single mentor or their current boss for development. This is particularly true for global leaders who must develop relationships across geographic and cultural boundaries. Successful global leaders build a network of relationships on which they rely for developmental assistance and support. These relationships can be lateral or hierarchical, within an organization or spanning organizations, ongoing or specific to a particular job transition, and job-related or career-related. Networks with stronger relationship ties that span more diverse subgroups will have more developmental power (McCauley and Douglas 2004).

To build global leadership competencies, participants in developmental relationships must focus on the specific global issues and skills involved in their work. Key elements in developmental relationships are assessment, challenge, and support (McCauley and Douglas 2004):

- *Assessment* provides day-to-day, ongoing feedback on how a person is doing in seeking to learn new skills or perspectives.
- *Challenge* pushes people beyond their comfort zone to enliven their thinking.
- *Support* from other people is needed to help with the struggles of a developmental experience.

Developmental relationships generally are a source of assessment information and a resource for interpreting and understanding that information. They challenge an individual directly or provide access to challenging assignments. They also are a primary means of support for development. In the Corporate Leadership Council's 2001 Leadership Survey of more than 8,000 managers, leadership development activities grounded in feedback and relationships (mentoring, administrator coaching, and interaction with peers) were rated as more effective for development than job experiences and education (McCauley and Douglas 2004).

**Feedback-Intensive Programs**

A feedback-intensive program is a comprehensive assessment of an individual's global leadership, generally in one or more sessions, using multiple lenses to view numerous aspects of personality and effectiveness. It is a blend of methodologies, combining such assessment-for-development tools as 360-degree feedback, experiential interactions, direct teaching of practical content from leadership research, and peer and staff coaching. It occurs within a supportive learning environment to maximize interaction among participants and faculty (Guthrie and King 2004).

> All of Johnson & Johnson's development functions use 360-degree feedback evaluations as a part of leadership development. Facilitators assess a multiple choice behavioral questionnaire, in which participants rate their performance in many areas and get ratings from supervisors, peers and subordinates. Plans may be made for participants to be coached later or to engage in activities to strengthen weak areas. (Ohlott 2004)

Leading global organizations view leadership development as an ongoing process based on the assumption that no single developmental event, no matter how powerful, is enough to create lasting change in an individual's approach to leadership tasks (Van Velsor, Moxley, and Bunker 2004). They view training as only one component of the development process and have expanded their portfolios to include targeted stretch assignments, developmental relationships, and 360-degree feedback; in short, the full range of developmental experiences described (Van Velsor et al. 2004).

### Address Specific Human Capital Challenges

Leading global organizations stay alert to human capital challenges. Achieving a more diverse workforce and maintaining global leadership capacity when a large percentage of senior administrators are retiring or will be eligible to retire over the next several years are two issues of particular urgency for federal agencies operating in the global environment. The current demographic shift in the federal workforce and the shift to a global marketplace present an opportunity as well as a challenge. While the retiring cadre of administrators may be less familiar with the need for global leaders, the successor generation has "grown up" in the era of globalization and so will be more receptive to global leadership development practices.

Diversity can be an organizational strength that contributes to achieving results in the global environment. Specifically, organizations that promote and achieve a diverse workplace can attract and retain high-quality employees wherever they are. For public organizations, this translates into effective delivery of essential services to communities with diverse needs.

Leading global organizations understand that they must support their employees in learning how to effectively interact with and manage people in a diverse workplace. They recognize the impact that diverse clients will have on the success or failure of an organization. In an effort to foster an environment responsive to the needs of diverse groups of employees, leading global organizations identify opportunities to train managers in techniques that create a work environment that maximizes the ability of all employees to fully contribute to the organization's mission (McCauley and Douglas 2004).

> The United Kingdom's Cabinet Office created Pathways, a two-year program that identifies and develops senior managers from ethnic minority populations who have the potential to reach the senior civil service within three to five years. The program is intended to achieve the governmental goal to double (from 1.6 percent to 3.2 percent) the representation of ethnic minorities in the service by 2005. Pathways provides administrator coaching, skills training and the chance for participants to demonstrate their potential and talent through a variety of developmental activities, such as projects and short-term work placements (GAO 2003).

Global leadership development programs should link and contribute to diversity by providing program participants with training and experiences that develop diversity competencies such as diversity awareness. At the Internal Revenue Service, diversity awareness is defined as having the following attributes:

- Values and embraces diversity.
- Demonstrates confidence in self and others.
- Considers different perspectives and experiences of the workforce and customers.
- Ensures that the organization builds on these differences and that employees and customers are treated in a fair and equitable manner" (Thompson and Rainey 2003, pp. 51–52).

This competency includes:

- *Willing to Learn from Others.* Solicits ideas and opinions to help form specific decisions or plans. Demonstrates self-confidence. Promotes team cooperation, showing positive regard for others who are different from oneself.
- *Open to Diversity.* Respects, treats with courtesy, and relates well to people of diverse backgrounds. Is sensitive to, and shows tolerance for, others' views. Applies knowledge of equal employment opportunity rules and regulations to promote and maintain a fair work environment.
- *Values Diverse Perspectives.* Encourages group members to contribute. Values and encourages contributions from others who have varying perspectives, experiences, or needs. Understands the underlying causes

for someone's feelings, behaviors, or concerns. Promotes consensus decision making.
- *Fosters Diversity.* Uses understanding of others to create an environment that values, encourages, and learns from various perspectives and experiences. Works to resolve conflicts between individuals with diverse perspectives. Models behavior that demonstrates the importance of diversity and supports diversity efforts.

(Thompson and Rainey 2003, p. 52)

### *Evaluate the Impact*

Because global leadership development is a function for which organizations invest significant resources, it is absolutely critical that the impacts of this function be assessed. Assessment is needed for the dual purpose of continuously improving and determining whether these functions effectively support individual and organization performance.

When succession planning and leadership development programs are aligned and move away from the "replacement" mindset of the past, measuring success becomes a long-term matter. No longer is it sufficient to know who could replace the chief administrator officer; instead, an organization must know whether the right people are moving at the right pace, into the right jobs, at the right time, and doing the right thing over time. In addition, organizations need to know for which jobs individuals are being groomed to avoid stretching the candidate pool too thin.

Leading organizations always assess the impact of their leadership development process. The Kirkpatrick Four-Level Model of Evaluation (participant reaction, knowledge acquired, behavioral change, and business results) is typical (Kirkpatrick 1994). Participants, human resources development staff, consultants, and sometimes financial staff conduct the assessments, the last weighing program expenditures' return on investment.

Generally, there are four essential steps in the evaluation process: (1) identifying key stakeholders, (2) performing needs assessment, (3) designing the evaluation, and (4) implementing the evaluation. The crucial point is that initiative design and the evaluation ideally should occur together, as part of an iterative process, so that each can be modified as necessary and the two pieces can be integrated (Martineau 2004).

### Conduct Systematic Program Management

Leading organizations build on their program management activities by developing an integrated and systematic program management process for succession planning and leadership development programs. This process can contribute to maintaining and improving the programs by addressing how the organization:

- Develops annual and longer-term training and developmental activities based on skills and competencies that the current and future workforce needs, and the degree to which training and development can address competency gaps;
- Identifies the appropriate level of investment to provide for succession planning, training, and development efforts, and prioritizes funding so that the most important needs are addressed first;
- Incorporates employees' developmental needs and goals in its planning processes and develops a business case for succession planning, training, and development solutions, setting forth expected costs and benefits of the performance improvement investment and providing decision makers with essential information needed to allocate necessary resources;
- Provides an appropriate mix of centralized and decentralized approaches for developing and delivering leadership development activities;
- Collects data and monitors implementation of specific succession planning and leadership development programs and activities in its strategic organizational and human capital plans; and
- Assesses, reports, and uses workforce profile and other data to help ensure that strategic and tactical changes are promptly incorporated in succession planning, training, and development efforts.

**Conclusion**

The most important elements of any successful organizational improvement initiative are the demonstrated commitment of top leaders to change and effective management to support leadership. Leaders and managers are primarily responsible for the success of global leadership development initiatives because they:

- Provide the visibility and commit the time and necessary resources;
- Communicate the organization's support for these functions in newsletters, policy statements, speeches, meetings, and websites;
- Send a clear message to others in the organization about the seriousness and business relevance of leadership development; and
- Create and maintain a leadership culture that differentiates individual performance.

Developing global leaders cannot happen in a vacuum. Global leadership development should be rooted in an organization's systems and processes such that all employees can develop to their fullest potential, take initiative, and:

- Act more like owners and entrepreneurs than employees or hired hands;
- Solve problems and act with a sense of urgency;
- Accept responsibility for meeting commitments and living the values of the organization;
- Share a common global leadership philosophy and language that include tolerance for contrary views and a willingness to experiment; and
- Create, maintain, and adhere to systems and procedures designed to measure and reward these distributed leadership behaviors. (O'Toole 2001)

The net result of all the above is a high-performance organizational culture with a global orientation that encourages talented people—at all levels—to take initiative in reaching their full potential.

There is urgency for public organizations to create and sustain such a culture. The combined and accelerating forces of globalization and technology have forged an increasingly interconnected world in which changes and threats—and the need to anticipate and respond to them—are both faster and more complex. More than ever before, the international and domestic issues and actions are inextricably linked. U.S. economic, military, and cultural power and influence made us a growing global presence by default well before 9/11, and therefore federal organizations and the people who lead them were finding themselves increasingly thrust into the global context.

A recent panel of professionals whose mission is to improve federal government performance stated:

> The most significant and challenging role and function changes facing federal managers in the twenty-first century involve increasing complexity of program missions and external environment . . . advancing technology . . . increased pace of change and need for speed; the increasing interdependency among federal agencies, private sector, and even global organizations . . . new expectations regarding accountability . . . shifting government-wide priorities (e.g., homeland security). (O'Toole 2001)

Indeed, the twenty-first century may very well become known as the century of the "global world" (McFarland, Senen, and Childress 1993).

# References

Bellamy, R. 2006. *Program Manager for Leadership and Knowledge Management.* U.S. Office of Personnel Management. Interview with Sydney Smith-Heimbrock.

Bikson, T. K., and G. F. Treverton. 2003. *New Challenges for International Leadership: Positioning the United States for the 21st Century* (Issue Paper). Santa Monica, CA: RAND Corporation.

Collins, Francis S., Eric D. Green, Alan E. Guttmacher, and Mark S. Guyer. 2003. "A Vision for the Future of Genomics Research." *Nature* 422 (24 April): 1–13.

Conger, J. A., and R. M. Fulmer. 2003. "Developing Your Leadership Pipeline." *Harvard Business Review* 81(12): 76–84.

Crabtree, H. R. 2001. "Take Me to Your Leader." In *Advances in Global Leadership,* eds. W. H. Mobley and M. W. McCall Jr., vol. 2, 49–75. New York: Elsevier Science.

Dorfman, Peter W. 2003. "Introduction." In *Advances in Global Leadership,* eds. W. H. Mobley and M. W. McCall Jr., 3–7. New York: Elsevier Science.

Fulmer, R. M., P. A. Gibbs, and M. Goldsmith. 2000. "Developing Leaders: How Winning Companies Keep on Winning." *MIT Sloan Management Review* 42(1): 49–59.

Gandossy, R., and M. Efron. 2004. *Leading the Way: Three Truths from the Top Companies for Leaders.* Hoboken, NJ: John Wiley and Sons.

Goleman, D. 2005. *Emotional Intelligence.* New York: Bantam Books.

Green, Stephen, Fred Hassan, Jeffrey Immelt, Michael Marks, and Daniel Meiland. 2003. "In Search of Global Leaders." *Harvard Business Review* 81(8): 38–45.

Greenberg-Walt, C. L., and A. G. Robertson. 2001. "The Evolving Role of Administrator Leadership." In *The Future of Leadership: Today's Top Leadership Thinkers Speak to Tomorrow's Leaders,* eds. W. Bennis, G. M. Spreitzer, and T. G. Cummings. San Francisco: Jossey-Bass.

Guthrie, V. A., and S. N. King. 2004. "Feedback-intensive Programs." In *The Center for Creative Leadership Handbook of Leadership Development,* eds. C. D. McCauley and E. Van Velsor, 2nd ed., 25–58. San Francisco: Jossey-Bass Wiley.

Hesselbein, F., ed. 2006. "Moving Peter Drucker's Works and Wisdom Around the World." *Leader to Leader* 41(Summer): 4-6.

Hollenbeck, G. P. 2001. "A Serendipitous Sojourn Through the Global Leadership Literature." In *Advances in Global Leadership,* eds. W. H. Mobley and M. W. McCall Jr., vol. 2, 15–48. New York: Elsevier Science.

Hollenbeck, G. P., and M. W. McCall. 2003. "Competence, Not Competencies: Making Global Administrator Development Work." In *Advances in Global Leadership,* eds. W. H. Mobley and P. W. Dorfman, vol. 3, 101–119. New York: Elsevier Science.

Hormats, R. D. 2003. "Abraham Lincoln and the Global Economy." *Harvard Business Review* 81(8): 58–67.

Kesner, Idalene F., Susan Burnett, Mike Morrison, Noel M. Tichy, and David Owens. 2003. "Leadership Development: Perk or Priority?" *Harvard Business Review* 81(5): 29–38.

Kettl, D. F. 2005. "The Next Government of the United States: Challenges for Performance in the 21st Century." Transformation of Organizations Series. Washington, DC: IBM Center for the Business of Government.

Kirkpatrick, D. 1994. *Evaluating Training Programs: The Four Levels.* San Francisco: Berrett Koehler.

Lawler, E. E., III. 2001. "The Era of Human Capital Has Finally Arrived." In *The Future of Leadership: Today's Top Leadership Thinkers Speak to Tomorrow's Leaders,* eds. W. Bennis and G. M. Spreitzer, 14–25. San Francisco: Jossey Bass.

Martineau, J. W. 2004. "Evaluating the Impact of Leader Development." In *The Center for Creative Leadership Handbook of Leadership Development*, eds. C. D. McCauley and E. Van Velsor, 2nd ed., 234–269. San Francisco: Jossey-Bass Wiley.

McCauley, C. D., and C. A. Douglas. 2004. "Developmental Relationships." In *The Center for Creative Leadership Handbook of Leadership Development*, eds. C. D. McCauley and E. Van Velsor, 2nd ed., 85–116. San Francisco: Jossey-Bass Wiley.

McFarland, L.J., S. Senen, and J. R. Childress. 1993. *Twenty-First Century Leadership*. New York: Leadership Press.

Ohlott, P. 2004. "Job Assignments." In *The Center for Creative Leadership Handbook of Leadership Development*, eds. C. D. McCauley and E. Van Velsor, 2nd ed., 151–183. San Francisco: Jossey-Bass Wiley.

O'Toole, J. 2001. "When Leadership Is an Organizational Trait." In *The Future of Leadership: Today's Top Leadership Thinkers Speak to Tomorrow's Leaders*, eds. W. Bennis and G. M. Spreitzer, 158–177. San Francisco: Jossey Bass.

Ready, D. A. 2004. "How to Grow Great Leaders." *Harvard Business Review* 82(12): 92–100.

Senge, P. 2006. "Systems Citizenship: The Leadership Mandate for This Millennium." *Leader to Leader* 41(Summer): 21–26.

Shrader, A. R., ed. 2006. "Celebrating Ten Years of Leader to Leader." *Leader to Leader* 41(Summer): 7–10.

Sirota, D., L. A. Mischkind, and M. I. Meltzer. 2005. *The Enthusiastic Employee*. Philadelphia, PA: Wharton School Publishing.

Steinhardt, B. 2006. *Director of Strategic Issues*. U.S. Government Accountability Office. Interview with Sydney Smith-Heimbrock.

Stewart, T. A. 2001. "Trust Me on This." In *The Future of Leadership: Today's Top Leadership Thinkers Speak to Tomorrow's Leaders*, eds. W. Bennis and G.M. Spreitzer, 67–81. San Francisco: Jossey Bass.

Stewart, T. A., and L. O'Brien. 2005. "Execution Without Excuses." *Harvard Business Review* 83(3): 102–110.

Thomas, D. A., and R. J. Ely. 2001. "Making Differences Matter." *Harvard Business Review on Managing Diversity*. Cambridge: Harvard Business School Publishing.

Thompson, James R., and Hal G. Rainey. 2003. *Modernizing Human Resource Management in the Federal Government: The IRS Model*. Washington, DC: IBM Endowment for the Business of Government.

United Nations. 2003. *Leadership and Social Transformation in the Public Sector: Moving from Challenges to Solutions*. New York: UN Publications.

U. S. Government Accountability Office (GAO). 2003. *Human Capital: Insights for U.S. Agencies from Other Countries' Succession Planning and Management Initiatives*. Report GAO-03-914 (September). Washington, DC. Available at http://www.gao.gov/htext/d03914.html (accessed November 27, 2007).

Van Velsor, E., R. S. Moxley, and K. A. Bunker. 2004. "The Leader Development Process." In *The Center for Creative Leadership Handbook of Leadership Development*, eds. C. D. McCauley and E. Van Velsor, 204–234. San Francisco: Jossey-Bass Wiley.

# 10

## Government Personnel

### Foreign Affairs

Thomas R. Pickering

Our nation continues to face many challenges and crises. Some of the most pressing and dangerous are outside our borders. Having the right people correctly prepared to meet and deal with these challenges is a central requirement for our national security. This is a complex task and involves seeking and developing many attributes, talents, and skills not part of a regular bureaucracy devoted to administering the large, complex area of the internal administration of our government. In this chapter I want to look at some of those requirements in detail and to propose some solutions. I hope to draw not only from my experience in the U.S. Foreign Service but also from time spent in the private sector.

Foreign affairs and national security is complex work, even in simple countries with simple economies. In large states with varied interests and significant engagements around the globe, it is doubly complex. But there are some useful overall precepts that can help guide the basic approach to the issues.

In the United States, many departments and agencies of government play a role in this activity. Each of them has charge of its own hiring, training, and promotion of personnel. Some have joined the State Department (State) in using the Foreign Service and its special, more flexible rules and approaches to meet the special needs of working outside the United States. Others have attempted to adapt and modify traditional civil service rules and requirements to meet those needs. State itself is staffed by both services, and in recent years there has been more mixing and matching to meet our overseas staffing requirements than previously was the case.

Second, it is important that in carrying forward this work, it be done under an umbrella of clearly understood objectives and goals. A system for making this clear is in place—put there in part by the National Security Act of 1947, as amended. It plays a useful role in setting up a structure for decision making and implementation. Over the years, there has been much debate over the success and failures in this system. Recent studies have indicated both when it works and why it has failed. The current U.S. approach is postulated on interagency cooperation, led by the national security advisor on behalf of the president and on presidential decision making after meetings, reviews, and recommendations by the leaders of the major departments and agencies. The specific elements of the process in the area of national security policy are decided by each presidential administration, usually in the form of an initial directive prepared at the outset of the administration.

Some have seen it as too restrictive, some as too loose. Some have complained that too much detail is pushed too high in the bureaucracy and too little preparatory and spadework is done in preparation for meetings and decisions. Others have argued, given the sensitivity of the decision making and implementation process, that consideration needs to be at a high level—cabinet officers or their immediate deputies—to ensure that the President is being well served and his or her policies are effectively being carried out.

Two points are clear here: each president will determine what he or she wishes to have in place as a system to do this and who will staff and serve him or her in that system. There will not be full satisfaction on the part of all departments and agencies with any one system.

A third point is also key: strong presidential leadership is required to ensure that a compatible group of advisors is chosen or that the system with varying and different views is operated on an efficient basis. This requires a strong national security advisor or a presidential determination to make *primus inter pares* one or more of his or her major cabinet secretaries or advisors for a particular subject area or issue.

In the end, any system and its personnel need to be judged at rock bottom on the ability to meet the first stricture of the medical profession expressed in the Hippocratic oath: "First of all, do no harm."

## Knowledge Requirements

It should go without saying that cultural, ethnic, language, and religious knowledge, along with a background in the history, politics, and economics of major countries and regions, is the foundation for successful foreign policy leadership. While geographic orientation has been the bedrock of our foreign policy, in today's rapidly changing world, the need for functional knowledge around specific areas—space cooperation, labor law, international finance questions, and the environment, to name a few—is also essential for success.

Without these capacities, the capability to deal effectively with complex issues will be lacking and the credibility of our diplomats and others will be broadly questioned and widely suspect.

What does this mean in practical terms? You will need to learn about and absorb as much of the culture in which you will be working as you possibly can. There are many ways to do this, and some will be addressed later. However, circumstances will arise when you will be asked and will want to know, "I wonder why they did that." Cultural background can often help explain the answer.

The need to understand and be able to explain what issues and ideas on the other side will impact your own objectives and goals in dealing with them will be more complex as well. This is explicitly true in problem solving, but it is more subtly true in anticipating reactions to policy choices that you might recommend and that your government might accept. Often these historical and cultural lessons can be overlooked or forgotten and, for extraneous reasons, help seriously set back or doom a policy you might otherwise feel to be fully in the national interest.

Simple examples abound. Suggesting that a non-French speaker might be a good candidate for secretary-general of the UN ignores the fact that the French, with a veto over the selection, have always insisted on good knowledge of the French language as a criterion for selection.

These requirements for knowledge and proficiency fit closely with many of the key tasks that need to be performed in foreign affairs and the national security field—whether collecting, reporting on, and analyzing information; delivering U.S. views to a foreign interlocutor; negotiating agreements or an end to a problem or crisis; or just performing the myriad tasks that are required to keep an embassy afloat and operating.

One special area of knowledge requires a few additional comments. Language and language skills are very significant to success. Most foreign diplomats know English better than we know their languages. The advantages of understanding and speaking a foreign language are substantial. Most foreigners feel complimented by the effective use of their language by non-native speakers. Catching nuances, checking interpretation, being able discuss things face-to-face without need for interpretation all help to speed the work and enable innovation and creativity when the time comes or the need arises. Many negotiations have broken down on the basis of linguistic misunderstandings, but some have been rescued through persistent work by multilingual diplomats.

Other advantages are less obvious. I have always felt that language learning provided clues about patterns of thought and ways of thinking in foreign societies. These are subtle, but important. One locus in which it is sometimes easier to see this point immediately is in the use of idiomatic expressions, often for concepts that in other languages are translated with straightforward, direct word-for-word expressions. Russians use an expression that means "with me" to express "I have" in English.

The need for avoiding gaffes and faux pas, which sometimes make diplomatic success harder, is perhaps easier to see. This may be true even among English speakers, where I learned what words in American English were acceptable in Australia and which ones were not.

There are also clear differences in the level of language skills. Some are adequate for finding your way in travel, others for social conversation, and still others for complex diplomatic and other forms of business. A good diplomat learns not to confuse them and insists on an interpreter if he or she is going to be in over his or her head. And indeed, in many foreign offices as a matter of national pride, diplomats from that country will insist on speaking their language with you even if they know English well.

Working with an interpreter is also an acquired skill. While good interpreters can handle long monologues, short bites work best. Making sure the interpreter knows the subject matter and understands as much of the context as possible is also valuable. Some of the best interpreters can handle conversation on a "voice-over" basis, almost as if they were using electronic equipment and headphones to convey the conversation. Don't try to correct your interpreters in the middle of a conversation, but do consult with them quietly if you have any doubts. Their credibility and yours will be enhanced. Some have seen the successful use of interpreters—even if you know the foreign language—as a way to get two bites of the apple. For most practiced diplomats, this is an advantage but not a huge one, because your knowledge of the issue—what you already know about it—is what counts and cannot easily be supplemented from outside sources in the middle of a discussion.

For those spending more than a year abroad in a foreign environment and who hope to work successfully, language study or already established capacity is a wise requirement. Most people underestimate the difficulty in learning a foreign language well. There are many aspects—pronunciation, grammatical control, and mastery of vocabulary, among others. Some are gifted in this area while others are not, although my experience has been that the more you study foreign languages, the more you find parallels and other clues that will help. Latin languages and Semitic languages, respectively, have many vocabulary items in common, but one always needs to be aware of "false friends"—words that may be the same in pronunciation but that have different meanings from one language to the next.

Language study also can be stressful. Years ago I read a newspaper story about the Marine Corps wanting to test a platoon's ability to deal with stress. The formula they came up with was to isolate them together and give them two weeks of intensive Spanish language training. The stress level was very high, especially at the end, which proved the point.

## Skills and Their Development

There are many skills that can serve well in diplomacy and in dealing with foreign colleagues and friends.

Listening is one of these. Many of us want to control the conversation, do most of the speaking, and ignore or fail to understand the value of hearing what the other side is thinking and saying. Until you can master their side, you cannot begin the process of making the suggestions, steps, proposals, or promotions of the ideas that will bring them around to your side.

Skill at understanding the other side's case and preparing your own is also an acquired attribute. You need practice, as well as some assistance and training, to do this well. What questions to ask, how to prepare the conversational field, and how to respond are all part of paving the road to success, just as much as making a successful first strike pitch. And indeed, almost all first strike pitches end up in failure unless and until you understand not only what is on the mind of the other side, but also where they are vulnerable and where they will need to realign their case to meet your concerns and criticisms. Understanding that approach is the beginning of the development of the people skills that are necessary in diplomacy.

Humor is another attribute well worth cultivating. However, one has to be careful. Humor doesn't translate easily. Humor has its own cultural boundaries that are not easily crossed. Humor about the subject you are both dealing with is better and likely to have a positive result than humor that is metaphorical and abstract.

Finally, in personal relationships you should always keep your eye on the objective. Often the objective is not to "win" the debate but rather to bring the other side's thinking on an issue closer to your own. Many tend to forget this and as a result waste much meeting time and a lot of good effort.

## Negotiations

Negotiations are a special area of activity that requires much experience, training, and skill to conduct successfully. While different fields of negotiation have different ways of going forward, many of the skills and techniques will work across a spectrum of fields if carefully deployed.

To begin, you need to know your objective clearly. This means that you must have a good idea of what your side will settle for on the issue. You must also begin to have a good idea of what the other side will find acceptable. Early discussions sometimes help to clarify this. Often in complex subjects, early discussions will remove illusions about how simple or easy it will be to bring the sides together.

Negotiations on behalf of governments are often many-sided. In the United States, it is often true that the Executive Branch is not fully in accord on where to come out. This creates allies and opponents for the negotiators on their own side, and they must skillfully manage those differences to find what will be an acceptable result. Congress also plays a large role here, especially if treaty ratification or legislative action for implementation is required. On the other side, the situation can be equally if not more complex.

Many still approach negotiations as if compromises may not be required. While there is a difference between what is said between the sides in negotiations and the reality that a compromise will be needed to resolve the issue, the latter reality must be absorbed by the negotiator and his or her principal sources of instruction in the government. The trick often is to find—as much as can be accomplished—a "win-win" solution. Most tough issues won't produce one of these easily or they wouldn't be tough issues requiring hard work to reach a settlement.

It is a good idea to canvass in detail, even if you have to do this alone or with a trusted confidant, those issues on which you can give, those on which you believe the other side can give, and what general shape the settlement can take. You can then often put together packages of proposals over time to make that happen.

You should also be aware of the cultural requirements of negotiation. Even in the straightforward West, as opposed to the more bazaar-oriented East, some haggling, some give and take, and some time must pass before a deal can be struck so that at a minimum the negotiators can claim to have done their job. This makes negotiating under very tight time pressure much more difficult, but the needs to meet the process requirements are often dictated by the negotiating circumstances as much as they are about standard views on timing. President Clinton, in a one-day negotiation with Nawaz Sharif, then prime minister of Pakistan, was able to secure an agreement to retreat from a Pakistani military incursion into Indian-held Kashmir on July 4, 1999. The time pressure helped, although many feel that the deal later led to Sharif's demise as prime minister.

The negotiating process is also interesting and, if extended, provides many opportunities for movement forward and new tactical considerations. Some of these include:

- private side conversations;
- ways to mobilize leverage;
- when to break off the talks or threaten to break off the talks;
- ways to counter the other side when it threatens to break off or does break off;

- when to introduce new ideas or approaches;
- how to keep the process synchronized by managing your side and the other side's approaches and activities;
- how and what to report about what is going on, and how to shape the outcome without misleading;
- how to break bad news to the other side or back home;
- whom to rely on for advice and support above and below your own level;
- who are your allies—on your side and on the other side—and who are your opponents;
- how to gauge and improve the value of personal chemistry in the process;
- what arguments are effective and which are failing and why, and whether there are new or unseen facets of an issue that can have tactical significance; and
- what do you do when the process gets really stuck?

The latter point is an interesting one. It is best addressed by a statement that I first heard from then Secretary of State George Shultz: "When you are in a deep hole, stop digging." In effect, it means that on one plane you have two options. One is to widen the deal and see if by bringing in more elements you can find a way to break the deadlock. A second is to narrow the deal, and by paring away divisive and irreconcilable elements, you can find a way to get to a positive conclusion. Both tactics have advantages and disadvantages.

On widening, you can increase the number of divisive points and, if you are not careful, make the process harder to handle. Another way of expressing this is that you have added too many moving parts in the deal for the other side, and sometimes your own, to absorb and make use of creativity to reach a solution.

On the other hand, paring down the number of elements can help but may leave key elements of the deal unresolved with the more difficult issues staying on the table. One example is in 1962, early in the Kennedy administration, when the United States was looking for a comprehensive nuclear test ban treaty. It was hard going. To make real progress the United States offered the Soviet Union a treaty covering tests in all areas except for those underground. We achieved early success in the limited treaty, but a comprehensive treaty has still escaped us even though there is a current commitment to a moratorium on all testing for most nuclear powers.

In sum, negotiations require much study, practice, learning, and preparation. Much of modern diplomacy still involves a great deal of learning on the job. It is true that some new and innovative courses are being offered within the government, especially at the State Department's National Foreign Affairs Training Center in Arlington, Virginia, and at universities and graduate schools around the country, but much still depends on participating and observing skilled and experienced players in action.

There are also a wide series of personal qualities to be looked for in finding successful practitioners of this art. Many are the same we look for in the domestic governmental arena, but some, mentioned above, include a devotion to and serious interest in the profession, background knowledge, interest in world events and developments, analytical ability, language skills, and strong "people" capabilities.

## Interagency Relations

Teamwork and the ability to mobilize, work with, and lead teams is important, as is the ability to efficiently manage organizations and their activities.

Throughout this process, the U.S. government is fortunate to have embassies, missions, and consulates in place around the world that are generally staffed by employees who have learned the profession well and can be relied on to perform. They are centers of interagency activity in the best sense of the word. The ambassador is charged with all U.S. relationships with a foreign country or international organization, except for those of a military commander engaged in active combat. This means that interagency teaming in the field is often ahead of where it is in Washington, DC. This raises new and exceptional challenges.

Over the last four years of the Clinton administration it was my pleasure to frequently address senior-level groups of government officials from my own and other agencies, including new ambassadors going out to the field and Department of Defense participants in the capstone course for newly minted general and flag officers. Invariably, this gave me an opportunity to talk about an issue that disturbed me: the lack of a pattern and process for organizing cooperation between the military and civilian portions of the U.S. government, particularly in pre- and post-conflict situations.

I noted that our military colleagues had worked over the past three decades in building "jointness" in our military operations—full cooperation between the services in dealing with combat operations and related activities. This now had to be amplified and enlarged, first by the addition of U.S. civilian activities and then by the further addition of international players, including organizations such as the United Nations and our allies and friends. This would be much harder, take longer, and requires a level of commitment, which was then and is still to some extent today absent from our government. Unfortunately, Bosnia, Kosovo, Afghanistan, and now Iraq have condemned us repeatedly to relearn in a painful way what the lack of such coordination can mean for success or failure in these operations.

And in mentioning preconflict situations, I was as serious as in mentioning postconflict activities. The use of diplomacy, backed by military force to resolve a conflict before it breaks out into fighting, is an important part of our national security effort. This in turn involves working out the coordination arrangements, the command-and-control activities, the method of mutual support, and many other details. The State Department, with congressional backing, has organized an office to deal with these issues, which is a good if slow start.

To be successful in this arena requires excellent people who are well schooled in a wide variety of skills, including politico-military relations. In that regard, commitment at the top is essential. Training and the use of games and simulations can go far to carry the process forward. The development of operational procedures, communications networks, doctrine, and theories of employment are all necessary. In the Clinton administration, PD-96, the politico-military scenario and assessment paper, marked a good beginning for successful activities of this type, but there is still a significant void and much catching up to do to avoid fighting the last war all over again as we address increasingly complex problems.

## Career Considerations

Early on I referred to the Foreign Service. It provides a flexible tool for the development of cadres on the civil side to deal with the problems of the new diplomacy or, as Secretary Rice has called it, transformational diplomacy. The service is much like the military, with rank in person rather than position, a commitment to assignment anywhere around the world, and frequent changes of assignment to avoid "localitis" overseas or too much U.S.-based perspective in this country. All officers are regularly considered after short periods of service in the present grade for promotion based on a selection board of Foreign Service officers slightly senior to them, which also includes an outside "public" member and another from one of the other U.S. foreign affairs agencies.

Members of the Foreign Service receive training in many of the skills they need, but also must pass a highly competitive test of their knowledge and capacity in the foreign affairs area to enter. New opportunities are opening up in this country as we pay increasing attention to our declining language skills. The terrorist attacks of September 11, 2001, brought home the extreme short of expertise in languages such as Arabic, Farsi/Dari, Urdu, and Malay, to name just a few.

The business community is also becoming more aware of these needs and personnel requirements. After retiring from the government in 2000 I spent five years with the Boeing Company, building a capacity at the corporate level to support the further globalization of a large company that traditionally has been the United States' largest exporter. Here, unlike the government, we had the opportunity to search for and hire non-Americans in an effort to build our relationships overseas.

Our focus was to support the sales and marketing activities of the firm and to develop new opportunities to work overseas in areas such as information technology in India, engineering and designing new airplanes in Russia, and the manufacturing of aircraft assemblies in Japan and China.

Our strategy was to build a program around three words beginning with the letter "p": people, presence, and process. People were by far the most important for us, and I believe the same is true for the government. We sought the best we could find and looked for people with good access to the government and industry in twenty selected countries. While of the first ten hired, five came from within Boeing, most of the next fifteen came from outside the United States.

Presence related to two factors: the selection of proper locations within which to work—countries with large markets and strong capabilities to contribute to aircraft design and manufacturing—and the setting up of a team built around members representing all Boeing activities in that country, the "country team" concept borrowed from the State Department.

Process was the need to construct a Boeing strategy for the country, spearheaded by the leader we had chosen and used by that leader to build the Boeing team in and around the country or region.

One of our most challenging issues was how to integrate these leaders back into the business organization at home in the United States. It has taken time, but we have done so through a series of tactics with a significant measure of success.

**Conclusion**

Foreign affairs is one of the most challenging areas of personnel management and training. Highly skilled and capable people are needed for important leadership positions for the country and its businesses. New ways of doing business are constantly emerging. To keep up with those challenges, a broad understanding of the field and the processes and ways of doing business are essential. Government has much to learn from the private sector, but in international relations, perhaps the private sector has even more to learn from government. How well we fare in the future will depend heavily on our educational system. Nowhere can we afford to ignore or to fail in the necessary preparation of our young people to meet the challenges they will face. Finally, we must build and strengthen our in-house capabilities at training and improve our interagency working relations if we are to meet the heavy burdens that the twenty-first century is placing on us all.

# 11

## Competency for Global Leadership

### Experience of the U.S. Foreign Service

Daniel Spikes

The Foreign Service Act of 1980, which governs the organization and management of the Foreign Service of the United States, requires the Department of State (State) and other foreign affairs agencies to establish precepts for selection boards to use in the evaluation and promotion of members of the Foreign Service. State, the federal agency with the largest number of Foreign Service employees, defines those precepts as skills in six broad categories with detailed subcategories (see Table 11.1 at end of this chapter). These standards, commonly known as "core precepts" or "core competencies," include leadership skills, managerial skills, interpersonal skills, communication and foreign language skills, intellectual skills, and substantive knowledge. The precepts are important because they illustrate the competencies State requires in its Foreign Service employees and because they form the basis for their individual assessment in annual performance reviews. Management and labor, represented by the American Foreign Service Association, regularly discuss the precepts to ensure that descriptions are current; however, the six basic categories have remained constant for over twenty-five years. State incorporates the core precepts in counseling, evaluation, and training, and employees, who must confront them every year in their evaluation reports, are familiar with their substance. This system, which involves considerable time and effort from all concerned, provides the department and its Foreign Service with a competitive, merit-based personnel system of long standing. It also provides an interesting example of what the leading U.S. foreign affairs agency regards as the competencies for global leadership in the modern world.

State presents the competencies in a chart with the six skill groups divided into subcategories, with the level of accomplishment expected for each at different grades; that is, entry level (generally through FS-04 [GS-11 equivalent]), midlevel (generally through FS-01 [GS-15 equivalent]), and senior level (FE-OC and above [SES equivalents]). The standards, in each case, are progressive and cumulative: as employees advance in grade, the development of their skills and abilities must follow suit if they expect to compete successfully for promotion in their careers. In 2005, State also established a program of career development that is being phased in over several years for employees who wish to compete for promotion into the Senior Foreign Service. The career development program, which complements the existing standards of the core precepts, encourages employees to acquire experience over time in a way that State deems important for success as senior managers. The program requires officers to gain breadth of experience through service in different regions and functions, to demonstrate abilities as leaders and managers, to sustain proficiency in foreign languages, and to take assignments to posts where there is a critical service need. The six categories of the core precepts, which naturally lie behind the principles of career development, are straightforward enough and by themselves do not add much, if anything, to what a reasonable person might suppose would be needed for employees in almost any profession. A short review of the subcategories and their contents, however, provides a larger and more informative picture.

*Leadership Skills* include subcategories for innovation, decision making, teamwork, openness to dissent, and institution building. In each case, the emphasis is on the creative and critical application of experience to making decisions, acting on them, and being responsible for their consequences. The emphasis is not only on individual accountability but also on being a member or leader of teams and knowing how to present or accept dissenting views. *Managerial Skills* embrace organizational effectiveness, management of personnel and material resources, customer service, support for equal opportunity and merit principles, and proper treatment of classified information. Some of the key ideas in this section are accountability, commitment and courage, achievement of goals and objectives, adequate internal controls, and support for diversity at all levels. The section on *Interpersonal Skills* covers abilities and behaviors that include persuasion, negotiation, and representational skills, as well as adaptability and perceptiveness in the workplace. The subcategory on representational skills includes a sine qua non of diplomatic service—the ability to identify, cultivate, influence, and assess persons and institutions that are important to U.S. interests. *Communication and Foreign Language Skills* naturally include the ability to speak, write, and listen with a purpose. This section also covers the requirements for foreign language skills, another basic distinction of the Foreign Service, as well as the ability to participate in public outreach, including through the media, as part of the responsibility of Foreign Service officers to participate in public diplomacy work abroad. *Intellectual Skills* include the ability to collect, evaluate, analyze, and present information, to identify and address key issues, and to formulate policy options. This section also stresses the need to improve those skills through training, education, and other forms of professional development. *Substantive Knowledge* essentially covers technical skills and the knowledge of how institutions work and relate to one another. This category also has an important subcategory titled "knowledge of foreign cultures," which stresses the need to understand the cultural, political, economic, and public norms of other countries.

The distinguishing features of the competencies for the Foreign Service fall into three broad categories: (1) those that are common to most professions, (2) those that are institutionally specific to State or to the federal government more generally, and (3) those that are professionally specific to the Foreign Service, however much they might be applied fairly to other groups as well. The majority of competencies, such as accountability, managing for results, teamwork, leadership skills, communications skills, and technical knowledge, are common ones. The same is true for the support of diversity and merit principles. Respect for dissent and the expectation that employees will contribute to the development of their colleagues and to the vitality of State as an institution may not be unique to State, but the principles they embody certainly have formed an increasingly important part of the culture of State and its employees in recent years. More interesting, however, are the passages on skills and abilities that lie at the heart of diplomatic work at home and abroad: substantive knowledge and appreciation for foreign cultures and societies, foreign language skills, identification and cultivation of persons and institutions, analytical and policy skills, and participation in public advocacy overseas for U.S. policies and positions. These are basic and reasonable requirements, easy to assert but more difficult to attain, that anyone with responsibility for international issues, however slight or intermittent, would do well to consider.

# Appendix

## Decision Criteria for Tenure and Promotion in the Foreign Service

The core precepts provide the guidelines by which selection boards determine the tenure and promotability of U.S. Foreign Service employees. These precepts will be in effect for the 2005–2006, 2006–2007, and 2007–2008 rating cycles. The precepts reflect the principles of the Career Development Program, with its emphasis on operational effectiveness, leadership and management effectiveness, sustained professional language and/or technical proficiency, and responsiveness to service needs.

The precepts enlarge upon the headings found in existing Employee Evaluation Report (EER) forms, defining the specific skills to be considered and the level of accomplishment expected at different grades. They distinguish between apprentice, journeyman, and master level—the junior-, mid-, and senior-level ranks.

The precepts are arranged in a grid; the left column defines the skill; the progressive possession and exercise of that skill are captured in boxes from left to right. The skills are cumulative; the descriptions for each level assume the employee has mastered those at the lower level(s). The rating employee should review descriptions at lower levels before making an evaluation. For example, in rating a mid-level employee, the rating employee should review the descriptions both for "mid-level" and for "entry-level."

Because progression in some specialist skill codes is capped at the midlevels, the senior Foreign Service column does not apply to those specialists.

Table 11.1

**Decision Criteria for Tenure and Promotion in the Foreign Service**

**Leadership Skills**

| Entry Level | Mid Level | Senior Level |
|---|---|---|
| **Innovation** | | |
| Takes initiative to go beyond assigned tasks; identifies problems and proposes creative solutions; seeks to improve job and organization performance | Develops insights into situations and applies them in the workplace; devises innovative solutions to make organizational improvements and policy adjustments; *engages staff in process of improving effectiveness of organization* | Creates an organization-wide environment that encourages innovation; takes a long-term view and acts as a catalyst for constructive change; conceives and institutes organization-wide policy and program initiatives; anticipates and prepares for the future |
| **Decision Making** | | |
| Identifies issues within context of own job, which require decisions or other action; arrives at recommendations in a logical, orderly manner; acts confidently and decisively within own purview, consulting others as appropriate; is sensitive to needs and opinions of others | Makes reasoned, effective, and timely decisions after considering all relevant factors and options, even when data are limited or conflicting or will produce unpleasant consequences; implements decisions and evaluates their impact and implications, making adjustments as needed | Integrates policy and administrative factors into problem solving and decision making in a manner enhancing the entire organization; *actively works to achieve Department's goals and objectives*; encourages staff to accept responsibility |
| **Teamwork** | | |
| Applies what he/she learns about team building to be an effective team member; is open to views of others; works in collaborative, inclusive, outcome-oriented manner with U.S. and foreign colleagues; accepts team consensus | Is an effective team leader who *creates an environment that facilitates full participation and an open exchange of ideas*; fosters cooperation and collaboration among U.S. and foreign colleagues; motivates and guides team members toward a common goal; *actively develops the skills of subordinates, counsels them, and makes optimum use of their talents* | Is an effective team motivator who inspires all staff to participate and contribute; encourages and develops a *sense of pride* and cohesiveness among staff; resolves work-related problems by mobilizing team skills and resources; *develops and implements strategies to improve the workplace, morale, skills, and achievements of team members* |

| | | |
|---|---|---|
| **Openness to Dissent** Demonstrates the intellectual integrity to speak openly within channels and a willingness to risk criticism to voice sensible dissent; publicly supports official decisions, even when disagreeing with them | Discerns when well-founded dissent is justified; engages in constructive advocacy of policy alternatives; guides staff to do the same | Accords importance to well-founded dissent and defends its appropriate expression |
| **Community Service and Institution Building** Participates actively in outreach or "community service" activities that contribute to employee welfare; for example, volunteers for post or department programs, initiatives, ceremonies, special events, blood and fund drives, and other activities | Participates actively in performance evaluation decision making and resource allocation activities (for example, serves on Selection Boards or on post-EER Review Panel); works on resource allocation committees (for example, Housing Board); counsels/mentors personnel more junior in grade | Participates actively in "institution building" activities that strengthen the Department as an organization (for example, recruits for the Department, serves as Diplomat-in-Residence or on the Board of Examiners); works on the Selection Boards; participates in department mentoring program |

**Managerial Skills**

| Entry Level | Mid Level | Senior Level |
|---|---|---|
| **Operational Effectiveness** Plans, organizes, and directs activities effectively; ensures that projects within area of responsibility are completed in a timely manner; accepts supervision and guidance; provides feedback to supervisors; demonstrates commitment and moral courage by making difficult choices, by working with a sense of purpose, and by caring about the results | Produces results in most effective manner *in accordance with the Department's goals and objectives*; critically analyzes the organization's strengths and weaknesses, and takes appropriate action | Establishes effective management procedures and controls; encourages and rewards efforts of staff to enhance their effectiveness, *including their ability to contribute to the achievement of the Department's goals and objectives*; foresees challenges to, and opportunities for, the organization and takes steps in advance to deal with them |

*(continued)*

Table 11.1 *(continued)*

## Managerial Skills

| Entry Level | Mid Level | Senior Level |
|---|---|---|
| **Performance Management and Evaluation** | | |
| Participates in preparation of work requirements for self and works with staff in preparing their work requirements; develops plans to accomplish work requirements; ensures that staff are appropriately utilized, appraised, and rewarded; gives staff both formal and informal feedback on performance and potential; completes employee evaluations in accordance with standards and deadlines | Establishes *and clearly communicates* broad performance expectations for unit; manages staff effectively, focusing on results; monitors plans to accomplish work requirements; delegates appropriately; creates a productive work environment in which *employee's* contributions are valued and encouraged; *works to prevent and resolve personnel problems in a timely manner,* ensures that the evaluation process is properly conducted and that counseling occurs throughout the rating year | Establishes *and clearly communicates* organization-wide performance expectations *in accordance with the Department's goals and objectives;* inspires a high level of performance in staff; ensures the professional development and mentoring of staff; oversees possible improvements in human resource processes; ensures that the evaluation and counseling process is conducted effectively and in accordance with standards and deadlines |
| **Management of Resources** | | |
| Utilizes internal controls to protect the integrity of the organization and prevent waste, fraud, and mismanagement, reporting any instances where such problems occur; uses material and financial resources prudently; strives to produce highest return with lowest cost | Ensures that effective internal controls are in place and work correctly; allocates resources efficiently, equitably, and in conformity with policy and regulatory guidelines; *makes every effort to ensure that employees have the tools needed to work effectively* | Evaluates adequacy of internal controls and ensures implementation of improvements as warranted; holds managers accountable for the consequences of their resource policy decisions; seeks resource adjustments as needed |
| **Customer Service** | | |
| Responds professionally, courteously, and competently to both internal and external customers | Balances competing and sometimes conflicting interests of a variety of customers; anticipates and responds appropriately to customer needs | At the organization level, encourages customer-oriented focus; maintains or improves services organization-wide |

*(continued)*

## Support for Equal Employment Opportunity and Merit Principles

Takes diversity training and applies its principles to the workplace; treats all individuals with respect and without regard to race, color, gender, religion, national origin, age, disability, *marital status,* or *sexual orientation;* acts in compliance with U.S. Government and Equal Employment Opportunity Commission (EEO) policies

*Manages diversity by recruiting diverse staff at all levels and ensuring staff diversity training and awareness;* promotes diversity awareness through training; ensures by example and instruction, and verifies through monitoring and follow-up, that all employees are treated with fairness and respect; applies EEO *and merit principles* consistently; identifies and addresses situations giving rise to complaints and grievances based on issues of fairness in the workplace

Fosters an organization-wide environment in which diversity is valued and respected; *encourages the organization to realize the full potential of a diverse staff;* provides personal leadership and vigorous support for EEO, *merit principles,* and fair employment practices

## Management of Sensitive and Classified Material, Information, and Infrastructure

Practices good personal security; takes full responsibility for handling and safeguarding *sensitive and classified material, information, and infrastructure properly*

Encourages the practice of good personal security measures *and serves as a model for others;* takes full responsibility for handling and safeguarding *sensitive and classified material, information, and infrastructure properly;* ensures that effective procedures are in place to protect *sensitive and classified material, information, and infrastructure* and that established security regulations are being followed

Promotes the practice of good personal security measures by employees; takes full responsibility for handling and safeguarding *sensitive and classified material, information, and infrastructure properly;* promotes security consciousness on an organization-wide basis; evaluates and monitors procedures to safeguard *sensitive and classified material, information, and infrastructure* and ensures that necessary changes are made if current procedures are inadequate; holds managers accountable for the consequences of their security policy decisions

Table 11.1 *(continued)*

## Interpersonal Skills

| Entry Level | Mid Level | Senior Level |
|---|---|---|
| **Professional Standards**<br>Holds self accountable for rules and responsibilities; is dependable and conscientious; is composed, professional, and productive, even in difficult conditions; *treats all with respect* | *Holds others accountable for rules and responsibilities;* consistently maintains equanimity and a professional demeanor; maintains own motivation and encourages others to persevere in difficult circumstances | Sets the standard for integrity and workplace behavior by example and instruction; does not lose composure under stress or in crisis; *fosters a climate based on mutual respect and trust* |
| **Persuasion and Negotiation**<br>Learns to influence others; gains cooperation while showing, in the spirit of mutual respect, understanding of others' positions | Influences others deftly; fosters understanding of USG/Department views and positions *and/or procedures and requirements;* develops alliances with others; finds common ground among disparate forces and builds consensus; facilitates win-win situations | Negotiates effectively on a wide range of issues in internal, bilateral, and multilateral environments; manages and resolves major conflicts and disagreements in an interest-based manner; manifests a faculty for astute compromise without sacrificing ultimate goals |
| **Workplace Perceptiveness**<br>Demonstrates sensitivity in both domestic and foreign environments to status, protocol, and chain of command; responds considerately to the needs, feelings, and capabilities of others; shows respect for cultural differences | Understands and deals effectively with relationships and aspirations; anticipates how others will react; frames own responses to achieve results | Navigates easily in an environment of shifting relationships; anticipates socially sensitive issues *and potential conflicts of interest* and takes appropriate action |

| **Adaptability** | | |
|---|---|---|
| Adapts behavior and work methods as needed in response to new information, changing conditions, or unexpected obstacles; displays sensitivity to cultural differences | Guides staff in adjusting to new environments and different value systems and cultures, while maintaining own standards and identity | Anticipates and plans for change; exercises sophisticated cultural sensitivity in all circumstances |
| **Representational Skills** | | |
| Establishes and maintains purposeful and productive relationships with domestic and foreign contacts; interacts effectively in official and social encounters | Identifies and cultivates *professional relationships* with key individuals and institutions; advances U.S. interests through hosting and attending representational events | Moves with ease at all social settings and levels; ensures identification, cultivation, and periodic assessment of *professional relationships with* audiences important to U.S. interests |

**Communication and Foreign Language Skills**

| **Written Communication** | | |
|---|---|---|
| Writes succinctly; produces written materials that are thorough; conveys analysis that highlights essential points and clearly explains essence of subject to the intended audience—*whether mission management or senior Department official* | Writes *clearly and persuasively*; ensures that policy and operational issues are articulated in ways most helpful to *the intended audience*; assists staff to develop effective writing skills | Exhibits full mastery of written communication; shows sophisticated ability to analyze, synthesize, and advocate in a timely manner; edits others' texts judiciously |
| **Oral Communication** | | |
| Speaks in a concise, effective, and organized manner, tailored to the audience and the situation; speaks convincingly in groups and in individual discussion | Speaks authoritatively to all audiences, demonstrating comprehensive understanding of issues and options; articulates policy goals persuasively; fosters an atmosphere of open communication and exchange of ideas | Effectively argues complex policy issues; deals comfortably with the most senior levels of government and society |

(continued)

Table 11.1 *(continued)*

**Communication and Foreign Language Skills**

| Entry Level | Mid Level | Senior Level |
|---|---|---|
| **Active Listening** | | |
| Listens attentively; understands and absorbs others' messages; correctly reads nonverbal signals; summarizes others' views accurately and confirms accuracy of understanding; considers and responds respectfully and appropriately | Instills trust in others, which motivates them to speak openly and candidly; understands and respects cultural sensitivities and constraints in discussing issues and opinions; asks open-ended, incisive questions to ensure accuracy of understanding | Adeptly discerns the innermost meanings and nuances of messages that others convey |
| **Public Outreach** | | |
| Develops public speaking and writing skills by seeking appropriate opportunities to present U.S. views and perspectives | Seizes and creates opportunities to advocate U.S. perspective to a variety of audiences. Actively develops the skills of subordinates | Deals comfortably with the media; is active and effective in public diplomacy, both in the United States and overseas. Contributes to and implements strategies to encourage a fair hearing for U.S. views and perspectives |
| **Foreign Language Skill (Generalists; Specialists as Applicable)** | | |
| *Meets language probation requirements;* uses foreign language skills to enhance job performance; seeks to improve foreign language skills | *Attains general professional proficiency\** in at least one foreign language, *strives to acquire advanced level proficiency and/or general professional proficiency in additional languages;* uses that skill effectively to communicate USG themes and exercise influence; works to increase foreign language ability | Maintains and/or further develops proficiency in foreign language(s); uses skill to promote U.S. interests with a wide range of audiences, including the media |

## Intellectual Skills

| Entry Level | Mid Level | Senior Level |
|---|---|---|
| **Information Gathering and Analysis**<br>Locates, evaluates, and quickly assimilates *key information*; reorganizes information logically to maximize its practical utility and identify key underlying factors; recognizes when additional information is required and responds accordingly; considers a variety of sources, cross-checking when appropriate | Has a sophisticated understanding of sources and their reliability; knows what to report and when; accepts that it may not be possible to base recommendations, decisions, or actions on comprehensive information; considers downstream consequences; guides and motivates staff to refine their own analytical skills | Integrates fully a wide range of information and prior experiences in policy making; ensures that staff search out and evaluate information before making recommendations and decisions; recognizes situations in which information and analysis are incomplete, and responds wisely; accepts accountability for self and insists on it for staff |
| **Critical Thinking**<br>Identifies key information, central issues, and common themes; identifies the strengths and weaknesses of various approaches; outlines realistic options; distinguishes fact from opinion and relevant from irrelevant information | Isolates key points, central issues, and common themes in a mass of complex information *or procedures*; can determine the best solution or action from a range of options; is objective in analyzing problems and judging people | Analyzes and defines complex policy issues clearly, in terms that permit them to be dealt with in a practical way; encourages staff to analyze situations and propose options, giving constructive and instructive feedback; correctly senses when it is appropriate to take risks, and does so |
| **Active Learning**<br>Seeks out new job-related knowledge and readily grasps its implications for the workplace; seeks informal feedback and learns from mistakes; recognizes own strengths and weaknesses and pursues self-development | Develops own knowledge *through broadening experiences, whether work-related, academic studies, or other type of professional development; develops* plans to teach others in the workplace; provides informal feedback to colleagues and *seeks feedback on own performance* | Anticipates the need for new information or knowledge for self and others; identifies sources of new information; communicates these sources to staff *and facilitates access* |

*(continued)*

Table 11.1 (*continued*)

## Intellectual Skills

| Entry Level | Mid Level | Senior Level |
|---|---|---|
| **Leadership and Management Training**<br>Learns basic principles of effective leadership and management. Pursues formal and informal training opportunities | Uses training opportunities to improve personal leadership and management skills *and* to keep abreast of current theory and techniques. Applies the principles learned at Foreign Service Institute (FSI) *and other relevant courses* on the job (for example, by developing subordinates). | Actively promotes leadership and management training at the organizational unit level; applies principles of leadership and management training to foster organizational improvements |

## Substantive Knowledge

| Entry Level | Mid Level | Senior Level |
|---|---|---|
| **Job Information**<br>Develops and applies knowledge needed in current assignment; learns factors that impact work; understands how job relates to organizational goals and U.S. policy objectives; uses FSI *and other* training to improve individual performance | Has broad knowledge of job-related processes and practices; remains current on policies, *programs*, and trends that affect the organization; analyzes the interplay of forces influencing the achievement of policy and program objectives and makes reasonable recommendations; uses training and other means to improve programs; *supports continuous learning of employees through both training and work opportunities* | Integrates thorough knowledge of issues arising in job to formulate and implement policies and programs; monitors internal and external sources for information and ideas; uses job knowledge to shape outcomes; uses FSI training to raise level of organizational unit performance; *creates an environment and strategies to support professional development through both training and work opportunities* |

| | | |
|---|---|---|
| **Institutional Knowledge**<br>Understands institutional realities that may affect work; understands the role and power of various offices and people, both domestically and abroad; cultivates and utilizes contacts in other organizational entities; uses institutional understanding to get things done | Applies knowledge of institutional realities to policy and operational issues; crosses institutional boundaries in obtaining information and building support; operates on an equal footing with officials in other bureaus, agencies, foreign governments, business communities, academia, and media; assists staff to comprehend the institutional influences within which they work | Uses sophisticated institutional understanding to avoid problems and advance USG goals; *develops these same skills in subordinates*; ensures *employees* are mindful of the importance of proper and prudent process in securing desired outcomes |
| **Technical Skills**<br>Learns and uses technical skills and technology as appropriate in setting of job; understands the impact of technology on the workplace; seeks ways to use technology to enhance performance | Continuously enhances own and staff's understanding of work-related technical skills and technology and their applications; advances policy and program goals through the use of available and appropriate technology | Promotes own and staff's full utilization of technical skills and technology to achieve bureau/mission goals; devises efficient and cost-effective strategies to integrate technology into the workplace |
| **Professional Expertise**<br>Understands and applies *Department of State* procedures, requirements, regulations, and policies; assimilates Department of State and Foreign Service milieu; builds knowledge of the United States and foreign environments; uses developing expertise in work situations | Strives to deepen understanding of the Department of State and of the Foreign Service as a profession; uses expertise to evaluate policies and programs and to advise and develop others; is able to operate independently to further bureau/mission objectives | Combines mastery of U.S. policy objectives and knowledge of foreign environments to advance USG goals; assists staff to develop Foreign Service skills and expertise, promoting a work environment that enhances their professional development |

*(continued)*

Table 11.1 (continued)

## Substantive Knowledge

| Entry Level | Mid Level | Senior Level |
|---|---|---|
| **Knowledge of Foreign Cultures**<br>Develops and demonstrates knowledge of foreign cultures, values, and norms; appropriately applies foreign perspective to domestic assignments and host country perspective to assignments abroad | Has sophisticated grasp of foreign political, economic, cultural, and information environments; relates knowledge to fulfillment of bureau/mission goals | Uses thorough knowledge of foreign environments to identify and seize opportunities to advance USG goals; *develops subordinates' understanding of how best to advance U.S. interests in a foreign environment* |

*Generalists, to cross senior threshold, must attain S/3-R/3 (*i.e., general professional proficiency*) in one language.

# Part IV

## New Political Appointees

# 12

# Getting New Government Leaders on the Fast Track to Success

## A Framework

Frank DiGiammarino

A proven leader, Admiral Thad Allen took over as the principal federal official for the Gulf Coast recovery in the aftermath of Katrina. The environment he entered was one of chaos and confusion. The Bush administration, considered by many to lack focus and direction, was concerned that the response to this natural disaster would define the president's domestic legacy. Admiral Allen's charge was to restore order and to recover from the disaster while negotiating the challenges of a new, undefined position.

Admiral Allen successfully navigated this complicated political landscape by establishing credibility, acknowledging and working within the constraints of the office, focusing his efforts, and aligning his strategy and people on key issues. Through his efforts, he serves as a model for all government leaders who assume leadership positions.

Today, our government leaders enter into an environment intensified by a global war on terror, an escalating budget deficit, and an American citizenry that has growing needs and expects results. In addition, the work of today's government is more complex, given the increasing speed of communication and demanding needs of a global world. As a result, there is greater need for government leaders to lead. The nation needs more great leaders like Admiral Allen. However, the question is: How can government leaders assume their responsibilities and get to meaningful and positive action fast?

Through interviewing twenty-five political appointees and careerists (see p. 230), reviewing current literature, and analyzing elements and behaviors that contribute to successes and failures, this chapter presents a four-step framework (Figure 12.1) tailored to the new government leader. This framework positions

Figure 12.1   **Steps in the Fast Track to Success**

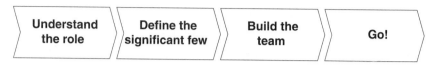

| Understand the role | Define the significant few | Build the team | Go! |

the new political appointee and senior careerist to achieve the following outcomes to leverage the full capacity of his or her office.

- Role clarity and understanding of the system.
- Focus on a limited number of initiatives that will have the most impact.
- Team alignment for consistent and efficient execution.
- Organizational commitment and plan for action.

Government leaders have significant control over their legacies. This chapter is designed to help them start with credibility and build a sustained plan of change over their tenure. Through the following four-step framework, this chapter covers the acceptance of the job through establishing and launching the vision for the organization. Like most frameworks, it presents one way to solve the problem; the framework will need to be customized to specific situations. In using it as a starting point, however, new government leaders can be better positioned to build the legacy they want from their time in office.

### Step 1: Understand The Role

> The government is like the pony express,
> but at each station they change riders instead of ponies.
>
> —*Anonymous*

There are many risks and challenges associated with accepting a leadership role in government today. Most of the negative focus is on the political appointee. Paul Light (Light and Thomas 2001), Congress (U.S. Government Accountability Office [GAO] 2000), and others often speak to the excess of political appointees and their inability to help the system. David Cohen (1998), in his article, "Amateur Government," goes so far as to label it mismanagement.

> It is *not* such a small price, and it does a *lot* of harm. The costs are enormous in confusion, inefficiency, lost time, wasted effort, low productivity, excess bureaucracy, and unnecessary personnel . . . . Even more damaging, the myth is reinforced that government itself does not or cannot work (p. 478).

Table 12.1

**Participants in the Study Offer Insights for a New Government Leader**

- Conduct research and delineate the boundaries of the organization. Political appointees and Senior Executive Service are entering a complex system.
- Respect the careerist. Careerists are critical to one's success. Early credibility with them is essential.
- Take the job only if passionate and knowledgeable about the subject matter.
- Conduct an all-hands meeting and articulate principles. A leader has one chance at a good first impression. Take advantage of the opportunity to build buy-in.
- Set the tone by focusing on the work, not the office. Don't overdo the trappings of the office by focusing on furniture and decorations in the first few days.

Public perception is that "Americans have a mixed view of presidential appointees as both well-meaning public servants and self-interested political operatives" (Labiner 2001, p. 6). A recent study from the Woodrow Wilson School of Public and International Affairs at Princeton University states that "the senior executive-run federal programs get systematically higher grades than those run by political appointees" (Gilmour and Lewis 2003, p. 1).

In addition, many of these appointees reside in their position for a period of eighteen to twenty-four months (Light and Thomas 2000). This is considered a short tenure for many who believe that "to make significant change, it takes at least three years and a couple of budget cycles" (Council for Excellence in Government [CEG] 2000, p. 17).

Political appointees and senior careerists inherit a multifaceted system from their predecessors that includes established budgets, programs, goals, and organizational standards. For example, the Government Performance and Results Act of 1993 compelled agencies to enact four- or five-year strategic plans, making it difficult for mid-term political appointees to initiate major course changes. It is essential that new government leaders understand the constraints and boundaries of an office and organization before they begin work.

This section addresses what the interview subjects (Table 12.1) and literature depicted about the leader's role and some of the lessons learned while assuming the responsibilities of his or her office. The outcome from this section is for the new government leader to achieve role clarity and understanding of the system.[1]

***Do the Research and Delineate the Boundaries of the Organization.
Government Leaders Are Entering a Complex System.***

Appointees and senior careerists enter office in different ways and times throughout an administration. This chapter concerns mostly those appointed at the start of a new administration and those who replace others in mid-term appointments. The theories can apply to political appointees and careerists assuming new responsibilities.

A majority of government leaders focus on particular areas that impact their ability to be credible and effective in their role on day one. It became apparent through the interviews for this research that a critical step of all government leaders was to delineate the boundaries of their role before they assumed it.

This clarity is not something that can simply be handed to the leader on the first day of work. It is more challenging, due to the complexity of the political/administrative system that appointees have entered. In addition, there is often no "boss" sitting over the government leader making sure that he or she "gets it." In many cases, new leaders find that their bosses have plenty of fires to fight and want the new leader to go solve their own problems. Government leaders, therefore, are frequently on their own in terms of understanding their role and defining their way ahead. It is imperative that these new government leaders take the initiative as quickly as possible to begin to understand and define their role.

In order to analyze that information and to understand the role of political appointees, this chapter develops a model for assessing the most critical levers of the organization. These levers which make up the boundaries of the organization are:

*Mandate.* The mandate consists of the rules and authorities that govern the office. The mandate is set first by program statutes, then historical precedents and the political expectations of that office. The precedents are set by the legislation and the directives that established its existence. In addition, it is important to have the historical context of why the office was established, what problems it was designed to solve, and how its role has changed over the years. The president sets global political expectations, whether it's through campaign speeches on subject matter that is related to the organization or specific goals that are laid out in his or her management agenda. The agency head sets agency expectations.

*Stakeholders.* Stakeholders represent the constituencies the leaders must work with and serve while in office. Stakeholders often come in many forms but are commonly represented by the White House and the Office of Management and Budget, Congress, professional associations and advocacy groups, labor unions, and sister agencies or programs that work on similar issues.

*Money.* Money represents the budget of the organization. It is essential to know who gets what from Congress and on what it is to be spent. If the leader knows where the money goes, then he or she will know what is important to Congress and the agency. A critical aspect of this is to understand the budget process and rules of government spending. While the budget process is inherently complicated and may present more problems than are outlined here, the following are some key insights on budgets.

- The budget that the new leader steps into was developed by a predecessor. Therefore, funding is in place for a set of initiatives that are important to the previous leadership team. Understanding what was important to the predecessor is essential in managing the organization going forward.
- While the budget of the agency is fixed, the allocation of that budget is not. Stronger government leaders have exhibited an ability to reallocate funds. The key is to find the discretionary dollars and, when ready, move those dollars to put energy behind new agenda items.

*People.* These represent the team that the leader works with to deliver on the mandate. This team is made up of careerists, other appointees, and contractors. The new leader should seek to understand who is working in his or her organization and what they are looking to accomplish. Consistently, interview subjects identified that the agency's legal counsel and budget person are good persons with whom to build an early relationship. The legal counsel will have knowledge of some of the "*Washington Post*" issues within the organization—the activities within the organization that a leader does not want to hit the front page of the newspaper. This is important since the new leader may be asked to represent the organization on Capitol Hill or to the media on any of these topics. The budget person will educate appointees on the financial situation and assist in managing resources. The framework also considers an approach to meeting people within the organization. Below are some insights.

- Some of the other people to get to know at the start are the next highest authority, the Senior Executive Service (SES) or G-15 who manages under the leader, authorities who affect the operation but are not controlled by the leader, the union steward, and any leaders who can work with the leader to move his or her agenda forward.
- There is more flexibility in managing staff than most political appointees assume.[2]
- Find the core competencies of the organization and the staff. For example, the weather bureau is not good at "weather," per se, so much as it is great at modeling and analyzing weather systems.

There is a significant amount of data available to new government leaders that will help them interpret the boundaries described above. The interview subjects for this chapter consistently indicated that the following are some of the best sources for information[3]:

*Congressional Record and the Latest Appropriations Bill.* Public record can present a good overview of how Congress views the agency. For example, congressional committee reports give good insight into current congressional activity and the Congressional Budget Justification is the most essential source for understanding the budget. On assuming office, most leaders receive copies of pertinent legislation and regulations that indicate what they can, cannot, and might do. This is also generally summarized in the Code of Federal Regulations for their program or agency. There are almost always briefing books prepared by the staff for the new appointee and sometimes by outside stakeholder groups. It is useful for new leaders to get copies of briefing books and other materials that are presented to previous leaders of their new office.

*Predecessors.* The most information about the role and an understanding of the current environment comes from the position's predecessor. Regardless of politics, the predecessor will want to see the organization be successful since it is important to his or her legacy. Even if there is an administration change and the politics are high, it is recommended that new leaders take the initiative and reach out to their predecessors for this connection to take place.

*Past Studies.* Consultants, the GAO, the Inspector General for the agency, advocacy and professional groups, and think tanks provide perspective on the perceived focus of the office and areas of challenge. In addition, there are superb materials available at organizations such as the National Academy of Public Administration (www.napawash.org) that can give a sense of the role, history, and expectations.

*Presidential Management Initiatives.* Each administration sets its goals based on the president's top priorities.[4] The Bush administration, for example, has the Presidential Management Agenda (PMA).

*Existing Strategies and Business Plans.* Most organizations have some documentation that outlines the principles of why and how the organization is executing today. In addition, most agencies have a five-year strategic plan, an annual performance review, and business-operating plan. The Government Performance and Results Act of 1993 (GPRA), the Program Assessment Rating Tool, and PMA-related documents provide context on strategic directions and policy for agencies and programs. Finally, most programs have handbooks and guidance, especially when the program interfaces with outsiders.

*Journals with Examples of Agency Work.* There are many periodicals that cover the issues of the office. Periodicals are a good place to start to get a sense of the accomplishments and challenges in the agency's area of interest.

Delineating the boundaries is difficult. The goal is to have symmetry in the boundaries—as in Figure 12.2—of the organization. The equal balance of all four sides creates clarity and stability in executing the mission. More than likely, however, government leaders will find that their boundaries often take

Figure 12.2 **Boundaries of an Organization**

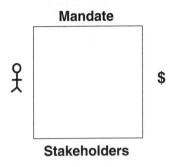

Figure 12.3 **Stretching Beyond the Mandate**

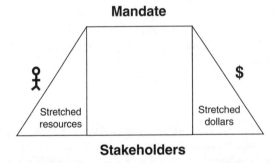

on some interesting shapes. A common organization shape is the trapezoid, depicted in Figure 12.3, in which the agency is trying to manage a stakeholder group and a set of programs that are beyond the scope of its mandate. The consequence is that the resources (people and money) are stretched thin. The mandate is only addressed in this instance by the organization rallying to the problem.

A common mistake among new leaders is to assume a reactive position in addressing problematic situations. As will happen over the course of a month, numerous problems crop up. A congressperson needs clarity on an issue, the secretary needs help preparing for a critical speech, or an incident occurs that requires the specialty skills that reside in that office. A leader in a reactive pattern will address the challenge by diverting people and focus to solving each demand. Over time, the reactive leader will constantly be assigning people to the latest challenge, and it won't be long before the leader's staff and budget are consumed with reacting to problems. The danger here is that the leader's strategic priorities will wither under all these distractions.

A focused leader, clear on the constraints of his or her office, will understand the balance that exists in the office and will proactively manage resources and challenges. It is this symmetry that allows the government leader to success-fully execute his or her most significant strategic initiatives while addressing tactical problems.

Many government leaders coming in the door have the expectation that they are there to drive policy for the president or the agency head. An impor-tant lesson learned from our interviews is that successful political appointees have recognized that they are managers as much as they are policymakers. The stronger managers have recognized the need to establish boundaries. They must identify which stakeholders and program activities are outside the scope of the mandate. The trapezoid in Figure 12.3 portrays a clear image of misalignment. As mentioned above, the challenge for the leader is to get all four sides into balance and symmetry.

It is the leader's job to work within the community and spheres of influ-ence to help the organization understand that something needs to change. The community, however, must take charge of that change. Distraction from this will lead to confusion within the organization and to mission failure. While some of the stakeholder community will be frustrated, the leader understands that in order to be successful, he or she must meet the mandate and balance resources accordingly.

It is important to note that coming in the first day, the new government leader will not have boundaries fully delineated. Some appointees have plenty of time prior to their appointment with access to staff and materials that allows them to analyze the levers depicted previously. For many appointees, it is common prac-tice to be brought on as consultants to the agency before they become appointed and confirmed. Others, however, do not have this luxury and must delineate the boundaries as they go. If the government leader does not initially take time to analyze and define these boundaries, his or her credibility is jeopardized. Leaders will always be lost in the firefights of the office and will never truly make an enduring impact on the strategic direction of the agency. For long-term success, it is important that government leaders are aware of the levers and know which ones they should focus on pushing and pulling first.

### Respect the Careerist.

When entering the organization and delineating the boundaries, the interview subjects consistently referred to the importance of the careerist to the orga-nization. The consistent theme was that the U.S. system of government has been in place for over 200 years and, while not without its challenges, has been able to consistently meet many of the needs of Americans at home and abroad. A majority of the interview subjects indicated a significant amount of respect for the system and the careerists that run it.

> Recognize that nothing seems to collapse when there isn't an appointee present. Careerists know what they're doing.
>
> —*Anonymous*

> Change would have been impossible without a significant number of career people who already wanted change.
>
> —*Anonymous*

The significance of careerists was the most consistent lesson learned from the appointees who were interviewed.[5] The following are some comments from political appointees about careerists.

- A vast majority of careerists are apolitical and loyal to the organization.
- Enter the organization knowing appointees can depend on career people. Too many appointees waste time trying to weed out the "bad careerists." This is a distraction that will cause political appointees to lose momentum and support.
- Success depends on a productive partnership with the career bureaucracy.

The majority of interview subjects believe that the careerists are so important to political appointees that losing credibility with them is the first indicator that the appointee will not be successful. While every careerist will not necessarily "be on the appointees' side," options such as repositioning of a careerist do exist. For example, it is possible to assign a careerist to another position of similar responsibility somewhere else in the agency, or an employee, particularly at the GS-15 level, could be rotated for more appropriate experience in another agency.

### Take the Job Only if Passionate and Knowledgeable About the Subject Matter.

For many of those interviewed, there appears to be a direct correlation between their credibility with the careerists and passion for the job. If government leaders do not have passion for what they are doing, our interview subjects noted that the careerists will tag those appointees as seeking more of a resume credential than wanting to make an impact. If the leader is not passionate about the subject matter, he or she is advised to reject the offer and to turn the president or agency director down because the work is too hard and the demands are too significant. Careerists and appointees consistently indicate that appointees who take the job without knowing the subject matter and/or who take the job for the glory of the role are usually the most ineffective.

A majority of our interview subjects also believe that it takes at least a year for new government leaders to understand the role and system if they do not have knowledge in the subject matter.

### Conduct an All-Hands Meeting and Articulate Principles. A Leader Has One Chance at a Good First Impression. Take Advantage of the Opportunity to Build Buy-in.

Several interview subjects involved in this study acknowledged the need to address the staff early on. Again, this is a crucial moment and speaks to the adage of "you only have one chance at a good first impression." The more time government leaders have to do research and to delineate the boundaries of the organization, the more comfortable they will be speaking at this time. The advice from the interview subjects is to not delve into subject matter as much as share personal experience. It is a critical moment for leaders to share *who* they are, *why* they are there, and *what* principles they believe are important in leading the organization.

In some instances, this time was used not only to be clear about principles, but also to give themselves some space and credibility by detailing their plan for the next few months. The next section will talk about that plan, but new leaders are setting the expectation that they are going to get to know the staff and the system before making any statements regarding change in the direction of the organization.

### Set the Tone by Focusing on the Work, Not the Office. Don't Overdo the Trappings of the Office by Focusing on Furniture and Decorations in the First Few Days.

To further build first impressions, there were some interesting stories about trappings of new government leaders coming in the door. Careerists look at this time as an indicator of whether their new boss will be successful. Interestingly enough, there are several key moves on the first day that will set the tone. Leaders should keep the following in mind as they enter office.[6]

- Focus on the work, not the furniture. If they hand over the furniture catalog, ask for the business strategy.
- Recognize that this is a temporary job that will last only as long as the leader is effective and/or the bosses hold office. As such, be good stewards of the office.

- Keep the door open. It will tell a lot about the leader's communication style and approach to management.
- Prepare to learn all over again. Recognize that government leaders are stepping into the biggest and most complicated system in the United States. Anything done before this outside of government cannot compare.
- Employees will know what is important to follow by what is on the leader's calendar.
- Have an open mind to the way things have been done. Don't start by changing "the way things work around here."
- Don't abuse the power of the office (and personal ethics) by overdoing it with privileges.
- Check "small-picture" politics at the door. "Small-picture" is defined as low-level political arguments that typically serve minor interests and do not support the overall management of the agency. While "big-picture" politics (including high-level vision and ideology) must remain a foundation of the leader's tenure, "small-picture" politics must be left behind. Even if the appointees were part of the campaign, they are now part of organizations that exist despite politics. Mission should win out over politics every time.
- Do not name drop, self-promote, or be too partisan.
- Everyone knows the leader is the boss; do not look for ways to prove it.
- Leave preconceptions about careerists at the door and make judgments based on personal experience.

### Step 2: Define the Significant Few

> Leaders establish the vision for the future and set the strategy for getting there; they cause change. They motivate and inspire others to go in the right direction and they, along with everyone else, sacrifice to get there.
>
> —*John Kotter*

What does the new government leader want to get done? The job itself can be all consuming. Many of the interview subjects described it as everyone wanting a piece of you every day with very little time for yourself. New leaders can elect to constantly get caught up in this whirlwind and always react in the moment or, from the start, define an agenda that they want to achieve during their tenure.

This section speaks to building on a credible start and describes an approach for establishing a customized program that will become a lasting legacy. The outcome from this section (summarized in Table 12.2) is for the new govern-

Table 12.2

**Participants in the Study Offer Insights for a New Government Leader**

- Spend time in the organization and learn how it works.
- Conduct one-on-one meetings with the staff.
- Meet all external stakeholders.
- Select the significant few (3 to 5) things that are the top agenda items.
- Choose the "inner-circle" and evaluate the agenda items with them.
- Despite the desire to communicate, put the infrastructure in place to execute on these initiatives prior to sharing them with the organization.

ment leader to achieve focus on a limited number of initiatives that will have the most impact during his or her tenure.

### Spend Time in the Organization and Learn How It Works.

Every organization has its own rhythm and culture. Where are the power centers? What is the reporting structure? What are the organization's values and norms? What does it take to play well with others? Who are the most respected careerists? Is decision making centralized or decentralized? Which issues can appointees take head-on, and which ones are politically suicidal? There is much to understand about organizations before appointees can lead them with credibility.

While there is no defined timeframe for understanding it all, most people interviewed believe it takes four to eight weeks to get a sense of the tempo and culture of the office. In addition to answering some of the questions above, the leader is looking to see how the staff conducts business, to understand what the office produces, and to discover how that office prioritizes its work. At this stage, new leaders continue to validate the boundaries (mandate, stakeholders and programs, money, and people). It is critical, however, that the role of new appointees is to not cast judgment, but to understand how people work and why.

### Conduct One-on-One Meetings with the Staff. If It Is a Small Staff, Meet Them All.

> Give the careerists the opportunity to solve problems, because they often come up with ideas better than you.
>
> —*Anonymous*

A critical aspect of achieving this understanding is to conduct one-on-one meetings with the staff. It is a unique period to get to know the people who will work for the government leader. It is important to note that in this initial interaction, the new leader will not know truth from fiction. These sessions are not designed to solve this, but to compile an impression of the organization and the people in it.

There are some people within the organization to get to know first. As mentioned earlier in this chapter, the agency's legal counsel and budget person are the people whom new leaders may need to rely on early in their tenure. One recommendation from the interviewees is to meet with the budget person and immediately carve out some discretionary dollars. New leaders will find that they will want these dollars available for special projects and investments to get their most important programs launched.

Besides these two critical people, the consistent recommendation from the interview subjects is to meet with as many staff as possible. At the very least, the new leader should go two levels down into the organization conducting one-on-one sessions. Sessions should focus on understanding what they do, what their challenges are, and what they think are the most important things to achieve over the next four years. As the new person, this is the time when there are limited biases and baggage to navigate; it is a "free" conversation. Ask questions that will help further delineate organizational boundaries as well as those that will make apparent the consistent themes and challenges facing the agency.

### Meet All External Stakeholders. This Is the Time to Understand the External Landscape and Build Important Relationships.

In addition to people internal to the organization, it is imperative to meet with the key external stakeholders; they play an important role in shaping demands on appointees while in office. In meeting these stakeholders, know that this is the time to build a relationship with someone that the leader will probably rely on in some capacity during his or her term in office. Similar to internal meetings, the first meetings with the external stakeholders are a great opportunity to discuss their concerns and issues. This conversation will have a few nuances to it. Many external constituencies will use this time to test leaders on what they know and to push them to think about issues like they do. Understanding their perspective on the issues that are important to the office will be essential in future interactions and possibly critical for future negotiations.

In conducting these interview sessions, do not only cater to the party in power and/or ignore specific stakeholders. This can cause immediate disenfranchisement and may cause long-term damage. A new government leader should make sure to take the time to build an accurate list of everyone in the ecosystem of the agency. Use the careerists to help build this list.

Many of those interviewed expressed some level of regret in not aggressively working their external stakeholder network. One spoke to it as recognizing that while an internal focus reaped rewards, they could have done more for the people in the organization if they had better relationships externally during some of the heated battles. Looking back on it, one interviewee said that if he were to do it all over again, he would have spent more time externally and built stronger relationships. Stakeholders are valuable to government leaders. They are sources of information, both technical and political; they are useful in marshaling support for policy and programs. In some cases they are also constituents, such as block grant recipients.

> Careerists do the work. My job is to help facilitate getting the job done.
>
> —*Anonymous*

> You need to be seen by your people as someone who can intercede with others when they can't.
>
> —*Anonymous*

These quotes raise an important characteristic of the job of the new government leader. The careerists are constantly looking to appointees and SES leadership to be engaged in the community and to break down barriers that interfere with execution of the mission. In this capacity, the leaders need to be able to pick up the phone and speak to other leaders and influencers in the community and get problems back on track. The initial weeks in office are the time to lay the foundation for those relationships.

### Select the Significant Few (3–5) Things That Are the Top Agenda Items.

After four to eight weeks, new leaders should have a strong sense of the organization and the internal and external pressures facing it. They will have delineated the boundaries, spent time in the agency, and met with both internal and external stakeholders. At this point, the new leader's job is to step out of the daily routine and assess the top three to five things that need to get done in the organization. There is no magic to this moment—it is the time for leaders to define their priorities and the impact they want to have during their tenure.

Many of the interview subjects indicated that the first version of this list is not collaborative. It is what the leader knows needs to be done. The new leader has heard from all aspects of the community, witnessed the organization's performance, and measured the limits of the office. At this juncture, it is time to weed out the many insignificant issues and focus on the significant few that will have the most impact.

One interview subject, in the early months of his tenure, could have spent all his time responding to stakeholder inquiries and daily fire drills. His observation was that to continue operating in a reactive mode would mean that the organization would continue to work as it always had. His success was driven out of his ability to step back and define what he wanted to get done while in his role. This allowed him to manage the organization and to drive true change as opposed to always reacting to issues of the day.

The thing that *is* essential appears to be the number of initiatives. Three to five is the consistent number of how many initiatives a leader *and* an organization can handle at any given time. Too many initiatives cloud the vision of the organization and can potentially bring progress to a standstill. Other guidance on initiatives is to:

- Understand that while new leaders cannot fully control their agendas, it is imperative that they choose three to five initiatives on which to concentrate.
- Listen to the ideas that exist within the organization. Most success comes from listening to the organization and understanding what is there that can be leveraged. Ideas that have already percolated in the organization are often more successful.
- Make initiatives part of the budget. Several of our interviewees spoke to the power of budget as an indicator of an initiative's future success. Lead with the return on investment of an initiative and broker support for it.
- Use existing program dollars. Find the programs that are most similar to the top initiatives and use those dollars to execute the top initiatives. Appropriating new money will take too long.
- Pick a few things that can be accomplished within the president's remaining time in office.

### Choose an "Inner Circle" and Evaluate the Agenda Items with Them.

The selection of the significant few presents the new leader with the opportunity to draw in some of the other key players in the organization. This group will become the new leader's inner circle. At this stage, the leader must pick a few people from the organization with whom to share his or her agenda. Much as a name is released to the press prior to an appointment, this step allows the leader to pulse the organization and get a sense of the agenda's plausibility. Some important lessons learned from the interviewees when building this group are:

- It should include an organizational cross section. The new leader must resist the temptation to always work with the current leadership team and should reach out across the organization, as well as down into its lower levels, to solicit a good cross section of input. This cross section should also include those who do not necessarily agree with all the leader's policies.
- There are some key players that need to be on board; make sure the leader's boss, the finance person, and informal influencers in the organization are included.

The leader will know who the informal influencers are from the one-on-one interviews. There is no set number to the size of the leader's inner circle. Some people take a few members as counsel, while others want to get a broad cross section of the organization. This is dependent on how the leader believes that he or she has assessed the organization and what comfort level is needed in knowing that the leader has hit the most salient areas.

### Despite the Desire to Communicate, Put the Infrastructure in Place to Execute on These Initiatives Prior to Sharing Them with the Organization.

Once leaders have closed on the significant few and have vetted them with some of the inner circle, they may feel like they are ready to go public with the plan. The risk at this stage is that the communication is abrupt and without full context. Just because there is a set of initiatives does not mean that the organization is ready to react to them. Should the leader push some of these thoughts as an edict out to the organization, the employees will not know how to react.

For example, the appointee who has defined the boundaries and identified the significant few is much further along than the organization. He or she is in position to move quickly and wants to strike while the "iron is hot." The problem is that the organization does not know as much as the leader. The system has not vetted the material and put its stamp of approval on it. The system will most likely listen with anticipation to the leader's words of wisdom and then go back to doing their "real work" until they understand who is to do what, how it will be measured, and when it will get done. Until the significant few initiatives have context and meaning for the organization, it will not adopt them and nothing will get done.

It is imperative that leaders judge the appropriate time to communicate based on their perception of the respective agency and when they feel as though the agency should be included in order for it to give its best efforts. The next section addresses building the team and the context that will help implement that vision.

Table 12.3

**Participants in the Study Offer Insights for New Government Leaders**

- Identify the manager and navigator(s).
- Get the manager and navigator aligned to the appointee's agenda. All three roles must become interchangeable and speak with a consistent voice.
- Work with the manager and navigator and a small cadre of others where necessary to build a road map for implementation.

## Step 3: Build the Team

> The way a team plays as a whole determines its success. You may have the greatest bunch of individual stars in the world, but if they don't play together, the club won't be worth a dime.
>
> *—Babe Ruth*

At this stage of the framework, the new government leader is about to get on the field and play the game. Until now, he or she has been in the locker room getting ready. Like any good athlete, however, he or she can't do it alone; a team is needed.

This section (summarized in Table 12.3) speaks to how the new leader can build a team of complementary skills. To drive lasting change for the organization, this team will need to want to accomplish the same goals *and* to work well with each other. The outcome here is for the leader to have team alignment for consistent and efficient execution.

### *Leadership Triangulation.*

Consistently, our interviewees depicted a team that was extremely powerful and successful. This team of three distinct roles was referred to by one of the interviewees as the triangulation of leadership (Figure 12.4).

- *The Leader.* Sets the vision and strategy for the organization. The leader is ultimately responsible for the success or failure of the organization. The leader is also the external face to the organization and is passionate about its direction and success.
- *The Manager.* Makes the trains run on time. This person understands the operations of the organization—who owns what, and how to get things done. The manager is often the "deputy" or "chief of staff."
- *The Navigator.* Understands the community and culture of the organization and knows how to negotiate through the complex ecosystem. Through experi-

Figure 12.4  **The Power of Three**

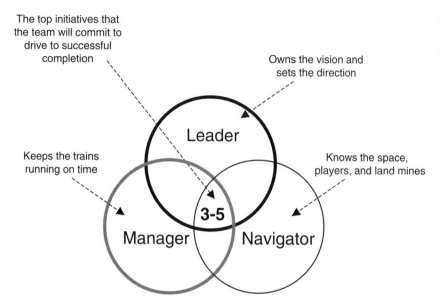

ence, this person has credibility and understanding of the issues, represents the mission, and embodies the culture of the organization. Depending on the complexity of the issues, there can often be multiple navigators.

It is at the intersection of these three roles that work gets done. Ability to drive the significant few initiatives rests in the hands of this team. If they are unified in their understanding and commitment to these initiatives, then they will be achieved. The opposite holds true as well. Not having all three of these roles and alignment on what to execute leads to fractures in the foundation of the leadership team and an inability to get the most important work done.

### *Identify the Manager and Navigator(s).*

Success as a leader lies in building the right team. The first step in building the team is to be clear about roles. In this model, appointees are the leaders.[7] The leader's job is to set the direction of the organization, align people to his vision, and motivate them to get there. The more clarity leaders have over their role, the easier it will be for the appointees to identify the manager and navigator.

While going through a cycle of the organization and one-on-one interviews, the manager and navigator should stand out. In addition, these people will most likely be a part of the inner circle that reviews the leader's vision and initiatives. As leaders watch their participation and thought process during that time, their selection will become more apparent.

Often, the manager is already in the role as a deputy or chief of staff. This is more common if the leader is a political appointee. A manager can be either a political appointee or a careerist. From the interviews, the navigator was often another appointee, but it is important to note that this varies greatly across agencies and programs. At the end of the day, however, the navigator needs to completely understand what the leader is trying to do, participates as a key part of the program, and is the person who is committed to getting things done. The leader must understand that this type of relationship between an appointee and the deputy is the ideal goal, but it is not always possible because of separate political lines of influence, protectors, and background.

> Appointees often tell me that taking my advice to find a mentor, coach or
> set of personal advisors was the best step they ever took entering office.
>
> —*Jan Piercy (CEG 2000)*

More than any other role, interviewees raised the navigator component as a "must have" individual in the organization. Often referred to as a consigliore or coach, this person knows the organization and its ecosystem inside out. A majority of the time, this person is a careerist. In this light, the navigator can act as the go-between for political appointees and the career staff, ensuring that the political appointees act in accordance with organizational norms and with a wide array of support.

In many cases, leaders have navigators inside and outside the organization. Whether they are from the private sector or nonprofit organizations, navigators can come from many places. The most essential piece is to find navigators who can align to the leader's agenda and be the trusted advisor who coaches the leader through the implementation of this agenda. Many times, interviewees noted that having the navigator(s) on board was an indicator of having a particular initiative succeed.

### Align the Manager and Navigator to the Leader's Agenda. Have All Three Roles Become Interchangeable and Speak with a Consistent Voice.

> We don't accomplish anything in this world alone . . . and whatever
> happens is the result of the whole tapestry of one's life and all the weavings
> of individual threads from one to another that creates something.
>
> —*Sandra Day O'Connor, Supreme Court Justice*

On any successful team, every member knows his or her role, the roles of teammates, and the expectations placed on those teammates in achieving the mission. When action is necessary, each person knows what to do and executes with precision. On an effective team, members can play (at least in part) other positions. Interchangeability is enabled by agreement on the mission and the top three to five initiatives, as well as by constant communication. It also demonstrates a commitment to understanding teammates' roles in the organization and consistently supporting them. If one team member is absent, the organization remains consistent on direction and continues to make progress.

### *Work with the Manger and Navigator and a Small Cadre of Others Where Necessary to Build a Road Map for Implementation.*

A common pitfall at this stage is for an executive team to hold an off-site retreat and spend a great amount of time getting to know employees through team-building exercises. While some of those exercises have their place, these senior executives will get to know much more about each other and commit at a deeper level if there is a problem they need to solve together.

The best way to build this team is to spend time working the leader's vision and initiatives with the manager and navigator. Depending on the organization, leaders may want to expand this group beyond the manager and the navigator. That will be a call the leader will make through his or her sense of the inner circle.

Within the inner circle, some strong interaction is needed to gain agreement on the initiatives, the meaning of success, and how the work will get done. At this stage, the leader is building a plan of action. This small group of individuals is starting to collectively own the problem, solutions, and action steps to successfully complete the initiatives. Strategically aligning the leader's innercircle in this way will ensure that everyone is on the same page going forward.

### Step 4: Plan, Align, and Go

> You need to manage well and market brilliantly.
>
> —*Anonymous*

At this stage, the new leader should be ready to launch. The leader has a draft implementation plan and is probably bursting at the seams to make the vision a reality. This section (summarized in Table 12.4) lays out a few of the lessons learned about launching those initiatives and making critical moves to ensure the leader's success. The outcome from this section is for the new

Table 12.4

**Participants in the Study Offer Insights for New Government Leaders**

* Put the best people on the most difficult problems.
* Assign cross-functional teams to support the solution of the problem.
* Manage the change.
* Empower the organization by removing barriers to success.

government leader to have organizational commitment and a plan for action on the most important initiatives.

### *Put the Best People on the Most Difficult Problems.*

Leaders know that success always comes down to having the right people. In *Good to Great,* James Collins (2001) emphasized that to be successful an organization must have the right people on the bus in the right seats. Most government leaders are concerned about how to effectively employ those at hand. To reinforce an earlier point, career civil servants are some of the best people with whom our interview subjects have ever worked. Their passion for the mission of the agency, knowledge of their subject matter, and commitment to the American people and system of government were recognized as critical aspects of the appointee's success.

A critical move at this stage is building effective teams to deliver on the leader's initiatives. When a leader finds that some of the right people are not in the right roles to achieve these initiatives, the interview subjects indicated, time and again, that the only move at this point is to take the "A" players from across the organization and put them on the A initiatives. If there are careerists who are out of place or don't seem to be on board with the agenda, do not focus on them. Recognize their value and have someone else work with them to find a better-suited role. The leader's job is to focus on the three to five initiatives and what it will take to make them successful.

### *Assign Cross-Functional Teams to Support the Solution of the Problem.*

With the right people leading these teams, it is important to provide them with the best support. Many of the leaders we spoke with indicated that another core aspect of success was to reach across the organization to pull some of the best and brightest to assist in these initiatives. In 1993, Joe Dear, the head of the Occupational Safety and Health Administration (OSHA), said this about getting input from across the organization:

We brought in people from all over the organization—frontline workers, senior managers, internal union representatives. We had them talk about problems and suggest solutions on the first day. On the second day, we made decisions about the proposed changes. I got a set of recommendations which we then began implementing. It was an important signal that I was going to manage OSHA differently, that we were going to listen to everyone in the agency. (CEG 1993)

Dear, through efforts similar to the one he described above, had a large impact at OSHA during a critical time, and his team won a Ford Foundation award for innovation in 1996.

These powerful cross-functional teams not only get the work done but also bring useful perspectives from across the organization to the problems at hand. This is helpful in developing creative solutions as well as getting buy-in from numerous constituencies that want to make sure their voice is heard throughout the change.

### *Manage the Change.*

At this stage of the framework, leaders should be focused on their overall approach and principles of management. Communicating a direction without clarity of vision and without a framework for execution is a recipe for organizational confusion. The assumption at this point, however, is that the leader now has sufficient detail to inform the organization of what he or she sees as shaping the next several years of his or her life. With clarity on the initiatives, the timeframe for execution, and the people assigned to lead the initiatives, it is time to start implementing a large change-management effort.

To deliver on the vision and execute against their initiatives, leaders must involve the entire organization. They are looking to raise awareness about what is important to them and the leadership team. Change management is not only about raising this awareness but about building support for action. Across the organization, leaders will need to direct a campaign to get people involved in what they are trying to build.

Classic change management at this point is a one-way street. Leaders often believe that telling a subordinate something will be enough information for the employee to take action. If a leader wants to have support and full organizational action on an initiative, communication must involve more than a one-way message about the leader's intent. It needs to be an open dialogue that helps employees understand why something is changing and what that change will specifically mean to them. For this reason, communication often occurs multiple times to multiple audiences across multiple mediums.

Figure 12.5   **Context for Communication**

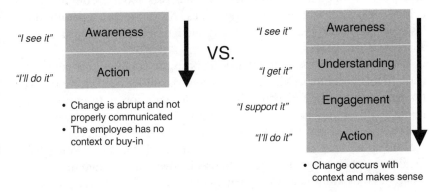

A few thoughts follow on steps appointees can take to build a change management plan.

- Conduct a brief review to understand current and former change strategies, measures, and effectiveness (strengths and weaknesses).
- Outline principles and objectives for the entire change effort.
- Define key stakeholders, their needs, and desired outcomes.
- Develop a communication process and plan. Ensure there are mechanisms to provide the right message, at the right time, and for the right stakeholder over the life of the work effort(s).
- Tailor the key points of the message to address your stakeholders' core needs.

One of the key points from our interviews about managing change within the organization was to play to the self-preservation component of the culture. People need to have a case for change that is compelling enough to act. In government, this case often involves ensuring relevancy—that they are a necessary and critical part of the system. In today's environment, if the agency is not relevant, its functions may be terminated. Another comment around communication spoke to the importance of enlisting the president and agency secretary in the initiative(s). In this way, leaders are ensuring that their work will be tied to the political agenda and seen as an important cornerstone of the administration's success.

***Empower the Organization by Removing Barriers to Success.***

> The career staff do know how to get it done, but they are only as good
> as the political leaders will allow them to be.
>
> *—David Cohen (1998, p. 453)*

As discussed at the start of this chapter, this framework was developed through discussions with political appointees and careerists about lessons learned in being or working with political appointees. At this stage, hopefully those lessons have taken on a deeper meaning and have better positioned political appointees for success.

Leaders are the bridge to other leaders in the communities they influence. With this connectivity comes the responsibility of clearing the path for those who work for them. Daily, the leader's job is to check on the progress of the initiatives and to determine how to help the organization and people overcome obstacles. The weight of the office and the power of the role grant leaders access that those who work for them do not have. Leaders must leverage this access to break down barriers and to build the outcomes they know need to happen. In the end, this is how leaders achieve the legacies they want.

## Conclusion and Recommendations

> The best way to predict your future is to create it.
>
> —*Anonymous*

The challenges for today's government leaders are daunting. The complexity of the ecosystem within which political appointees work and the significance of the problems they solve demand clear guidance for how to assume their responsibilities. For better or worse, there are massive amounts of data available to today's government leaders. The question we continued to ask, however, was: How can the new leader distill that information and structure his or her environment for success?

What has emerged from the interviews and research is a framework that can assist new government leaders in the early months of their tenure. Through the steps outlined above and depicted in Figure 12.6, this chapter concludes that there are specific actions leaders can take to establish themselves as effective during their tenures in office.

While some of these steps can be applied to the private sector, there are nuances to political appointees that warrant special attention. Most notably these are the:

- levers that constitute the boundaries of the organization;
- complexity of the ecosystem that political appointees enter when taking office;
- importance of credibility in assuming the role, especially with careerists;

Figure 12.6  Getting to Action Fast

| Understand the role | Define the significant few | Build the team | Go! |
|---|---|---|---|

**Key insights**

**Understand the role**
- Do the research and delineate the boundaries of the organization; government leaders are entering a complex system
- Respect the careerist; careerists are critical to one's success; early credibility with them is essential
- Take the job only if passionate and knowledgeable about the subject matter
- Conduct an all-hands meeting and articulate principles; a leader has only one chance at a good first impression; take advantage of the opportunity to build buy-in
- Set the tone by focusing on the work, not the office; don't overdo the trappings of the office by focusing on the furniture and decorations in the first few days

**Define the significant few**
- Spend time in the organization and learn how it works
- Conduct one-on-one meetings with the staff; if it's a small staff, meet them all
- Meet all external stakeholders; this is the time to understand the external landscape and build important relationships
- Select the significant few (3–5) things that are the top agenda items
- Pick an "inner circle" and evaluate the agenda items with them
- Despite the desire to communicate, put the infrastructure in place to execute these initiatives prior to sharing them with the organization

**Build the team**
- Identify the manager and navigator(s)
- Align the manager and navigator to the leader's agenda; all three roles must become interchangeable and speak with a consistent voice
- Work with the manager, navigator, and a small cadre of others where necessary to build a road map for implementation

**Go!**
- Put the best people on the most difficult problems
- Assign cross-functional teams to support the solution of the problem
- Manage the change
- Empower the organization by removing barriers to success

**Outcomes**

| Role clarity and understanding of the system | Focus on a limited number of initiatives that will have the most impact | Team alignment and consistent and efficient execution | Organization commitment and plan for action |
|---|---|---|---|

- necessity of observing the organization and getting to know all the stakeholders tied to it;
- need for leadership triangulation, especially the navigator; and
- various approaches to aligning support and managing people.

This framework is focused on preparing the new government leader for assuming his or her responsibilities and for preparing him or her to take action. The framework is designed to lay the foundation for change and to leave space for additional discussion on how to execute change.

As with most frameworks, it is at best an ideal or outline that every practitioner has to adapt to his or her particular situation. In reality, the work of assuming a leadership position is far from sterile and will never be as smooth as this framework depicts. Each leader will need to assess his or her situation and determine which aspects of the framework will best apply to his or her needs.

Based on conversations with these interview subjects, however, it is possible that with measured guidance and some careful first steps, success is within reach. Political appointees and senior careerists are essential elements that make the U.S. government work. Predict your own future and take these steps to develop the legacy you want.

**The Study**

The impetus for this study came from an observation that there had to be a way to get new government leaders to take action fast. The initial focus of the study was on the political appointee. In a time when the tenure of the political appointee is less than two years, the belief is that it is essential that appointees, with the right approach, can start from a positive place and have positive results. The leadership and guidance that an appointee provides is too important to have that leader start from a negative situation. The difficulty that these appointees have in achieving success is as damaging to those people working for them as it is to the important missions they drive for the country. In this vein, this chapter sought to find out what techniques other leaders had deployed in their efforts and to see if there were any patterns that offered insight into how to shorten the length of time it takes a leader to get up to speed, as well as how to increase effectiveness upon entry.

This chapter, therefore, presents the results of a study that collected observations from 25 former and current political appointees and career civil servants (15 political appointees, 10 careerists) from various White House administrations, backgrounds, and agencies. Within this group, 21 performed their duties in a civilian agency and 4 were military. Represented agencies included the

Department of Homeland Security (Coast Guard), General Services Administration, Department of Defense, Department of Transportation, Department of Commerce, Internal Revenue Service, and the Office of Management and Budget. Sixteen separate agencies are represented in this study. In addition, the interview subjects were fairly balanced across Democratic and Republican administrations. Political appointees were selected based on having served in office for over 2.5 years. The careerists in this study represented a broad brush of agencies and are long-time civil servants. All interview subjects provided their insights on what makes new political appointees successful when coming into office. Analyses of their responses led to the creation of this chapter.

## Notes

I would like to thank all the senior government officials who were so generous with their time and for their open, frank, and insightful views that helped shape this study's findings. I have kept their names anonymous. For all of his assistance through interviews, brainstorming, and evolving the body of this work, I would like to thank Chuck Rubin. For their support and assistance in evolving the content and direction of this chapter, I want to give a special thanks to Terry Buss, Frank DiGiammarino II, Peter DiGiammarino, Daniel Forrester, Sara Gilbert, Michelle Lally, Kathryn Newcomer, Ian Portnoy, Mike Prosser, Carmie Rogers, Dan Sheehan, Leif Ulstrup, and Barry White. I would also like to thank Morgan Kinghorn, Howard Messner, and the National Academy of Public Administration for their support in publishing this material. On a personal note, I would like to thank Carol, Catherine, Maya, and Ellie DiGiammarino for their continued love and support for me through this entire effort. I would also like to thank my parents for not only setting outstanding examples of leadership and for mentoring me on how to "get to action," but for always supporting and encouraging me in everything I do.

1. The system in this chapter refers to the dynamic and interrelating complex of people, systems, and communities that are associated through their focus and commitment to a particular issue. The system constitutes all players both internal and external to the organization.

2. There are current personnel reform efforts toward the Senior Executive Service (SES) evaluation and compensation structure that will impact how government employees are rewarded for performance. In addition, it is important to know the rules that govern employees. These rules typically vary by agency and often have been built into organizational myths. Clarifying the myth can sometimes lead to increased options.

3. Another good list of research materials is located in CEG (2000, p. 21).

4. Under the current administration, this is called the President's Management Agenda, and each agency's progress is measured against President Bush's top five management priorities for his administration.

5. Most of the literature on this subject concurs. One publication out of the PriceWaterhouseCoopers Endowment for the Business of Government, titled *Becoming an Effective Political Executive: 7 Lessons from Experienced Appointees* (Michaels 2001), stated, "91 percent of the PAS's surveyed rated their career subordinates 'generally' or 'greatly' helpful in major aspects of their work."

6. There is an excellent list on pages 19 and 20 of the CSIS Report by Norman R. Augustine (2000), titled *Managing to Survive in Washington: A Beginner's Guide to High-Level Management in Government.*

7. The political appointee as the leader is the most common model. It is important to note, however, that there are times when the appointee could be the manager in another appointee's team.

## References

Augustine, Norman R. 2000. *Managing to Survive in Washington: A Beginner's Guide to High-Level Management in Government.* Washington, DC: Center for Strategic and International Studies, the CSIS Press.

Cohen, David M. 1998. "Amateur Government." *Journal of Public Administration Research and Theory* 8(4): 450-497.

Collins, James C. 2001. *Good to Great: Why Some Companies Make the Leap—and Others Don't.* New York: Harper Business.

Council on Excellence in Government (CEG). 1993. *Building a New OSHA.* Washington, DC: Author.

———. *A Survivor's Guide for Presidential Nominees.* 2000. The Presidential Appointee Initiative. Washington, DC: Author.

Gilmour, John, and David Lewis. 2003. *Political Appointees and the Quality of Federal Program Management.*

Labiner, Judith M. 2001. *A Vote of No Confidence: How Americans View Presidential Appointees.* A Report on a Survey Conducted by Princeton Survey Research Associates on Behalf of the Presidential Appointee Initiative. Washington, DC: Brookings Institution Press.

Light, Paul, and Virginia Thomas. 2000. *The Merit and Reputation of an Administration: Presidential Appointees on the Appointments Process.* A Report on a Survey Conducted by Princeton Survey Research Associates on Behalf of the Presidential Appointee Initiative. Washington, DC: The Brookings Institution Press.

———. 2001. *Posts of Honor: How America's Corporate and Civic Leaders View Presidential Appointments.* A Report on a Survey Conducted by Princeton Survey Research Associates on Behalf of the Presidential Appointee Initiative. Washington, DC: Brookings Institution Press.

Michaels, Judith E. 2001. *Becoming an Effective Political Appointee: 7 Lessons from Experienced Appointees.* The PriceWaterhouseCoopers Endowment for The Business of Government. Washington, DC: The Center for The Business of Government.

U.S. General Accountability Office. 2000. *Confirmation of Political Appointees* (GAO/GGD-00–174). Washington, DC: Author.

# 13

## A Leadership Agenda for Newly Appointed Senior Officials

Cindy Williams, F. Stevens Redburn, and Terry F. Buss

> Drive your business, or it will drive thee.
>
> —*Benjamin Franklin*

In 2005, the Department of the Navy asked the National Academy of Public Administration (NAPA) to advise senior management on what actions they might take on assuming a leadership role over a major program, department, or agency. NAPA convened a panel of leaders who had all distinguished themselves at the highest levels of government in their careers. In this chapter, we report on the top ten things a leader should accomplish upon taking command.

You've just been confirmed as the new assistant secretary of a federal agency. You want to develop a strategy that will achieve your personal goals and those of the administration, while at the same time serving the American people and your constituents. Whether or not you have extensive management experience guiding large, complex organizations in the federal system, here are ten things (Figure 13.1) to consider in launching a new administration or in reinvigorating an existing one at mid-term or one that is simply transitioning. (Each item is discussed in detail in subsequent pages.)

### 1. Build Strategic Relationships . . . and Nurture Them

> The most important single ingredient in the formula of success is knowing how to get along with people.
>
> —*Teddy Roosevelt*

---

Figure 13.1   **The Top Ten Leadership Agenda Items**

1. Build strategic relationships and nurture them.
2. Understand what you can and cannot do.
3. Identify key issues where you personally can make a difference.
4. Institute a strategic planning process early in your tenure.
5. Manage against a few key performance measures.
6. Link rewards to organizational performance goal attainment.
7. Create an environment that fosters and rewards integrity.
8. Encourage and reward creativity and innovation.
9. Understand the policy cycle and its implications.
10. Travel and speak regularly and talk with the civil servants and your constituents.

---

### Build Relationships Within the Department

Build relationships with key department leaders, including the secretary, administrator or director, other assistant and under-secretaries, and senior executives. Know how they operate, learn what their priorities are, and determine how best to work with them. Develop relationships based on trust and respect. Nurture and strengthen these relationships, among other things, by being sure you personally attend important meetings involving these individuals.

### Foster Communities of Interest

Form a community of interest with key stakeholders, including public interest groups, professional associations, and officials in comparable federal programs or organizations. Interacting with stakeholders and others makes it much easier to accomplish your goals and to fulfill your mission when you understand the major players and they you.

### Build Relationships with Congress

Build relationships with the congressional committees of jurisdiction. Understand that Congress has both an oversight role and a partnership role. Don't mix or confuse roles.

## 2. Understand What You Can and Cannot Do

> When you have got an elephant by the hind leg, and
> he is trying to run away, it's best to let him run.
>
> —*Abraham Lincoln*

### Know What Your Job Entails

You may have significant authority under statute or delegated authority under a secretary or administrator. Early in your tenure, re-read or examine the scope and breadth of your authority. Areas where you have no authority can affect your success directly. Especially when you do not have primary responsibility for policymaking and budgeting, which will affect your success directly, build strategic relationships with those who are responsible wherever possible (see point 1 above).

### Work Within Your Authority

Your goals and commitments should reflect both the breadth of and the limits of your authority. Working within another's authority can cause conflict that can focus your attention too much on politics and not enough on mission. Before you decide to exercise your authority in areas where there is a vacuum, understand why the vacuum exists and what the implications of filling the void will be.

### Educate Others About Lines and Boundaries of Your Authority

Authority patterns in agencies often grow and change over time, independently of what statutes require and often based on personalities occupying key positions. There may be an informal system of authority in place paralleling the formal one. Find out quickly how both systems work, and use them to achieve your personal and administrative goals.

## 3. Identify Key Issues in Which You Personally Can Make a Difference

> Surround yourself with the best people you can find, delegate authority, and don't interfere as long as the policy you've decided upon is being carried out.
>
> —*Ronald Reagan*

### Be Careful What You Delegate

Your subordinates can handle many issues with you as reviewer and supervisor, but a few issues deserve your personal attention. These may include issues that are high risk or controversial, high priority for the administration, or part of your personal management agenda. Never forget that when you delegate responsibility, you remain accountable for actions of subordinates.

## Pursue a Tightly Focused Management Agenda

Early in your tenure, try to identify a few key issues—probably no more than five in which you can personally make a difference and bring about lasting change. Choose these issues carefully. Hopefully all will interest you and will be consistent with the goals of your superiors. In addition, add some issues to your list that will be of particular interest to those up the chain of command. Choose those over which you have authority, or over which you can build partnerships or coalitions.

## Talk to Everyone in Developing Your Management Agenda

Some managers, upon assuming office, ignore the opposition—political, bureaucratic, or philosophical—when setting up operations. Although you might not want to adopt their agenda, they can provide you with valuable insights about their positions and what to expect from them, and which agenda issues you might want to work on. Starting off de novo can be counterproductive.

## Discipline Rationing Your Time

Discipline your activities so that you can invest time in key issues. You will be besieged by near-term issues—program reviews, budget meetings, Hill testimony, and many more—that are important and require your attention. Be sure, however, that you devote a significant portion of your time to long-term issues that can make a lasting difference in your organization or department. Set a goal of spending a minimum amount of time—probably no less than 30 percent—on these long-term issues.

## Set up a Strategy to Manage Change

It is not sufficient to issue directives to re-engineer organizations or publish a strategic plan (see fourth item below), then hope that they succeed. There should be a well-defined strategy for managing change that is well known and widely accepted by stakeholders. This plan is in addition to the organizational strategic plan below. People are less likely to resist change if they understand the plan and have bought into it. Essential is the development of a *communication plan* that keeps everyone informed continuously through the change process. Do not assume that when no one responds to your communications you ought to abandon them. Lack of response may be interpreted as satisfaction with the process. At any rate, communication is a cost of doing business.

## Hit the Ground Running

Most assistant secretaries do not complete a four-year term, regardless of the agency. Many leave in mid-term, some are appointed late in an administration. You have a relatively short period to figure out what you want to accomplish and then accomplish it. It is imperative to "hit the ground running" if you want to contribute. Advice in this memo should be vigorously pursued.

## 4. Institute a Strategic Planning Process Early in Your Tenure

> Plans are nothing. Planning is everything.
>
> —*Dwight D. Eisenhower*

### Work Collaboratively

Work collaboratively with stakeholders to develop a strategic plan. Unless stakeholders feel a sense of ownership in the effort, they may not support it and in some cases may oppose or subvert it. In the federal service, they may simply bide their time until a new appointee takes over the organization.

### Process and Product Are Equally Important

Recognize that the process is part of the product in strategic planning. The process brings stakeholders together to form shared directions and responsibilities. It elicits commitment and support. Process should never be viewed as a waste of time or as a compliance exercise. Your process should include one or more off-site meetings with key clients and stakeholders. Having understood that process as critically important, do not forget that you must produce something—policy, decisions, program design, or the like. Production, in the end, is the result of process.

### Vision Is Important

> I skate to where I think the puck will be.
>
> —*Wayne Gretzky*

Develop a clear vision statement that reflects the breadth and limits of your authority and responsibility that your clients and stakeholders can understand and to which they can relate. Vision should tie into department and administration perspectives, as well as into subordinate offices in your organization. Make sure vision derives from mission and that it fits into your strategy.

## Use Process to Identify Priorities, Issues, and Opportunities

Develop a process that will help identify issues requiring attention, including those key issues worthy of your personal attention. Too often, process focuses on organizational weaknesses and threats—negative things. Use process to also identify opportunities. The process can also be used to devise an action plan to address issues.

## Generate Some Initial Successes to Build Confidence in Your Leadership

When assuming leadership of an organization or when undertaking a new strategic initiative, it is important to create some early successes that will help build your credibility. Do not design a process that leads to results only in the distant future, especially if it is likely to extend into another administration. People will lose their momentum or become discouraged or indifferent. Again, some will simply wait until a new administration takes charge.

## Establish Some Immediate Benefits for Cooperation

To demonstrate your seriousness when taking over and launching your management agenda, deliver to your subordinates and, to some extent, your superiors some "added value" to their operations. Scout the landscape to find out what other managers need to perform their duties well. Decide what needs you can make good on. Meet with managers individually and discuss their needs. Then deliver on some needs as soon as possible after your meetings.

## 5. Manage Against a Few Key Performance Measures

> You can't manage what you don't measure,
> and what you don't manage doesn't get done.
>
> —*Peter F. Drucker*

## Reach Consensus with Stakeholders Early On

On the one hand, some key stakeholders may be reluctant to be pinned down on how they will judge your success and are generally resistant to performance measurement. On the other hand, early agreement with Congress and the Office of Management and Budget on specific measures by which your organization will be judged will allow you to focus management of the organization to achieve results. This communication/negotiating challenge should not be overlooked.

### *Limit Performance Measures, Focus them on Outcomes*

Key performance measures should be limited in number, both to ensure focus on the most important outcomes and to bound the reporting burden they impose on the organization. Measures will differ widely depending on your mission. Even then, there are a wide variety of possible measures. Some measures need to be kept in place because they represent historical trends. But where you have discretion, choose measures that help define your management agenda, keep it on track, and demonstrate success on accomplishment.

### *Don't Ask for Data That Will Never Be Used*

Ask only for performance data you intend to use to manage operations. When data are not used, management and staff will not take data requests seriously. Over time, collecting useless data will undermine strategic planning and performance-based management, both of which are data-driven. Publicize, whenever possible, how data were used to plan or manage, and why they were important.

### *Set Long- and Short-Term Targets*

Set specific long-term and interim annual targets for improving results for major business lines. You cannot afford to wait until year's end to determine how operations are going, particularly in fluid environments.

### *Link Targets to Resource Allocation*

Use targets to drive resource allocation decisions that are under your control and as an indication to others of how effectively resources are being applied.

### *Properly Resource Performance Initiatives*

Ensure that performance management efforts are properly resourced. Do not ask your managers to engage in extensive data gathering and reporting efforts, then deny them the means to perform. Inevitably, they will divert resources away from operations to comply with your directive or will not take the assignment seriously.

*Assign Responsibility for Goal Attainment*

Assign responsibility to ensure the accuracy and timeliness of data produced for performance measures; then hold that person accountable. Build an independent or alternative means of data verification wherever possible.

*Understand PART and GPRA, and Take It Seriously*

Government Performance and Results Act of 1993 (GPRA) and Program Assessment Rating Tool (PART) requirements necessitate considerable expenditure of resources whether done properly or not. Some officials take these seriously as planning and evaluation tools; others treat them only as a compliance exercise. Although GPRA and PART may have problems, they also offer opportunities to manage more effectively. Because you will have to expend resources to comply, it makes more sense to use both processes to further your management agenda.

## 6. Link Rewards to Organizational Performance Goal Attainment

> I have yet to find the man, however exalted his station, who did not do better work and put forth greater effort under a spirit of approval than under a spirit of criticism.
>
> —*Charles Schwab*

*Define Rating and Reward System, Then Act on It*

The rating and reward system should clearly define performance expectations for each manager, and use these as a basis for ratings and rewards. Managers, in turn, should do the same for their staff where appropriate. Do not reward poor performance unless there is a compelling reason not to do so. Conversely, do not promise rewards for performance and then not deliver.

*Tie Your Goals to Those of Subordinates*

Performance expectations, against which key subordinates are held, should reflect your own key issues (see item 3). While this advice may sound obvious, it is not. The performance measures of key Senior Executive Service personnel may not reflect your management goals.

*Negotiate Goals with Senior Management*

Reach agreement with senior program managers on how their offices' performance will be measured, and establish specific improvement targets consistent with the targets established through your performance management process.

### Tie Your Goals to Those of Your Superiors

Effective managers should be able to show how their mission, vision, goals, and strategies fit into successively higher levels of the department or organization. Having your agenda succeed in supporting superiors ought to ensure rewards for your entire team—management and staff.

### Evaluate Performance at Mid-term

Do not wait until an annual performance review to give subordinates feedback on their performance. Conduct a mid-year assessment to identify those areas that are on track and those that are not. Making annual changes in course is a dangerous practice.

### 7. Create an Environment that Fosters and Rewards Integrity

> In looking for people to hire, you look for three qualities: integrity, intelligence, and energy. And if they don't have the first, the other two will kill you.
>
> —Warren Buffet

### Build Stakeholder Confidence in Integrity of Business Process

Work to sustain the confidence of your stakeholders, clients, and the public in the honesty and fairness of your business processes. Organizations enjoying reputations for high integrity will usually be given the benefit of the doubt.

### Ensure that Everyone Knows Laws and Regulations

Numerous statutes, regulations, and directives govern your operations specifically, or generally, as a federal agency. There is good reason for this—past actions gone awry led to corrective policies. Ensure that you and your subordinates are aware of applicable laws, regulations, and directives. Follow them. In many agencies, you may find that there is no single source of statutes, regulations, and directives—you may have to hunt them down. It is better to spend time finding guidance than in violating laws and regulations.

### Speak Out About Integrity

Often, integrity in organizations is determined by the standards set by management; lax management leads to lapses in integrity. Use your speaking engagements to reinforce the message that integrity of your business processes is crucially important to you personally. Also reflect importance of integrity in every written communication you can.

### Create Processes That Enforce Compliance

As one of your key management goals, consider reviewing and, if necessary, developing processes that foster and reinforce compliance. Continually review and test processes to see that they compel compliance. Ensure that checks and balances are built into all processes in which bias, manipulation, or conflict of interest might occur.

### Eliminate Conflicts of Interest as High Priority

Carefully review conflict-of-interest procedures within your organization. Build procedures that guard against conflicts of interest.

### 8. Encourage and Reward Creativity and Innovation

> When all think alike, then no one is thinking.
>
> —*Walter Lippman*

### Reward Creativity and Innovation

Encourage and reward managers who develop creative solutions. Rewards do not necessarily need to be monetary. Reward innovation publicly at recognition events, in newsletters, on websites, and in reports. Make sure rewards are real and merit-based. Do not set up a process to elicit innovative ideas and then fail to act on them. However, be prepared to field some very bad ideas.

### Reward Innovation Among Outside Stakeholders

Encourage and reward stakeholders who develop creative solutions to problems that are important to your operations. Sometimes your staff are too close to issues or too constrained by organizational culture to innovate.

Figure 13.2.  **The Policy Cycle**

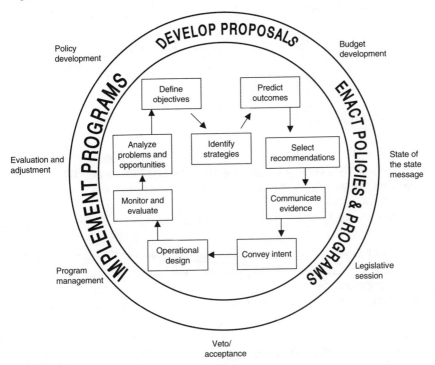

## 9. Understand the Policy Cycle and Its Implications

### Become Well-Versed in the Policy Cycle

Programs, policies, and budgets have their own rhythms in the policy or budget cycle (Figure 13.2). If you arrive late in the cycle, you will have to wait until the appropriate stage in the process. If you arrive early, you will need to take advantage of opportunities. Understand where you are in the cycle, and balance accordingly.

### Focus on a Few Priority Items

Should you arrive at an early stage in the policy or budget cycle and are able to make proposals for new, big-ticket items on your agenda, choose only a handful to pursue. The process is easily clogged when too many proposals are driven through the system. The more proposals floated, the lower the likelihood of success. Agencies always have more proposals than funding.

## 10. Travel and Speak Regularly . . . and Talk with the Civil Servants and Constituents

> The day soldiers stop bringing you their problems is the day you have stopped leading them.
>
> —*Colin Powell*

### *Speak Out Whenever You Can*

You will receive many invitations to speak to groups within and outside government. Try to accept as many as you can. Assistant secretaries government-wide tend to lead through persuasion as much as through authority.

### *Develop Model Speeches That Support Your Agenda*

To permit you to travel and still accomplish your other duties, develop a "stump speech" or two that is good and, once prepared, can be delivered and re-delivered without too much preparation. The speeches should tie into your management agenda and reflect those things you want to achieve as high priorities.

### *Get to Know Staff at All Levels*

When you visit or speak, try to schedule some time to meet with working people in your organization. For example, walk through a program management office and take a moment to ask each individual what they do and how they are doing. Ask them how each of your key initiatives is faring. People will greatly appreciate your taking time to say hello personally. In addition, candor increases with the square of the distance from Washington, DC, and you will occasionally uncover a nugget of information during these walk-through meetings.

# Part V

# Approaches to Public Leadership Development

# 14

## A New Vision for Public Leadership

### The Case for Developing Transformational Stewards

James Edwin Kee, Kathryn Newcomer, and S. Mike Davis

> Leaders create change, and they help organizations and people navigate through change to produce results. Spurred by technology, globalization, down-sizing, economics and public expectations, this is a time of change that calls for leaders.
>
> —*National Academy of Public Administration (NAPA) 1997*

Public service today is characterized by extensive organizational change that requires public leaders to be agents of change—what we refer to as *transformational stewardship* (TS). Public servants at all levels of government face many transformational conditions and requirements, including the following:

- rapid communications that penetrate traditional barriers to information sharing;
- increasing transparency and public scrutiny around government issues, results, and opportunities for improvement;
- evolving information technology, breaking down organizational silos, and connecting and integrating organizational functions in ways not previously possible;
- changing strategic influences and mission requirements, exacerbated by the nature of cross-jurisdiction, cross-sector, and cross-functional interdependencies;
- expectations for more agile and performance-oriented work and organizations;
- increasing top-down, government-wide guidance and coordination of operational standards and improvement priorities; and

- a workforce characterized by shifting demographics and blended public–private partnerships.

We argue that the need for change leaders and managers requires a new way of thinking about public leadership. In addition, a more comprehensive approach to the development of transformational leadership competencies is necessary if we are to meet current and future governance challenges.

## Public Leaders as Transformational Stewards

Over the past decade, government leaders have become increasingly aware that being a public servant also requires being a leader of change. This recognition has rested on the implicit assumption that traditional leader and manager roles, development approaches, and competency profiles are sufficient to support change leadership. Looking more closely at whether managers and leaders are equipped to meet the challenges of change, however, reveals that government's ability to determine skill requirements for the evolving change challenge is a game of "catch up."

Historically, government improvement initiatives have consistently lacked a requisite consideration of the leadership skills and abilities necessary to accomplish the changes that are proposed (NAPA 2002). Recent events involving Federal Emergency Management Agency and National Aeronautics and Space Administration, for example, have also exposed government agencies' inabilities to learn from mistakes and effectively implement change. This argues for a reconsideration of ways of thinking about public sector leadership and management development. From new mission requirements to current succession planning and broader human capital management assessments, agency leadership development programs are in need of realignment and expansion to meet contemporary change competencies.

By exploring government change through case-based research, interviewing current and former public sector change leaders, and dialogue with government executives, we have developed a new approach to change leadership. We refer to this new vision of a public sector change leader as a "transformational steward"—a unique combination of change-related roles that are particularly suited to meeting the challenge of change in government. In this chapter, we draw on previous work (Kee, Newcomer, and Davis 2007) that defined the TS's role and responsibilities, and extend that discussion to consider the related developmental needs and educational approaches necessary to develop TSs.

Why TS? Most government leaders and managers recognize that leading and managing change is a core part of their role as public servants. Many training and development programs have taken this to heart as well and have begun to incorporate competency models and instructional designs addressing the skills needed for change leadership. Yet, government leaders and managers often report that while the instruction they receive in this area is generally "on topic," it frequently fails to provide skills and approaches that survive the reality of constant change that is their daily experience. Collaboration and interorganizational information sharing is taught; yet when the *ideal* of open, articulate, trusting stakeholders is contrasted to the *real* operational environments of complex issues and sometimes hostile stakeholders, managers and leaders are often left feeling that survival requires them to vastly scale back or even to abandon these collaborative approaches.

The public leader has the responsibility to effectively implement change while simultaneously working collaboratively with affected populations to address their possible resistance in a constructive manner. Unfortunately, many current training and development options that are available to public leaders and managers focus on collections of specific leadership and management "competencies" that when developed individually fail to adequately equip civil servants to meet the complex trade-offs of the government change landscape.

This is where the need for TS is most clear. Instead of presenting traditional competency models that represent a collection of more or less separate yet complementary abilities, TS begins with a set of attributes that represent the general characteristics of TS practice and then uses these attributes as a backdrop to consider challenges presented by the requirements to lead and manage change. These requirements are expressed through processes such as "initiating change" and "implementing and sustaining change." In each process, there is a dynamic equilibrium in which the manager or leader must manage risk and find a practical balance between moving transformation forward while stewarding the stakeholders and organizational interests involved in the issue.

Because the heart of change at any point is about the risk of leaving the old for the new, the equilibrium of TS is a reflection of the nature of change itself. TS is an opportunity for public managers and leaders to understand and develop the necessary skills and abilities regarding the trade-offs that they must make as they deal with the challenges of change. In this way, TS is a way to reframe traditional competencies, validate the core requirements and related skills and abilities of change, and then develop and apply these tools in the context of competing influences to broker an effective balance—creating a dynamic equilibrium that reconciles the need for change with the competing needs of stakeholders and the institution.

### Transformational Stewardship and Leadership Development

Given this basic framing of the TS concept, we now consider several fundamental observations about change leadership training and development as a prelude to the more detailed discussion of successfully developing TS. At the basic level, the ultimate objective of TS is to enhance successful transformation and to mitigate change-related risks. To accomplish this, development strategies, programs, and practices should focus on two very basic objectives:

1. Cultivating leaders and managers' awareness of the purpose, nature, and dynamics of organizational change.
2. Channeling that awareness by providing leaders and managers specific approaches, skills, and abilities that enable proactive, integrated action.

This chapter is a practical guide for those in leadership and management positions who are faced with change-related challenges that require transformational acumen, and also for directors of training and development organizations who are seeking to create and improve programs to enable leadership and management of change in their organizations. Discussion thus addresses five key questions.

1. What are the general TS attributes and characteristics that help facilitate effective change leadership and management?
2. What functions, responsibilities, and related abilities and skills are necessary to enable successful TS?
3. How do these factors relate to current leader and manager development standards?
4. What knowledge and experiences does a leader or manager need to effectively accomplish TS responsibilities and put TS abilities and skills to use?
5. What developmental approaches are best suited to accomplishing TS capability development?

### The Essence of Change-Capable Leaders and Managers: Transformational Stewardship Attributes

TS attributes present a general context that describes the nature and characteristics of leading change in the public sector (Kee, Newcomer, and Davis 2007). Taken together, TS attributes provide the basis of more detailed discussions of how TS can be developed in public leaders and managers so that they can more effectively steward change. This initial discussion explains TS through an exploration of the attributes that define this practice.

TS, in the broadest sense, can be thought of as a leadership function in which those exercising leadership (those with "legitimate" authority and others throughout the organization) have developed certain attributes that guide their actions. These attributes reflect leaders' personal outlook or beliefs (their inner-personal beliefs or traits), how they approach a situation (their operational mindset), how they involve others in the function (their interpersonal actions/interactions with others), and their commitment to change and innovation (their change-centric approach).

The "trait" theory of leadership is one of the most persistent concepts about what makes a good leader. Some argue that individuals are either born with leadership traits (such as intelligence) or not. Others argue that the most important leadership traits are those that can be learned (such as understanding the job or task at hand). Among the recent proponents of the trait theory of leadership are the "emotional IQ" or maturity approach of Goleman, McKee, and Boyatzis (2002), who believe that leadership traits can be learned through self-evaluation and mentoring. We believe that the attributes of transformational stewardship are ones that can be part of a person's development—education, skills development, feedback from mentors, and the ongoing experiences of leadership. While one could make a case for many different leadership attributes, Table 14.1 lists the fifteen attributes important for TS and leading change.

### Inner-personal Leadership Beliefs/Traits

We believe the most important personal leadership beliefs/traits are not ones that we are born with, but those that develop throughout our lives and provide us with continuing guidance on how to act in a particular situation—they become inner-personal guides to our actions. The most vital traits for TS are ethical conduct; a reflective, continuous learning attitude; empathy toward others; and the foresight or vision to lead an organization toward a preferred future.

Ethics and moral standards have their roots in the principles we learn throughout our lives, either from parents or mentors or from our own inquiries into what constitutes a just action. It is not a matter of doing what your "conscience tells you" but knowing what ethical principles might apply in a particular situation and possessing the skills to apply them (Badaracco 1997).

Self-reflection is a key to personal growth. Wheatley (2005) suggests that we need to "pause long enough to look more carefully at a situation, to see more of its character, to think about why it is happening, and to notice how it is affecting us and others" (p. 215). Thompson (2000) argues, "Beyond a certain point, there can probably be no personal growth, no individualization, without the capacity for self-reflection" (p. 152).

Table 14.1

## Attributes of Transformational Stewardship

| Attribute | Description |
| --- | --- |
| **Inner-personal Traits/Beliefs** | |
| Ethical | Maintain high standards of integrity for themselves and their organization, elevating organization to a "higher plane" |
| Reflective/Learning Oriented | Able to step back from the situation and consider alternatives; learn from success and failures; self-aware and tolerant |
| Empathy | Demonstrate concern for others, both within and without the organization, over self-interest; self-deprecating |
| Visionary/Foresight | Able to look beyond the current situation and see big picture for the mission and the organization; creating vision for the future |
| Trustee/Caregiver | Hold position and organizational resources in trust for others—the public, in general, and future members of the organization |
| Mission Driven | Fiercely and courageously pursue the mission of their organization; creating "common purpose" |
| Accountable | Measure results in multiple ways, in a transparent fashion, and share with those who contribute to the organization's success. Transformational stewards take responsibility for the results |
| Attention to Detail | Able to sort out those that impact people from the "red tape" that slows change |
| **Interpersonal Abilities** | |
| Trust Builder | Develop community and maintains trust—with the members of their agencies, their constituents, and their principals (Congress and political leadership) |
| Empowering | Decentralize authority and real decision-making throughout the organization so others can become co-leaders and stewards in fulfillment of the public interest |
| Power Sharing | Rely less on positional authority and more on persuasion, moral leadership, and group power to achieve goals |
| Coalition Builder | Recognize the importance of building coalitions with others, within government, in the nonprofit and for-profit sectors |
| **Change-centric Approach** | |
| Creative/Innovative | Focus is on the change needs for the organization, rather than who leads the change; open to new ideas, intuition, inspiration; willing to take risks |
| Comfortable with Ambiguity | Conflicting organizational objectives and priorities often require a balancing act—continuity and change, efficiency and equity, etc. |
| Integrative Systems Thinking | Understanding forces for change and interrelationships; ability to find integrative rather than polarizing solutions |

A TS demonstrates concern for others, both within and outside the organization. Empathy is more than just being a "good listener"; although it is an important skill, leaders must both hear and understand. Thompson (2000) explains, "If by that we mean only that we have learned certain skills and techniques that make the other person feel heard, we have still largely missed the point. To empathize is to both hear and understand, and to grasp both the thoughts the other person is trying to convey and the feelings he or she has about them" (p. 181).

A transformational steward is also able to look beyond the current situation and see the big picture and potential vision for the organization. Mary Parker Follett referred to the need for leaders to "grasp the total situation. . . . Out of a welter of facts, experience, desires, aims, the leader must find the unifying thread . . . the higher up you go the more ability you have to have of this kind. When leadership rises to genius it has the power of transforming, transforming experience into power" (Follett in Graham 2003, pp. 168–169).

## Operational Mindset

Transformational stewards recognize that they hold their position and use organizational resources for others, not for their own self-aggrandizement. The broad concept of public interest, while not always easy to define, must be a constant touchstone for the leader. Public servants, whether elected, appointed, or part of the large civil service system, are only temporarily in charge of their resources and responsibilities. They hold them in trust for the public (both current and future generations); hence, they serve the public and must act in the public's interest, not for self-interest.

Transformational stewards fiercely and courageously pursue the mission of their organization. In most cases, they act as agents of those who established that mission—the legislature, the chief executive, or the courts. Sometimes, conflicting goals and agendas require the public servant to arbitrate (Kee and Black 1985). Public managers can find this common purpose by engaging the people with their agencies, citizens, and other stakeholders who will assist the leader in defining the agency's mission or core values—in effect, determining the public interest.

Transformational stewards measure their performance in a transparent fashion and share those results with those who can affect the organization and its success. This is consistent with efforts at the federal level to get agencies to articulate and measure progress toward their performance goals (e.g., the Government Performance Results Act of 1993). Transformational stewards support processes such as performance-based budgeting, balanced scorecards, and other efforts to measure program results in an open fashion and subject them to periodic review and evaluation. What is important is not measurement for the sake of measurement or the creation of short-term output measures, but measurement for the sake of legitimate feedback and program revision aimed at attainment.

Transformational stewards know that details do matter (Addington and Graves 2002). Details are often the way in which government programs ensure adherence to important democratic values, such as equitable distribution of public benefits or access to public programs. Process "red tape" is often the means to ensure adherence to procedural imperatives; however, it should not be used as cover or excuse for poor performance.

### Interpersonal/Interactions with Others

Leadership theories increasingly stress the importance of the leader's interaction with others. The chief goals for transformational stewards are empowerment and engendering trust in employees throughout the organization. Transformational stewards build program success through developing and maintaining trust with the members of their agencies, their constituents, and their principals. Developing trust is about building community within their organizations, engendering trust with the citizens they serve, and developing the confidence of the principals (executives and legislatures) to whom they report.

The concept of empowerment is closely related to trust. Trust demands empowerment of agency employees and, where possible, decentralization of authority—real decision making—throughout the organization. To the extent that leaders empower others (employees and citizens), the others become co-leaders and stewards in fulfillment of the public interest. This creates a fundamental role and opportunity for transformational stewards throughout the organization.

Transformational stewards rely less on positional authority for their power and more on personal power sources, persuasion, and moral leadership to effect change. Beyond personal power, transformational stewards rely on "group power." Follett claimed, "It is possible to develop the conception of power-with, a jointly developed power, a co-active, not a coercive power. . . . The great leader tries . . . to develop power wherever he [sic] can among those who work with him [sic], and then gathers all this power and uses it as the energizing force of a progressing enterprise" (Follett in Graham 2003, pp. 103, 173).

Transformational stewards recognize that they cannot fully meet their mission with given resources (people, dollars, etc.) without involving others. They know that horizontal relationships and coalition building with other organizations within government, in the nonprofit sector, and in the for-profit sector are essential for the success.

### Change-centric Approach

Building on trust, empowerment, coalition building, and power sharing, transformational stewards are able to be change-centric, focusing on the needed change itself, rather than the source of the call for change (from the leader, top-down, or from the followers, bottom-up). What matters is finding the proper balance of top-down and bottom-up management that leads to successful change (Kee and Setzer 2006). Achieving positive change should be the focus, not assigning inflexible leadership roles. The focus of change-centric leadership is on the successful change effort itself, which is not to say leadership does not have an important role. On the contrary, the leader or leaders of an organization serve as facilitators of change. They should strive to be cognizant of when change efforts require more initiative from the top and when the success of change efforts may hinge on allowing more employee participation in formulation of the change vision. To be change-centric, trans-formational stewards need to be creative, innovative, and comfortable with ambiguity and with navigating complex systems.

Transformational stewards do not wait for a crisis to innovate and create; they attempt to build an environment that values continuous learning in which workers constantly draw on current and past experiences to frame a new future for the organization. Vaill (1996) acknowledges that "creative learning" is seemingly a contradiction in a world of institutional learning where people who "know" transfer knowledge to people who do not know. However, in a change environment there often is no "body of knowledge" to transfer; thus, it is up to the transformational steward to create the knowledge. This requires an inquiring mind that is willing to explore options. Just as an artist might not always know what the final product will look like, transformational stewards must be open to the unknown, willing to surprise themselves, and willing to recognize "in that surprise is the learning" (Vaill 1996, p. 61).

Transformational stewards recognize that conflicting organizational objectives and priorities often require a careful balancing act of competing interests and obligations. Public managers, like their private counterparts, live in an era of "permanent white water," bombarded by pressures from both within and outside the organization (Vaill 1996). Transformational stewards recognize that their "solutions" are among many plausible alternatives and that they must be continually reassessed and adjusted as conditions change.

Thanks largely to Peter Senge's book, *The Fifth Discipline* (1990), systems thinking has become one of the most important concepts in the field of leadership. However, systems thinking is not an easy concept to grasp or apply. Vaill (1996) notes that evidence demonstrates an absence of systems thinking: our tendency to think in black and white, to believe in simple linear cause–effect relationships, to ignore feedback, to ignore relationships between a phenomenon and its environment, and to ignore how our own biases frame our perceptions. Vaill (1996) sees the core idea of systems thinking in the balancing and interrelating of three levels of phenomenon: first, the "whole," or phenomenon of interest itself; second, the inner-workings of the whole—the combining and interacting of the internal elements to produce the whole; and third, the world outside the whole that places the phenomenon in its context—all moving dynamically in time (pp. 108–109). Vaill argues that the key to learning systems thinking—and we believe it can be learned—is "understanding oneself in interactions with the surrounding world" (p. 110).

## Meeting Change Leadership Development Needs:
## The Transformational Stewardship Leader Profile (TSLP)

As we examine the attributes of a transformational steward and contrast that to current approaches for developing leaders of change, we find three significant shortcomings.

1. Insufficient linkages that tie the work of organizational change to the required skills, abilities, and developmental efforts necessary to accomplish that work. This may be the result of insufficient attention to ensuring employee skills match the requirements of evolving roles in achievement of changing agency missions.
2. Inaccurate or incomplete definitions of what is and is not involved in organizational change. This is often due to a lack of fluency with organizational change dynamics and processes.
3. Training and development approaches that fail to convey the necessary real-world skills for effective change leadership, and/or that develop related skills and abilities without sufficiently exploring the change-related interdependencies and practical challenges involved. This is often due to the lack of experiential learning as part of a leader development plan.

In this section, we outline the components of a Transformational Stewardship Leader Profile (TSLP) as a step toward addressing these deficiencies. Drawing on the TS attributes as a foundation, the TSLP is a framework that defines the nature of TS roles and practices, as well as the fundamental components of leadership development related to leading change and transformation. Our discussion will initially focus on a consideration of how we can best structure the elements of TS in a comprehensive and integrated way, and then turn to the specific organizational change functions and processes that transformational stewards must learn. Following this orientation to the two basic aspects of the framework, we will discuss specific TS competencies.

## 1. How Do We Define and Structure Transformational Stewardship Skills, Abilities, and Developmental Efforts to Support Successful Organizational Change?

The TSLP organizing framework, depicted in Figure 14.1, includes six inter-related elements: functions, responsibilities, abilities, skills, knowledge, and developmental experiences. The elements of the framework articulate the ingredients of TS, as well as the "nuts and bolts" necessary for translating the vision of TS into an operational reality in public sector organizations.

We group the six organizing elements of the Leader Profile into two distinct dimensions. The first "Requirements and Competencies" dimension includes consideration of the functions and responsibilities of transformational stewards, as well as required skills and abilities. These first four elements relate specifically to the "work" of leading and managing change, with the path from the function element to the skills element a progression of increasing detail and tactical specificity. The second "Learning and Development" dimension of the framework includes two elements—knowledge and developmental experiences. These elements outline the necessary knowledge that transformational stewards must gain, as well as the experiential aspects required to put TS skills into practice. These two elements provide a baseline for leadership development programs to incorporate.

## 2. What Are the Phases of the Organizational Change Process That Present Different Challenges for Transformational Stewardship Practice?

We conceptualize the change process in three general phases: (1) initiating transformation, (2) implementing and sustaining transformation, and (3) stewarding organizational growth and renewal. The specific details involved in accomplishing each step of these general processes are discussed below.

The first phase begins when the need for change is recognized and the stewardship responsibilities relate to *what* to change, *who* will play *what* roles in the change process, and *how* to proceed. Leaders need skills in strategic awareness, risk assessment, and appreciation of common stakes and current capabilities. While this aspect of the change process often becomes

Figure 14.1  **Transformational Stewardship Leader Profile (TSLP) Organizing Framework**

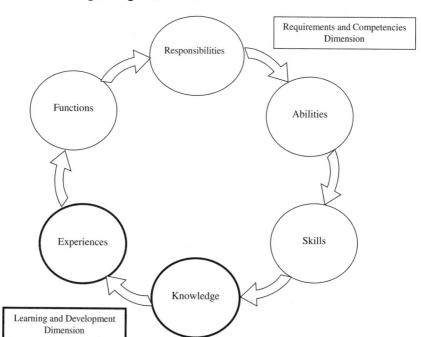

(as it should) a structured and organized proceeding, the initial dialogue is frequently informal, and this informal discussion is a constant backdrop of this and subsequent stages in the change process.

The second phase picks up with the determination of *how* to proceed with a plan to implement changes. This is usually the point in which the initial dialogue of *why* and *what* has led to a collective focus on a particular priority for action. This stage of the change process requires leadership with an awareness and fluency with the nature of changing work and the workforce, an ongoing appreciation for stakeholder needs and interests, and an ability to proactively manage risks. This second stage concludes roughly when there is a transition from the implementation activities to the more operational conditions of sustaining the change.

Finally, the third phase of the change process is that of continual organizational growth and renewal. As this conceptualization suggests, growth and renewal is not necessarily a sequential aspect but rather an ongoing process that should ground organizational dialogue at all levels. Different from the other two phases of change process, "growth and renewal" is not characterized by activities undertaken to accomplish a particular change but rather by strengthening institutional mechanisms that ensure reinvention and "change-centric" behavior in the organization. Leadership qualities that support this growth include an emphasis on reflective practice, agile organizing structures, strengthening relationships and transparency, and continual alignment and improvement. Having described the fundamental processes of organizational change and the related requirements for TS, we now turn to a more detailed discussion of the TSLP as it relates to each aspect of organizational change.

## The Requirement to Initiate Change

The initiating phase of organizational change includes the tasks and related competencies of determining *why* and *what* to change. This stage begins with the assessment of strategic influences and trends that drive the need for change and concludes with the creation of a change implementation plan that defines and structures the work of change effort. Like the other steps of the organizational change process, the elements of this stage are not always sequential. Rather, they often occur simultaneously, unfolding gradually throughout the initiation process.

The initiating phase is probably the most commonly recognized part of the change process—almost everyone is familiar with the process of "strategic planning," building "business cases," "environmental scanning," and "scoping" a project. Yet, while some of the tasks in this stage are part of many management vocabularies, the actual scope and nature of transformation-specific activities during this stage are much more detailed than most leadership training. Initiating change is not easy in any organization, and this challenge can be particularly complicated in government, where rules and procedures may explicitly govern the collaborative process among stakeholder groups. Similarly, the unique nature of career civil servant and political stakeholder interests establishes a very subtle and complex backdrop for change initiatives. Difficulties notwithstanding, the requirement for an integrative, collectively supported change is inherent in our government and is a fundamental expression of the nature of the TS challenge.

### *The Balancing Challenge*

To initiate change successfully, transformational stewards balance working within structural bureaucratic limitations, satisfying (to the extent possible) the diverse, complex interests of stakeholders, and maintaining appropriate political accountability while consistently moving forward with a practical change agenda that enhances agency effectiveness. Leadership development approaches have traditionally sought to address this need by providing general collaboration, negotiation, and ethics instruction. We feel that a more complete understanding of the requirements and mechanics of change at this stage illuminates the need for a much richer array of skills and experiences.

By understanding the nature of initiating change more completely, transformational stewards can develop a much broader array of practical tools and approaches for creating a balanced process that moves the agency forward, all the while recognizing and appreciating the complexity of the issue involved. More exclusive competency-focused development often misses this mark, providing leaders and managers with skills that are necessary but insufficient.

Table 14.2 outlines how the initiation requirement translates into attributes, abilities, and skills. The table also displays how these aspects translate into specific learning and development activities. In the discussion that follows, we consider the elements of the initiation competency profile in greater detail, exploring several important links that are critical to developing successful transformational stewards.

### The Initiation Process: From Functions to Responsibilities, Abilities, and Skills

Two core functions define the change initiation phase: defining the context and requirements for change, and designing realistic, comprehensive change strategies and plans. The key transformational-steward challenge during this phase is to balance the need for change while appreciating current organizational strengths and synthesizing stakeholder interests and concerns. This is no easy task, but there are leaders and managers who are able to work together effectively to accomplish this balance. What are the characteristics of these successes?

We begin with the "attributes" exhibited by TS leaders and managers. Like all aspects of the TS approach, attributes during the change initiation stage are interdependent and integrative in nature. As depicted in Table 14.2, three key attribute clusters are most important for supporting the actions of initiating change: (1) visionary perspective and foresight; (2) empathetic ways of relating to others and coalition-building abilities; and (3) integrative, systems awareness, and attention to detail. While specific attributes are more important for meeting specific requirements, these three clusters are generally representative of behaviors that are consistently of top importance across all phases of organizational change. During the initiation phase, these attributes help the transformational steward articulate the need and nature of change, understand and appreciate the needs of others involved in the process, and craft a realistic transition strategy.

Table 14.2

**Initiating Change**

**Phase 1: Initiate Transformation**

| Relevant TS Attributes | Competencies and Standards Dimension | | | Learning and Development Dimension | |
| --- | --- | --- | --- | --- | --- |
| | Responsibilities | Abilities | Skills | Knowledge | Developmental Experiences |
| Visionary/ foresight; integrative systems thinking; mission driven | Determine change drivers | Ability to assess internal and external strategic influences, define organizational change implications, and design and manage strategically aligned change initiatives | Assess strategic influences and implications driving organizational change; translate strategic drivers into mission requirements/ requirements for change | Be aware of and understand current strategic public sector influences and trends | Conduct environmental scan and trend-identification exercise |
| | | | | Understand the relationship of strategic trends to mission requirements, vision, and the implied requirements for change; understand methods for identifying strategic influences and trends | Conduct a strategic organizational assessment and define organizational change requirements |

*(continued)*

Table 14.2 *(continued)*

| | Competencies and Standards Dimension | | | Learning and Development Dimension | |
|---|---|---|---|---|---|
| Relevant TS Attributes | Responsibilities | Abilities | Skills | Knowledge | Developmental Experiences |
| | Set change vision | Ability to grasp the total situation (whole and the parts) in a changing environment, and draw on that understanding to create a vision for the future that creatively meets mission requirements and clearly defines the context for change | Determine and articulate project/ team vision | Understand how to define an organizational vision that is representative of stakeholder needs and effectively articulates a future state that can frame and guide change | Conduct a vision-setting exercise |
| Empathy; power sharing; coalition building; trust building | Facilitate identification/ realization of common interests and objectives | Ability to design and steward stakeholder collaboration forums and processes, synthesizing and brokering stakeholder needs to forge common, collectively defined change efforts | Conduct stakeholder audit; structure partnership agreements; negotiate and broker common objectives; develop Common Case for Change (CCC); facilitate stakeholder forum | Understand stakeholder interests, perceptions, and expectations; understand approaches to designing and managing stakeholder collaboration; understand methods for conducting stakeholder assessments | Conduct a stakeholder audit to identify stakeholders and stakes for a change issue; facilitate a stakeholder forum; meet and engage stakeholders to understand needs and expectations; articulate a CCC allowing facilitation/ dialogue |

| | | | | | |
|---|---|---|---|---|---|
| Foresight; accountable | Set and manage specific change objectives, measures | Ability to define, implement and manage clear, credible measures and objectives; ability to employ measures and performance information to identify impediments and successes | Define change objectives and measures; track and manage performance information | Understand nature and types of change-related performance measures, including normative perceptual variables as well as project and process-based implementation measures | Develop change strategy, objectives, and measures for change project or initiative |
| Integrative systems thinking; attention to detail; foresight | Anticipate the scope required for integrated total systems change | Ability to anticipate potential scope of impacts resulting from planned changes and determine a baseline estimation of required scope of transition activities that will be necessary to accomplish objectives | Map systems influences, interdependencies, and impacts | Understand systems dynamics of organizations; interdependencies across organizational systems and strategy, structure, process, skills and culture/climate; understand approaches to mapping systems variables and impacts | Complete an impact/complexity analysis exercise related to a particular change event, in order to determine the potential impact footprint of the change |
| Integrative systems thinking; attention to detail; foresight | Accomplish change within capacity limitations and with maximum return on resources | Ability to assess dimensions of organizational capacity and cost against requirements; determine change priorities; allocate resources and manage available capacity to achieve objectives | Assess current organizational capacity, and change capacity requirements as defined by impact change footprint; determine Return on Investment (ROI) | Understand types of organizational capacity and limitations of capacity; understand methods for assessing/ balancing capacity through priority-based resource allocation and decision-making; understand costs and benefits, methods for assessing ROI | Complete a capacity assessment and cost-benefit/ROI analysis |

*(continued)*

Table 14.2 (continued)

| Relevant TS Attributes | Competencies and Standards Dimension | | | | Learning and Development Dimension | |
| --- | --- | --- | --- | --- | --- | --- |
| | Responsibilities | Abilities | Skills | | Knowledge | Developmental Experiences |
| | Limit unanticipated impacts of change | Ability to assess change-related risks and identify potential high-risk areas | Conduct risk assessments for complexity, capability, and stakes dimensions | | Understand change-related risk factors and dynamics across project complexity, stakeholder relations, and organizational change capability areas | Conduct change risk assessment and identify change risk areas |
| | Develop change implementation and risk mitigation plan | Ability to draw on change complexity/scope analysis to design realistic transformation efforts including communications, workforce transition, and stakeholder alignment activities | Create transition plans/design transition activities | | Understand transformation strategies and approaches to affect organizational change | Develop a change implementation and risk management plan |

While many skill-building approaches address any single attribute or combination of these attributes separately, we feel that truly successful transformation can only emerge from the reciprocal support that each of these elements provides to the whole. In this way, TS is grounded in a definition of change as a state in which individuals determine whether to risk leaving the comfort (or familiar discomfort) of the present for the potential of better conditions in the future. Here in the initiation process is where balancing begins, and TS attributes create a solid foundation for effectively employing specific transformational skills.

"Responsibilities" are the next level of detail depicted on the matrix as flowing from function requirements. For the initiation stage of change, we have defined seven specific responsibilities of the transformational steward. In general, they represent task areas that the transformational steward must accomplish. The TS role during this stage is to establish a strategically aligned, collectively supported change agenda. The TS responsibilities are intended to contribute to creating shared value. It is important to note the distinction between this role for transformational stewards as opposed to widely accepted visions of the task of managing change. The nature of the transformational steward's responsibility through the initiation process is explicitly collaborative and service-oriented. This is different from the common conception of "managing" change during initiation as a task primarily concerned with using persuasion to gain minimally sufficient "buy-in" to implement a mostly predetermined, one-sided agenda that if necessary may contain a carrot or two for potentially threatened stakeholders.

As part of identifying the context for the change initiative, TS requires scanning and assessing change drivers, setting the change vision, and developing common values and interests among affected stakeholders. During the design phase, TS requires the development of specific change objectives and measures, development of an integrated change plan, the efficient use of organizational capacity, and the mitigation of change risks.

Flowing from these responsibilities, the transformational steward must have the ability to identify and assess various strategic influences on the change landscape. Regardless of whether the change is at the organizational, interorganizational, or team level, strategic influences must be translated into change requirements. Developmentally, leaders and managers must understand strategic management principles and the process of determining operational requirements from strategic factors. Even at the most tactical levels, having the ability to translate strategy into the need for change is critical when interacting with stakeholders.

The second cluster of skills and abilities requires transformational stewards to create the conditions for stakeholder interests to be expressed and vetted with regard to the need for change. The leader must facilitate stakeholder collaboration, broker diverse interests to identify common interests and objectives, and craft a stakeholder relationship strategy that maximizes mutual gain and minimizes loss. While all stakeholders may not support the effort with total commitment, the collaborative process itself provides stakeholders with an opportunity to guide the change process, while simultaneously legitimizing and improving the likely results of change efforts.

During this phase of the change process, the balance that the transformational steward must maintain is one of appreciating what is working while illuminating what is not. Particularly in government, the limited tenure and frequent turnover of top leadership means that the norm is a completely new agenda with each new leadership team. This has, in effect, created a pervasive anxiety of government civil servants surrounding organizational change. In many instances, new leadership paves over and even contradicts efforts that civil servants are attempting to implement from previous change efforts. By including an appreciative, empathetic focus throughout the strategic assessment and stakeholder collaboration processes, transformational stewards can more effectively achieve the dynamic equilibrium necessary to effect positive change.

In practice, the initiation process requires that transformational stewards be proficient at conducting stakeholder assessments/audits, planning and facilitating stakeholder forums, and developing a resulting "common" case for change. These tasks require the foundational knowledge of stakeholder relationships and the dynamics of collaborative processes, with an understanding of methods for analyzing stakes to understand how to best strategically move change forward. Experientially, the tasks of conducting a strategic assessment, facilitating stakeholder dialogues, determining requirements, and making the "case" for change all provide practical venues for the initiating competencies to be developed.

The third competency group for the initiation phase involves abilities and skills associated with bringing the collaborative process to realization through practical strategies and plans for change. These activities are supported by the attributes of attention to detail and integrative systems thinking. Beginning with the articulation of change objectives and measures, the result of inputs from the stakeholder collaboration process, TS requires the ability to develop a specific approach to change that not only defines an implementation approach, but also anticipates and mitigates change-related risks and is supported by available organizational capacity. To accomplish these objectives, transformational stewards require an understanding of change-related risks associated with change complexity, stakes, and organizational change capability; and an understanding of the interdependencies that link impacts across strategies, organizing structures, work processes, reporting relationships, job/role requirements, and developmental needs. This awareness is gained and refined by conducting risk analyses and impact assessments on proposed change approaches.

### The Initiation Process: Learning and Development Dimension

The competencies necessary to support TS while initiating change are substantially limited in the current developmental tracks available to most federal leaders and managers, save basic strategic planning and interpersonal collaboration skills. For the most part, the requirement to lead and manage change is included as either a general aspect of broadly defined leadership abilities or as a technical or functional responsibility tied to a particular area of practice such as e-government or financial management. The more detailed change competencies noted here as necessary for initiating transformation, including the corresponding challenge of reconciling competing interests, are not recognized or sanctioned in any consistent manner. This includes the familiar Executive Core Qualifications (ECQs) that outline federal executive competency requirements. The initiation process is very conducive to experiential learning and scenario-based exercises, since leaders and managers can refine many complementary skills in a process of responding to change drivers when given a set group of stakeholders and resource limitations.

While learning and development can come from "book knowledge," we would argue that the most valuable development is experiential learning—whether in the classroom or on the job. Developing a vision statement is something you can learn about, examine illustrations, and understand the process. However, unless a person actually participates in this attempt by trying to find a common set of values and norms among competing interests, full development is unlikely to occur. This is somewhat akin to the question: "How do you get to Carnegie Hall?" Answer: "Practice, practice, practice." TS requires practice. Thus, understanding how to define an organizational vision is no substitute for facilitating a vision-setting exercise that incorporates change and transformation.

Similarly, transformational stewards have a responsibility to facilitate the identification of common values, interests, and objectives of the organization's stakeholders. Individuals can learn about how to do this, how to conduct a stakeholder audit, how to facilitate collaborative processes, and how to develop a "common case for change." However, unless a person has actually attempted to do this, the transformational steward will have inadequate skills to adapt to the many and various conditions and issues that are likely to come up. Again, while case studies can provide one method of "gaining experience," there is no substitute for actually conducting a stakeholder "audit" and facilitating a stakeholder meeting to develop common interests. Those wishing to become transformational stewards should complement their book knowledge by volunteering to participate in these activities, thereby gaining the experience and confidence to fulfill their TS responsibilities.

## Implementing and Sustaining Change

The second set of TS competencies relate to aligning the processes, structures, policies and procedures, and roles and jobs of the organization or team. As noted in our discussion of the initiation phase, implementation ideally begins when the initial dialogue of why and what to change has led to a collective focus on a particular priority for action. Complete consensus is not frequently a luxury that transformational stewards experience; nevertheless, general agreement is critical to keep the risks of unanticipated, undesirable consequences to a minimum.

The need to manage change-related risk, in combination with the requirement to navigate the interdependencies and systems impacts of changing work and workforce roles, emerge as the two core driving functions during implementation. And as with initiation, these functions are set on the backdrop of the principal attribute clusters of (1) maintaining constant awareness of the "bigger picture" or long-term vision; (2) translating feedback, challenges, and decisions empathetically to maintain a commitment to relationships and mutual ownership; and (3) applying an integrative systems awareness and attention to detail. In this stage, the empathetic, interpersonal attributes are a function of the need to effectively communicate, act with transparency, and understand and engage evolving interests and sources of resistance. The integrative systems attributes relate expressly to the transformational steward's ability to understand, anticipate, and navigate the risks and required transition activities resulting from work and workforce changes.

Change is unsettling to some degree, regardless of the context of how well it is led and managed. During implementation, the transformational steward must address the upheaval and uncertainty of changing work with a consistent and unwavering commitment to maintain focus and clarity, empathically recognize and understand capacity limitations and the needs expressed behind statements of resistance, and facilitate dialogue in which everyone owns a part of the process.

### *Implementing and Sustaining: From Functions to Responsibilities, Abilities, and Skills*

In implementing and sustaining transformation, transformational stewards have the following chief responsibilities: establishing transparency, engagement, and collective ownership; appreciating, understanding, and addressing resistance; aligning organizational capabilities; and partnering to successful implement transformation. These responsibilities are the complementary influences of transformation and stewardship.

Over the past fifteen years of emerging interest in technology implementation and project management, the requirements for TS have had the tendency to be shaped into a more limited, tactical focus on "managing" the change process. While this focus has pushed leaders and managers to consider the mechanics necessary to manage project-based transformation, it has also somewhat concealed the more holistic aspects of successfully leading and managing. In one sense, this technical concentration has been a backlash of sorts to the more "touchy-feely" practices that were proposed by organizational psychologists in the late seventies and early eighties. In our view, change leadership during implementation (as in other phases) is neither purely tactical and technical nor exclusively facilitative and subjective. Rather, as the represented responsibilities, abilities, and skills depict here, TS requires fluency in technical and tactical and strategic and traditional aspects of organizational management. Moreover, the function of dynamic equilibrium proposed by the TS concept is fertile ground for starting to tie the range of disparate change competencies together in a practical framework of specific, concrete developmental actions. And while many current leader development approaches present a singular, separate, and "definitional" focus on specific competencies, the TS development experiences in Table 14.3 should provide an initial gateway to exploring the details of operational proficiency.

The competency requirements for implementing transformation are relevant for all leaders and managers involved in the implementation process—not merely the transformation implementation team itself. During the initial span of the implementation process, it is critical that organizations' business process owners and program managers who are involved in the change are invited to participate in shaping and guiding the transformation. In addition, contractors or other extra-organizational partners should be involved in this step. This "blended-workforce" reality of most change situations involves core and extended teams of transformational operatives working together to jointly design and implement the transformational initiative. The collaboration, risk mitigation, and alignment responsibilities in Table 14.3 point to this need. Many change efforts involving diverse actors without this type of global transformational proficiency are fatally wounded early in the implementation process, ambling on as "Trojan horses" until a later point when implementation-related risks bring unstable foundations into play more visibly and the project begins to collapse.

Table 14.3

**Implementing and Sustaining Change**

**Phase 2: Implement and Sustain Transformation**

| | Competencies and Standards Dimension | | | Learning and Development Dimension | |
|---|---|---|---|---|---|
| Relevant TS Attributes | Responsibilities | Abilities | Skills | Knowledge | Developmental Experiences |
| Empathy; coalition building; trust building | Establish transparency, engagement, and collective ownership | Ability to identify communications needs; design, deploy, and manage change-related communications | Conduct a communications needs assessment; create a communications strategy and plan; manage communications across multiple channels and audiences | Understand communications types, channels, and audience segments; understand planning and management of change communications | Conduct a communications needs assessment and develop a change communications plan |
| | | Ability to establish mechanisms for ownership and collective engagement in the implementation process | Create and manage participative implementation planning, decision making, and issue resolution processes | Understand decision making and issue resolution methods and approaches; understand dynamics of trust and methods for establishing transparency | Complete role-play and scenario analysis exercises related to issue resolution and determining balance of execution and participative deliberation |

271

| | | | | |
|---|---|---|---|---|
| Appreciate, understand, and address resistance | Ability to recognize, understand, and address obstacles to change, including overt and covert stakeholder resistance, culture and climate variables, and organizational defensive routines | | Understand needs/ "meta-messages" underlying resistance; understand forms of organizational defensive routines, self-sealing behaviors, and limiting mental models, as well as approaches for addressing resistance and using it in positive manner | Conduct role-play and resistance-response exercises |
| Integrative systems thinking; attention to detail | Align organizational capabilities | Ability to assess and understand workforce impacts and to plan and manage workforce transition activities; plan and manage job/role restructuring and requisite training and development efforts | Determine process, role and skill workforce impacts, and related transitional requirements | Understand process, role and skill interdependencies, and business process improvement approaches | Complete a work/workforce impact analysis, business process improvement, and workforce transition plan |
| | | | Conduct job/role/task analysis | Understand workforce transition requirements and approaches | |

(continued)

Table 14.3 *(continued)*

| | Competencies and Standards Dimension | | | Learning and Development Dimension | |
|---|---|---|---|---|---|
| Relevant TS Attributes | Responsibilities | Abilities | Skills | Knowledge | Developmental Experiences |
| Creative/innovative; coalition building | Partner to successfully implement transformation | Ability to design and manage blended implementation efforts as part of change-related procurement actions or inter-agency/intersector partnerships | Create and manage participative implementation planning and execution, including interagency/sector joint efforts and procurement-related plans and efforts | Understand partnership agreement methods and approaches, including interagency and intergovernment-al partnerships, as well as procurement vehicles for addressing change needs | Complete blended implementation scenario exercises and/or role-plays involving procurement partnerships and interorganizational change partnerships |

Transformational skills are everyone's responsibility, and comprehensive transformational competency is a necessity to ensure successful change initiatives. When such capability is absent in the larger community of involved stakeholders and responsibility for change success is restricted to more central, authority-wielding officials, the tendency to focus on official accountability may overshadow the need for collective ownership and diffused transformational acumen. In the federal government, for example, change efforts that involve significant procurement aspects—such as e-government systems- implementation initiatives—can fall into the trap of focusing accountability and risk-mitigation activities on the contract vehicle and the requirement for the vendor to deliver. While this aspect of change projects is important, emphasis on procurement accountability may lead agency leaders to undervalue the need for their managers and leaders at all levels to possess the transformational ability to implement the change and make the project a success. While contracting relationships and public–private partnerships present their own unique risks, failed implementation is easy to pin on irresponsible contracting when it is frequently a result of ineffective collaboration and transformational capability at each point where public leaders and managers interact with implementation partners.

Two important, complementary transformation skills are worth additional consideration—the ability to anticipate change impacts and the ability to understand and mitigate transformational risk. Both of these aspects are grounded in the attributes of integrative systems thinking and attention to detail. Foremost during implementation, transformational stewards must be adept at assessing the "scope" of change that achieving a management objective requires. This is not to be confused with the "project scope," traditionally used as a gauge of what is involved in a project. Rather, change scope is a more specific aspect that if not carefully considered often leads to underestimating the project scope.

To determine change scope, the transformational steward must have the ability to draw on the explicit, objective-driven definition of the project and then deduce the requirements for process, policy, procedure, structure, and competency changes that are necessary. This ability requires that the transformational steward be proficient at using a systems approach to identifying the primary and secondary impacts of the effort. A transformational steward who possesses this ability is then able to apply that knowledge to anticipate key change-related risks and structure necessary transformation plans. These resulting activities are represented in Table 14.3—ability and skills descriptions—with corresponding developmental experiences.

In addition to the TS competencies related to change scope and risk identification, successful TS during implementation also requires an empathetic connection to the pulse of the stakeholders participating in the initiative. Through communications planning and management, participative decision making and issues resolution, and obstacle/resistance awareness, the transformational steward can strike a balance that builds and sustains trust and commitment while still moving forward with change. While much of listening, communicating, and being obstacle-aware are intuitive, we have pointed out in our definition of skills and experiences for this stage that there are discreet, practical tasks the transformational steward must execute if he or she is to create conditions for successful implementation

## *Implementing and Sustaining: Learning and Development Dimension*

As Table 14.3 describes, effective implementation and sustaining requires a combination of both foundational knowledge and practical experience. The complementary and reciprocally reinforcing nature of these two components is necessary to provide the transformational steward with a solid base for applying competencies. For example, one key responsibility of TS is creating a transparent environment in the organization with informed and involved stakeholders. From books, we can learn about various approaches to communications, how to develop channels of information flowing both down and up through the organization, and how important it is to involve others in the implementation of change and transformation. But for a transformational steward, these activities must be more than pro-forma. There is no substitute for facilitating specific transformational planning, decision making, and risk management approaches in operational circumstances similar to what the leader/manager would normally encounter. This is an area of practice that training and development programs can implement, as well as the more informal developmental expectations between leaders/managers and their supervisors.

### Continual Growth and Renewal

The final phase for TS is the growth and renewal of both the organization and the individual transformational steward. In this phase, all of the TS attributes are in play; however, some are more important to the organization while others are more important in the growth and renewal of the individual. The challenge during this phase for both organization and the individual is to balance the need for continuity with the need to improve and evolve. Constant change that occurs without meeting the need for closure, recognition of success, and establishment of process maturity is unhealthy and disruptive.

Yet, neither the organization nor the individual can remain complacent, with an imbalance toward security and comfort at the expense of evolving to meet stakeholder and customer needs. Growth and renewal involve balancing tradition and consistency while scanning for improvement opportunities and creative solutions.

This phase is different from the two other phases discussed in this chapter, as leaders focus on building transformational capability, both individually and organizationally, rather than focusing on the successful execution of a particular change. We feel that the role of the transformational steward includes responsibility for accomplishing both—in fact, an organization without both cannot realize its transformational potential. This responsibility to nurture transformational capacity requires both change-centric ways of perceiving and relating (creativity, comfort with ambiguity, and integrative systems thinking) as well as interpersonal abilities that emphasize extending the concept of TS throughout the organization (especially building trust, empowering, and power sharing). Collectively, these attributes reflect the transformational steward's ability to create an organization that is open and adaptive to change, with people throughout the organization willing to assume leadership in the constant renewal of the organization.

Transformational stewards are also responsible for their own nurturing—something that in the crush of work often gets less attention than it should. In this case, the continued development of a person's "inner-personal traits and beliefs" is vital, including ethical reasoning, self-reflection, empathy, and vision or foresight. In addition, attributes related to developing a change-centric approach are also important (creativity/innovation, comfort with ambiguity, and integrative systems thinking). Development of these attributes should continue throughout a person's life and career. Their development often comes only when a person is willing to take the time to step back and assess where he or she is, what is going well, and what could be improved. Personal retreats, conferences, sabbaticals, courses taken at a university, keeping a journal, and ongoing dialogue with a mentor are methods of self-improvement that have their advocates. Similarly, assessment instruments that query an individual and/or team's transformational skills are helpful to become more aware of one's transformational proficiency. These methods can be applied through organizational training and development programs or informally by individual leaders and managers seeking to become more confident and effective; ideally, a combination of formal and informal means provides a broad transformational awareness for further skill development.

Table 14.4 breaksdown the functions and responsibilities of transformational stewards for growth and renewal of themselves and their organizations.

Table 14.4

**Growth and Renewal**

**Phase 3: Growth and Renewal**

| Relevant TS Attributes | Competencies and Standards Dimension | | | Learning and Development Dimension | |
| --- | --- | --- | --- | --- | --- |
| | Responsibilities | Abilities | Skills | Knowledge | Developmental Experiences |
| Systems thinking; creative/Innovative | Facilitate organizational learning, improvement, and innovation | Ability to scrutinize current practices and develop new ideas and approaches; ability to design and implement organizational learning mechanisms such as feedback channels, after action reviews, etc.; ability to identify lessons learned and align practices accordingly | Conduct project close-out/after action review; establish feedback channels and forums for reflective practice; facilitate creative problem solving/innovation | Understand organizational learning and innovation dynamics and mechanisms; examples of organizational learning lessons, successes, and challenges | Review a historical change project and develop project and after-action profile of lessons and recommendations |
| Empathy; ethical | Establish an environment of collaboration, information sharing, and relational responsibility | Ability to develop approaches to collaboration over competition, create a sense of team unity, structure rewards for collaborative behavior | Conduct team building activities; lead and manage task-organized multidisciplinary teaming arrangements and work structures; encourage teamwork and information sharing; establish mentoring practices and other efforts to enhance relational responsibility | Understand group dynamics and team development and accountability approaches, social capital and information sharing, and problem-solving networks | Complete coaching and leadership self-assessment exercise |

| Empowerment; power sharing; coalition building; trust building | Establish change implementation management practices, structures, and strategies | Ability to understand, implement and manage processes for assessing change and change-risk; ability to create roles for individuals and units that encourage transformational practices | Establish institutional processes, policies, and procedures for determining strategic change drivers and change scope, planning, and managing communications; leading workforce transition and project governance activities | Understand change implementation management approaches and institutional best practices for enhancing resiliency and agility | Seek new areas of responsibility and/or share existing areas with others in the organizations |
|---|---|---|---|---|---|
| | Develop change-centric leaders and managers | Ability to institutionalize practices to develop TS competencies and awareness in other employees, managers, and leaders | Adopt TS competency profile and standards; assess leader and manager TS competencies; create TS competency development plans and training exercises; establish TS-focused rotational assignments | Understand TS requirements, competencies, and developmental strategies | Initiate a 360-degree evaluation in which attributes of transformational stewardship are included |

Table 14.4

| | Competencies and Standards Dimension | | | Learning and Development Dimension | |
|---|---|---|---|---|---|
| Relevant TS Attributes | Responsibilities | Abilities | Skills | Knowledge | Developmental Experiences |
| Ethical; empathy; foresight; reflective/learning oriented | Develop a transformational ethic | Ability to be acutely aware of both the strategic and evolving nature of the mission/agency, as well as the commitment and responsibility to the stakeholder needs and interests involved in pursuing change | Speak, write, and act in a transformationally aware, accountable, and responsible manner | Recognize and appreciate one's transformational responsibilities as a steward to the larger purpose of public service and the requirement to work toward synthesizing the collective interests of stakeholders; understand one's own skill and ability level and limitations through self-assessment, and the developmental activities required to further develop transformational competencies | Complete role simulation/scenario exercises that extend awareness to multiple perspectives and roles; complete competency self-assessment and audit; develop individual transformational steward development plan |
| Comfortable with ambiguity; integrative systems thinking | Fulfill the role of managing change-related risk | Ability to perceive operational and strategic challenges in terms of systems-originating obstacles and opportunities rather than mere locally occurring, limited status quo conditions and causes | Assess change-related complexity, stakes, and capability risks; identify high change-related risk areas and establish risk mitigation plans; manage risk | Understand the TS role of managing change-related risk and how that role is critical to successful leadership and management of change | Complete role simulation/scenario exercises that extend awareness to risk obstacle and opportunity variables |

### Renewal and Growth: Moving from Attributes to Responsibilities, Abilities, and Skills

We have listed seven areas of responsibility for TS for renewal and growth—four for organizational renewal and three for personal growth. For the organization, the TS responsibilities are to create a learning organization; enhance ethical collaboration; create change-centric practices, systems, and strategies; and develop other change leaders. For the individual, the transformational steward responsibilities are to develop a commitment to change and transformation, to become fluent in change management, and to become "risk aware"—learning to recognize and deal with risks that emerge as a result of change.

Each of these responsibilities is associated with particular abilities and skills. Just as with the attributes, there is some overlap; however, there is enough differentiation to provide guidance to a person wanting to exercise TS. For example, responsibility of creating a learning organization is associated with the ability (and willingness) to scrutinize and question current practices and to be open to new ideas and concepts. It means creating feedback mechanisms within the organization to encourage a learning behavior. It means not punishing mistakes but learning from them. Reflective practice requires developing specific skills and implementing realistic approaches for assessing experience, identifying lessons, and taking action to address deficiencies.

Similarly, in personal growth and renewal, the responsibility of becoming risk-aware means that a person is able to perceive strategic and operational change initiatives in terms of both opportunities and obstacles and is able to weigh the risks associated with different change strategies. Specific skills include both ability to assess risk and creativity to manage risk to minimize its potential negative consequences.

### Renewal and Growth: Learning and Development Dimension

As with the other phases of TS, learning and development require a combination of knowledge and practice—both important to a full understanding of TS. Two examples provide illustrate how the two work in concert.

Transformational stewards are responsible for enhancing ethical communication and collaboration within their organizations. To accomplish this, transformational stewards must understand workplace standards, good ethical practices, and approaches to mentoring and individual development, as well as the ability to structure team and collaborative awards. However, this knowledge serves as the frame for providing mentoring, coaching, and individual and team development—practices all managers and leaders should follow, particularly those wishing to practice TS.

Transformational stewards, as mentioned, are also responsible for their own growth and renewal. Reading books on aspects of change and transformation or attending conferences on that subject can provide a foundation for personal development in this area. However, more personal self-reflection is in order. A person wishing to practice TS might initiate a 360-degree evaluation of his or her abilities and skills regarding transformation and change. This would involve attaining feedback from supervisors, peers, and those employees for whom the person has supervisory responsibility. The 360-degree evaluation might specifically focus on TS attributes as part of the evaluation process. Once data are in hand, the person might then develop a personal development plan that includes strengthening those aspects in need of improvement.

## Reinforcing Transformational Stewardship Development Efforts

Understanding TS competencies and institutionalizing an effective developmental strategy is a solid step in the direction of more capable leaders and managers of change. In addition, aligning key aspects of complementary organizational systems can significantly strengthen an agency's transformational capability. Two such areas include staffing and succession planning and selection and advancement processes. Foremost, an agency cannot develop TS capability if change leadership and management is not legitimized, recognized, and appreciated within the organization. In many agencies, positions of leading and managing transformational projects are staffed by selecting individuals who are interested in stepping outside mainstream career development paths—this can be a privilege in many cases, but it can be an undesirable channel as well. In such instances, top leadership of change may be selected for their skill and distinguished as top performers, while mid- and senior-level managers are not rewarded if they choose such roles since it removes them from the officially sanctioned track for developing line management abilities. It is important that agencies reward and value the experience of change leadership at all levels.

Similarly, as suggested in the selection aspect above, when transformational competencies and experiences are recognized explicitly as requirements for promotion, leaders and managers are much more likely to consistently seek out and commit to investing time and effort in pursuit of such skills. As an example, in the early days of the "Six Sigma" process improvement initiative at General Electric, Chief Executive Jack Welch established the requirement that to be promoted into a management position, one had to complete process improvement and reengineering training and had to accomplish a successful transformation project. The result was understandable: Would-be managers got the training and went out in search of opportunities to lead change.

"Valuing" of transformational proficiency is an area in which the federal government could stand to make significant gains. For example, current Senior Executive Service candidates are expected to report their experience and ability for each of a range of competencies to achieve acceptance into top leadership ranks. A full range of transformational competencies is not represented in federal ECQs; however, several such as collaboration and communication have made it into the profile. Yet, the typical process that candidates complete is to sit down with the categories and to fill in the experiences that they feel relate, as they look back across their experience in government. While this reflective aspect is beneficial, it does not push leaders and managers to expand their range of abilities and to actively seek out developmental opportunities related to transformation. If the range of practical challenges and experiences noted here as important to TS were included as an integrated aspect of the ECQ/development process, leaders would be more likely to enter top ranks with a stronger transformational foundation.

## Conclusion

In this chapter, we have attempted to make a case that the traditional approaches to leadership development in the areas of change and transformation are insufficient for today's challenging public service environment. We have argued for a way of understanding change leadership in the public sector, which we have called transformational stewardship (TS). We also have indicated specific attributes we think are closely identified with this concept and have indicated how they underscore the various phases of change and transformation: initiating, implementing and sustaining, and growth and renewal. Finally, we have presented a developmental framework including the requirements and competencies that define TS and the learning and development aspects involved in meeting these requirements.

Transformation is difficult, even with the necessary skills and abilities. We feel that the ability to lead and manage change successfully is such an important task that we cannot continue to merely "wing it" and rely on more traditional, comfortable definitions of public leadership and management. Basic responsibilities, abilities, and skills that we have identified here are necessary ingredients to the success of all organizations, and particularly those entrusted to serve the public interest. Approaching this challenge in an informed, comprehensive manner is critical, and a combination of enhancing transformation knowledge and learning from developmental experiences is needed to make these competencies a reality.

## References

Addington, Thomas, and Stephen Graves. 2002. "The Forgotten Role." *Life@Work.* 1(6): 25–33.
Badaracco, Joseph. 1997. *Defining Moments: When Managers Must Choose Between Right and Right.* Boston: Harvard Business School Press.
Goleman, Daniel, Annie McKee, and Richard Boyatzis. 2002. *Primal Leadership: Realizing the Power of Emotional Intelligence.* Boston: Harvard Business School Press.
Government Performance and Results Act of 1993, Pub. L. No. 103-62, § 20, 107 Stat. 285 (1993).
Graham, Pauline. 2003. *Mary Parker Follett: Prophet of Management.* Washington, DC: Beard.
Kee, Jed, and Roger Black. 1985. "Is Excellence Possible in the Public Sector?" *Public Productivity Review* 9(1): 25–34.
Kee, James Edwin, and Whitney Setzer. 2006. "Change-Centric Leadership." Working paper. Washington DC: Center for Innovation in the Public Service, George Washington University.
Kee, James Edwin, Kathryn Newcomer, and S. Mike Davis. 2007. "Transformational Stewardship: Leading Public Sector Change." In *Transforming Public Leadership for the 21st Century,* eds. Ricardo S. Morse, Terry F. Buss, and C. Morgan Kinghorn, 154–188. Armonk, NY: M.E. Sharpe.
National Academy of Public Administration (NAPA). 1997. *Managing Succession and Developing Leadership: Growing the Next Generation of Public Service Leaders.* Washington, DC: Author..
———. 2002. *The 21st Century Federal Manager: A Study of Changing Roles and Competencies.* Washington, DC: Author
Senge, Peter. 1990. *The Fifth Discipline.* New York: Doubleday.
Thompson, C. Michael. 2000. *The Congruent Life.* San Francisco: Jossey-Bass.
Vaill, Peter. 1996. *Learning as a Way of Being.* San Francisco: Jossey-Bass.
Wheatley, Margaret J. 2005. *Finding Our Way: Leadership for an Uncertain Time.* San Francisco: Berrett-Koehler.

# 15

## Designing and Delivering Leadership Programs

### Challenges and Prospects

Richard F. Callahan

> I brought hope and a vision back to my organization.
>
> —*Sierra Health Foundation Leadership program participant*

Bringing "hope and vision" back to an organization is an outcome of each of the programs that the University of Southern California (USC) delivers. The question addressed in this chapter is how to design and deliver leadership training programs that have impact not only on the participants but also on the communities they serve and the organizations they lead. The transformation of the public sector calls for growing leaders who can thrive in ambiguity and work across the public, nonprofit, and for-profit sectors to lead effective change (see Appendix, p. 341).

This question of how to grow leaders is addressed by drawing on my personal experience designing and delivering leadership programs at the national, state, regional, county, and municipal government levels, as well as for a foundation in the nonprofit health sector. In the past year, USC's work has been with over 600 professionals at all levels of public service and in health nonprofits. Over 2,000 participants have engaged in this leadership training over the past five years. Participants have been from a wide range of professional fields.

Design and delivery lessons are drawn from a rich set of observations, including formal program evaluations, focus group interviews with program graduates, pre- and post-leadership assessment tests, narrative inquiry, end of program interviews, alumni observations and interviews, daily feedback forms (thousands), debriefing of presenters, individual conversations with participants during and after programs, and discussion with program sponsors. This data collection occurred over the past seven years.

Drawing on these observations and experiences in designing and delivering programs, this chapter seeks to facilitate the following outcomes for the reader:

1. Increased ability to design and deliver effective leadership programs;
2. Knowing how to design and implement training to push out ineffective and toxic leadership (Reed 2004); and
3. Competencies to stimulate leadership conversations, creating tipping points (Gladwell 2002) of core-value–driven leadership practices and impacts.

The discussion is structured into four sections: design challenges, curriculum drivers, leadership drivers, and leadership outcomes.

## Epistemological Primacy

> The door to novelty is always slightly ajar; many pass it by with barely a glance, some peek inside but choose not to enter, others dash in and dash out again; while a few drawn by curiosity, boredom, or rebellion, or circumstances, venture so deep or wander around in there so long that they can never find their way back out.

> —*Tom Robbins,* Villa Incognito

Profound challenges are involved in designing and delivering leadership programs. First and foremost is the challenge best described as the assertion of epistemological primacy. No one uses those words outside the halls of philosophy. In the professional world the challenge is stated in varied ways, always to the effect that one's own profession is uniquely situated, with specific demands. The implication of this assertion is that leadership practices can only be taught—or at the least are best taught—by trainers and faculty from that world. This concern finds knowledge unique to a professional field, or even a particular agency, as precluding the possibility of learning from other fields.

In drilling down on this concern, the root appears to be previous bad training experience. The occasions when a faculty member from a different academic discipline has been irrelevant to the professional practice of the participants profoundly affect future willingness to invite outside perspectives in training. In addition, the profound challenges faced in the public and nonprofit sector, often with life-and-death consequences, foster a sense that few can understand the daily pressures experienced in working in a particular profession. Past bad training experiences only reinforce this perception.

Since learning can only occur by invitation—recall the story of Confucius pouring tea till it is overflowing and telling the young man he cannot learn until he empties his cup—offering a leadership program must initially address the assertion of epistemological primacy. This challenge is less acute in leadership programs designed for participants from across different fields, as opposed to a program offered exclusively to participants from one profession. But even then, say at the state government level, the challenge lurks, sometimes in the form of profound skepticism that lessons can be learned from outside the level of government or outside the sector, for example, the nonprofit sector.

## Focus Groups

The design of a leadership curriculum can address this issue through a focus group process. Pulling together leading professionals in the field to discuss the leadership challenges allows two important processes to emerge. First, the focus groups discuss the leadership processes needed and the priority in that field or sector; for example, skills needed for creating an improved organizational culture. Second, focus groups also raise the content areas specific to the field, knowledge of which is essential for emerging leaders; for example, new legislation or funding guidelines specific to the field. The focus group process allows for development of the balance in the curriculum between the amount of time spent teaching leadership processes that are not specific to the participants' professional field and the amount of content specific to the profession of the participants.

Engaging in this focus group process results in two critical outcomes. The first result is a curriculum tailored to the specific professional leadership processes. The focus group process allows participants to know that the curriculum is designed for them, not an imposition of topics important to outside faculty or trainers.

The second important outcome is buy-in from the leaders in the professional field who helped design the curriculum. The leadership program becomes credible because of their participation in the design. Most important, this allows established leaders to become champions for the program. They can identify and recommend staff who should attend the leadership program. These leaders become vested in the program's success in developing leaders.

Addressing the assertion of epistemological primacy through focus groups of professional leaders allows the design to not simply overcome potential participant resistance; more significantly, it facilitates offering a program that can draw resources from across academic disciplines and professional fields. For example, consider drawing on public management and business administration in a program for mental health executives or drawing on corporate strategy models for nonprofit health directors.

An interdisciplinary approach advances leadership essentially as a creative act. This approach trains leaders to engage in interdisciplinary problem-solving approaches to generate new solutions to complex problems. This approach moves beyond simply teaching best practices to delivering a program that deliberately sparks creativity through the connection of previously separate domains (Johansson 2004). The conclusions reached by Malcolm Gladwell's *Tipping Point* (2002) suggest the value of reaching across disciplines and professional fields to both understand the dynamics of social change and the potential for leaders as connectors to create positive social epidemics.

Finally, to overcome aversion to reaching out for leadership training, note that the focus group process models two important leadership practices. First is customer-focused leadership. As stated well by a remarkably successful university president, USC's Steve Sample (2002), this involves working for the people who are working for you. The process models engaging the professionals closest to a challenge in crafting approaches to address that challenge. Second, the process also models leadership as inquiry. As succinctly stated by long-time leadership trainer Laree Kiely, leadership is developed most effectively around questions, not certainty. The focus group process models leadership as asking the right questions.

## Curriculum Drivers

> Wooden-headedness, the source of self-deception, is a factor that plays a remarkably large role in government. Wooden-headedness is also the refusal to benefit from experience.
>
> —*Barbara Tuchman*, The March of Folly *(1984, p. 7)*

Leadership training builds on the premise of leadership as learned mastery, neither inherited nor accidental. The insight developed by Bennis and Thomas (2002) of a crucible experience not merely shaping the leader but as being essential to becoming a leader strongly supports the possibility of learning leadership skills. Likewise, Perkins's (2000) research on "leadership at the edge" finds challenging circumstances calling forth extraordinary leadership. Leadership training builds on this seminal role of experience in developing leadership skills. Of course, trapping aspiring public sector leaders in the Antarctic ice like Ernest Shackleton is not a realistic possibility (Perkins 2000).

The importance of experience in developing leadership skills strongly suggests that the right type of experiential exercises in a leadership program can develop a participant's leadership skills, capacity, and impact. Typically, well-designed simulations, role-playing games, group exercises, and negotiation practices are among the various experiential learning exercises that are incorporated into leadership programs. Reading, analyzing, and developing recommendations based on the study of others' experiences and factual situations in the form of case studies is also suggested as a form of experiential learning.

In the design and delivery of curriculum, four features can amplify leadership skill development:

1. Delivery over several months;
2. Participant reflections;
3. Group projects; and
4. Designed reentry of participants.

## Program Delivery

Offering a leadership program over a six-month period offers a range of advantages. The most overwhelming learning impact is the ability to assimilate and apply learning at work between sessions. Second, the participants can bring back questions and insights for the trainers and for their colleagues in the program. Third, the participants can model the assimilation and application of the leadership practices for each other.

The modeling of leadership for colleagues in the program is an enormously powerful mechanism for leadership programs. Trying new leadership approaches that were initially learned in a leadership program exemplifies the most important of principles: leading by examples. These examples also develop an expectation that the concepts and practices from the training are designed for applications at work. The examples by participants, the peer questions, the participant successes, and the failures also invite accountability to each other for applying the leadership principles. Finally, allowing time for participants to bring back application between sessions demonstrates that leadership is possible.

## Participant Reflections

Leadership reflections by participants during the program become an important mechanism for leadership development. Initially, reflections discussed at the start of each day practice the leadership skill that Warren Bennis (1989) describes as one of the most important functions of leaders: creating shared meaning. Reflections by participants create shared meaning about their learning in the program, about the challenges of applying new leadership practices, and about their aspirations.

In his most recently published research on leadership, Marcus Buckingham (2005) concludes after interviewing hundreds of leaders that the most important practice shared by successful leaders is taking time to reflect on their experiences. Structuring such reflections in a leadership program allows participants to practice the skill, experience its benefit, and learn how to bring practices of learning through reflection back to their organization. This practice facilitates participants' personal development and their development of their agency as a learning organization.

### *Group Projects*

The design of group projects into leadership programs offers a considerable challenge. Not the least of the potential objections of participants is that there is no time for an additional overlay of work on top of an existing job and that excessive time is taken from work and family to participate in program requirements. Participant reluctance to engage in group projects calls for careful design of the project process and a clear nexus to personal leadership development.

Clarity about the process and the outcomes for group projects allows participants to move from feeling overwhelmed to seeing an opportunity for personal and professional contributions. Presenting the group project process as a chance to practice leadership skills during the course of the program helps participants to find a clear connection with leadership development. Clearly outlining the expectation that the presentation of the group project is as much about reflections on the leadership processes used (e.g., forming teams, communications, and negotiations) as it is on the outcome, encourages participants to view the process as opportunities outside the workplace to try new leadership practices and develop new skills.

Presenting projects as an opportunity to contribute to a community good also can connect leadership participants with the projects as opportunities to make a difference—the core value of contribution. Projects can be developed by nominations from outside groups, program sponsors, and the participants. Allowing participants to voluntarily select—as opposed to being assigned—the project on which they will work further addresses an initial reluctance for added work.

Offering expert consulting at the start of the process and throughout allows participants to focus on a set of skills that will readily transfer to the workplace. Typically, learning from the project consultant includes a process for moving from problem to proposal, recognizing the importance of scoping a project, presentation practice, and how to design a problem-solving network. Typically, when reflecting on the group project process, each of these items looms large as having a significant impact on the process.

### Designed Reentry

Drawing on a metaphor from the National Aeronautics and Space Administration (NASA) space experience aptly describes the experience of leadership program participants returning to work. After leaving and returning to Earth's orbit, on reentry, the Apollo astronauts faced the challenge of successfully moving through Earth's atmosphere. Entering Earth's atmosphere at too sharp an angle would cause the Apollo capsule to create so much friction that the ship would incinerate. Entering at too shallow an angle would cause the capsule to bounce off Earth's atmosphere into deep space, never to return. Similarly, a leader returning at too sharp an entry risks burning up quickly within an atmosphere that has not changed. Likewise, a leader returning with too shallow an approach risks not getting through and having no impact.

A well-designed leadership program can address this set of issues through a number of mechanisms. Acknowledging the reality of the reentry challenge to participants is an important first step. Encouraging participants to tell their colleagues at work that the leadership program has encouraged them to try new leadership practices and skills offers an initial license to try new practices on reentry to their workplace. Using the structured reflections of participants in class to talk through ways participants are introducing new practices between sessions models successful practices and allows debriefing on less than successful attempts. Including group projects offers an intermediary place to practice new skills outside the classroom but not yet at work. And, finally, meetings with alumni help participants calibrate their reentry actions.

### Leadership Drivers

> This transformation will take time, and the difficulty of changing a decades-old culture in the second largest bureaucracy in the federal government should not be underestimated.
>
> —Dr. Kenneth W. Kizer, Vision for Change (1995, p. 7)

The design and implementation of leadership programs aim to develop leadership skills from a variety of directions, but they need to converge around a fundamental question: How do you develop the capacity in individuals to move forward into profound uncertainty? By definition, leaders go where the road has not been paved or perhaps even surveyed. Leaders are not following others. Fundamentally, leaders chart new courses rather than navigate by following the fixed directions of others.

Nothing is wrong with following or with mastering processes that have been developed. However, that is not leadership; it is management. Strong management skills are needed in the public and nonprofit sectors. But leadership is fundamentally more. Leaders move forward, and they do so deliberately into the unknown. The fundamental skill that sets leaders apart is the ability to bring clarity where there is uncertainty (Buckingham 2005).

Leaders intentionally invite change. Again, if an individual is improving on existing processes, refining current practices, or following an established direction that has been proven successful, that person is practicing management. That is a needed and vital skill set. However, managing existing processes is not leadership. By definition, leaders are moving an organization in a direction that is different than the one currently being followed. Leaders invite change not as an accident but by design (for recent examples, see Dahle 2005.)

The challenge for leadership programs becomes preparing individuals to operate in arenas where outcomes are not certain, where success is not guaranteed, and where there are followers expecting clarity and who are only comfortable with certainty. At their essential core, leadership programs develop an individual's capacity to intentionally design change and make change stick.

### Designing Change

Three processes prepare participants for leading change: identifying strategy, embracing dissent, and designing networks.

The role of intentionality in leadership needs to be learned. Being "at cause" rather than being "caused" is a more abstract way of conceptualizing this skill set. In the world of leadership practices, this is the skill set of strategy. Development of such skill is not the same as teaching strategic planning. Rather, this is learning an applied strategy model: developing the capacity of leaders to be at cause for measurable outcomes that have sufficient assets realized through targeted behaviors to achieve those outcomes (Logan and King 2001; Logan 2005). Leaders move into profound uncertainty through the application of a strategy model that takes into account all that is known and creates accountability in the leader for achieving outcomes. Strategy facilitates a leader's overcoming the natural resistance to change by marshaling assets and instituting behaviors committed to change (see Appendix, p. 341).

The second important process for moving into "swampy conditions" is to invite dissenting views (Biller 2005). The fear of change—or the fear of "dropping your tools" (Weick 1996)—profoundly shapes how a leader is received. The insight on which leadership programs can build is facilitation of skills that first allow a leader to recognize this fear and then skills needed to seek out and embrace dissent—early and often.

The third leadership process that facilitates moving into profound uncertainty is the deliberate design of personal and interorganizational networks. The design of networks is different from simply the admonition to get to know powerful people through networking. The first leadership difference is recognizing networks as a significant problem-solving tool, with an understanding of how fundamentally networks change the capacity to move information (Barabasi 2003) and to move people (Gladwell 2002). This recognition builds on the insight of the seminal value of connectedness developed by Chester Newland (2000) through the core values of rule of law and respect for human dignity for advancing public administration. The second difference is the value of mapping networks between organizations. Clearly understanding the varied ways organizations are connected through referrals, resources, and other factors, and mapping the intensity of those connections (Provan and Milward 1995) develops leadership capacity for deliberately designing more effective interorganizational networks. Teaching the skill of connecting individuals around what they care most about—their core values—into three-way relationships that are the building blocks of individual networks builds leadership capacity for having the relationships needed as assets in strategy to move forward into uncertainty.

## Making Change Stick

In leading organizational change for the largest health-care provider in the United States, the Veterans Health Administration, Dr. Kenneth Kizer (1995) noted that beyond the challenge of introducing change was the challenge of getting change to stick in a "decades-old culture" (p. 7). Kizer observed that change involves much more than reorganizing structure. The challenge for leadership development is how to make change stick through changing organizational culture: creation of effective organizational culture. The 2005 symposium on leadership by the National Academy of Public Administration described this as leadership that will "embed the values in the organization" (see Appendix).

The fundamental assumption is that strategy is not sufficient. Leadership training can focus on developing the skills to find leverage points in moving from diagnosis of organizational culture to changing the culture. One approach builds leadership capacity through coaching individuals in changing the types of conversations within the organization (Logan and King 2001). This approach to leadership development builds on the seminal insights of Burns (1978) that a leader elevates an organization as a teacher. In addition, training builds on Bennis's (1989) insight of the leader's role in creating shared meaning. In practice, leaders develop skills to move conversations in an organization from being self-focused to team focused and from ineffective to vital (Logan and King 2001).

Training a leader to move organizational culture calls for creating shared meaning around core values. Developing the leadership skills to move strategy forward driven by core values fundamentally addresses the problem of resistance by connecting to what individuals care most about—their core values. In effect it is "revealing what is good in them and ultimately giving them hope" (O'Toole 1995, p. 10). In the example of Dr. Kenneth Kizer's (1995) leading change at the Veterans Health Administration, he appealed to the core value of compassion through quality care for veterans and the core value of contribution through improved access and patient-centered care for veterans (p. 8). That shifted the focus from the bureaucracy to the patients; from structure and entrenched culture to the values of public and health service.

Leading from core values calls for developing powerful listening (O'Toole 1995, p. 29; Sample 2002, p. 21) and the ability to relate core value stories. Leadership programs that develop these capacities allow leaders to create vital organizational cultures through core-value–driven conversations, pushing out gossip, toxic conversations, and self-promotional toxic leadership (Reed 2004). Organizational culture is changed through core-value–driven conversation.

**Levels of Leadership**

> Have you forgotten that life is a treasure, not a trial?
>
> —*Jimmie Dale Gilmore*

Leading from core values can span the complex and varied approaches to leadership that are apparent from any walk down the aisle of a bookstore or quick Google search of the topic. What is needed is a way to sort through the bewildering arrays of suggestions for leaders that are found in books as biographies, metaphors, survey research, and literature reviews, and from large data set analysis. A comprehensive leadership model suggested by Van Wart (2004) starts with the observation, "First, the sheer number of competencies required of leaders is daunting" (p. 175).

To bring clarity to the daunting array of leadership suggestions, the design and delivery of leadership training can be organized around the suggestions of Nobel Prize winner Herbert Simon, who outlined five levels of society. A systematic approach to leadership development that recognizes complexity but does not overwhelm participants can be developed around the following levels: individual, group, organizational, community, and institutional (Simon

1952). This framework offers a coherent approach and suggests the close connections of each level, which Simon describes as a set of boxes within larger boxes, touching on all sides. Most important, this approach starts with two important premises: one, a movement from the heroic leadership genre in which individual level skills and personal attributes are presented as sufficient for all leadership challenges; and two, understanding that different circumstances call for different types of leadership skills.

Levels of leadership development can be organized around the following:

- *Individual:* Leading through core values, decision-making styles, communication techniques, interpersonal designed network, and Myers-Briggs and other instruments.
- *Group:* Forming high-performing teams; roles, negotiations, and customer-focused approaches, with instruments such as Leadership Effectiveness Assessment.
- *Organization:* Changing structure, culture and symbols, human resources, and political frames (Bolman and Deal 2003); systems thinking, finance, and interorganizational networks.
- *Community:* Working with a board of directors, strategic planning, creating public value (Moore 1995), and fund development.
- *Institutions:* Influencing the "rules of the game" (North 1990) through advocacy, working with legislative representatives, initiatives, and the courts (Garrett 1997).

The sequence in delivering training at varied levels allows participants to move from the most familiar (i.e., personal level skills) to the more abstract (i.e., organizational and institutional level skills). Focusing a session, typically over two days, on each level facilitates participants' seeing the distinctions related to that level.

The individual and group levels are always the easiest for participants to relate to in training. These levels are tangible, and participants are able to see themselves and each other as individuals and teams. The community level is typically easy to relate to in both nonprofit programs (as clients) and in government programs (as constituents). In addition, sequencing a program to go from the individual, to group, to community level facilitates starts at levels that resonate more easily with participants, and it then allows the organizational-level training to focus on how to better connect the organization to constituent or community considerations. Likewise, with the institutional level, training on legislative advocacy works better when leadership processes for accessing the needs of the community or constituents have been developed in previous sessions.

## Leadership Outcomes

Designing and delivering leadership programs around varied levels allows participants to develop both the skill set needed at a particular moment and other skills that they may need later in their careers; in the language of a proverb, digging wells before being thirsty. An outcome of this approach is twofold: first, an appreciation of the varied skills needed at different times to achieve different outcomes; and second, an improved ability of participants to create future leaders.

Designing leadership programs around outcomes models the practices being taught in leadership strategy. These outcomes can range from reinvigorating participants' commitments to public or nonprofit service to designing networks that break down the silos that exists across different public agencies. However, the metric of leaders creating other leaders as an outcome of any program becomes the basis of transformational leadership (O'Toole 1995, p. 11). This outcome metric facilitates participants' looking backward to mentors in their own leadership and how opportunities for leadership were created for them, as well as looking forward to design their legacy for impacts as leaders.

An outcome from the design and delivery of leadership programs for creating future leaders becomes the basis for an epidemic of leadership that advances varied social goods driven by core-value leadership. In training programs, the challenge is to shift the focus from the individual to the outcome the individual can create. Designing leadership programs to address different skill sets at different levels allows for a vibrant heterodoxy in the curriculum, calling on participants to actively shape their learning and applications of the learning. Designing leadership programs around the expected outcomes of leaders creating leaders aligns the curriculum with impacts beyond the individual; it facilitates leadership skills that work for the community. In an era of working not only in the public or nonprofit sector, but with the need for skills to work across sectors (Salamon 2005), developing leadership capacities through multilayered, experiential learning prepares participants to have impact in serving their varied communities by interacting across the nonprofit, for-profit, and public sectors. Developing core-value–driven leaders allows communities to connect across sectors about which they care most. Connectedness through core values can define the legacy of a successful leadership program.

## References

Barabasi, Albert-Laszlo. 2003. *Linked: How Everything Is Connected to Everything Else and What It Means for Business, Science, and Everyday Life.* New York: Plume, Penguin Group.

Bennis, Warren G. 1989. *On Becoming a Leader*. Reading, MA: Addison-Wesley.

Bennis, Warren G., and Robert J. Thomas. 2002. "Crucibles of Leadership." *Harvard Business Review* 80(9): 39–45.

Biller, Robert. 2005. "Change and Leadership." Presentation at Leadership, 21, San Gabriel Valley Council of Governments. City of San Gabriel, CA.

Bolman, Lee, and Terrance Deal. 2003. *Reframing Organizations: Artistry, Choice and Leadership*, 3rd ed. San Francisco: Jossey-Bass.

Buckingham, Marcus. 2005. *The One Thing You Need to Know*. New York: Free Press.

Burns, James McGregor. 1978. *Leadership*. New York: Harper & Row.

Dahle, Cheryl. 2005. "The Change Masters: How Do You Solve the World's Problems?" *Fast Company* 90 (January): 47–58.

Garrett, Elizabeth. 1997. "Tushnet on Thurgood Marshall." *Journal of Supreme Court History* 22(2): 140–149.

Gladwell, Malcolm. 2002. *The Tipping Point*. Boston: Little, Brown.

Johansson, Frans. 2004. *The Medici Effect: Breakthrough Insights at the Intersection of Ideas, Concepts, and Culture*. Boston: Harvard Business School Press.

Kizer, Kenneth. 1995. *A Vision for Change: A Plan to Restructure the Veterans Health Administration*. Washington, DC: Department of Veterans Affairs.

Logan, David. 2005. "A Strategy Model." Presentation for Sierra Health Foundation. Grizzly Creek Ranch, Portola, CA.

Logan, David, and John King. 2001. *The Coaching Revolution: How Visionary Managers are Using Coaching to Empower People and Unlock Their Full Potential*. Holbrook, MA: Adams Media Corporation.

Moore, Mark. 1995. *Creating Public Value*. Cambridge: Harvard University Press.

Newland, Chester A. 2000. "The Public Administration Review and Ongoing Struggles for Connectedness." *Public Administration Review* 60(1): 20–38.

North, Douglass C. 1990. *Institutions, Institutional Change, and Economic Performance*. New York: Cambridge University Press.

O'Toole, James. 1995. *Leading Change: The Argument for Values-Based Leadership*. New York: Ballantine Books.

Perkins, Dennis. 2000. *Leading at the Edge: Leadership Lessons from the Extraordinary Saga of Shackleton's Antarctic Expedition*. New York: American Management Association.

Provan, Keith, and H. Brinton Milward. 1995. "A Preliminary Theory of Interorganizational Network Effectiveness: A Comparative Study of Four Community Mental Health Systems." *Administrative Science Quarterly* 40(1): 1–33.

Reed, George. 2004. "Toxic Leadership." *Military Review* 84(4): 67–71.

Salamon, Lester. 2005. "Training Professional Citizens." *Journal of Public Affairs Education* 11(1): 7–19.

Sample, Steven B. 2002. *The Contrarian's Guide to Leadership*. San Francisco: Jossey-Bass.

Simon, Herbert A. 1952. "Comments on the Theory of Organizations." *American Political Science Review* 46(4): 1130–1139.

Tuchman, Barbara W. 1984. *The March of Folly: From Troy to Vietnam*. New York: Ballantine Books.

Van Wart, Montgomery. 2004. "A Comprehensive Model of Organizational Leadership: The Leadership Action Model." *International Journal of Organizational Theory and Behavior* 7(2): 173–208.

Weick, Karl E. 1996. "Drop Your Tools: An Allegory for Organizational Studies." *Administrative Science Quarterly* 41(2): 301–313.

# 16

## Learning How to Learn

### Action Learning for Leadership Development

Robert Kramer

Each year, federal, state, and local governments in the United States invest hundreds of millions of dollars in university leadership courses, executive development programs, and off-site retreats for mid-level managers; yet, leadership continues to be cited as the weakest link in public service, resulting in poor agency performance, scores of billions of taxpayer dollars wasted, and low employee morale (National Academy of Public Administration [NAPA] 2002; U.S. Office of Personnel Management [OPM] 2005; Walker 2005).

**Transfer of Learning Problem**

Traditionally, leadership development for mid-level managers has been seen as taking place outside the workplace in university classrooms (Denhardt and Campbell 2005, p. 174), weekend retreats, or off-site settings. But leadership development conducted as courses, retreats, or off-sites is rarely transferred when managers return to their high-pressure jobs at 8 A.M. the following morning. No one else's leadership has been "developed." The existing organizational culture is often so strong that it is virtually impossible for managers returning from even a well-designed program to translate classroom learning into practice. "[I]n some cases, less than 5 percent of learners claimed to use their instruction" (Raelin and Coghlan 2006, p. 671).

In universities, traditional executive master of public administration (MPA) curricula use a teacher-centered model of academics providing lectures and a sprinkling of experiential exercises, role plays, and case studies—in topics such as government ethics, administrative law, budgeting, statistics and program evaluation, organization theory, politics, and policymaking. However, case studies, role plays, and classroom exercises bear no direct relationship to real-time (not simulated) organizational predicaments and do not test the always unpredictable consequences of action taken by managers during real-time challenges. Few executive MPA programs, even those with adjunct faculties of distinguished practitioners, provide participants with an opportunity to practice classroom learning *holistically* in real time, under real working conditions, in the gritty here-and-now of collaborating with others struggling to solve real problems, when no one knows what to do but there is an urgent need to take action. For managers, real time is the only time that counts. The organization, not the university, is the best classroom.

## The Permanent White Water of Public Service

Managing in the turbulent context of today's public service means immersion into "permanent white water" (Vaill 1996). Under such conditions, splitting the process of leading from the process of managing—following the conventional wisdom of Zaleznik (1977)—is not helpful. I do not want to diminish the importance of either skill, as some writers now do by glorifying leadership and minimizing management. In recent years, too many writers have split "leading" and "managing" as if one were the calling of Martin Luther King, Jr., and the other merely the work of an accountant. You cannot succeed as a manager unless you are skilled at leading people, and you cannot succeed as a leader unless you meet your budget and timetables. We need both skills in one person. According to Yukl and Lepsingh (2005), "integrating leading and managing is essential for organizational effectiveness" (p. 361). Managers must know how to lead and leaders how to manage (Fairholm 2006, p. 343). Following Vaill (1996, p. 52), I call such public administrators "managerial leaders." Permanent white water means that managerial leaders face daily predicaments that as a regular course they cannot even define with clarity, much less resolve, and yet require which immediate action. Today, according to Vaill (1996, pp. 10–12), permanent white water characterizes public service organizations in five ways.

1. Permanent white water conditions are full of shocks and surprises.
2. Permanent white water conditions produce novel predicaments with no single correct solution.
3. Permanent white water conditions feature wicked problems that are messy, ill defined, unpredictable, and difficult to solve.
4. Permanent white water conditions are expensive.
5. Permanent white water conditions tend to recur.

In this permanent white water environment, where the only constants are surprise, pain, and confusion, *leadership for public service must be reframed as the capacity to learn continually*. And learning how to learn in such a fluid environment is perhaps the single most important requirement for leading others to perform effectively in public service.

Managerial leadership, according to Vaill (1996), cannot be taught or learned: *"managerial leadership is learning"* (p. 126). But how do managers in bureaucracies, where leadership power is positional and adherence to rules takes precedent over the purposes for which they were developed, learn how to learn? "Bureaucracies have been defined as organizations that are too rigid to learn from their errors," wrote McCurdy (1977). "A bureaucracy, by design, is an organization that cannot correct its behaviors by listening to its errors" (p. 86).

> A bureaucratic organization is not only a system that does not correct its behaviors in view of its errors; it is also too rigid to adjust without crises to the transformations that the accelerated evolution of industrial society makes more and more imperative. (Crozier, cited in McCurdy 1977, p. 95)

In bureaucracies, ownership for taking action is impeded by the boxes on organization charts. Responsibility is easy to avoid in any hierarchical system. "The power of any official to oversee another depends completely on their relative position in the official hierarchy; it has nothing to do with their personal skills or competence" (Crozier, cited in McCurdy 1977, p. 75). As leadership educators for public administrators trapped in the "iron cage" of bureaucracy, how do we address the tremendous learning challenges of managerial leaders in public service? How do we plant the seeds of a learning organization in an anti-learning culture?

University courses and off-site retreats promote leisurely reflection but do not involve real-time action since, by definition, participants are "out" in three senses: they are out of context, out of commission, and out of touch. Is it any wonder that executive participants off-site cannot seem to stay away from their Blackberries, e-mails, voice mails, and cell phones? When they return to work, these managerial leaders tend to act frenetically, but often little is resolved or learned in the process of taking action, resulting in endless recycling of the same problems.

Within recent years, the nation has seen public administrators fail to manage recovery from Hurricane Katrina; to implement billion-dollar computer systems at the Internal Revenue Service, Federal Bureau of Investigation, and Federal Aviation Administration; to intercept hijacked planes on 9/11; to build an effective Department of Homeland Security; to win the peace in Iraq; and to learn from any of these failures. Unless quantum leaps in learning occur in the mindsets of our public managerial leaders, catastrophes such as these, or worse, will haunt us for the rest of the twenty-first century.

## What "Develops" in Leadership Development?

As leadership educators, how do we develop managerial leaders who show the creativity, open-mindedness, and emotional intelligence to meet the learning challenges of performing the public's work in conditions of permanent white water? Before I unpack this critical question, I want to pose a related one: What, exactly, *develops* in public service "leadership development"? Knowledge? Competencies? Best practices? A set of skills?

Based on my twenty-five years as a public administrator, including a stint on Vice President Gore's task force to reinvent government, I have come to believe that, more than anything else, what must "develop" in leadership development is the *capacity to learn in real time, in the here-and-now, while continuing to act in the swirling midst of permanent white water.* Like the false dichotomy between managing and leading, learning and working can no longer be separated. Learning is the work of the twenty-first century.

Drawing on decades of empirical research, students of managerial leadership, such as Kouzes and Posner (1987), argue that practices of leaders at their best include: (1) challenging the process, (2) inspiring a shared vision, (3) modeling the way, (4) enabling others to act, and (5) encouraging the heart.

> Leaders find the common thread that weaves together the fabric of human need into a colorful tapestry. They seek out the brewing consensus among those they would lead. In order to do this, they develop a deep understanding of the collective yearnings. They listen carefully for quiet whisperings in dark corners. They attend to the subtle cues. They sniff the air to get the scent. They watch the faces. They get a sense of what people want, what they value, what they dream about (Kouzes and Posner 1987, p. 115).

Without a doubt, public managers need to learn and demonstrate these five practices of leaders at their best (see Van Wart 2005). But executive educators who care about leadership *development* must focus on one additional objective: *helping our participants develop the capacity to learn how to learn and, even more, helping them develop the capacity to teach others around them to learn how to learn.*

### A Story About Developing Leaders Who Can Learn How to Learn

Let me share a personal story of how I learned to develop the capacity of public administrators to learn how to learn. From 2002 through 2005, I served as director of American University's executive MPA program, which for thirty years had been offered on weekends. Participants were managerial leaders—average age forty, with at least ten years of experience—working in mid-level or senior positions. An executive cohort at American University usually consisted of twenty-two participants, of whom about 50 percent were female and 30 percent African American. Most worked in federal, state, or local government, with the rest coming from nongovernmental organizations. On taking over in 2002 as director, my first leadership challenge was to address the problem of transfer of learning from the classroom to the workplace, a problem that had languished at American University—and at every other university—for decades.

Traditionally, after twenty months of intensive weekend courses, the executive MPA program culminated in a rigorous "comprehensive" exam, which required executive participants to prepare detailed answers in academic writing style over a forty-eight-hour period to a set of questions. The director was supposed to formulate these questions from facts woven into a three-page case study drafted by a rotating group of faculty. No matter how hard they tried, however, the faculty who graded the exams could rarely reach consensus on the "right answers" to these questions. Since the case study was always too brief to explore the full context of the problem and none of the actors identified in the case could be interviewed, faculty always saw the "right answers" through the lens of their functional discipline—conflict management, policy formulation, government ethics, administrative law, politics, or research and evaluation, etc.—leading to interminable disagreements in grading and to not a few near nervous breakdowns by executive participants.

As my first act of leadership, I decided to abandon this comprehensive exam, the main result of which seemed to have been to infantilize adults, who were being forced to answer questions about problems they cared nothing about and, in any event, could take no action to resolve. But what should take its place? How do I inspire a shared vision for a more action-oriented philosophy of executive education among my faculty and participants? For years I had been an active member of the Organizational Behavior Teaching Society (OBTS), a vibrant learning community of 650 management and leadership educators worldwide who hold a teaching conference each year. Before deciding on a replacement for the exam, I spoke with many of my OBTS colleagues, all of whom were experienced in applying adult learning models in university settings (Merriam and Caffarella 1999). As an outcome of many rich conversations, I chose to replace the executive MPA comprehensive with action learning. I would now require each of my executive participants to negotiate a "learning contract" with me for the conduct of a real-time work-related project. (For an example of a learning contract, see Appendix at end of this chapter).

What is action learning? Action learning is a group process that promotes learning in the "here-and-now" while participants tackle a real challenge with real work colleagues in real time. While people are working in a small group to solve an urgent problem, action learning simultaneously plants the seeds of a learning organization. Action learning is not new. Widely adopted over the past decade by Fortune 100 companies, the methodology of action learning was first designed by Reginald Revans (1971, 1980, 1982, 1983) in England over sixty years ago and was substantially improved in recent years by Michael Marquardt (1999, 2000, 2004). Revans intended the word "action" to refer to changes in the organizational culture that the group effected in the workplace; and the word "learning" to changes that emerged in the mindset, assumptions, beliefs, and emotions of group members.

The basic principle of action learning is that only those who have learned how to change their own mindsets—their own taken-for-granted assumptions, beliefs, and attitudes—can change the taken-for-granted assumptions, beliefs, and attitudes embedded in the culture of an organization. "Those unable to change themselves," wrote Revans (1983, p. 55), "cannot change what goes on around them." Action learning builds a community of learners that allows group members to transfer what they learn in the process of solving an urgent problem today to solve other, even more complex, workplace problems tomorrow.[1] The optimal group size in action learning is five to seven, and meetings usually take place at least one day a month, but sometimes weekly or even daily, over the course of a project (Dilworth and Willis 2003).

Conventionally, directors of executive master's programs in public administration have assumed that to develop leaders, participants needed to be taught academic theories and facts in government ethics, team building, administrative law, budgeting, leadership, and policy evaluation. Universities excel at this kind of teaching, which, in practice, means the transmission of what Revans called "programmed knowledge" (Weinstein 1999, p. 36) by means of lectures, textbooks, PowerPoint slides, case studies, classroom exercises, and role plays.

Programmed knowledge consists of the set of consensually agreed-on concepts, ideas, theories, models, and conclusions accumulated through the process of peer-reviewed research and publication in any academic discipline. University professors trained in the language and methods of their disciplines are comfortable in teaching about and lecturing on programmed knowledge. Conversations on public administration topics led by a professor with a "more participative, collaborative Theory Y style of behavior" (Newman 1996, p. 19) are useful in helping executive participants gain a level of intellectual grounding in the concepts and practices of the field. But the process of teaching programmed knowledge is incapable of transforming any participant's inner-world. Leading in conditions of permanent white water cannot be learned by "depositing" programmed knowledge about public administration theory and practice into the memory banks of those who want to become public service leaders (Newman 1996).

In contrast to the "banking model of education" (Freire 1970, p. 58), action learning is designed to develop learners in real time by transforming their internal, "invisible" psychic worlds while they are engaged in transforming the external visible practices and systems in their organizations. What, exactly, is "invisible" about the psychic world of human beings? Everything.

> We can all see another person's body directly. We see the lips moving, the eyes opening and shutting, the lines of the mouth and the face changing, and the body as a whole expressing itself in action. The person *himself* is invisible. . . . All our thoughts, emotions, feelings, imaginations, reveries, dreams, fantasies are *invisible*. All that belongs to our scheming, planning, secrets, ambitions, all our hopes, fears, doubts, perplexities, all our affec-tions, speculations, ponderings, vacuities, uncertainties, all our desires, longings, appetites, sensations, our likes, dislikes, aversions, attractions, loves and hates—all are themselves invisible. They constitute *"oneself"* (Nicoll, cited by Pedler 1997, pp. 34–35).

In adopting action learning, I was not merely replacing the "comprehensive" with a real-time leadership and learning project. I was radically transform-ing the purpose of executive education at American University from one that poured programmed knowledge into a space between the ears of our partici-pants to one that facilitated their real-time capacity to learn how to *examine, reflect on, and transform their own mindsets* at the same time that they were struggling to change the culture of their organizations. Kurt Lewin, the first theorist of organization development and the learning organization, famously said, "You cannot understand a system unless you try to change it." Likewise, I have come to believe that *you cannot understand your own mindset until you try to change it.*

The purpose of the executive MPA, as I envisioned it, was not merely to master the knowledge contained in the academic silos of public administration: administrative law, human resource management, statistics, policy evaluation, and budgeting. We would continue to require that executive participants study public administration through the traditional lenses and vocabularies of each of these functional courses, some of which (such as leadership, team building, and conflict management) are designed around experiential exercises and role plays in order to enhance practical skills. According to Kegan (2000), functional courses such as these are valuable because they represent "learning aimed at increasing our fund of knowledge, at increasing our repertoire of skills, at extending already established cognitive capacities" (p. 48). This is what Kegan called "informational learning"—learning that deepens our knowledge about an *existing* frame of reference. "Such learning is literally in-*form*-ative because it seeks to bring valuable new contents *into* the existing *form* of our way of knowing" (p. 49). However, learning of this kind, no matter how useful, does not encourage an epistemological transformation or mindset shift in learners. It is not "transformational learning," which, according to Kegan radically shifts the frame of knowing itself by questioning the taken-for-granted assumptions of the existing epistemology. This is "trans-*form*-ative" learning, where the frame of reference itself—the "form" of knowing—undergoes a radical and discontinuous shift (see Figure 16.1).

Informational learning, although valuable because it can stimulate "a change in behavioral repertoire or an increase in the quantity or fund of knowledge" (Kegan 2000, p. 48), cannot stimulate a change in mindset. In essence, informational learning is closely correlated with the received wisdom, accepted beliefs, standard models, or prevailing ideologies held by public administration academics.

To inspire a new shared vision about the possibility of transformational learning for our participants, rather than merely continue the existing practice of informational learning, I encouraged my faculty colleagues, many of whom were distinguished adjuncts teaching part-time, to redesign their course syllabi around the core values of a new, overarching, and systemic educational philosophy for the executive program. To become more effective facilitators of transformational learning, I invited the faculty, full-time and part-time, to infuse each of their functional courses with their own personally designed, holistic philosophies of real-time adult learning (Knowles, Holton, and Swanson 2005). How they did this was up to them. I was determined not to encroach on their academic freedom by mandating that they follow my own predilections.

Foremost, by adopting action learning, I envisioned our purpose as executive educators not merely to graduate ethically grounded, technically competent, and constitutionally literate public administrators but to *grow leaders who learn and learners who lead*. In other words, I saw our purpose as growing *learning leaders in public service*.

What, exactly, are the characteristics of a learning leader?

- A learning leader is a person who models inquiry and critical reflection while grappling with wicked public problems under conditions of permanent white water, when no one knows what to do, but immediate action must be taken.
- A learning leader is a person who learns all the time, not merely for the

purpose of applying one of the functional tools of public administration to get a job done.

- A learning leader is a person who demonstrates a high level of sensitivity to the difficulty others (especially subordinates) may experience in learning and who possesses the emotional intelligence—that is, self-awareness, courage, creative will, and empathy—to teach others how to learn.

These characteristics of a learning leader led me to formulate a second, equally vital outcome for executive education: in addition to growing learning leaders, we were going to grow *teaching leaders in public service.*

What does a teaching leader teach? Not programmed knowledge or the conventional wisdom found in public administration texts or learned through prepackaged experiential exercises or role plays. By definition, programmed knowledge deals only with past solutions to past problems. Programmed knowledge is what the dominant culture says is the right thing to do when you face a problem that has been solved at least once before. Programmed knowledge, however, is not sufficient for those who need to learn continually under conditions of permanent white water, when fresh problems arise that have never been considered by anyone and, therefore, cannot possibly have programmed answers (Heifetz 1994).

So what does a teaching leader teach? A teaching leader teaches—in day-to-day, face-to-face relationships with subordinates, peers, and superiors in the workplace—*learning as a way of being* (Vaill 1996). Learning leaders, in short, model the way for others to learn continuously.

I wanted my newly minted learning leaders to see that as public managers their most important responsibility, beyond learning how to learn for themselves, was to *grow other learning leaders* in their workplaces. They would never be able to meet the learning challenges of public service and the missions of their organizations, acting by themselves as solo operators. They needed to build communities of learners all around them in an ever-widening 360-degree circle. Therefore, they were personally responsible for planting the seeds of a culture of learning in their organizations. Unless they did it, no one else would. Leadership development *is* organization development. Growing a learning culture throughout the organization was a *leadership responsibility,* not something to be delegated to agency staff in the personnel or human resource branch.

Therefore, I required each executive participant to *teach the action learning model to others inside their organization.* As they taught action learning to other organizational stakeholders, they were stretching their capacity to lead. Not surprisingly, as they got better at teaching, they would find that they were *learning how to lead.* Learning how to teach would constitute, in part, learning how to lead. And learning how to lead would merge, finally, into learning how to learn. Managerial leaders in public service do not see themselves as adult educators, as teachers, or as learners. Yet leading, teaching, and learning are, at bottom, synonyms. "Leading" adults is the same as "educating" adults. The word "educate" is derived from the Latin *educare,* out, and *ducere,* lead.

## Leading = Teaching = Learning

For the successful completion of their action learning comprehensive examination, my executive participants would need to demonstrate to me that they had developed the creative will and courage to make a huge paradigm shift—to transform themselves from mid-level or senior bureaucrats trapped helplessly in the iron cage into learning leaders and teaching leaders. I made clear to them that there was no such thing as failure in the conduct of this final project, since whatever they learned during the process was the right thing for them to learn. How could it be otherwise? Each participant would be undertaking a unique leadership, learning, and teaching journey. I invited them to reflect deeply on the following questions in the course of conducting their leadership journey.

- During this project, what am I learning about myself?
- How are these learnings evolving over the course of the project?
- How does my mindset influence the data I am seeing, the decisions I am making, and the results I am achieving?
- What am I blind to? What do I still need to learn?
- In what specific ways am I growing or changing as a leader? What experiences are leading to these changes?
- In what specific ways am I growing or changing as a learner? What experiences are leading to these changes?
- How am I demonstrating that I have the capacity to learn how to learn?
- What am I learning about leading others to learn for themselves?
- What am I learning while teaching the action learning model to my team?
- To what extent do I now see myself as a learning leader? What evidence can I provide to support my self-assessment?
- To what extent do I now see myself as a teaching leader? What evidence can I provide to support my self-assessment?

By instituting action learning, I was creating conditions that allowed my executive participants to practice *in real time* what they learned and to learn *in real time* from what they practiced. Obviously, this comprehensive examination would have to be taken in the participant's own work organization, not sitting in a classroom on the university campus. There was nothing artificial about this examination. It was not a case study. It would not partialize managerial leadership into the contextually isolated knowledge areas taught by faculty compartmentalized in the silos of academic public administration, no matter how "in-*form*-ative" such teachings might be. It was holistic. It was work-based. It was learner-centered. The project would require learners to tap into their deepest emotions and thoughts and deploy every ounce of their leadership energies, courage, and creative will. It would involve real risk, real action, and real results.

Over the course of a five-or six-month project, the personal identities of the participants would transform dramatically. With the empathic support of colleagues in their action learning groups, they would experience many profound, disorienting learning moments, during which they came to question their own mindsets or frames of reference—that is, their previously unexamined assumptions and beliefs about who they were, what leading in their organizations meant, and what they were capable of accomplishing in public service. From managers who did not see their task to be one that demanded challenging their own preconceived notions of how they saw reality, they came, slowly, to transform the way they apprehended knowing and knowledge itself. They changed their epistemologies, their meaning perspectives. Epistemologies are how we make sense of the world. Meaning perspectives are the psychosocial filters that shape, usually without our awareness, how we see ourselves, our interpersonal relationships, our ways of knowing and problem solving, our ways of responding to crisis and permanent white water, and our ways of being and becoming. From managers entrenched in bureaucratic silos, they were breaking through the anti-learning bars of their "iron cages" *from the inside* and transforming themselves, day by day, with increasing confidence, into learning and teaching leaders.

In the setting of action learning, the anti-learning assumptions of Weberian bureaucracy—a model of organizing that has long been seen as contributing to "occupational psychosis,"[2] "trained incapacity,"[3] "professional deformation" (Warnotte 1937), and "bureaupathology" (Thompson 1961)—could be questioned by these managerial leaders for the first time. "This is a process of emancipatory learning—becoming free from forces that have limited our options, forces that have become taken for granted or seen as beyond our control" (Cranton 1996, p. 2).

My executive participants were learning how to learn and becoming skilled at teaching others to learn how to learn—perhaps the most valuable leadership skill they would need to succeed for the rest of their careers in public service.

Whatever else leaders do, their primary role is to keep learning and to facilitate the learning of those around them . . . Constant change requires something beyond managing to stay on a predetermined course. It requires leading, i.e., learning whether changing conditions are altering the landscape of needs and opportunities and requiring a change in existing plans or goals; learning which alternative courses might be possible or desirable; learning which direction to go; learning what it takes to get there; learning, learning, learning. In this sense, the crucial question in leadership development is not just *what* to learn, but how to *learn how to learn* (Antonacopoulou and Bento 2004, p. 82).

In the remainder of this chapter, I look more closely into the process of how action learning does this.

## How Does Action Learning Promote Learning How to Learn?

As we have seen, action learning involves a small group of five to seven people working in real time on an urgent organizational problem, asking questions, learning from beginning to end, and taking action to implement a set of solutions.[4] At succeeding meetings, the group asks questions such as, "What happened after the action was taken? What worked? What could we have done better? What did we not see? What more do we still need to do to resolve this problem? Are we becoming more effective as problem-solvers? As leaders?" (Marquardt 2004, pp. 77–80). Action learning builds a leadership culture for people to collaborate in the process of continuing to learn how to learn long after the project is completed (Raelin 2006). How does it do this?

The power of action learning comes from the many ways it develops the skills and habits of participants in questioning, listening, and reflection. Questions are more important than answers during action learning. At first, action learners engage new ideas by asking questions to frame and reframe the presenting problem (Bolman and Deal 2003). A frame is a mindset, a way of seeing the world, a paradigm, a form of knowing—an epistemology. A frame is a lens on experience that filters how group members see personal and organizational behavior and the meanings they construct from what they see. Unlike conventional problem-solving approaches, action learning is a process of finding, rather than accepting at face value, what is presented as the right problem:

Action learning emphasizes finding the right problem. . . . To find the problem, people engage in an active investigation that produces information, upon which they reflect. This leads to a reexamination of the problem, in a cycle that recurs three or four of five times before the project group can agree on a redefined problem. (Marsick 1990, p. 32)

As action learning sessions unfold while consciously framing and reframing the presenting problem—that is, finding the right problem—participants are, at a preconscious level, also beginning to learn *how to unlearn*. Learning how to unlearn means that participants will be repeatedly revisiting taken-for-granted values, assumptions, beliefs, and biases, and becoming more and more open to questioning their own personal mindsets. What is a "mindset"? Without entering the thicket of neuroscientific research, a "mind" may be said to consist of a "set" of beliefs, ideas, thoughts, concepts, intuitions, assumptions, perspectives, uncertainties, presentiments, and puzzlements—all of which are soaked through and through with a range of emotions. "To break open the shell of complacency and self-righteousness," Kurt Lewin (1951) wrote, "it is sometimes necessary to bring about deliberately an emotional stir-up" (p. 229). In the field of intellectual history, no one has articulated the need to unlearn old, worn-out beliefs better than Isaiah Berlin, the preeminent twentieth-century historian of ideas:

> We are enslaved by despots—institutions or beliefs or neuroses—which can be removed [or unlearned] only by being analyzed and understood. We are imprisoned by evil spirits, which we have ourselves—albeit not consciously—created, and can exorcise them only by becoming conscious and acting appropriately. (cited by Weinstein 1999, p. 17)

In what way are we "enslaved" by institutions, beliefs, or neuroses? Berlin suggested that each of these "despots" is somehow related to the other two. Therefore, a deeper question is: In what way is an institution or belief like a neurosis; and what, exactly, is neurosis?

In the early 1930s, Otto Rank, a founder of the modern object-relations approach to psychotherapy (Kramer 1995a), challenged Freud's then-reigning *psychology of likeness,* which had reduced all human beings to the same biological drive of sex, and proposed, instead, a *psychology of difference* that focused on releasing the "creative will" that lay buried underneath the inhibitions, symptoms, and anxieties of his clients—many of whom were blocked artists such as Anaïs Nin and Henry Miller. As an overarching organizing principle, Rank replaced Freud's biological drive for *procreative reproduction* with the human urge to create—the drive for *creative production.* "The creative artistic personality," Rank said (1989), "is thus the first work of the productive individual, and it remains fundamentally his chief work" (p. 28).

Despotic institutions and beliefs deaden the living creative energies of human beings, according to Rank, and foster a neurotic mindset that reinforces complacency and self-righteousness. So how do we break open the shell of our complacency? How do we let go of our self-righteousness and our bureaucratic neurosis? How do we unlearn what, in essence, is part and parcel of our own identity? In the banking model of learning, information is deposited "into" people by breaking into their shells from the outside. But unlearning (or what Kegan calls trans-*form*-ation) "can be gained only by breaking out from your own shell, from the inside" (Casey 1997, p. 223).

Comparing the process of unlearning to the "breaking out" process of birth, Rank was the first psychologist to suggest that a continual capacity to separate from "internal mental objects"—from internalized institutions, beliefs, and neuroses; from the restrictions of culture, social conformity, and received wisdom—is the sine qua non for lifelong creativity:

> Life in itself is a mere succession of separations. Beginning with birth, going through several weaning periods and the development of the individual personality, and finally culminating in death—which represents the final separation. At birth, the individual experiences the first shock of separation, which throughout his life he strives to overcome. In the process of adaptation, man persistently separates from his old self, or at least from those segments off his old self that are now outlived. Like a child who has outgrown a toy, he discards the old parts of himself for which he has no further use. . . . The ego continually breaks away from its worn-out parts, which were of value in the past but have no value in the present. The neurotic [who cannot unlearn, and, therefore, lacks creativity] is unable to accomplish this normal detachment process. . . . Owing to fear and guilt generated in the assertion of his own autonomy, he is unable to free himself, and instead remains suspended upon some primitive level of his evolution. (Rank, in Kramer 1996, p. 270)

Unlearning involves separation from one's self, as it has been culturally conditioned to conform to familial, group, occupational, or organizational allegiances. According to Rank (1989), unlearning or breaking out of our shell from the *inside* is "a separation [that] is so hard, not only because it involves persons and ideas that one reveres, but because the victory is always, at bottom, and in some form, won over a part of one's ego" (p. 375). Separating from one's self is an experience of creativity or frame-breaking, not a matter of informational learning—of adding to what we already know—according to Rank (1978). "This knowing differently about ourselves, about our own psychic processes is . . . a new interpretation of ourselves, with which and in which we free ourselves from the old, the bygone, the past, and above all from our own past" (p. 40).

In the organizational context, learning how to unlearn is vital "because what we have learned has become embedded in various routines and may have become part of our personal and group identity" (Schein 2004, p. 321). We refer to the identity of an individual as a "mindset." We refer to the identity of an organizational group as a "culture." Action learners learn how to question, probe, and separate from both kinds of identity—that is, "individual" selves and their "social" selves. By opening themselves to critical inquiry, they begin to learn how to emancipate themselves—how to unlearn. The slow process of breaking out of one's self-imposed iron cage, of separating from one's internalized objects, constitutes unlearning, which inevitably carries with it fear and pain. "Your pain," said the poet Kahlil Gibran, "is the breaking of the shell of your understanding" (cited in Casey 1997, p. 223).

On commencing action learning, participants are likely to be emotionally attached to the unconscious assumptions, beliefs, and values inculcated into them during a lifetime of socialization into various roles—family, community, religious, educational, professional, and organizational. Bringing into awareness and questioning, and, *where necessary*, unlearning, these values, assumptions, beliefs, and expectations is essential for effecting personal and organizational change.

Questions, according to Revans (1983), the founder of action learning, open up the minds and heart of participants.

> [They] ensure that no member of their set is allowed to coast along on the presentation of the others. All, with inexorable certitude, will be called upon to disclose much that they had for many years successfully hidden from themselves, such as what (if anything) they really believe in . . . or why they say the things they say, and do the things they do. (p. 135)

During sessions of action learning, the "contents" of mindsets and organizational subcultures emerge, usually in fragments or short statements, during the mutual questioning process in the form of "perceptual frameworks, expectations, world views, plans, goals, sagas, stories, myths, rituals, symbols, jokes and jargon" (Nystrom and Starbuck 1984, p. 55). While participants are learning about and unlearning their own taken-for-granted norms and behaviors, they are learning how to inquire into the collective assumptions of the organizational culture.

In essence, participants in action learning dialogues are learning the capacity for self-reflection and culture reflection. They are learning how to change mindsets—their own and those of their fellow group members—by examining taken-for-granted assumptions. They are increasing their capacity for mindful learning and unlearning. They are making conscious what is not conscious, making visible what is invisible. "How can we know if we do not ask? Why should we ask if we are certain we know? All answers come out of the questions. If we pay attention to our questions, we increase the power of mindful learning" (Langer 1997, p. 139).

Through questioning, participants are also learning that not knowing an answer does not make them an ineffective manager or leader. Not-knowing is reframed in action learning as an opportunity for learning, not as a sign of weakness, as it is traditionally seen by leaders who feel obligated to "have all the answers." Valuing not-knowing can inspire them and others in the organization to take committed action even in the face of unknowable outcomes. Traditionally, successful managerial leaders have seen themselves as "answer" people rather than "question" people. As problem solvers, they are comfortable diagnosing problems swiftly and proposing ideas and quick solutions. This is not action learning.

By willing to be open to transforming their own mindsets, participants are creating transitional spaces for themselves and their group colleagues to learn and unlearn (Argyris and Schön 1978, 1996). They are becoming learning leaders. Their learning is being inextricably tied to real organizational work. Working and learning are fusing into the same activity: self-transformation and organizational transformation (Kramer 1995b). They are planting the seeds of a learning organization.

### Reflection: "Stepping Out of the Frame of the Prevailing Ideology"

The heart of action learning is asking higher-quality questions (see Figure 16.1) to promote deeper levels of reflection to "discriminate between beliefs that rest upon tested evidence and those that do not" (Dewey 1933, p. 97). Questions allow group members to "step out of the frame of the prevailing ideology" (Rank 1989, p. 70), reflect on their assumptions and beliefs, become more self-aware, and reframe their choices as managerial leaders. The process of "stepping out" of a frame, out of a form of knowing—a prevailing ideology—is analogous to the work of artists as they struggle to give birth to fresh ways of seeing the world, perspectives that allow them to see aspects of the world that no artists, including themselves, have ever seen before (Fox 2002). The most creative artists, such as Rembrandt, Beethoven, Michelangelo, and Leonardo, know how to separate even from their own greatest public successes, from earlier artistic incarnations of *themselves.* Their "greatness consists precisely in this reaching out beyond themselves, beyond the ideology which they have themselves fostered" (Rank 1989, p. 368).

Through the lens of Otto Rank's work on understanding art and artists,

Figure 16.1   **What Is Transformative Learning?**

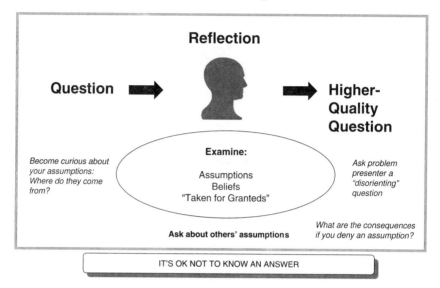

leadership "development" in action learning can now be seen as the never-completed process of learning how to "step out of the frame" of the ruling mindset, whether one's own or the culture's—in other words, of learning how to unlearn. "When this happens," explains brain researcher Andrew Newberg, associate professor of radiology and psychiatry at the University of Pennsylvania, "one's sense of self is temporarily lost" (Newberg and Waldman 2006, p. 236).

The most powerful questions have an almost poetic impact: they allow us the uncanny possibility of becoming "other" to ourselves. "I have learned to put myself on the other side of what I believe," one manager said (Taylor 2000, p. 154). On being asked his name, the poet Rimbaud replied, "I am an other" (Mason 2003, p. 27). To become "an other" is to become trans-*form*-ed—to become qualitatively and epistemologically a different person. "We have met the enemy," a federal manager said to me in the midst of an action learning session, quoting the famous line from Pogo, "and it is us" (personal communication, September 2006).

Because creativity is a process of continual "flow" (Csikszentmihalyi 1996), a surrender to the fluidity of emotional experience, the best outcome of a question in action learning often is not an answer but a higher quality, more thoughtful question.

"A world of questions," according to Adams (2004), "is a world of possibility. Questions open our minds, connect us to each other, and shake outmoded paradigms. . . . Our orientation would shift from one of answers and opinions to one of questions and curiosity. We would see quick judgments, fixed perspectives, and old opinions give way to exploration, discovery, innovation and cooperation" (pp. 7–8).

Questions open our minds and hearts for learning about ourselves and others and re-imagining both. Participants in action learning can transform their own mindsets and organizations by changing their questions. The changes implemented in the organization are called "action," while the transformations in mindset, beliefs, biases, emotions, blind spots, and assumptions are called "learning." Since action learning solves real problems in real time, it simultaneously advances leadership development, team building, paradigm shifts, organizational learning, and culture change (Marquardt 2004).

Unraveling layers of the problem and learning about one's own belief systems and the taken-for-granted assumptions of the organizational culture is the central task. This can be done only through critical reflection (Cunliffe and Jun 2005).

Action learning makes inquiry and critical reflection central to the group as members learn with and from each other while taking action. Learning how to learn is a communal activity, done together with others in dialogue, and never alone.

What, exactly, is liable to be questioned in action learning? For starters: beliefs, assumptions, expectations, facts, habits, values, opinions, bottom lines, ways of doing, ways of being, ways of seeing, and existing power relations in the organizational culture (Vince and Lawrence 1993). What else can be questioned? Everything that is usually invisible: "Our scheming, planning, secrets, ambitions, all our hopes, fears, doubts, perplexities, all our affections, speculations, ponderings, vacuities, uncertainties, all our desires, longings, appetites, sensations, our likes, dislikes, aversions, attractions, loves and hates" (Nicoll, cited by Pedler 1997, pp. 34–35)

In short, what can be questioned is any idea, belief, feeling, or practice considered to be unquestionably true. Doubt rather than certainty is thereby legitimized as the essence of learning (Weick 2001) and courage defined as the creative will to question any organizational value, assumption, belief, practice, or ideology that has become embedded in the culture. As Rank (1989) observed in *Art and Artist,* "the ruling psychological ideology itself appears to be as much in need of explanation as the other spiritual phenomena which it claims, either wholly or at least satisfactorily, to explain" (p. xv).

Here are some examples of questions (adapted from Cranton 1996, p. 86) directed toward taken-for-granted beliefs (i.e., ruling ideologies) that are typically asked during action learning.

- Was there a time when you did not hold this belief?
- Can you remember when you first came to believe this?
- Was this belief prevalent in your family, community, or schooling?
- Is this a commonly held belief in the organization?
- If you did not believe this, how would you act differently?
- If you continue to believe this, how will you act?
- Which people in the organization do not share your belief?
- What would be the impact if you changed your belief?
- What would be the impact if others changed their belief?

Obviously, as a prerequisite for this kind of deep questioning of the prevailing ideology, psychological safety must be assured for participants. How is this accomplished? Marquardt's (2004) recent insightful contributions to advancing the theory and practice of action learning provide the best approach: under the most important ground rule of action learning, group members do not offer statements, opinions, or viewpoints *except in response* to another member's question (p. 76):

> This ground rule does not prohibit the use of statements; as a matter of fact, there may still be more statements than questions during the action learning meetings since every question may generate one or more responses from each of the other members of the group, or up to five to ten statements per question. (*ibid.*)

In a conventional task force, the purpose of asking questions is to get immediate answers. In action learning, rather than a quick fix, the group seeks to go deeper into the thinking and feeling process to uncover aspects of the problem embedded in the culture that may barely be visible. Sometimes, certain questions are so incisive, so powerful, that no one has an immediate answer. In action learning, it's OK not to know an answer.

The most successful questioners adopt the mindset of Rainer Maria Rilke, who advised in *Letters to a Young Poet* (1993, p. 35) that poets "try to love the questions themselves":

> Do not now seek the answers, which cannot be given to you because you would not be able to live them.... *Live the questions now.* Perhaps you will then gradually, without noticing it, live your way some distant day into the answer.

By questioning each other's assumptions and beliefs in a respectful but challenging way, with the support of an empathic learning coach (see below), group members can learn to see the problem more systematically. The group can make the invisible visible. Asking questions to open the minds of group members beyond the existing boundaries of their assumptions is the central method for problem solving.

Action learning invites participants to become as comfortable with not-knowing as they are with providing answers. Holding back from coming to quick closure is what poet John Keats (1936) called "Negative Capability"—the courage to remain "in uncertainties, mysteries, doubts, without any irritable reaching after fact and reason" (p. 193). Only by holding the tension between knowing and not knowing, only by "loving the questions themselves" without succumbing to the urge for quick action, can new thoughts and new intuitions and creative directions for action emerge. "Not-knowing is crucial to art, is what permits art to be made," suggested writer Donald Barthelme (1986). "Without the scanning process engendered by not-knowing, without the possibility of having the mind move in unanticipated directions, there would be no invention" (p. 24).

Action learning breaks down the biases and rigid preconceptions that managers normally bring to solving a problem. At first, not-knowing leads to discomfort; this is painful. Eventually, not-knowing becomes an opportunity to open everyone's mind and heart to asking higher-quality questions—the royal road to learning.

"If I had an hour to solve a problem and my life depended on the solution," Albert Einstein said, "I would spend the first 55 minutes determining the proper question to ask, for once I knew the proper question, I could solve the problem in less than five minutes" (cited in Revans 1980, p. 102).

## Role of Action Learning Coach

To promote "Negative Capability" and ensure psychological safety, at each session of the action learning group, one member serves in the role of action learning coach, a role that often rotates among members. The coach only asks questions. Practice is required before members become skilled in coaching. According to Marquardt (2004, pp. 133–158), an empathic coach is essential to promote safety in the real-time learning of the group. The coach does not direct, instruct, or correct the group; instead, the coach's task is to pose challenging questions to support the reflection, learning, and unlearning of the members.

Modeling the three conditions that Carl Rogers found necessary for transformation in any interpersonal situation (Kramer 1995a), the coach must be congruent, "fully present in the here and now, with no pretense of emotional distance, no professional façade" (p. 87), and show unconditional positive regard and empathy for members of the group as they struggle with questioning and unlearning beliefs that are no longer helpful.

When intervening with questions, the coach intends to promote "learning-in-action" and "learning-after-action." The word "action" in this sense refers not to the action that will be taken by the group to implement change in the organization but to "speech-action," or dialogue that takes place inside deliberations of the group.

It is important to realize that speech is, in fact, the only "action" that takes place during action learning dialogue.

> Speaking is the primary and most influential medium of action in the human universe—in business, in school, among parents and children, and between lovers. . . . People who speak of moving from talk to action are apparently not awake to the fact that talk is the essence of action. . . . The very best managers often have an intuitive appreciation for how much we are influenced by the nuclear dynamics of conversational action. (Torbert and Associates 2004, p. 27)

Periodically, to promote "learning-in-action," the learning coach will interrupt the group dialogue to pose questions such as: What are we doing well as a group? What might we do better? Are we clear on the nature of the problem? What is stopping us from taking initiative? How creative are our questions? What assumptions have we challenged? What can we do to be more creative? How do our mindset and assumptions influence our choices here? How might we expand our vision of what we can see about this problem?

At the end of every session, to promote "learning-after-action," the coach will ask members questions such as: What did we learn about problem solving during this session? About leadership? About team building? What did we learn that we can now transfer to other problem-solving settings in this organization (Marquardt 2004, pp. 133–158)?

**Acting on the Problem**

After each meeting of an action learning group, acting *beyond* speaking must also occur. The process of action learning is not merely an opportunity for Socratic questioning and unlearning. Action needs to be taken on the problem, no matter how provisional or incomplete its definition. Action must be tested against the limits of the real organizational culture, with all of its normal constraints, in real time. "There can be no action without learning," Revans insisted (1983, p. 16), "and no learning without action."

Action enhances and is imbued with learning because acting on the problem provides for deeper dimensions of inquiry and reflection when the group reunites to review outcomes of the action. Learning that occurs in the interval between adjournment and reunion of an action learning group is similar to the learning that occurs in the "after-action reviews" conducted in the wake of each battlefield maneuver by the U.S. Army.

After-action review, according to one Army commander, "has instilled a discipline of relentlessly questioning everything we do. Above all, it has resocialized three generations of officers to move away from a command-and-control style of leadership to one that takes advantage of distributed intelligence" (quoted in Mintzberg 2005, p. 220). *Resocialization* is sparked by the communal dialogue and reshaping of norms inherent in unlearning and learning. Unlearning may be another name for resocialization.

Action learning, therefore, often leads to surprisingly creative solutions in the "finding" or the "defining" of a problem. As Weick (2001) explains, army commanders often "fight empirically" against their enemies to discover, by retrospective sense-making, what is ground truth in the battlefield.

> Sometimes the officer will need to implement his or her solution with little or no problem definition and problem solving. Only after taking action and seeing the results will the officer be able to better define the problem that he or she may already have solved! (p. 98)

# Appendix 16.1

# Sample Learning Contract

**1. Title:** Enhancing Administrative Services at the Food and Drug Administration (FDA)

**2. Manager:** Executive Program Participant

**3. Sponsor:** Director, Office of Management, FDA

**4. Background**

The Department of Health and Human Services (HHS), in support of the President's Management Agenda, set a goal to consolidate administrative services within the HHS agencies as well as within the Department. As a result, in October 2005 the FDA implemented a "shared services" model for delivering internal administrative support functions in the agency. Under this model, many of the administrative functions formerly conducted at our local "Center" level were consolidated at the agency level in a new Office of Shared Services (OSS).

This resulted in a large reorganization of administrative services in my organization, the Division of Management Services (DMS), which is part of the Center for Drug Evaluation and Research (CDER) in FDA. Many positions were realigned from DMS to the new OSS, and new positions had to be created. The creation of OSS made it necessary for us to change our structure and functions in DMS to ensure that we were effectively aligned with the new environment created by OSS.

As part of this process, a new Interface Management Branch (IMB) was created in DMS, with liaison positions established within IMB to serve as the coordination point between our Center's programs and OSS. Other functions were brought into IMB as well.

The rapid turnover of staff has led to a lack of cohesion and identity within the organization. In addition, the major shift of functions has created confusion within and outside the organization over roles and responsibilities. As a result, resources are not being put to their optimal use.

**5. Provisional Statement of the Problem**

How can DMS create a cohesive organization with a sense of purpose that clearly communicates its role to the Center in the new shared-services environment? There are four possible core issues.

- Structural: How do we ensure that the new structure is the optimal structure for the organization? How do we obtain a more clear statement from OSS of our responsibilities vs. their responsibilities in the new environment?
- Human Resource: How do we involve each employee in clarifying his or her individual role? How do we most effectively utilize our human resources in the new organization? How do we effectively communicate our role and responsibilities to the larger organization? How do we move closer to becoming a "learning organization"? How do we move closer to becoming a "teaching organization"?
- Political: How do we align all internal FDA stakeholders and incorporate them appropriately? How do we manage conflict constructively? How do we align all external stakeholders (e.g., congressional staff and OMB examiners) and incorporate them appropriately?
- Symbolic: How do we build a common vision and purpose? How do we institute a high-performing culture of public service? How we do deploy the tools of action learning to grow *learning leaders?* How we do deploy the tools of action learning to grow *teaching leaders?*

## 6. Current Ramifications and Consequences

- Lack of cohesion among staff members
- Lack of identity within the organization
- Confusion within and outside the organization over roles and responsibilities
- Lack of a clear sense of purpose
- Inefficient use of human resources
- Poor communication
- Lowered morale
- Increased anxiety and conflict

## 7. Measures of Success

- Cohesion among staff members
- Strong identity within the organization
- Clarity within and outside the organization over roles and responsibilities
- Strong communication within and outside organization
- High morale
- Constructive conflict resolution
- Willingness to adopt action learning throughout the organization

## 8. Major Stakeholders

- FDA senior executives
- Congressional appropriation committees
- OMB budget examiners
- CDER program managers
- CDER administrative management team (management officers and program specialists)
- All CDER employees

## 9. Team Members

Director, Division of Management Services
Deputy Director, Division of Management Services
Chief, Interface Management Branch
Office of Real Property Services Liaison
Two contractors dedicated to support this project, in addition to group members

## 10. Resources Available to Support Effort

25 percent of my workday dedicated to this project over five months
Team members used to identify and solve problems, biweekly, June–October
DMS staff members
Program managers
Administrative Management Team members

## 11. Other Resources/Linkages

OSS staff contacts
CDER senior management
Office of Personnel Management staff
OMB budget examiners
Congressional staff

## 12. Potential Obstacles/Constraints

Heavy workload/competing priorities of participants
Lack of cooperation from OSS
Work culture differences among new DMS members
Future large-scale changes proposed for DMS

## 13. Team Norms

Members will commit to taking action after each meeting.

Members will commit to valuing learning and unlearning just as much as action.

Members will reserve at least 15 minutes at the end of each session to respond to learning questions from the coach.

Meetings will occur only when at least four members and a coach are present.

Dialogue will be earnest, but members will never attack one another.

All members will carry their share of the responsibility.

Members will practice active listening with one another.

Members will respect the confidentiality of the group.

## 14. Process for Action Learning

Essential Elements

- A problem
- The group
- The questioning and reflection process
- The commitment to taking action
- The commitment to learning and unlearning
- A coach to promote learning-in-action and learning-after-action

Common Understanding of the Problem

- Need to define and redefine the problem
- Full picture of problem and its context before attempting to solve it
- Underlying causes
- Obstacles and how to overcome
- Identify the true problem

Shared Vision/Alternative Future

- Short-range solutions
- Long-range solutions

Common Basic Assumptions

- Be self-aware of one's mindset
- Examine "taken-for-granted" assumptions of FDA culture

## 15. Teaching Action Learning to My Team

At the beginning of the project, I will model the role of action learning coach and teach the action learning model to team members.

## 16. Learning Journal

Over the course of the project, I will keep a learning journal to record my reflections. Entries in this journal will help me track my growth and development as a leader and learner. I will record my reflections after each meeting or session of my team. I will also record what I learned during the process of teaching the action learning model to others.

## 17. Written Report

Questions I will explore in my written report include:

- During this project, what did I learn about myself?
- How did these learnings evolve over the course of the project?
- How did my mindset influence the data I saw, the decisions I made, and the results I achieved?
- What was I blind to? What do I still need to learn?
- In what specific ways did I grow or change as a *leader*? What experiences led to these changes?
- In what specific ways did I grow or change as a *learner*? What experiences led to these changes?
- How did I demonstrate that I have the capacity to *learn how to learn*?
- What did I learn about leading others to lead and learn for themselves?
- What did I learn while *teaching* the action learning model to my team?
- To what extent do I now see myself as a *learning leader*? What evidence can I provide to support my self-assessment?
- To what extent do I now see myself as a *teaching leader*? What evidence can I provide to support my self-assessment?
- Which courses did I draw on in the process of conducting this project? At least four courses will be identified. Specifically, how did I apply these courses to the project? (For each of the courses, I will provide at least four references to the books, articles, or scholarly readings I used for that course. Not all books, articles, or readings need to be cited, but the

minimum number of references or citations in my written report will be sixteen. If I have doubts about what material to put in quotes, I will use the "four word" rule—more than four consecutive words will be set in quotation marks and cited. I will include a complete bibliography.)

I will add at least two more questions. The report will be no longer than thirty typed, double-spaced pages, excluding the appendix. I will seek help or coaching from others for copyediting. At least two coaches will read and comment on my drafts before I submit the final paper. In an appendix, I will explicitly identify my two coaches' questions and my responses. The editorial quality of the paper will be excellent—at a professional level. I will plan to spend at least one third of my time copyediting and improving the clarity of my response.

## 18. Course Work I Will Draw on for Action Learning

I will draw on the following four executive MPA courses:

Organizational Diagnosis and Change
Action Learning
Research and Evaluation
Legal Issues in Public Administration

## 19. Oral Report

In addition to a written report, I will make an oral presentation, sharing my most important learning. Because of time limits, I will choose a meaningful subset of the questions I explored in my written report.

## Notes

1. How do we evaluate the long-term effectiveness of action learning? Little research has been conducted on action learning in the private sector (McGill and Brockbank 2004) and virtually none in the public sector. I am in the midst of a two-year follow-up evaluation, using periodic, in-depth interviews with the graduating executive MPA cohort members and their supervisors, peers, and subordinates. Results will be reported in future publications.
2. A term attributed to John Dewey (see Burke 1984).
3. A term attributed to Thorsten Veblen (see Burke 1984).
4. For examples of action learning projects, go to http://spa.american.edu/key/action-learning.php (accessed November 27, 2007).

## References

Adams, Marilyn G. 2004. *Change Your Questions, Change Your Life.* San Francisco: Berrett-Koehler.
Antonacopoulou, Elena A., and Regina F. Bento. 2004. "Methods of 'Learning Leadership': Taught and Experienced." In *Leadership in Organizations: Current Issues and Key Trends,* ed. John Sorey. London: Routledge.
Argyris, Chris, and Donald Schön. 1978. *Organizational Learning: A Theory of Action Perspective.* Reading, MA: Addison Wesley.
———. 1996. *Organizational Learning II: Theory, Method and Practice.* Reading, MA: Addison Wesley.
Barthelme, Donald. 1986. "Not-Knowing." In *The Pushcart Prize XI: Best of the Small Presses,* ed. Bill Henderson. Wainscott, NY: Pushcart Press.
Bolman, Lee, and Terry Deal. 2003. *Reframing Organizations: Artistry, Choice and Leadership.* San Francisco: Jossey-Bass.
Burke, Kenneth. 1984. *Permanence and Change: An Anatomy of Purpose,* 3rd ed. Berkeley: University of California Press.
Casey, David. 1997. "The Shell of Your Understanding." In *Action Learning in Practice,* 3rd ed., ed. Mike Pedler, 221–228. Brookfield, VT: Gower.
Cranton, Patricia. 1996. *Professional Development as Transformative Learning: New Perspectives for Teachers of Adults.* San Francisco: Jossey-Bass.
Csikszentmihalyi, Mihaly. 1996. *Creativity: Flow and the Psychology of Discovery and Invention.* New York: Harper Perennial.
Cunliffe, Ann L., and Jong S. Jun. 2005. "The Need for Reflexivity in Public Administration." *Administration and Society* 37(2): 225–242.
Denhardt, Janet V., and Kelly B. Campbell. 2005. "Leadership Education in Public Administration: Finding the Fit Between Purpose and Approach." *Journal of Public Affairs Education* 11(3): 169–179.
Dewey, John. 1933. *How We Think: A Restatement of the Relation of Reflective Thinking to the Educative Process,* rev. ed. Boston: D.C. Heath.
Dilworth, Robert L., and Verna J. Willis. 2003. *Action Learning: Images and Pathways.* Malabar, FL: Krieger.
Fairholm, Matthew R. 2006. "Leadership Theory and Practice in the MPA Curriculum: Reasons and Methods." *Journal of Public Affairs Education* 12(3): 335–346.
Fox, Matthew. 2002. *Creativity: Where the Divine and the Human Meet.* New York: Jeremy P. Parcher.
Freire, Paulo. 1970. *Pedagogy of the Oppressed.* New York: Herder and Herder.

Heifetz, Ronald A. 1994. *Leadership Without Easy Answers*. Cambridge, MA: Belknap Press of Harvard University Press.

Keats, John. 1936. *The Letters of John Keats, 1814–1821, Vol. 1*, ed. Edward D. McDonald. New York: Viking. (Letter to George and Thomas Keats dated December 21, 1817.)

Kegan, Robert. 2000. "What 'Form' Transforms? A Constructive-Developmental Approach to Transformative Learning." In *Learning as Transformation: Critical Perspectives on a Theory in Progress,* ed. Jack Mezirow and Associates, 35–69. San Francisco: Jossey-Bass.

Knowles, Malcolm S., Elwood F. Holton, and Richard A. Swanson. 2005. *The Adult Learner: The Definitive Classic in Adult Education and Human Resource Development,* 6th ed. Burlington, MA: Elsevier Butterworth Heineman.

Kouzes, James M., and Barry P. Posner. 1987. *The Leadership Challenge: How to Get Extraordinary Things Done in Organizations.* San Francisco: Jossey-Bass.

Kramer, Robert. 1995a. "The Birth of Client-Centered Therapy: Carl Rogers, Otto Rank, and The Beyond." *Journal of Humanistic Psychology* 35(4): 54–110.

———. 1995b. "Carl Rogers Meets Otto Rank: The Discovery of Relationship." In *In Search of Meaning: Managing for the Health of Our Organizations, Our Communities, and the Natural World,* ed. Thierry Pauchant, 197–223. San Francisco: Jossey-Bass.

Kramer, Robert, ed. 1996. *A Psychology of Difference: The American Lectures of Otto Rank.* Princeton, NJ: Princeton University Press.

Langer, Ellen J. 1997. *The Power of Mindful Learning.* Reading, MA: Addison-Wesley.

Lewin, Kurt. 1951. *Field Theory in Social Science.* New York: Harper & Row.

Marquardt, Michael J. 1999. *Action Learning in Action.* Palo Alto, CA: Davies-Black.

———. 2000. "Action Learning and Leadership." *The Learning Organization* 7(5): 233–240.

———. 2004. *Optimizing the Power of Action Learning.* Palo Alto: Davies-Black.

Marsick, Victoria J. 1990. "Action Learning and Reflection in the Workplace." In *Fostering Critical Reflection in Adulthood: A Guide to Transformative and Emancipatory Learning,* ed. Jack Mezirow and Associates, 23–46. San Francisco: Jossey-Bass.

Mason, Wyatt, ed. 2003. *I Promise to Be Good: The Letters of Arthur Rimbaud.* New York: Modern Library.

McCurdy, Howard E. 1977. *Public Administration: A Synthesis.* Menlo Park: Cummings.

Merriam, Sharan B., and Rosemary S. Caffarella. 1999. *Learning in Adulthood: A Comprehensive Guide,* 2nd ed. San Francisco: Jossey-Bass.

McGill, Ian, and Anne Brockbank. 2004. *The Action Learning Handbook: Powerful Techniques for Education, Professional Development and Training.* London: Routledge Farmer.

Mintzberg, Henry. 2005. *Managers Not MBAs: A Hard Look at the Soft Practice of Managing and Management Development.* San Francisco: Berrett-Koehler.

National Academy of Public Administration (NAPA). 2002. *Strengthening Senior Leadership in the Government,* Panel of the National Academy of Public Administration for the U.S. Office of Personnel Management, Patricia W. Ingraham, Chair (December). Washington, DC: National Academy of Public Administration.

Newberg, Andrew, and Mark Robert Waldman. 2006. *Why We Believe What We Believe: Uncovering Our Biological Need for Meaning, Spirituality, and Truth.* New York: Free Press.

Newman, Meredith A. 1996. "Practicing What We Teach: Beyond the Lecture in a Public Administration Class." *Journal of Public Affairs Education* 2(1): 16–29.

Nystrom, Paul, and William Starbuck. 1984. "To Avoid Organizational Crises, Unlearn." *Organizational Dynamics* 12(4): 53–60.

Pedler, Mike. 1997. "Managing as a Moral Art." In *Action Learning in Practice,* 3rd ed., ed. Mike Pedler, 31–40. Brookfield, VT: Gower.

Raelin, Joseph A. 2006. "Does Action Learning Promote Collaborative Leadership?" *Academy of Management Learning & Education* 5(4): 152–168.

Raelin, Joseph A., and David Coghlan. 2006. "Developing Managers as Learners and Researchers: Using Action Learning and Action Research." *Journal of Management Education* 30(5): 670–689.

Rank, Otto. 1978. *Truth and Reality: A Life History of the Human Will.* New York: W.W. Norton. (Original work published 1929.)

———. 1989. *Art and Artist: Creative Urge and Personality Development.* New York: W.W. Norton. (Original work published 1932.)

Revans, Reginald W. 1971. *Developing Effective Managers: A New Approach to Business Education.* London: Longmans.

———. 1980. *Action Learning: New Techniques for Management.* London: Blond & Briggs.

———. 1982. *The Origins and Growth of Action Learning.* Bromley, UK: Chartwell-Bratt.

———. 1983. *The ABC of Action Learning.* Bromley, UK: Chartwell-Bratt.

Rilke, Ranier Maria. 1993. *Letters to a Young Poet,* trans. H. Norton. New York: W. W. Norton. (Original work published 1934.)

Schein, Edgar H. 2004. *Organizational Culture and Leadership,* 3rd ed. San Francisco: Jossey-Bass.

Taylor, Kathleen. 2000. "Teaching with Developmental Intention." In *Learning as Transformation: Critical Perspectives on a Theory in Progress,* ed. Jack Mezirow and Associates, 151–180. San Francisco: Jossey-Bass.

Thompson, Victor. 1961. *Modern Organization.* New York: Knopf.

Torbert, Bill, and Associates. 2004. *Action Inquiry: The Secret of Timely and Transforming Leadership.* San Francisco: Berrett-Koehler.

U.S. Office of Personnel Management (OPM). 2005. *What Do Federal Employees Say? Results from the 2004 Federal Human Capital Survey.* Washington, DC: U.S. Office of Personnel Management.

Vaill, Peter B. 1996. *Learning as a Way of Being: Strategies for Survival in a World of Permanent White Water.* San Francisco: Jossey-Bass.

Van Wart, Montgomery. 2005. *Dynamics of Leadership in Public Service.* Armonk, NY: M.E. Sharpe.

Vince, Russ, and Martin Lawrence. 1993. "Inside Action Learning: An Exploration of the Psychology and Politics of the Action Learning Model." *Management Education and Development* 24(3): 205–215.

Walker, David M. 2005. *21st Century Challenges: Transforming Government to Meet Current and Emerging Challenges.* Testimony before the Subcommittee on the Federal Workforce and Agency Organization, Committee on Government Reform, House of Representatives, GAO-05-83T (13 July). Washington, DC: Government Accountability Office.

Warnotte, Daniel. 1937. "Bureaucratie et Fonctionnairisme." *Revue de l'Institut de Sociologie* 2(April–June): 219–260.

Weick, Karl. 2001. "Leadership as the Legitimation of Doubt." In *The Future of Leadership: Today's Top Thinkers Speak to Tomorrow's Leaders,* eds. Warren Bennis, Gretchen M. Spreitzer, and Thomas G. Cummings, 91–102. San Francisco: Jossey-Bass.

Weinstein, Krystyna. 1999. *Action Learning: A Practical Guide,* 2nd ed. Burlington, VT: Gower.

Yukl, Gary, and Richard Lepsingh. 2005. "Why Integrating Leading and Managing Is Essential for Organizational Effectiveness." *Organization Dynamics* 34(4): 361–375.

Zaleznik, Abraham. 1977. "Managers and Leaders: Are They Different?" *Harvard Business Review* 55(3): 67–78.

# 17

## Transforming and Decentralizing Global Public Leadership Through Social Artistry

Lisa S. Nelson

Social Artistry is an approach to leadership development that builds creative capacities in a culture-specific context. Social Artistry uses a society's or organization's stories, music, and other arts in combination with a unique set of principles of human development to evoke enhanced awareness and access to the sensory, psychological, mythical, and integrative resources that are available to all humankind. Social Artistry is currently being delivered in several countries (Philippines, Kenya, Albania, and others) as a pilot leadership capacity-building program sponsored by the United Nations Development Programme (UNDP), and it is applicable to leadership training in all contexts.

Social Artistry harnesses the development of human capacities to the challenges and tasks faced by leaders across the world. In this critical period of world history, leaders seek the strategic actions that can move large organizations and make an important difference. Social Artistry helps leaders work on both shared and discrete situations by helping them become more aware of inherent personal and cultural resources.

Training in Social Artistry provides a framework for bringing new skills and understandings to light, including deep listening, awareness of how cultural gifts can be tapped for psychological and social development, and development of a profound sense of common purpose with others. Social Artistry encourages the decentralization of leadership and capacity development by affirming the unique contribution each individual has to offer in these challenging times and by training individuals to present the same experiential processes in their home organizations and societies.

Social Artistry creatively shifts leaders' understanding of themselves and their purpose and abilities. It celebrates the countless individuals who have developed creative responses to challenges facing their communities, such as taking stands for individuals with HIV/AIDS, for pedestrian-friendly cities, for storytelling and drama as a means of economic development, for the education of young women and girls, and for countless other steps toward a world that works for everyone. Social Artists are well linked to other Social Artists and are encouraged to draw on a wide range of expertise and resources to assist communities in tapping into their own emergent creativity to solve problems and celebrate achievements.

In this chapter, Social Artistry is presented as a path and a process for re-energizing the call to public service, and working to expand and deepen that core premise to tap a much broader range of cultural and human potential than has ever been tapped before at this scale. A favorite saying of Einstein's among Social Artists is that solving a problem has to occur at a different level from the level at which it was created. Training in Social Artistry is a way to reach that different level. This chapter provides a detailed account of the Social Artistry leadership model and the processes, experiences, and outcomes of the training programs that have occurred in various countries around the world. It highlights the principles and core competencies that will benefit public leadership in this new century.

**Personal Connection**

As a public administration professor and Master of Public Administration program coordinator, I first became aware of Jean Houston's Social Artistry work in the spring of 2004. I had been feeling a certain dullness toward the same-old, same-old in the literature of leadership and public administration, and in one sense was walking away from it, focusing instead on the day-to-day practice of involving students and mediating the needs of different individuals and institutions associated with a federal Community Outreach Partnership Center grant to my university. On a personal level I was feeling drawn toward yoga and related perspectives, and I had offered a short course on nonviolence and civil disobedience during the quarter in which the United States invaded Iraq. I began to wonder if these new directions were ultimately leading away from my previous commitments to the triad of scholarship, teaching, and service in public administration that I had made so deeply in graduate school. When I came across Jean Houston's paper on Social Artistry, written for the UNDP Re-inventing Government conference in Mexico City, I felt a sudden snap, as if the far perimeters of the personal and philosophical frontiers I had been wandering were in fact reintegrated into a tiny but potent core of experiencing and acting in a much larger universe (Houston 2003). I was once again in the center of my earlier commitment. I had to find out more.

A series of surprising events made it possible for me to attend Houston's

Social Artistry Intensive training session in the summer of 2004, and I was able to experience and practice the training processes referred to in her paper. There are many layers of possibility embedded in the training, and the more I have become engaged in her work, the more I see its helpfulness for public leaders in all venues. Over the next year I was better able to see how enriching it is to acknowledge and incorporate additional dimensions of human experience such as inner-awareness and the arts into the "business" side of public and community activity.

## The Social Artistry Leadership Model

The aim of Social Artistry is to implement the current transition towards creative change and growth in many arenas and in ways that will encourage and prepare stakeholders to more effectively accomplish the goals of decentralization. Its goal is to provide significant shifts through a variety of trainings: cross-cultural, human and cultural development, education in human and cultural development, education in human and cultural capacities and potentials and other activating factors aimed at directing both individual and social capital toward the creation of better societies and peoples. Social Artistry also aims at providing strategies that can work in an interconnected world, training effective leaders who can productively address interconnected public problems, given present day conditions of reduced fiscal resources, lack of consensus on options, and the necessary involvement of diverse, independent-minded stakeholders. (Houston 2003)

Defining Social Artistry is a bit difficult, as it is intentionally adaptable to specific persons, times, and places and is evolving with the added experiences of its practice. As a growing body of work, its authorship expands to include Jean Houston's close associates and many of her students who are working to apply it in their own professional and community settings. Social Artists have available to them a field book and a set of principles and core competencies with which to work; conference calls on different aspects of application; audio recordings of the Social Artistry Intensives; and the opportunity to attend the summer intensives (International Institute of Social Artistry 2006).

Jean Houston had extensive personal contact with Teilhard de Chardin, Joseph Campbell, and Margaret Mead in her youth and as a young adult (Houston 1996). Many of their intellectual and social contributions find expression in Social Artistry. De Chardin's (1959) vision of humankind evolving into a "no-osphere" of planetary consciousness enlivens a notion of creative responsibility for today's generations, empowered and overpowered by the Internet and other aspects of globalization. Margaret Mead's often-quoted remark is another touchstone: "Never doubt that a small group of thoughtful, committed citizens can change the world. Indeed, it is the only thing that ever has." Campbell's insights based on his detailed studies of the world's myths inform many of the key processes developed by Houston to evoke deeper understanding among social artists of the importance of myth and symbol in personal and social life.

The task for Social Artistry becomes, according to Houston, to enliven, enrich, and evoke the potential of individuals, groups, and societies to help the birth of the new global society. This includes a calling for skilled governance at every level, and thus, the decentralization of authority and decision making.

Houston calls Social Artists to participate in a jump into the future for humanity based on a repatterning of human nature, the regenesis of human society, the breakdown of the membrane, and the breakthrough of the depths (Houston 2004a). The repatterning of human nature involves awakening dormant capacities and committing to lifelong learning in new ways with concentration, mindfulness, and optimal physical performance. The regenesis of society is about the rise of all people to partnership in all of life's roles, communicating and including everyone in circles of civic participation rather than hierarchies, and understanding the world as an ecology of local and global systems. The breakdown of the membrane is the dissolving of barriers and the recognition of interdependence occurring so rapidly in our times. The breakthrough of the depths is witnessed in the spiritual renaissance occurring everywhere and the convergence of mythic and symbolic archetypes with the global pop culture. It is, according to Houston, a loaded "Jumptime" inviting us all to co-create new possibilities.

### Specific Elements of Social Artistry Training Processes

The foundational framework for expanding and deepening individual and group capacities is based on Houston's decades of research and teaching experience. Two organizing principles in this work are the Four Levels and the Hero's Journey.

The Four Levels and a sample of processes associated with each are discussed in depth in Houston's *The Possible Human* (1982). Essentially, the idea is that humans experience life at four levels of increasing depth. The level closest to the surface is the level of physical and sensory perception. Below this is the psychological or personal history level, followed by the symbolic, and finally, at greatest depth, the "unitive" or integrative level. Exercises are designed to extend the senses, to reap the capacities of different aspects of our individuality, to engage ourselves in mythically resonant work, and to perceive and operate within the source of life and being. Many of the exercises and processes in Social Artistry are designed to evoke greater capacities at each of these levels and thus to provide the participant with greater access to his or her inner resources.

The Hero's Journey was brought to light by Joseph Campbell as a common archetypal theme in the world's myths, legends, and religious and spiritual traditions. In these stories, a hero passes through several stages, beginning with the call and completing the journey with the return as master of both worlds (see Table 17.1). In Social Artistry, an individual, a group or organization, or even an entire society can take the journey. Seeing the transformation process as occurring in stages helps locate and alleviate stresses and feelings of despair at the size of the task. It also focuses attention on discovering the specific tasks that must be accomplished by the "hero" in order to complete the journey.

Two other elements of the training are used in multiple ways in Social Artistry training venues: the entelechy and the polyphrenic self. Both are sourced in the second psychological level of the training. The entelechy is the higher self, the part of one's persona that is the fully realized human, with all capacities fully developed. The entelechy of an acorn is the full-grown oak tree. Another way to express the idea is to have a person imagine himself or herself in the future looking back with compassion and wisdom to his or her current self. In the trainings, the participants are led through a process where they meet their entelechy and open themselves to the possibility of a conversation. The entelechy becomes a reference point for gaining a higher perspective on the specific issues and problems one is confronted with in his or her work as a social artist.

The polyphrenic self is also known as one's "inner crew" in which experts in various skills and knowledge sets can be called on to accomplish necessary tasks. One can approach understanding this concept by noticing the many hats we wear in our lives. A hilarious illustration has been provided by Houston's associate, Peggy Rubin, who acts out the personification of her inner cleaning woman who is called on periodically to accomplish work that Peggy normally does not enjoy. This woman is tough, ruthless, intolerant, and eager to discard that with which Peggy is reluctant to part. Peggy calls on her when it is time to do that kind of work.

The entelechy and inner crew, once introduced, are called on in a range of subsequent training exercises. As a preview to the training, participants are often asked to bring with them the idea of a project they are working on, with the idea that it will be worked on and developed in the workshop. The projects then become focal points to play off with the Four Levels, Hero's Journey, entelechy, and inner crew. The imagination muscles are stretched, and the linkages between present and potential are strengthened and sharpened. At times, the collection of processes has been referred to as "adult kindergarten," but with a joyful knowing rather than a dismissive sense.

Table 17.1

**Stages in the Hero's Journey and the Journey of the Social Artist**

| Hero | Social Artist |
|---|---|
| The call comes. | Feels impetus to make a difference in a troubled world. |
| The call is refused. | Finds all the reasons it cannot be done. |
| It persists; the Hero agrees and begins preparation. | Begins anyway, making a preliminary commitment and means of preparation. |
| Allies arrive. | Gathers the artist's tools. |
| The Hero reaches the threshold to the realm of amplified powers. | Avails himself or herself of study, people, groups who advance the commitment. |
| The Hero encounters/confronts the guardian of the threshold. | |
| Persuades/tricks, undermines the guardian and crosses the threshold. | Discovers entropy: "We've always done it this way." Futility sets in. |
| Falls into the belly of the whale. | Deepens study, makes choices, pulls away from all who say "no." |
| Emerges, renewed, to a road of adventure. | Vows to cross the threshold to fully embodied engagement, both Being and Doing. |
| Gains supernatural allies. | Recasts the self, hones the self, gains experience, learns a lot, may feel swallowed up. |
| Keeps undergoing challenges, grows to meet them. | Opens to empathy with others and learns to really listen. |
| Reaches the deepest place of at-one-ment with reality; sacred marriage of the soul; gains a great boon or gift. | Begins to understand the source issues, is carried to the depths, is required to find and tap inner resources. |
| Hears the call to return to "lesser existence"; tries to stay in the deeper realm. | Experiences intense challenges; difficult choices are required: to die, to give up, to go deeper. |
| Takes a magic flight back. | Finds fruition, delights, manifestation, community, sacred union with that community. |
| Lives as master or mistress of two worlds, giving the great gift to the "ordinary" world. | Gains new skills; finds acknowledgment at deeper levels. |
| Awaits the next call. | Galloping entropy arrives; the Social Artist feels (and is) attacked, blamed, disregarded. "Why did I bother? It's all for nothing." |
| [Thanks to Joseph Campbell] | Hangs in, holds on. |
| | Moves outward into other arenas, becomes more expansive, even explosive. New realizations keep arriving. |

*Source:* Adapted from Houston, 2004b.

## Complementary Training

In the past four years, the summer intensives have included presentations and mini-trainings from experts in compassionate listening, fundraising, international development, the use of art and mind mapping to track group process, and other specific skills and knowledge sets. Compassionate listening is important as a feature of expanding sensory and psychological capacities and is key to many of the partner and small group processes that make up so much of the training.

The Compassionate Listening Project was developed by Quaker-Buddhist Gene Hoffman, who learned of the value of simply listening nonjudgmentally as a visitor to Israel and Palestine during a period of intensified conflict. The project has been developed into a training program and has returned to the Middle East and Croatia. It is applicable in any situation of deep conflict, and the skills are foundational to breaking through the usual barriers to meaningful communication. The object is to actively and dynamically listen for common interests and needs and to stay open in one's mind to new possibilities and in one's heart to accept the other person, no matter what actions or positions are being expressed (Compassionate Listening Project 2004).

The leadership model promoted by Social Artistry presents a unique blend of human capacity development and cultural and global contextualization. It welcomes and celebrates the richness of both the inner and outer worlds. Additional aspects of the qualities of those engaged in this work are presented below in the section on training activities occurring in the United States. First, a discussion and illustration of its application in the training of leaders in developing countries is presented.

## Social Artistry and the Millennium Development Goals

Gazell (2005) developed a useful description of an emerging global ethic that grounds the idealism of public leadership and public service in principles that can be shared across conventional political boundaries. Consistent with this ethic is the Millennium Declaration approved by the United Nations in 2000, with its eight central Millennium Development Goals (MDGs). These goals (see Table 17.2) have been presented as a meaningful agenda for "a world that works for everyone" at the summer social artistry intensives.

### Recent Training Experiences with the United Nations

How has Social Artistry been applied to real world training and development needs? Consistent with the model described above, Social Artistry

Table 17.2

**The Millennium Development Goals**

Goal 1:  Eradicate extreme poverty
Goal 2:  Achieve universal primary education
Goal 3:  Promote gender equality and empower women
Goal 4:  Reduce child mortality
Goal 5:  Improve maternal health
Goal 6:  Combat HIV/AIDS, malaria, and other diseases
Goal 7:  Ensure environmental sustainability
Goal 8:  Develop a global partnership for achieving the goals

seeks and applies a society's unique cultural richness to leadership train-ing on a foundation of evoking individual and group capacities. It has been harnessed to the UN project of decentralizing work on the MDGs to the local leadership level.

### Albania: Framing the Training with a Well-Known Folktale

The frameworks of the Hero's Journey and the Four Levels were creatively combined through the use of an Albanian folktale known as "The Seven Brothers." In the version adapted for Social Artistry, seven brothers take up the task of rescuing a beautiful princess from an evil demon. Each brother has a unique magical skill, and the rescue requires each brother's skill. Using this framework of restoring the princess to her parents and the kingdom is a metaphor for restoring the society to its pretotalitarian days. Needing all seven brothers to accomplish the rescue is a metaphor for needing all segments of the entire society to bring their gifts in common purpose. Within the training, each of the skills of each brother becames a hook for a process further awakening the participants to an aspect of the Four Levels.

### Philippines: Extending the Sense of History; Calling on Art and Music to Evoke Commitments

Two examples of what Social Artistry is able to achieve are illustrated by the training that occurred in the Philippines during the summer of 2005. Most Filipinos are educated into a sense of history that begins with the Spanish conquest. There is little awareness of the precontact culture. In the course of the training sessions, there was an opportunity to visit some precontact petroglyphs. The trainers led a process right at the site that evoked a sense of continuity with the ancient indigenous linkages to the land. Participants reported this to be a powerful experience that extended their sense of time and deepened their purposes of building toward a healthier wholeness in their society.

The summer of 2005 was a politically tense time in the Philippines, as the president was facing demands that she step down for corruption in her administration. During the training, participants were seen to be constantly checking their text messages on their cell phones for news as it was taking place. In a closing ceremony for the training, a children's choir presented several songs that evoked a deep emotional response in everyone present. At the opposite end of the continuum from the petro-glyphs, the children reinforced the commitment to the future and the need to achieve the MDGs.

### Nepal

In addition to the UN's program experience with Social Artistry, the Institute for Cultural Affairs (ICA), a nonprofit organization with extensive develop-ment experience, has initiated Social Artistry training in Nepal. Training has been directed primarily at the MDGs of gender equality and HIV/AIDS prevention (Timsina 2005). The ICA–Nepal program has been endorsed by civil ministers and spiritual leaders for its attention to inner-human processes, linking traditional concerns of the East and West.

### Other Countries and Experiences

Social Artistry has also been presented in the West Indies and in Kenya. In these postcolonial and evangelically besieged settings, access to myth is difficult, and because of the predominantly white teaching staff (so far), establishing trust and connecting points is a challenge. In the West Indies, the sport of cricket emerged as a metaphor for tying human capaci-ties processes to the emerging social vision. In Kenya, a folktale about a star basket was modified to become the container for dreams of the new Kenyan society.

One of the more activating and exciting processes used in all Social Artistry training combines ideas from chaos theory, Buckminster Fuller's cybernetics, and evolutionary biology.

### Chaos Theory

Houston draws on chaos theory as an explanation for the turbulence we see in global politics, the economy, environmental impacts, the clash of archaic fundamentalisms, and the wide openness of cyberspace. In times of chaos, creative and insightful individuals can reach through the turbulence and pull out the new system that wants to emerge. Systems that are driven too far can produce something new to restore equilibrium. Chaos itself contains the seeds of a new, higher level of self-organization.

## The Trimtab

R. Buckminster Fuller, futurist and designer of the geodesic dome architectural structure, used a powerful metaphor for conveying the ability of an individual or small group to make a difference, congruent with Margaret Mead's point. Fuller ("Bucky") used the image of the trimtab rudder, the small rudder within the big rudder that steers large ships. Directing energy to this relatively small but well-designed and well-intended part of the ship creates much larger-scale change.

## The Keystone Species

The prairie dog is an example of a keystone species on the North American short grass prairie. The tunnels that prairie dogs dig become habitat for a large set of other species, from rodents to reptiles to insects, serving the food chain needs of larger mammals and raptors. Taking care of the keystone species simultaneously takes care of the ecosystem. Similarly, there are social artistry projects that are positioned to have an immediate but widespread impact on many other features of the social landscape.

The process that emerges and illustrates these concepts is one of the most memorable of all Social Artistry exercises. After a lecture presentation, audience members are asked to consider whether a project they are planning might be a trimtab or keystone species for a variety of other needs. A volunteer is selected and asked to come to the front of the room to describe or explain their project. The teacher/guide who is leading the process turns to the audience and asks, "Who can help make this happen?" Soon, person after person is coming to the front of the room, promising a variety of wonderful and surprising forms of assistance. Each person is physically joined to the original volunteer by placing a hand on the last person's shoulder or the shoulder of an earlier gifter, until a large group is gathered at the front of the room. Everyone, most especially the original "keystone" volunteer, is in awe of the flowering networked vision that has assembled. The keystone volunteer is asked to step out of the group and to turn and look at the assemblage. It is often a very emotional experience. The exercise is completed with an exchange of contact information and dance music in which the ideas and promises are "embodied" at a sensory level.

## Training and Practices in the United States and Australia

Who are the Social Artists? In one sense, Social Artists include anyone trying to make a difference in a creative way, to evoke the potential for the new global society. However, those who are self-consciously working on becoming "Social Artists" have participated in a variety of overlapping learning experiences, including summer intensives held in the United States and Australia, train-the-trainers intensives, and a master's degree in Leadership in Social Artistry. In addition, participants in each of these venues are eligible to join a variety of conference calls. Many people participate in more than one group, creating an overlap of emphasis and interest.

The Social Artistry principles shown in Table 17.3 are highly compatible with core values of public service and public leadership. The language is richer and speaks of subjective and intersubjective possibilities not commonly addressed in the mainstream literature. Is this boundary-crossing language acceptable for public leaders? Many scholars and practitioners refer to the importance of grounding their work in an ethos or spiritual tradition. What may be different in these principles is the assertion of a common unifying reality shared by all, a simultaneous respect for other cultures, and an acknowledgment of cultural "shadows" in the Jungian sense of a behavior or identity that needs to be addressed and transformed to serve the larger purposes of growth and development.

Table 17.4 addresses some of the skills that may form the toolkit or portfolio of the Social Artist. As a collection, these competencies suggest a pattern of leaders as evokers, whose main agenda is the fruition of human and social potential. Again, the individual elements are highly compatible with more familiar roles for leaders, but in brighter colors. Someone exhibiting these skills might appear charismatic and gifted, and they would be. Social Artistry provides a means to overcome the notion that leadership talent is innate rather than learned.

## Benefits of Social Artistry for Public Leadership

Public leadership becomes more and more challenging as global, regional, and local change accelerates. Solutions to problems are at best provisional; governance situations are so dynamic that almost everything is revisited (or should be) in increasingly tight timeframes. In such circumstances, building relationships helps sustain the commitment to continue addressing immediate

Table 17.3

**Principles of Social Artistry**
(compiled by Peggy Rubin)

The Social Artist sees, and persists in seeing, in everyone and helps to evoke in everyone the possible human creating the possible society in a possible world, a world that truly works for everyone.

The Social Artist is a skilled and dedicated orchestrator/choreographer of energy, mood, inner-personae, time, situations, patterns, and points of view, to inspire creativity, élan, delight, courage, and innovation in himself or herself and others.

The Social Artist is a devoted compassionate listener, capable of hearing the stories of others at many levels, while also attending to the stories that are beyond speech and body language. At the same time he or she acknowledges the presence of a new story asking to be born, a story that may be hiding within or under the old story.

The Social Artist maintains love, honor, and respect for his or her family, community, and country, while in the process of shifting conscious allegiance to the global family, the global community of sentient beings, and the living earth. The Social Artist is opening his or her consciousness to "think like a planet" and become a full planetary citizen.

The Social Artist is a lifelong learner committed to deepening his or her existing skills and gaining new ones—skills that open the powers, focus, dedication, values, and knowledge of a great artist on a scale that employs these skills for the well-being and nurturing of society.

The Social Artist is in love with people's cultural gifts to the world, although is fearlessly aware of cultural shadows and the ultimate need for a people to resolve such shadows creatively.

The Social Artist carries a profound knowledge of the source and resource levels of existence; he or she recognizes, acknowledges, and respects these unifying levels in others (even when they seem unable to do so); he or she maintains communion with these sourcing levels to sustain energy, commitment, passion, compassion, creativity, playfulness, alignment, and well-being.

and chronic issues. We need many leaders, not just better leaders. Unilateralism of power or of perspective, approaching problems with training grounded in the world of the 1920s, and adherence or retreat into well-trodden paths do not do justice to what is available without and within those persons who are either called or find themselves in positions of public leadership.

Social Artistry is a rich and powerful agent of change for those who experience it and take it on as a field of endeavor. Public leaders would do well to investigate it and encourage others as well. As a more diverse set of individuals

Table 17.4

## Social Artistry Core Competencies
(compiled by Theodosia Southern)

1. Ability to use story and build learning experiences around a story or myth
2. Internalize processes and deepen knowledge of Social Artistry, including:
   - four levels (sensory, psychological, mythic, spiritual)
   - compassionate listening and dialogue
   - the power of myth
   - the polyphrenic self or "inner crew"
   - the entelechy
   - the unitive/meditation
3. Ability to create exercises in all four levels in different cultural contexts
4. Ability to create workshops and learning environments that evoke the genius in individuals and groups
5. Ability to help people access their creativity, think "out of the box," and move beyond their comfort zones
6. Skill in using dance, drama, and music to energize groups and to help them integrate processes
7. Ability to help others be mobilized by a vision of new possibilities
8. Ability to create a sense of urgency and hope
9. Ability to help others shift from local to global, from internal to external perspectives, and to operate from "planetary consciousness"
10. Skill at creating partnerships, collaborative networks, and teaching/learning communities
11. Communication skills, including speaking, writing, and use of visual arts and computer technology
12. Ability to self-orchestrate in terms of voice tone, body movement, and expression to serve the outcome of the training
13. Strong group process and facilitation skills, including:
    - eliciting from the audience
    - paraphrasing, reframing activities
    - giving and receiving feedback
    - brainstorming and prioritizing
    - recording the results
14. Ability to set a tone of respect, honor, and learning delight in every context and culture
15. Ability to help people recognize operating paradigms or metaphors they use that are failing them
16. Ability to understand the importance of timing and discern trimtab opportunities
17. Workshop planning and follow-up skills
18. Cross-cultural fluency; ability to communicate and facilitate in diverse cultural contexts
19. Enabling people to create and initiate their own trimtab projects
20. Transforming communities, organizations, and institutions

around the world become familiar with it and begin to apply it in organizations and communities, we can expect to see the commitment to important projects such as the MDGs become enlivened with creative "trimtab" projects and expanded commitment.

## References

Campbell, Joseph. 1972. *The Hero With a Thousand Faces.* Princeton, NJ: Bollingen.

Compassionate Listening Project. 2004. Materials presented at 2004 Social Artistry Summer Leadership Institute. Available at www.compassionatelistening.org (accessed May 2, 2007).

De Chardin, Pierre Teilhard. 1959. *The Phenomenon of Man*, introduction by Julian Huxley (translation by Bernard Wall). New York: Harper.

Gazell, James A. 2005. "The Provenance and Development of a Global Ethic." *Public Administration and Management: An Interactive Journal* 7:1. Available at www.pamij.com (accessed May 2, 2007).

———. 1982. *The Possible Human: A Course in Enhancing Your Physical, Mental and Creative Abilities.* New York: Tarcher Putnam.

———. 1996. *A Mythic Life: Learning to Live Our Greatest Stories.* San Francisco: Harper.

Houston, Jean. 2003. "Applying Social Artistry to Decentralized Governance for Human Development." Paper presented at the Fifth Global Forum on Re-inventing Government: Innovation and Quality in Government of the Twenty-first Century. Mexico City, November 3–7. Available at www.jeanhouston.org/un.html (accessed May 2, 2007).

———. 2004a. *Jumptime: Shaping Your Future in a World of Radical Change.* Boulder, CO: Sentient Publications.

———. 2004b. Lecture notes and materials distributed at 2004 Social Artistry Summer Leadership Institute. June 17–26, Southern Oregon University, Ashland, Oregon.

Houston, Jean, and Janet Sanders. 2004. *Developing Your Inner Capacities. The Social Artist's Fieldbook: Book One.* International Institute of Social Artistry.

International Institute of Social Artistry. 2006. Homepage. Available at www.socialartistryinstitute.org (accessed May 2, 2007).

Timsina, Tatwa P. 2005. "ICA Launches Social Artistry Initiatives in Nepal." Available at http://www.socialartistryinstitute.org/Launching%20Social%20Artistry%20in%20Nepal%2005.pdf (accessed May 2, 2007).

# Appendix

## Can Government Grow Great Leaders?

### Results of a Symposium

National Academy of Public Administration

The National Academy of Public Administration (Academy) sponsors the Human Resources Consortium—a membership organization of top federal agency human resource managers that meets monthly to discuss pressing issues in human capital management. Leadership issues since September 11, 2001, have been "the" preoccupation among political elites in national government. Hurricane Katrina, the Iraq War, a deadlocked Congress, and more have fueled concern. In 2005, a panel of experts met to explore the question: Can government grow great leaders? The collective wisdom of the panel's deliberations is captured here.

Senior-level federal government senior executives and managers function in a world of constant change and transformation. Developing leaders to face these constant changes is perhaps the single most important component of effective human capital management. Over the past decade, the Academy has focused on the need for public sector organizations to strengthen their leadership development and succession planning programs. In particular, the Academy has published a five-volume series that produces a clearer picture of the behaviors, skills, and competencies of successful twenty-first-century federal managers. Likewise, a number of organizations have developed and implemented innovative leadership development programs, many of which focus on these same behaviors, skills, and competencies. The premise of these projects was that federal agencies should be able to strengthen their leadership teams and to create and sustain high-performing organizations. This symposium continues the Academy's focus on leadership.

As a part of the Academy's Executive Consortium, a symposium on June

23, 2005, was conducted that addressed key issues regarding federal leadership development. Discussing leadership issues was a panel composed of:

- Prudence Bushnell, Ambassador, Dean of the Foreign Service Institute, U.S. Department of State
- James E. Colvard, Faculty Member at Indiana University and former deputy director of the Office of Personnel Management (OPM)
- Mary E. Lacey, Program Executive Officer of the U.S. Department of Defense, National Security Personnel System
- Ronald P. Sanders, Chief Human Capital Officer, Office of National Intelligence
- David M. Walker, Comptroller General of the United States

The panel was moderated by C. Morgan Kinghorn, president of the Academy. Great leaders, in the words of the Academy, are:

> Individuals who help to create the future and strive for continuous improvement, with and through others while also discharging their stewardship responsibilities.
>
> —David Walker

> Those you follow because you want to, not because you have to.
>
> —James Colvard

> Ensure change and not put up with the same ways of doing business.
>
> —Ambassador Prudence Bushnell

> Engaged in finding talented front-line folks and nurturing them a year or two before they ever think about becoming managers.
>
> —Dr. Ronald P. Sanders

> . . . not just the top, it's the middle, it's the bottom, it's the unsung heroes, and we pay too little attention.
>
> —Mary Lacey

### Can Government Grow Great Leaders?

Government is in transformation. Successful leaders will emphasize and reward:

- measuring results, focusing on clients and customers, promoting employee involvement, working partnerships, and informed stakeholder relationships;
- developing human capital strategies and training programs that match business goals; and
- building leadership succession and development linked to performance.

Leadership requires global thinking and the modernization of today's OPM leadership competencies. For example:

- defining "who" leads must include all who contribute, not just "managers";
- mastering diverse cultural and multi-sector workforce challenges;
- dealing with ambiguity and working the "gray" areas across organizations; and
- balancing management and leadership strategies to have immediate impact.

The DNA of our organizations must be revitalized. This includes:

- leadership competencies linked to performance management systems;
- reward and recognition systems that hold leaders accountable;
- flat organizations demanding leadership at all levels;
- core values embedded in the organizational culture; and
- personnel authorities consistent with new organizational models and workforces.

"Stewardship" for growing great government leaders of the future means:

- building capacity for leadership at all levels;
- sharing power with many to identify the few who will excel . . . moving from a controlling to an empowering culture while managing the risks; and
- changing the people to "change the people." Move people around, not just up.

**Key Leadership Themes**

Various studies have underscored the importance of having agency leaders and managers with the skills and commitment to drive cultural change focused on results. Agency leaders, career and political alike, should be held accountable and should hold others accountable to ensure continuous effectiveness, constant improvement, and increased mission accomplishment within the agency. This leadership is critical for an agency to overcome its natural resistance to change, to marshal the resources needed in many cases to improve management, and to build and maintain an organization-wide commitment to improving its way of doing business.

> There are a lot of changes and challenges facing us that are going to require top leadership. The federal government is the largest, most complex, most diverse, and ultimately the most important organization on the face of the earth. You've got to have top-quality leadership running that operation. It's critically important to our economy. It's critically important to our homeland and national security. It's critically important to the world's economy and to stability around the world.
>
> —David Walker

Symposium participants stressed the importance of agencies focusing on ways to build and sustain leadership. Key themes identified by the panel and participants were as follows.

- New competencies are needed for the leaders of today and tomorrow.
- Federal agencies need to better transfer successful military leadership practices to civilian leadership development.
- The culturalization and institutionalization of leadership is critical.
- New personnel authorities are needed to enhance government leadership development programs.

These themes are discussed in more detail below.

**New Competencies Needed to Grow Great Leaders of Today and Tomorrow in a Changing and Challenging Landscape**

In its report *Leadership for Leaders: Senior Executives and Middle Managers* (NAPA 2003), the third of the five series *21st Century Manager* reports,

Figure A.1   **The Federal Workforce**

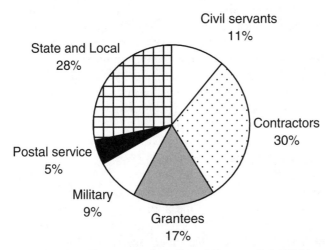

*Source:* Paul Light, "Fact Sheet on the True Size of Government" (Washington, DC: Brookings Institution, 2002).

an Academy panel provided a list of changing environmental factors that are creating the need for new leadership competencies. Symposium panelists emphasized many of these changes and the new competencies that will be needed to deal with them. These include managing a multi-sector workforce, network management skills, globalization, and a high tolerance for ambiguity. Panelists also pointed out how crisis situations provide opportunities for leadership.

## *Managing in a Multi-sector Workforce*

Increasingly, the federal workforce is not simply civil servants. The federal workforce is comprised of civil servants, contractors, grantees, state and local workers, and, with the Department of Defense (DOD), the military. Paul Light discussed this total workforce in his book, *The True Size of Government* (1999), and has developed estimates of its size. For example, he estimated the total federal workforce to be 16.7 million people, including 1.8 million civil servants, 5.2 million contractors, 2.9 million grantees, 1.5 million military, 900,000 Postal Service, and 4.7 million state and local employees, who work on federal programs and are paid with federal dollars. Thus, civil servants comprised only a little more than ten percent of the total workforce, as is depicted in Figure A.1.

Symposium participants said managing such a complex multi-sectored workforce requires new competencies. Leaders must lead their own civil servants, but they must also influence the work of a large number of other employees over whom they do not have direct control. The National Aeronautics and Space Administration (NASA) has had a lot of experience dealing with this type of workforce, especially in developing and deploying the Space Shuttle. Participants noted that the DOD is developing workforce planning processes for its workforce that is comprised of civilians, military, contractors, and foreign partners. It is systematically questioning each position and saying what needs to be civilian, what needs to be military, and what can be either, depending on the particular competencies needed for that position at a given point in time.

### *Leading through Effective Partnering*

Symposium participants pointed out that a key leadership skill to deal with the multi-sector workforce is the ability to manage networks. Such skills were described in Stephen Goldsmith and William D. Eggers, *Governing by Network: The New Shape of the Public Sector* (2004).

In the past, leadership primarily focused on a very singular mission—focus on getting A done, and then after A, do B. It was very linear, and agencies generally developed hierarchical organizations focused on a particular goal or sub-goal to manage this linear process. The world is not that simple anymore. Looking across the federal government, a merging of missions is starting, and there is more and more gray stage in what used to be black and white. Panelists noted there is a big challenge to refocus many federal organizations to address this ambiguity. Organizations should not get rid of the gray stage because it generates a lot of creativity. Yet in the process of making so much gray space, organizations have lost a little bit of black and white that is needed to maintain, sustain, and keep people focused on where organizations are going and what they should be doing.

Today, we need to develop a cadre of leaders that can operate across department missions and the gray stage that others have called networking. Governing, leading, and managing by networking are dimensions that have emerged in DOD in the past few years, as its organizations need to work together.

> It's no longer win/lose. It's work together, lead together to accomplish a greater good. I've seen organizations that have been at each other's throats for decades and in the last couple of years have started to emerge as partners, strategic partners, as they align for more complex missions. We can't go it alone anymore.
>
> —Mary Lacey

Symposium participants said that other federal agencies are also beginning to realize that they must work with each other and not just focus within their agencies.

### Globalization

Federal organizations and the people who lead them increasingly find themselves thrust into the global context. The combined and accelerating forces of globalization and technology have forged an interconnected world in which change and the need to anticipate and respond to it are faster and more complex, and where the international and domestic are inextricably linked. Key globalization leadership competencies include multicultural knowledge and sensitivity, understanding global macro- and microeconomics, and geopolitical boundaries.

This global aspect of leadership is critical. It was noted that the United States is at a threshold in terms of power and the issues that it faces, many of which are truly international and global. A panelist noted that 80 percent of the challenges that the United States faces are those that other countries face as well.

The United States is not number one in all things—it lags in such critically important things as K–12 education, while health-care outcomes often are not aligned with money spent. The United States is facing many challenges such as homeland security, national security, energy, environment, and fighting infectious diseases. These must be dealt with on a more multilateral basis Geopolitical boundaries are becoming less and less important.

### High Tolerance for Ambiguity

Increasingly, leaders need to have a high tolerance for ambiguity because many organizations are facing new and unique management challenges. The federal government's Senior Executive Service leadership competency model is more than a decade old. Although there are some enduring competencies in that model, it needs to be modernized. If leadership competencies are linked to vision and strategy, they can become much more powerful.

One of the leadership competencies that is far different from the decades-old model in use is a high tolerance for ambiguity. This is the ability to literally be plopped down in an organizational situation, reconnoiter, and have an impact quickly—being able to operate with literally a clean slate. Nobody's telling you what to do. You've got to figure it out. How do you define that? How do you develop it? How do you reward it?

*Crisis Provides Leadership Opportunities*

Panelists also discussed the role of crisis in bringing about leadership and the application of those leadership abilities to a crisis situation. They pointed out that as a new leader in an organization it is easier to make the transformation when there is chaos and uncertainty. That gives the leader the opportunity to transform—but not every leader or organization takes advantage of it. Leadership in crisis situations is easier than it is with an organization that is not experiencing major change, crisis, or transformation.

A panelist noted that the Internal Revenue Service (IRS) was under attack in the 1990s. There was a series of very visible hearings. And there was clearly a demand, not an expectation, for fundamental change. When new leadership came to the IRS, it knew it had to change the organization.

It is tougher to change when you do not have a clear and compelling external case and have to build a case for change. Where you have to convey to people we are on a "burning platform," the status quo is unacceptable and unsustainable.

## Transferring the Life-Cycle Military Career Approach to Civilian Leadership Development

In addition to new leadership competencies, a second major theme was the need to transfer successful military leadership practices to civilian leadership development. Panelists noted that there are great leadership models with both the military and the Foreign Service—where in both organizations it is far more of a life-cycle approach to leadership development. Both organizations look at senior leadership requirements, but more important, they focus on the pipeline of leaders all the way down to front-line employees, not just first-level managers.

The key reason the military does leadership development better is that the military is a career. It develops leaders with each assignment—assignments are made for the purpose not of just doing that job, but of developing the individual for the next job. Leaders are evaluated not just on how they are doing, but how they will do in the future. The entire personnel system in the military is geared toward leadership. However, it is far tougher to develop leaders on the civilian side where they are under the general schedule.

A panelist noted that DOD is identifying some of the best of what the military does with its leadership development and trying to transfer that to civilian leadership development. DOD is realigning its thinking around career competencies, career paths, and career fields. It is looking at the DOD workforce through a different set of lenses. Instead of looking at it just through the organization and the mission, DOD is looking at it through the career and the community, and across the entire broad organization. It is identifying the skills, knowledge, and abilities needed to be successful, as well as the interconnections needed across those communities. As a result, some of the aspects that have always been a part of the military culture are starting to migrate over into the civilian workforce.

In addition, DOD's new National Security Personnel System (NSPS) will be designed to focus on performance-based management and leadership. NSPS will have performance standards and performance factors. One of these factors will be for managers and leaders to assess how well they manage and lead. Using measurable results will enable DOD to put more visibility and granularity in defining the kinds of leaders that are needed. This way, the NSPS is also being informed by the military experience.

### The New Genetic Code—Culturalization and Institutionalization of Leadership Roles and Responsibilities

The third theme of the symposium was how to institutionalize change and leadership so that the positive traits will continue even with leadership turnover. A critical part of this goal is embedding the organization's culture with the ability to continue to change.

Panelists noted that institutionalizing positive leadership behaviors is critical to continued progress and achieving program results. Important components of this process are:

- the development of a strategic plan;
- an organization aligned to support the strategic plan;
- a redefinition of success based on results, clients and customers, people, and partnerships; and
- a competency-based performance appraisal system that is linked to the strategic plan that is linked to institutional units and individual performance measures.

Panelists noted that the institutionalization process needs to ensure that a genetic code of the right kind of leadership competency is embedded in the organization. An organization may have a great leader with the values and visions that that leader brings to an organization, but unless you want it to disappear when that leader leaves, it must be embedded in the system. It is not just the human resource system, but others (e.g., finance, information technology, procurement) that send cues to employees about what is valued. Those systems send the messages that help to embed the values in the organization.

> Unless you get it rooted in the organization and are around long enough
> so that the roots take hold, then it is not sustained. I've been part of too
> many organizations where, frankly, we just didn't have enough time to
> get the roots sunk deep enough to get the system.
>
> —Dr. Ronald P. Sanders

Linkages are critical to the institutionalization process. You can define and develop leadership, but unless it is linked, it is irrelevant. There are two dimensions to these linkages. First, it has to be linked to every other aspect of your human resource system, and second, it needs to be linked to the agency's vision, mission, goals, and objectives. The human resource system needs to link expectation setting, training, development, performance evaluation, and compensation to the desired values. If any one of those human resource system components is out of whack, they cancel all others out. Trainers know this instinctively. Organizations have wonderful leadership development courses that focus on desired behaviors, but these behaviors are inconsistent with the culture in the workplace. However, when the employee returns from training, the desired behaviors evaporate. Organizations must pay attention to linkage.

One way to promote that genetic code is to ensure that the performance factors in an appraisal system are promoting appropriate values. Such a performance appraisal system should not focus just on compliance issues but also on values that can stand the test of time. If the things used to measure people for rewards or promotions are consistent with articulated core values, this sends signals to both managers and employees that the organization is serious about these values.

Panelists said stewardship is another aspect of institutionalization and one of the key responsibilities of a leader. This is not just leaving things better off than when the leader assumed his or her position but leaving things better positioned for the future. That is a much higher bar. "Sharing power" can also assist with the institutionalizing process. Leaders must be willing to share power with their subordinates. Unless power is shared, subordinates will not be in a position to assume leadership. Panelists also said that moving people around helps to build an organizational culture. This is because an important part of embedding a culture in an organization has to do with making sure that more of the people know what the whole organization is about. People can only get that through experience.

Institutionalization is especially important in the government. Leaders have to be there long enough to know the job and to maintain continuity. Panelists noted that one of the biggest problems in government is that people who are the hierarchical leaders—the people who have the titles—typically are not there very long. Typically, they are policy oriented and do not really care that much about management issues.

The January 2003 Report of the National Commission on the Public Service (Volcker Commission), titled *Urgent Business for America: Revitalizing the Federal Government for the 21st Century*, noted that President George W. Bush was faced with identifying more than 3,300 individuals for political positions. The report noted that the number of political appointees had steadily increased from just 286 political appointees in the Kennedy administration. The commission recommended that Congress and the president work together to significantly reduce the number of executive branch political positions.

Embedding the leadership culture into the organization and linking it to human resource systems and the organization's vision and mission are especially important. The leader must promote this culture and change.

> The driving forces of that transition are the driving forces that bureaucracies need to have very different expectations. Leaders need to ensure change and not put up with the same ways of doing business.
>
> —Ambassador Prudence Bushnell

Finally, the leader is quintessentially the person who influences desired behaviors. Organizations should train to that behavior, but most of all, the leader must model the desired behavior. For example, a leader who has an open door policy had better keep his or her door open and "swallow his irritation at the people who walk through it"—because leaders align their behaviors and their intentions.

It was noted that a leader is somebody you follow because you want to, not because you have to. A boss is somebody you follow, but he or she may or may not be a good leader. If one looks at some of the greatest leaders in the world, many had very little authority.

> Nelson Mandela, who I submit was one of the greatest leaders of this century, spent most of his time in jail. He didn't have any authority. He didn't have any troops. He didn't have any money. He got things done. Leaders get things done through inspiring other people.
>
> —James Colvard

## New Personnel Authorities Needed to Enhance Government Leadership Development

A final theme of the symposium was a discussion of how limitations in certain aspects of Title 5 hamper the leadership process. This is particularly true of the classification process, which essentially requires that to give a technical expert more money the organization needs to promote him or her to a supervisor. These technical experts can often be poor supervisors.

Panelists explained that the promotion of those who do their job well technically are the ones who have traditionally been promoted to leaders. Federal organizations continue to believe that they are not training their technical employees well in leadership. It was posited that these technical employees may not have the capacity or the interest for developing their leadership skills. IBM, which probably has one of the largest and most successful research entities in the world, addressed this issue by creating a position of research vice president. These are individuals who are at the top of their field and are paid more than anyone else in the firm, including the CEO. These positions do not require the leadership or supervisory skills of line managers. In addition, IBM created a dual track compensation system that acknowledged technical skills and manager/leader skills were two entirely different, but equally valuable, skill sets. The compensation system gives them equal value.

A similar situation exists in the military with its "up or out" philosophy and strategy.

A panelist noted that one of the advantages of the NSPS will be changing the limitations of the classification system. DOD will be able to give people additional pay without requiring them to move into supervisor or manager positions and therefore break the mold created by the outdated Title 5 classification rules. DOD assessed the experiences of more than thirty years of demonstration projects. Those organizations created a career path for the technical depth and allowed employees to distribute along the continuum based on their competency.

A panelist noted that another limitation of Title 5 is the basic career profile. NSPS will create some needed flexibility, but additional flexibility is needed. Specifically, one flexibility that needs to be assessed further is a career profile change that an Academy panel outlined in a report released in February 2005, titled *NASA: Human Capital Flexibilities for the 21st Century Workforce*. This proposal would provide agencies with additional flexibility at the beginning and end of employees' careers. At the front end, the agency would be able to lengthen the probationary or trial period for up to five years depending on the nature of the position, a potential increase from the more traditional one year at NASA and most federal agencies. At the back end, retirement rules

In the navy, it's either up or out. For a very, very good fighter pilot, the next logical step is to take over a wing and then a series of wings. Well, some of these are great fighter pilots because they like to fly. And you get to a certain point in your military career, at least in the navy, and if you don't take that next leadership promotion, you don't take over the large wing, you don't become a desk jockey, you're out. Now, at this point in time, if somebody's an O5 or O6, we've got a couple of million dollars in training and development invested in this pilot. And they can walk out the door and get a job as a commercial pilot. And then we start spending a couple of million dollars to train the next pilot. During the early days of the Afghan situation, we had quite a number of Navy fighter wings that were over there. And we had quite a few reserve wings that were activated to supplement the forces. And guess which wing had the best record by order of magnitude? It was the reserve wing. This was the O5 that were told to get out. All they wanted to do was fly. So you had a whole wing made up of incredible flyers who didn't want to be the leader. But they were not the leader in name, they were the leaders in fact. They led in what they did. They had the competency. They knew what they wanted to do. They focused on that mission that they were assigned to. And they were very, very successful.

—Mary Lacey

could be changed to allow the agency to separate an employee eligible for optional retirement, if doing so would help it achieve workforce reshaping or downsizing goals.

**Summary**

Developing strong leadership in federal agencies and institutionalizing a leadership culture is the key ingredient in ensuring a high level of government performance. The final report of the *21st Century Manager Series*, *Final Report and Recommendations: The 21st Century Federal Manager* (2004), noted that today there is an enormous gap between what is expected of federal leaders and what they are capable of delivering. Closing this gap is essential to effective government programs and the overall fundamental well-being of the United States.

The results of this symposium provide real information of what is needed to help address this fundamental leadership need. This included ensuring leaders have new competencies to address today's and tomorrow's challenges, learning from the positive leadership development experiences of the military, culturalizing and institutionalizing leadership, and providing needed changes to personnel rules that could enhance leadership development.

## References

Goldsmith, Stephen, and William D. Eggers. 2004. *Governing by Network: The New Shape of the Public Sector*. Washington, DC: Brookings Institution.

Light, Paul C. 1999. *The True Size of Government*. Washington, DC: Brookings Institution.

National Academy of Public Administration (NAPA). 2003. *Leadership for Leaders, Senior Executives and Middle Managers*. Washington, DC: Author.

———. 2004. *Final Report and Recommendations: The 21st Century Federal Manager*. Washington, DC: Author.

———. 2005. *NASA: Human Capital Flexibilities for the 21st Century Workforce*. Report by a panel of NAPA for the National Aeronautics and Space Administration, James E. Colvard, chair (February). Washington, DC: Author.

Volcker, Paul A., et al. 2003. *Urgent Business for America: Revitalizing the Federal Government for the 21st Century*. Report of the National Commission on the Public Service. Washington, DC: Brookings Institution.

# About the Editors and Contributors

**Ricardo S. Morse** is Assistant Professor of Public Administration and Government at the University of North Carolina–Chapel Hill School of Government. His teaching and consulting work focuses on public leadership and community and regional collaboration. His publications include several articles and book chapters on collaboration and public participation. Rick received bachelor's and master's degrees in Public Policy from Brigham Young University and PhD in Public Administration from Virginia Tech.

**Terry F. Buss** is a Program Director at the National Academy of Public Administration. He earned a doctorate in political science from Ohio State University. He has managed public administration programs and research centers at Ohio State University, Youngstown State University, University of Akron, Suffolk University, and Florida International University, and has served as a senior policy advisor at the Council of Governors' Policy Advisors, Congressional Research Service, U.S. Department of Housing and Urban Development, and World Bank. He has published ten books and several hundred papers.

**Ruth Ann Bramson** has had a diverse career, which includes running a nonprofit organization, providing political commentary for a television station in a major media market, managing a statewide presidential political campaign, serving as deputy county administrator for a large county in Florida, and providing consulting and technical assistance to over fifty local governments around the country. She has taught in the public administration departments of University of South Florida and Florida State University, and for the past thirteen years at Suffolk University in Boston.

**Richard F. Callahan** is Associate Dean and Director of State Capital and Leadership Programs for the School of Policy, Planning, and Development of the University of Southern California. He has directed the design and delivery of graduate degree programs and leadership programs for all levels of government and nonprofits. Dr. Callahan serves on the Board of Directors of Sacramento Healthcare Decisions; the American Congress of Health Care

Executives, Sacramento Regents Advisory Board; and the Editorial Board of *Public Administration Review*. He has been published in the *Journal of Public Administration Research and Theory, American Review of Public Administration,* and *Public Administration Review*. He has over twelve years of local government and county government experience, including five years as a township administrator.

**James E. Colvard** has had a long and distinguished career with the federal government. He began as a physicist at the Ordnance Test Station in China Lake, California, and ended as a presidential appointee in the Reagan administration as the Deputy Director of the Office of Personnel Management. His career has spanned the spectrum from bench scientist to executive policymaker. During his career he has received numerous awards and was the first person to receive the Presidential Rank of Distinguished Executive from two presidents—Carter and Reagan. After his federal service, Jim served as the Associate Director of the Johns Hopkins University Applied Physics Laboratory and currently lectures for Brookings and the University of Virginia.

**S. Mike Davis** is a Senior Analyst at the U.S. Government Accountability Office. He has worked with and studied public organizations involved in transformation and change while serving in various leadership positions in government, the private sector, and academic and nonprofit organizations. He previously served as the Executive Director for the Center for Innovation in Public Service at the George Washington University School of Public Policy and Public Administration.

**Frank DiGiammarino** is a Vice President at the National Academy of Public Administration. He is an accomplished leader with a proven track record in helping senior government executives drive strategic change and increase organization potential. Prior to joining the Academy, Mr. DiGiammarino held positions of leadership at Touchstone Consulting Group, Sapient Corporation, and American Management Systems. Mr. DiGiammarino has a BA, cum laude, in Political Science from the University of Massachusetts, and an MPA in Science and Technology Policy Analysis from George Washington University.

**Brian E. Gittens** is Senior Associate Director of Business Operations and Strategic Initiatives at Virginia Tech, where he leads a team of professionals focused on business planning, organizational development, and learning. Brian began his professional career as a noncommissioned and later commissioned officer in the United State Marine Corps. After thirteen years of service as an administrative leader, he transitioned into higher education. Brian holds a bachelor's degree in Communications and a master's in Public Administration from Virginia Tech. He is currently a doctoral candidate in higher education administration at George Washington University with a research interest in leadership and organizational culture.

**Marc Holzer** is Dean of the School of Public Affairs and Administration and Board of Governors Professor of Public Administration at Rutgers University in Newark, New Jersey. Marc is a fellow of the National Academy of Public Administration and former president of the American Society for Public Administration. A leading expert in performance measurement and public management, he is the founder and director of the National Center for Public Productivity and founder and editor-in-chief of *Public Performance and Management Review*. He is the recipient of many national honors, including the National Association of Schools of Public Affairs and Administration Excellence in Teaching Award.

**James Edwin Kee** is a Professor in the School of Public Policy and Public Administration, George Washington (GW) University. Before joining GW in 1985, he had a twenty-year career in government. He was a legal assistant to Senator Robert F. Kennedy, a legal counsel to the New York State Assembly, and executive director of a New York legislative commission. From 1976 to 1985 he served in several executive-level positions in the State of Utah, as State Planning Coordinator, State Budget Director, and from 1981 to 1985 as Executive Director of the Department of Administrative Services,. At GW, Kee has been a department chair and the Senior Associate Dean and Interim Dean of the GW School of Business and Public Management. His teaching and research interests include leadership, public management, public–private partnerships, and administrative reform. Kee is the principal investigator of the "Public Sector Change and Transformation" project in the GW Center for Innovation in the Public Service. He published the book *Out of Balance* with former Utah Governor Scott M. Matheson and has numerous book chapters and articles in such journals as the *Harvard Law Review, Public Administration Review,* and *Public Budgeting and Finance.*

**Robert Kramer**, PhD, teaches action learning, leadership, and organization development at American University (AU). In 2004, he won the Curriculum Innovation Award of the American Society for Public Administration for instituting action learning at AU. In 2005, he taught action learning to the entire U.S. Presidential Management Fellows (PMF) cohort of 400 participants. He is now teaching action learning to officials at the European Commission in Brussels and consulting to public administration faculty at the following three universities to design leadership curricula employing action learning: Roger Williams University (Bristol, RI), University of Sharjah (United Arab Emirates), and Corvinus University (Budapest, Hungary).

**Lisa S. Nelson** is a Professor in the Political Science Department at California State Polytechnic University, Pomona. She teaches public administration, American government, research methods, and electives related to environmental and natural resources policy and management. Nelson is also a Social Artist, working with networks promoting community sustainability. She received her bachelor's degree from Brown University and master's and PhD degrees from Arizona State University.

**Stephanie P. Newbold** is Assistant Professor of Public Affairs at the University of Texas at Dallas. Her research interests include constitutional theory, ethics, administrative history, and the legal environment of public affairs. She is part of the Constitutional School of Public Administration. She received her bachelor's degree from Elon University and master's and PhD degrees at Virginia Tech.

**Kathryn Newcomer** is the Director of the School of Public Policy and Public Administration at the George Washington University, where she teaches public and nonprofit program evaluation, research design, and applied statistics. She conducts research and training for federal and local government agencies on performance measurement and program evaluation. Dr. Newcomer has published five books and numerous journal articles. She is a Fellow of the National Academy of Public Administration and President of the National Association of Schools of Public Affairs and Administration for 2006–2007. Dr. Newcomer earned a BS in education and an MA in Political Science from the University of Kansas, and a PhD in Political Science from the University of Iowa.

**Thomas R. Pickering**, a Career Ambassador in the Foreign Service of the United States, served as Undersecretary of State for Political Affairs; U.S. Ambassador to the Russian Federation, India, Israel, El Salvador, Nigeria, and the Hashemite Kingdom of Jordan; and U.S. Ambassador and Representative to the United Nations in New York in a diplomatic career spanning five decades. He also served as Executive Secretary of the Department of State and Special Assistant to Secretaries William P. Rogers and Henry A. Kissinger. He was on active duty in the U.S. Navy from 1956 to 1959. After leaving government service, Ambassador Pickering joined Boeing as Senior Vice President for International Relations.

**F. Stevens Redburn** is former chief of the Housing Branch at the Office of Management and Budget, Executive Office of the President. He and his staff helped coordinate administration policy and review the budget and management of the Department of Housing and Urban Development (HUD) and other federal agencies. He earned his PhD in Political Science from the University of North Carolina–Chapel Hill. Redburn's scholarly contributions include co-authoring a book, *Responding to America's Homeless,* that helped shape the nation's understanding of a complex problem by delineating subgroups within the homeless population and differences in approaches to service delivery required for each group. His federal service began in 1979 at HUD, where he led field studies in the Office of Policy Development and Research to evaluate major programs. His most recent book is a collection of essays, coedited with Terry Buss, *Public Policies for Distressed Communities Revisited.* He is an elected fellow of the National Academy of Public Administration.

**Sydney Smith-Heimbrock** is a PhD candidate in political science at Miami University of Ohio. She served with the National Academy of Public Administration during her candidate development program for the Senior Executive Service. She is currently with the U.S. Office of Personnel Management.

**Daniel Spikes** is the Director of the Global Leadership Consortium at the National Academy of Public Administration. The Consortium is a research and learning network that supports federal agencies in developing leaders who can excel in the global environment. Partners include the Federal Executive Institute and the Graduate School, U.S. Department of Agriculture. Before joining the Academy, he served for twenty-five years as a Foreign Service Officer for the U.S. Department of State and the U.S. Information Agency, with assignments to Naples, Rome, Budapest, Poznan, and Washington, DC.

**Carl W. Stenberg III** is Professor of Public Administration and Government and Director of the Master's of Public Administration program at the University of North Carolina–Chapel Hill School of Government. Previously, he served as Dean of Yale Gordon College of Liberal Arts, University of Baltimore; Director of the Weldon Cooper Center for Public Service, University of Virginia; Executive Director of the Council of State Governments; and Assistant Director of the U.S. Advisory Commission on Intergovernmental Relations. He is former features editor of *Public Administration Review,* co-author of *America's Future Work Force* (Greenwood Press, 1994), and co-editor of *Managing Local Government Services: A Practical Guide* (ICMA, 2007). Stenberg is a Fellow and former chair of the Board of Directors of the National Academy of Public Administration and past president of the American Society for Public Administration.

**Larry D. Terry** was a giant in the field of public administration and author of *Leadership of Public Bureaucracies,* now in its second edition (2003, M.E. Sharpe). Larry was a Fellow of the National Academy of Public Administration and editor of *Public Administration Review* from 2000 to 2005. He was Vice President of Business Affairs at the University of Texas at Dallas at the time of his untimely death in the summer of 2006. A tribute to Larry can be found in the December 2006 supplement to Volume 66 of *Public Administration Review.*

**Vaughn M. Upshaw** is currently a faculty member in Government and Public Administration at the University of North Carolina's School of Government. Upshaw has twenty years of experience working with public and nonprofit governing boards at the local, state, and national levels. Upshaw helped establish and then directed the Association for North Carolina Boards of Health and was instrumental in establishing the National Association of Local Boards of Health (NALBOH). She served as President of NALBOH in 1999 and has been in national leadership positions, serving as a member of the Public Health Foundation's board, Turning Point's Public Health Law Collaborative, the National Association of City and County Health Officials' workgroups, and the Centers for Disease Control and Prevention's National Public Health Performance Standards Program. Dr. Upshaw received her doctorate in Education from North Carolina State University in 1997, doctorate and master's of Public Health from University of North Carolina–Chapel Hill in 1999 and 1984 respectively, and bachelor of arts degree from Ohio Wesleyan University in Delaware, Ohio, in 1982.

**Donna Warner** is an adjunct instructor with the Institute of Government at the University of North Carolina–Chapel Hill. She works with faculty to design and implement education and training programs for city and county managers and elected officials. She brings expertise in budget and management analysis, strategic planning, human resource administration, and retreat facilitation. Donna has conducted planning and board retreats for multiple North Carolina municipalities and counties, helping boards plan and work together to solve public problems. Donna earned her BA from the University of Virginia and her MPA from the University of North Carolina–Chapel Hill.

**Cindy Williams** is a Principal Research Scientist of the Security Studies Program of the Massachusetts Institute of Technology. Formerly, she was an

Assistant Director of the Congressional Budget Office. Dr. Williams has served as a director and in other capacities at the MITRE Corporation in Bedford, Massachusetts; as a member of the Senior Executive Service in the Office of the Secretary of Defense at the Pentagon; and as a mathematician at RAND in Santa Monica, California. Dr. Williams holds a PhD in mathematics from the University of California, Irvine. She is the coeditor, with Curtis Gilroy, of *Service to Country: Personnel Policy and the Transformation of Western Militaries* (MIT Press, 2007), and the editor of *Holding the Line: U.S. Defense Alternatives for the Early 21st Century* (MIT Press 2001) and *Filling the Ranks: Transforming the U.S. Military Personnel System* (MIT Press, 2004). She is an elected fellow of the National Academy of Public Administration and a member of the Naval Studies Board, the Council on Foreign Relations, and the International Institute of Strategic Studies. She serves on the advisory board of Women in International Security and on the editorial board of *International Security.*

**Ruth Zaplin**, President of the Zaplin Group, specializing in leadership development; strategic, policy, and program development; innovation; organizational transformation; human capital management; and business process improvement. She has more than twenty-five years of experience working nationally and internationally in both the private and public sectors and has developed and led large-scale government reform initiatives, enterprise-wide transformation plans, workforce restructuring, and work redesign initiatives. She founded the National Academy of Public Administration's Global Leadership Consortium and serves as the Academy's lead on corrections initiatives. Dr. Zaplin holds DPA, MPA, MA, and BA degrees.

# Index